Silenced Communities

Silenced Communities
Legacies of Militarization and Militarism in a Rural Guatemalan Town

Marcia Esparza

berghahn
NEW YORK · OXFORD
www.berghahnbooks.com

Published in 2018 by

Berghahn Books

www.berghahnbooks.com

© 2018 Marcia Esparza

Library of Congress Cataloging-in-Publication Data

Name: Esparza, Marcia, author.

Title: Silenced communities : Legacies of militarization and militarism in a rural Guatemalan town / Marcia Esparza.

Other titles: Legacies of militarization and militarism in a rural Guatemalan town

Description: New York : Berghahn Books, [2017] | Includes bibliographical
references and index.

Identifiers: LCCN 2017037762 (print) | LCCN 2017044724 (ebook) | ISBN
9781785336881 (ebook) | ISBN 9781785336874 (hardback : alk. paper)

Subjects: LCSH: Chichicastenango (Guatemala)--History. | Civil-military
relations--Guatemala. | Guatemala--Militia--History. | Guatemala--Armed
Forces--Demobilization. | Guatemala--Armed Forces--Civic action. | Human
rights--Guatemala. | Militarism--Guatemala. | Guatemala--History--Civil
War, 1960-1996--Influence.

Classification: LCC F1476.C45 (ebook) | LCC F1476.C45 E86 2017 (print) | DDC
972.8105/31--dc23

LC record available at https://lccn.loc.gov/2017037762

British Library Cataloguing in Publication Data

A catalogue record for this book is available from the British Library

ISBN 978-1-78533-687-4 hardback
ISBN 978-1-78533-688-1 ebook

I dedicate this book

to the courageous Maya campesinos who, despite their wretched lives, organized to tell what had happened to them during the Cold War's genocide and kept promoting their vision of a better life for themselves, their families, and their communities while they fought against the militarization of their communities. With them, I learned a new meaning for the term "humility." I hope this study will shed light on the tragedy that besieged those Maya communities who were coerced into lending their support to the same non-Indigenous state that regards them as inferior during the war and in the postgenocide and postwar years.

to the Association for the Progress of All (APA) leaders, who opened my eyes to how the army's mentality had seeped into their everyday lives and how they have learned to live with it.

to Henry R. Huttenbach, who helped pave the way for the integration of Latin American Cold War cases of extreme forms of violence within the genocide scholarship.

to my beloved cousin Marjorie Lilian Stansfield Calderón, whose smile always got brighter even during hard times and whose memory I deeply treasure.

Contents

Illustrations

Maps

Figures

Tables

Acknowledgements

Over the years when I've worked on this book, at different time periods and geographical locations, I've been very lucky and honored to have bright and committed research assistants who helped me tremendously. In particular, I want to thank Ximena Navarrete, Luisa Fernanda Alvarez, Diana Belmont, Lina Rojas, Kristy Sanandres, and Francisca Vargas for compiling tables and reading sections of the manuscript.

I owe to Guatemalan anthropologist Luz Bonilla most of the searches in military journals and newspapers at the Hemeroteca Nacional de Guatemala, Clemente Marroquín Rojas, and the Academia de Historia y Geografía in Guatemala City (2010–2011). Awesome translators Miguel Falquez-Certain and Alejandro Arriaza undertook the painstaking task of making sense of narratives from Spanish into English with tremendous challenges because the Spanish versions were already a translation from Maya-K'iché. The many editors and readers—Stephanie Damoff and, especially, Lydia Shestopalova—shared with me their incisive comments that shaped and enriched the manuscript. Alex R. Steers McCrum edited most of the final manuscript, offering indispensable and unwavering help, along with his witty enthusiasm, after tirelessly going over several versions of the book. Last, but not least, I want to thank Brian Gawley, who helped edit the final manuscript.

Many scholars and practitioners provided insightful advice during the production of this long-overdue book. Among them were Nate Woodill, a former student from John Jay College and an Iraq War veteran, offered poignant observations on various chapters, providing clarification of how the military, in general, promotes its goals and strengthens its ideology and structures. Emily B. Campbell also provided important feedback about the urgent task of reckoning with the lingering effects of militarization and militarism.

In Guatemala, Maya peasant and popular organizations took the time from their busy everyday lives to share their war and genocide experiences. Some of them were the Comité Nacional de Viudas de Guatemala, the National Coordination of Widows of Guatemala (CONAVIGUA), the Mutual Support Group (GAM), the Rujunel Junam Council of Ethnic Communities "We Are All Equal" (CERJ), the Association of Family Members of the Detained Disappeared of Guatemala (FAMDEGUA), and the National Council of Displaced Guatemalans (CONDEG).

Above all, this study wouldn't have been possible without the support of local human rights organizations and activists from Santo Tomás Chichicastenango. My deepest gratitude goes to the Association for the Progress of All (APA), whose trust in this study meant that I felt safe while carrying out interviews with army collaborators. I am also thankful to the Auxiliatura Indígena, which opened up its doors to networks of communities' authorities. I am also thankful to the Academia de Geografia e Historia de Guatemala in Guatemala City and to the Oficina Municipal de Planificación (OMP) in Chichicastenango for sharing important socioeconomic information about communities. My deepest appreciation also goes to the numerous scholars and human rights activists who generously offered their views to this study: Fernando Lopez, Maria Martín, Maribel Rivas Vasconcelos, Miguel Angel Urbinas, and Father Ricardo Falla.

I want to name some of my dear friends who have provided me with their kind support every time I cried out for a respite during the years it took me to complete the manuscript: Nina Schneider, Horacio Leyton, Maria José Fierro, Barry Spunt, Olga Teplukova, Jennifer Harbury, Liza Rosas-Bustos, Juan José Hurtado Paz y Paz, Angelica Macario, the Pixcar family, Yolanda and Reginaldo, and Amílcar Méndez. Special thanks go to Carlos Edén-Maiden (Peteyem)—a survivor of the Kawesqar, an Indigenous Chilean group in the process of extinction—who offered insider knowledge of what it means to be a military Indigenous man—confirming many of this book's central arguments. Tamar Fortuna Theiler enthusiastically elaborated diagrams. I am humbled by the encouragement of my former mentees and now close friends, a source of true inspiration, Stephanie Alfaro and Jenny Escobar, whose sustained friendship reminds me of the true meaning of solidarity. Jenny also offered critical insights to the final manuscript.

I could not have completed this book without various funding support. A Faculty Research Award from the National Endowment for the Humanities (NEH) allowed me to carry out archival research at the Mesoamerican Center for Research, CIRMA, in Antigua, Guatemala (2011–2012), where I found a research home under the leadership of Thelma Porres. Support from John Jay College's Office for the Advancement of Research (OAR) generously contributed to the completion of this book.

In New York City, my friend and colleague Alessandra Benedicty, who I met at a 2012–2013 seminar on poverty hosted by the Andrew W. Mellon Foundation at the Center for the Humanities at the Graduate Center (CUNY), provided me with the unconditional support and unique insights into my analysis of inequality, militarization, and postcoloniality. A summer semester in 2014 as a visiting scholar at the University of Konstanz, Germany greatly facilitated the time to work on various chapters. I thank Andrea Betzenbichler for assisting me with map details while finishing her master's degree. I am also indebted to the generous reviewers making important comments on this book and to Chris Chappell, Berghahn editor, for trusting this project and for making himself available for my telephone calls while I traveled across Latin America.

To Pierre-Yves Linot goes my eternal gratitude for his companionship through this long and seemingly endless journey in the making of this book. I am also grateful to him, Vince Heptig, and Derryl Bazzy for generously allowing me to use their photos in this book. Daniele Volpe, also a photographer, generously took pictures at the Hemeroteca in Guatemala City. Last, I thank my beloved Rosita and Daniel for their patience and unconditional support of my work. I take full responsibility for all the errors and omissions.

Chichicastenango Research Area

Map 0.1. Guatemala

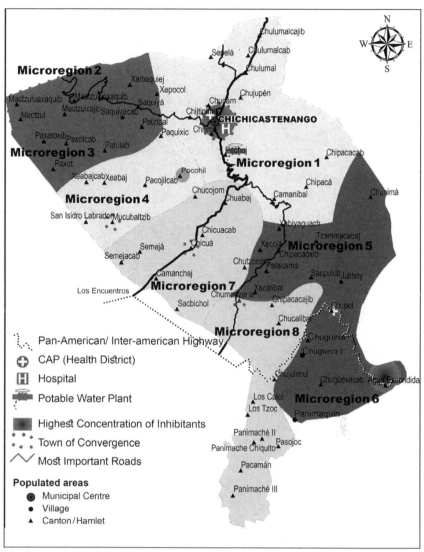

Map 0.2. Santo Tomás Chichicastenango, East and West Regions.

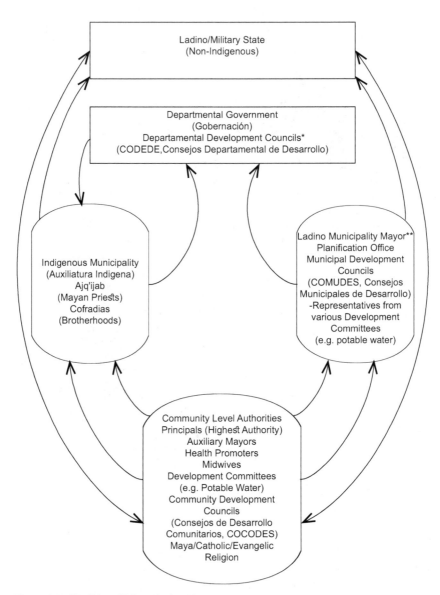

Figure 0.1. Traditional Maya Authorities

"My Soul Is a Military Soul"

Through the lens of the early aftermath of war and genocide in Santo Tomás Chichicastenango, a nearly all-Maya municipality in Guatemala's western highlands, or altiplano (1997–2004), I empirically explore the long-lasting legacies of violent militaristic practices impacting rural communities. This critical ethnography took place in the context of my fieldwork with the United Nations' Commission for Historical Clarification (in Spanish, La Comisión para el Esclarecimiento Histórico [CEH]) a year after the UN-sponsored Peace Accords ended the bloody war (1962–1996) between the state and the left-wing Guatemalan National Revolutionary Unity (URNG).

To verify compliance with the accords, the United Nations' Observer Mission in Guatemala (MINUGUA) was established in 1997. The commission concluded that the military launched vicious, U.S.-trained, financed, and equipped counterinsurgency campaigns against real or imagined subversives. In the eyes of the army, Maya communities became the country's "internal enemy" in its rallying Cold War rhetoric, allegedly menacing the country's national security and capitalist development. Across the region, the anticommunist National Security Doctrine (NSD) promoted by the United States, and to a lesser extent by the French Counterinsurgency Doctrine, was embraced by local armies, Daniel Feierstein asserts.[1] As Mexican philosopher Leopoldo Zea points out, "The Cold War was the ideological pretext used to dehumanize, imprison, torture, and kill anyone demanding higher salaries or land reforms."[2]

In Guatemala, this doctrine was used to squelch a widespread uprising that coalesced with the rebels. As a result, beginning in the late 1970s the state committed 626 massacres—half of them in the Department of El Quiché's deep mountain areas where I collected testimonies. The war left 200,000 people dead—many tortured, sexually assaulted, and thrown into unmarked graves.[3] Some 50,000 victims disappeared, the whereabouts of their remains still to be disclosed by the perpetrators, showing the widespread impunity embedded within institutions and society at large. Most victims belonged to one of the twenty-three Maya groups. More than 1.5 million people escaped the bloodshed by crossing into Mexico and the United States.

Guatemala: Memory of Silence, the Truth Commission's final report, concluded that the Ladino (or non-Indigenous state)[4] had committed acts of genocide between 1981 and 1983, a period remembered as "La Violencia."[5] The Archdiocese of Guatemala's 1998 *Guatemala: Never Again!*, known as the Proyecto Interdiocesano de Recuperación de la Memoria Histórica (Interdiocesan Project for the Recovery of Historical Memory), REHMI Report, reached a similar conclusion. In Colombia, La Violencia refers to the period 1948–1953, when 200,000 to 300,000 left-wing labor activists were killed. During the Cold War era, 30,000 people were tortured in Chile, while some 70,000 were killed in El Salvador, leaving behind a trail of polarization, widespread impunity, dehumanized social relations, and—this book hopes to show—the lingering footprints of grassroots militarization and militarism. In retrospect, growing up under General Augusto Pinochet's dictatorship (1973–1990) somehow prepared me to become a privileged witness to survivors' experiences with war and genocide. Over time, I began to reconnect with my own political history and experience with deep socioeconomic inequalities.

Local Contexts: Santo Tomás Chichicastenango

A few months before the end of my stay in El Quiché, I was assigned by the commission to carry out an in-depth historical analysis of Santo Tomás Chichicastenango ("Chichi," for short) about 145 kilometers (90 miles) northwest of Guatemala City.[6] Locals are called Maxeños or Chichicastecos. Every Thursday and Sunday are *día de plaza,* or market days, when the administrative center, *el pueblo* or *cabecera municipal,* located 1,965 meters above sea level, transforms itself into a bustling commercial center for local farmers and artisans selling colorful merchandise such as the handmade embroidered *huipiles* worn by Maya women.

Chichi is a preferred tourist destination for Guatemalans and foreigners alike, who pour into the otherwise forgotten streets, snapping photos of traditional Maya authorities dressed in colorful ceremonial garb. This is particularly the case during celebrations every 21–22 December honoring the town's patron saint, Santo Tomás, when the Cofradías, a religious brotherhood, carry the Santo Tomás statue to the loud sound of marimba music. Images of these festivities are sold on colorful postcards by the Guatemalan Institute of Tourism (INGUAT), which also promotes trips to nearby Pascual Abaj, where Mayan priests celebrate ceremonies showing how the Maya religion has survived in "syncretic forms." For many, Chichi is also known as the place where the Maya-K'iché *Popol Vuh,* or the *Book of the Community,* which records K'iché's pre-Conquest traditions, was recovered in the early eighteenth century by Fray Francisco Ximénez.[7]

Once I was done collecting interviews, I mapped out testimonies and I asked myself why fewer than 2 percent of all registered human rights crimes corresponded to communities roughly located in the western area (see front map). What had prevented western communities from testifying before the commission? These are located in the hinterlands, far from the paved Interamerican Highway (known also as Panamerican, or CA-1) spanning the country from Guatemala City to Northern El Quiché. Compared to the more remote western communities, most eastern communities considered in this book are along, next to, or just off the highway.

This geographical and political schism had already been noted in the 1930s by anthropologist Ruth Bunzel when she asserted, "A tradition of hostilities existed between them … a mysterious division, each with its own responsibilities, maps … traditional highest authority, the principal."[8] But the phenomenon was left largely unexplained. Today, as well as by the time of this study, this east-west division also applies to rural settlements being administratively divided into microregions, a partition facilitating communities' access to the few public services available in the countryside (see front map).

"My Soul Is a Military Soul"

In late 1999, I went back to Chichi to investigate this overarching silence. This second time in Chichi, I faced an utterly boisterous army, which showed no signs of guilt for its past human rights crimes. A year earlier, for instance, the army had "defamed"[9] spokesman Colonel Otto Noack for asserting that the army should apologize for past human rights crimes. Quite the opposite, it was emboldened by the rise to power of the hardline Guatemalan Republican Front (Frente Republicano Guatemalteco, FRG) party, created in 1989 by General José Efrain Ríos Montt, the very same dictator who had unleashed callous counterinsurgency campaigns during the genocide (1982–1983). To the dismay of local and international observers, including me, his handpicked candidate, Alfonso Portillo Cabrera, was sworn in as president on 14 January 2000. Cabrera vowed to bring peace and security to the country, giving continuity to the national security state.

Although it seems counterintuitive, this sustained post-Peace Accords, top-down militarization helped pave my way into a tight network of pro-army authorities, I term the "amigos," who were serving at the time in community and municipal-level posts. I rented a cozy room at Posada Conchita, conveniently located adjacent to both the non-Indigenous municipality (or municipal board) and the Indigenous mayor's office (known as the Auxiliatura Indígena or Alcaldia Indígena), from which the *principales* Elders Council (Tzanabe in Maya-K'iché) impart their traditional authority over religious, administrative, and political affairs. The Auxiliatura Indígena is a unique form of Maya organization that still prevails in some townships in El Quiché, Sololá, and Totonicapán. At the community level, each village system of authority—which can be traced back to colonial times—is made up of a principal, auxiliary mayor (coordinating with the Auxiliatura Indígena) and variously named ad hoc committees responsible for administering infrastructure and community chores (see front diagram, Traditional Maya Authorities).

As I discuss in Chapter One, my fieldwork took place within an eerie climate shrouded in the utmost secrecy, which made it feel as if the war was still going on. Moreover, my access to western community authorities, through the army's local Civil Affairs and Local Development Division (S-5) maintaining relations with the locals, can be seen as still more evidence of the overwhelming control exercised by the military over communities. On 14 July 2000, sipping a hot cup of coffee, I interviewed Rigoberto, acting as president of the Friends of the Army Association, Amigos del Ejército.[10] Rigoberto proudly showed me a photograph of himself dressed in military gear that was hanging around his neck on a loose lace. When I asked him why he was not wearing a uniform during our encounter, Rigoberto boasted, "I do not need this uniform [as he grabbed his photograph] any longer because my soul is a military soul. That is what is important."[11]

Since 1987, Rigoberto had been tied to the nearest army outpost in different military capacities. First, he had served as a military commissioner, a type of plainclothes rural police, the lowest-ranked military personnel and reservist, rounding up young men for military service and acting as informant, the army's "eyes and ears." Second, Rigoberto was a former member of the civil self-defense patrols (Patrulleros de Autodefensa Civil, PACs), a plainclothes auxiliary force made up of poverty-stricken Maya peasants linked to the army's chain of command. Nearly 80 percent of the rural population became unpaid patrol members by 1983.[12] According to the commission, PACs perpetrated 18 percent of all human rights crimes committed between 1962 and 1996. Officially, PACs were disbanded following the 1993 Human Rights Accord and the 1996 Agreement on the Strengthening of Civilian Power and on the Role of the Armed Forces in a Democratic Society.[13] In the early aftermath, across El Quiché, however, some unofficially activated pockets of ex-patrols and ex-military commissioners continued targeting human rights groups.

Informed by the human rights literature emphasizing victimhood, I found it difficult to fathom Rigoberto's identification with the army, as well as other pro-army authorities I soon would interview, who had brutally killed and looted families and communities. What could explain Rigoberto's veneration of the army?

Aims of This Book

Based upon the failed dismantling of the patrol system, this timely book will challenge the transitional justice and posttransitional paradigm that ignores the fact that the "old order" terrorizing the population was, in fact, not destroyed. Scholars focusing on Latin America have largely been seduced by legalistic responses to reckon with the past bloodshed and have left unexamined the unbroken relations between the army and sectors of the population across the region.

As I argue in *Legacies of State Violence in Latin America,* since 2000, the transitional justice field can be seen as a Janus-faced paradigm because it has been used as a rallying cry by human rights organizations, while at the same time it often has been co-opted by international and domestic elites. This co-optation has hindered grassroots attempts to achieve historical memory, truth, and justice for victims of human rights crimes. Moreover, the field has been criticized for overlooking the continuities of structural inequality and economic exploitation.[14] I hope to show that it also has diverted attention away from the study of the revival of war's destructive "abiding legacies,"[15] in the words of historian Frank Biess when analyzing the aftermath of WWII.

To go beyond the legalistic field of transitional justice, I discuss the often-disconnected fields of postcolonial, military sociology and the interdisciplinary field of genocide to tackle the legacies of enduring community-level militarization and militarism. This entrenched military control creates not only silences regarding war and genocidal atrocities themselves but also silences linked to relations between the oppressed and the oppressor that preceded the genocide. As I discuss in Chapter Two, a growing body of literature emphasizes the conquistadors' grappling with the pivotal importance of having the Indigenous peoples cooperate in warfare.[16]

In *Indian Conquistadors,* historians Laura E. Matthew and Michel R. Oudijk highlight the particular colonial racist ideology justifying the use of Indian allies, the "amigos," in their capacity as fighters, interpreters, and scouts to usurp Indigenous lands.[17] Historian Philip Wayne Powell succinctly points out, "The Indians of America were the conquerors—or destroyers—of their own world, to the advantage of the European invaders."[18] I use the term "Indian" to refer to colonial Maya and "Maya" to their descendants, as discussed by Victor Perera.[19]

I tease out the powerful meaning of the deafening silence concealing the army's fascist ideology—surprisingly little studied in the Latin American experience with right-wing violence. While there are various types of fascism, I use the term to imply state control over every aspect of national life, an ideology having as key elements "racism, the masculine, military, radical nationalism rehearsed … by symbols from flags to uniforms."[20] To achieve this control, fascism deceptively calls for the national unity of social classes but actually promotes the division of people by ethnicity, age, sex, gender, culture, nation, or religion.

A central thesis in this book is that the Cold War militarization—through training, arms sales, and ideological propaganda—added another layer of internal colonialism to Maya communities. It deeply strengthened unequal postcolonial ties between the oppressed and the oppressor, as the army reified its racist views of Indigenous peoples. Following Alex Alvarez and others, I define the crime of genocide as unfolding in various stages over time, rooted in a "destructive and deadly form of state policy" against a targeted group perceived historically as "the other," its defining characteristic.[21]

As Holocaust scholars long have observed, aftermaths are a specific historical stage of the process of genocide. They have different historical temporalities that shape collective memories and silence during which, as in the wake of the Reconstruction Era in the United States (1865–1877), gains toward social justice can be rolled back. Aftermaths are time periods when the "ideological garbage" takes on an afterlife of its own, if it is not fully disentangled and perpetrators are not held accountable for their past wrongs.[22] From a postcolonial viewpoint, embodied in the writings of Martiniquais-French Frantz Fanon focusing on postcolonial Africa, the immediate aftermath of regime change involves unrealized promises previously made by militants fighting for independence.[23]

As opposed to later aftereffects, I distinguish at least three immediate aftermaths: after each massacre or collective disappearance, after the height of the genocide (1981–1983), and in the war's early wake (1997–2004). While particular to historical periods, aftermaths are all part of larger, ongoing postcolonial legacies in which current iterations of colonialism are interconnected to the genocides of the Conquest and the Cold War.

Sociologically, my emphasis is on communities' collective responses to the Cold War patrol system reenacting colonial collaboration, the colonial practices of "divide and conquer," and the brutality committed against native populations. In this regard, Latin America is composed of a series of historical déjà vu, with a long tradition of praetorianism and coup d'état armies conniving with local amigos to quell organized opposition demanding social justice, resulting in crimes against humanity. Yet, *Silenced Communities* is less about patrols as human rights perpetrators as it is about systems of exploitation inherited from colonial times that have continuity to this day.

As elsewhere, Indigenous communities in Guatemala are highly vulnerable to outside pressures "that cause 'closure' under pressure but permit 'opening' in its absence," as anthropologist Carol Smith argues.[24] Far from adopting an apologetic posture toward oppressive pro-army groups, however, I examine how grassroots' militarization and militarism can create silence and how these are reinforced by the oppressed themselves. As Christopher Browning has asserted, "Explaining is not excusing; understanding is not forgiving."[25]

Explaining the Civil Self-Defense Patrols (PACs)

At the time of the commission in the late 1990s, the prevailing view regarding the participation of peasants in the patrol system was suggested by anthropologists David Stoll and Paul Kobrak, who argued that villagers felt "trapped between the two forces demanding their cooperation."[26] This ill-informed notion of being "caught between two evils," found elsewhere in Latin America, equates state armies supported by the United States with poorly armed left-wing guerrillas. Most troubling, this approach strips Maya peasants of political consciousness. Stoll wrongly suggests that patrols disintegrated in the late 1980s.

Recently, Kobrak's analysis of the patrol system in Colotenango, Huehuetenango does not problematize those factors, except fear of the army, leading to villages "enthusiastically accepting the army's call to organize."[27] A more nuanced historical picture explaining the patrols' collaboration developed by anthropologists Matilde González, Simone Remijnse, and Ricardo Sáenz de Tejeda's examinations of Joyabaj, El Quiché and in Huehuetenango suggests that responses to patrolling varied according to each community's unique local history, preexisting militarization, and local consciousness.[28] Despite their heterogeneity, however, patrols' responses were constrained by their subordinated position to the army's ironclad control. I will use the terms "postcolonial" and "neocolonial" interchangeably to denote legacies rooted in colonial times.

Unusual Dialogues: Postcolonial and Military Sociology

While postcolonial studies in the region are today a vibrant field, as exemplified by the scholarship of Walter Mignolo, Anibal Quijano, Silvia Rivera Cusicanqui, Boaventura De Sousa, and Karina Bidaseca, among others, the field has grown disconnected from military sociology and genocide studies that could account for why the subjugated mimicked and continue to mimic their oppressors in the war's aftermath. In fact, Andrew Hussey, the director of the Center for Postcolonial Studies (CPCS) has criticized the field for being "too textual and theorized" and has called for more empirical research investigating the lived experience with "coloniality," a term that encompasses the continuity of colonialism linked to urgent socioeconomic and political themes, not just cultural and literary ones.[29]

The Scourge of Internal Colonialism

Surprisingly, while the United States' imperialist policies in the region, which date back to the 1823 Monroe Doctrine, have been thoroughly documented, few studies have focused on how local armies exploit the internal colonialism produced by these policies to gain communities' collaboration. In the 1960s, Mexican sociologists Rodolfo Stavenhagen and Pablo González Casanova coined the term "internal colonialism," asserting that Latin American independence from Spain did not translate into the end of the "coloniality of power." Accordingly, a self-proclaimed, light-skinned, dominant national group uses systems of exploitation to control the original ethnic population's lands and resources, which are affected by systematic disadvantages, such as disparities in education and health. Shaping this internal colonialism are "labor repressive systems" that often lead to fascism, as explored by Barrington Moore's benchmark study *Social Origins of Dictatorship and Democracy.*

In the case of Guatemala, Jeffery Paige's Marxist analysis points to the unequal concentration of land and production maintained by the oligarchy of coffee processors, manufacturing capitalists, and the financial and commercial class, all part of "one elite." For Paige, "Guatemala constitutes ... an extreme case of a country dominated both by a landed elite and by its pre-Columbian past."[30] Paige illustrates this point by noting that coffee production in Guatemala is less efficient than in El Salvador because the elite continue utilizing an oppressive agrarian system to maintain control over the socioeconomic infrastructure of the state.[31] The elite, to uphold its privilege, maintains the illiteracy of the Indigenous people through a feudal agrarian system, which does not allow them to acquire a critical consciousness. Privilege, Tunisian Albert Memmi writes, is at the "heart of the colonial relationship."[32]

This aggressive agrarian system caused extreme poverty and enormous social inequality in the Guatemalan highlands that impacted, for example, children's health, as reflected by their below average height.[33] In 1979, 2.6 percent of the population controlled 64.5 percent of the land; in 2000, four years after the accords, 1.5 percent controlled 62.5 percent.[34] Framed by both the internal conditions of colonialism maintained by the Coordinating Committee of Agriculture, Commercial, Industrial, and Financial Associations (CACIF), the landowners' association (AGA) and the broader globalized extractive economy (mining, natural gas, petroleum, hydroelectric), lending institutions such as the World Bank, and a host of multinational corporations, militarized groups that maintain order for the army continues relentlessly.

Peasants are faced with the growing threat of landlessness rooted in their exploitation as "peasants," defined as small-scale farmers holding plots of land that are smaller than two acres who "engag[e] in the production of ... food crops for family needs or for sale at a local market."[35] Elucidating how the organizing principles of internal colonialism intersect can shed light on how they shape peasants' forced and voluntary collaboration with their local army outpost. This voluntariness is illustrated in the little problematized fact that in 15 percent of all the cases, PACs acted alone, that is, unaccompanied by the army.[36] Against a historical context of enduring military control through conscription and counterinsurgency campaigns, peasants became dependent on the army building an "implacable dependence, [which] molded their respective characters and dictated their conduct,"[37] as suggested by Memmi in his analysis of the relations between the colonizer and the colonized in postcolonial Algeria.

Memmi and Fanon long have argued that internal colonialism enables the army's exploitation of peasants' extreme poverty to compel them to collaborate in reenacting a longstanding paradox: the oppressed collaborate with the oppressor in his own exploitation, forging a warped and distorted relationship. In *The Colonizer and the Colonized*, Memmi points out the inherent ambiguity characterizing postcolonial relations and famously notes that the colonizer frames the colonized into "concrete situations, which close in on the colonized."[38] From this perspective, Indigenous peoples are born into a pre-designed coercive situation framing their war and genocidal roles and molding what I term, "subordinated alliances," with the army.

While Memmi had the French rule of Arab territories in mind, his insights are nonetheless relevant to how colonial institutions allocate roles to the subjugated, and they are particularly useful in explaining what is, ultimately, a colonial and postcolonial paradox: the oppressed who are forced to act out these roles against their neighbors during war and genocide and their aftermath. Furthermore, in the case of Peru, Kimberly Theidon points out the "intimate killings" involving an enemy who was "a son-in-law, a godfather, an old schoolmate or [from] the community that lies just across the valley."[39]

This paradox initially created by the Conquest has prevailed over time and is poignantly illustrated by Richard Arens in the case of the early 1970s genocide against the Ache in Paraguay, when the army "order[ed] the captive Aches to hunt the free Aches ... if they wished to achieve recognition as humans."[40] The coercive situation leading the oppressed to turn against their own kin does not mean that each individual is a passive recipient, an insight long understood through subaltern studies in India, convincingly challenging the monolithic image of the colonized. This sociological insight has great relevance because it leaves space to explore not only the oppressed's collaboration but also peasants' acts of collective resistance to the army's violence and exploitation, an engagement that is limited to neither complete assimilation into the oppressors' ideology nor outright violent revolt.

As Memmi observes, "It is common knowledge that the ideology of a governing class is adopted in large measure by the governed classes."[41] Decolonization, as suggested by Fanon in *The Wretched of the Earth*, implies challenging the "colonial situation."[42] This points to the need to consider its continuity in the postwar years to begin tackling the mutual dependence maintained between the Guatemalan army and pockets of former patrols, both of whom fear each other but are simultaneously bound, with devastating consequences for impoverished communities.

By contextualizing the collaboration of Indigenous peoples with the military, we can attain a more nuanced understanding of the deeply violent ties the army maintains with Maya peasants. Uncannily, these ties were encouraged by Liberal public projects and, later, Cold War civic action programs, which involved psychological operations (PSYOP), all part of a multipronged strategy used to gain the collaboration of "white communities" or "pro-army communities." These military operations illustrate the efforts the army undertook to persuade the subaltern to support its patrol system. As scholars point out, even the colonizer is forced to negotiate spaces, as there are various types of colonizer-colonized relations. In the process of delivering this aid, the army reconfigured its image as the friend of Maya communities (Chapter Three). Charles H. Wood and Marianne Schmink also have suggested that the army rewarded peasants to win over the population in the Brazilian Amazon.[43]

Grassroots Militarization and Militarism: The Missing Link

Cultural anthropologists dominating the study of the postwar years in Guatemala, while acknowledging the precarious life engulfing rural areas due to neoliberal policies, have argued that the "countryside has been demilitarized."[44] In contrast, political scientists, such as Jennifer Schirmer, have argued for its continuation, which she refers to in her groundbreaking work *The Guatemalan Military Project* about the army's long-term control over rural areas.[45] Following Andrew Ross's distinction between militarization and militarism, I define militarization as a step-by-step process composed of military expenditures, arms imports and production, and, in general, military buildup.[46] To differentiate it from militarization, Ross defines militarism as the ideological marks resulting from military values, loyalty, patriotism, and due obedience being instilled, surpassing the true military purpose of defeating the enemy,[47] and "carrying military mentality and modes of acting and decision into the civilian sphere," as Alfred Vagts suggests.[48]

Pivotal for my study is Ross's assertion that *militarism* can occur in the absence of *militarization*. That is, at the local level, people can remain militarized because a military mindset and social practices have been normalized. I link militarization and militarism experienced at the local level to the reenactment of deeply rooted racist ideology and violent practices that shape the aftermath of wars, even when military "buildup" is not apparently present or robust.

The field of military sociology lags behind in the study of legacies of militarization and militarism, neglecting the use of critical ethnography that can account for entrenched military control and military-Indigenous relations. Instead, it has overly emphasized a top-down approach, examining the state system or interstate conflicts through quantitative, cross-national research an approach that ends up avoiding the difficulties involved in carrying out the complicated and dangerous fieldwork of militarized contexts.

Military sociologists have been faulted for "standing in harmful isolation" not only in relation to the social sciences[49] but also within the humanities and war and genocide studies. Conversely, the field of genocide focusing on Latin

America has overlooked the study of militarization and militarism as shown, for example, in a special volume, *Debates from the Latin American Margin*, that ignores the need to examine ongoing, and unequal, grassroots military-civil relations in the aftermath of the Cold War.[50]

A postcolonial-military sociology needs to pay more attention, for example, to the role of the rural police and state-sponsored Indigenous militia forces carrying out genocidal policies. These forces are similar, in the sense that they were members of local communities, to the Janjaweed in Sudan, the Interahamwe in Rwanda, and rural militias assisting the German Einsatzgruppen in Poland and Russia.[51] Military commissioners and their auxiliaries largely resembled the rural police in Europe in World War II, such as the Gemeindepolizei or Gendarmerie, which were under the Order Police Main Office, the small-town local police hunting Jews.[52]

Civilian-military relations are defined in Kurt Lang's words: "The attitudes of uniformed men and the civilian population toward one another ... and the political alliances between military and civilian groups help determine what influence the armed forces will exert, not only in politics, but also on social life generally."[53] Samuel Huntington's theory of civilian-military relations in the United States has dominated discussions over the subordination of the army to civilian power. In *The Soldier and the State,* he asserts that the professionalization of an army serves to render the military "politically sterile, neutral ... ready to carry out the wishes of any civilian government."[54] In contrast, Morris Janowitz's *Professional Soldier* argues that armies will become a pressure group but nonetheless can be "responsible, circumscribed, and responsive to civilian authority."[55]

Brian Loveman and Thomas M. Davies argue that in the Latin American case, politics for the military has historically meant "class conflict and instability," which has encouraged the army's intervention "to cleanse the body politic of political corruption."[56] In the early twentieth century, "professionalized" armies maintained ties to traditional elites. What is needed to modify their corrupted nature, a modernizing view argues, is to "expose foreign militaries to the modern, professional training embodied by the U.S. military."[57] The standard to professionalize the military is a form of U.S. imperialism because the underlying assumption is that a Eurocentric way of behaving is the norm.[58] However, as elsewhere in the region, in Guatemala, the historical role of the army in perpetrating crimes against Indigenous communities refutes the notion of the army as "professional."

Espousing this approach of the Guatemalan army as professional is Richard N. Adams, a scholar of civilian-military relations, who asserts, "The identification of the military with the nation, and the creation of a career for officers, have produced an increasingly professional officer."[59] For Adams, the army's identification with politics is not an obstacle as much as the fact that the salary system is insufficient for "ambitious individuals ... [who] expected to see additional incomes."[60]

As Fanon suggests, a postcolonial view of the military, such as that in post-colonial Algeria, implies that politicizing the army, the "dividing line ... represented by the barracks and the police stations," compartmentalizing the world of the colonized, could be eradicated.[61] This is because the army was an institution that could erase inequalities in addition to "rais[ing] the level of national consciousness," where recruits would aid in the reconstruction of the country, while militias would be mobilized in the "case of war."[62]

Ignoring the postcolonial continuity of military control—with the exception of Loveman's work—military sociologists have made poor assumptions about the nature of democracy in the region. Since the 2000s, arguing for the "complete transition" into democracy, David Pion-Berlin has said, "At the dawn of the new century, civil military relations ... are more stable than they were a decade or two ago." He argues that the "coup or no-coup question is not the defining one for this era."[63] Pion-Berlin has asserted that the "completed transition" has driven scholarship to focus again on "the patterns of civilian-military relations developing under democratic auspices."[64] However, an analysis of the patrol system will suggest that prolonged militarization hinders the subordination of the army to civilian power at the grassroots level since people themselves reproduce militaristic worldviews and practices.

As Karen Remer suggests, scholars "moved from the study of democratic breakdowns to the study of ... transitions without pausing to analyze the authoritarian phase that came in between."[65] Regarding Central America, Pion-Berlin has argued, "Militar[ies] are smaller, more compliant, and less interventionist than they once were."[66] Most studies have focused on military prerogatives, remnants of the authoritarian regimes, such as in Argentina and Brazil, entrenched at the state level, and referred to in the literature as the "authoritarian enclaves."[67] However, on the one hand, these views largely overlook the persistent role that unequal civilian-military relations play in shaping collective memory and constructed silence at the community level, long after formal civilian control has been attained. On the other hand, the underlying assumption that armies have become subordinated to civilian regimes since the end of the Cold War ignores how local armed forces now play a prominent role in U.S.-led wars against drugs and global terrorism in communities reeling from the legacy of state violence.

Recruitment of the Internally Colonized

While Indigenous groups recruited by the colonizer are generalized phenomena, this is not always problematized by scholarly discourses, with some valuable exceptions.[68] In Spain, Moroccan soldiers and militias were recruited to fight imperial wars during the Franco regime.[69] Similarly, France recruited the Harkis in Algeria, who were prompted by extreme poverty to ally with the French to support their families.[70] For many, conscription into the colonizer's military was advantageous because it seemingly offered a way out of a precarious life, as U.S. activist Winona LaDuke argues in the case of Native Americans who "voluntarily" serve in the U.S. military despite compelling reasons to resist enlistment.[71]

Past scholarship focusing on civilian-military relations in Guatemala points out "the recruitment of Indigenous males into the army, mainly from rural areas, by coercive means."[72] For many peasants, "the military provided their only access to education ... [resulting in] Kaqchikel's renewed confidence to stand up to Ladino persecution."[73] And while "few Mayan men looked forward to military recruitment," because of the brutal treatment received from the army,[74] anthropologist David Carey argues that Kaqchiquel men remember that under General Jorge Ubico Castañeda (1931–1944), they "gained confidence from their military service."[75]

In the case of service in the Cold War patrol system, the assertion that recruitment into the patrol made Maya peasants feel, to paraphrase Kobrak, newly enfranchised in the Guatemalan nation, suggests that army-Maya peasant relations are inherently exploitative. Yet, men are, the argument goes, at the same time empowered by military service to fight back against abuses from the Ladino elite.[76] These suggestions are highly problematic because they ignore that the cost of this "empowerment" has been Indigenous peoples' dehumanization and that their oppressors have benefitted. The perverse outcome of this practice is most aptly summarized in the words of Fanon: "It is the 'peoples of color' who annihilated the attempts at liberation by other 'peoples of color.'"[77]

Cold War Ideology, Propaganda, and Myth Making

Research has established that policies of annihilation require the support of the population. But how do armies maintain grassroots political support? As past studies have shown, in addition to a longstanding suspicion of outside institutions, Maya communities were shocked into silence by the fear of a violent death, which many barely survived during the war. As Beatriz Manz notes, "The purpose of the terror ... was to intimidate and silence society as a whole, in order to destroy the will for transformation, both in the short and long term."[78] Less discussed in the literature, as anthropologist Diane Nelson notes, is why "indigenous people [have] actively engaged in counterinsurgency campaigns?"[79] Instead, as Alvarez and others have suggested, we need to examine the role of ideologies in helping create and organize the "justification needed for populations to engage in genocide."[80]

Propaganda campaigns disseminating rumors about the war enabled the army to co-opt and recolonize right-wing peasants' and communities' historical memory by usurping masculine representations of pre-Hispanic warring pasts while, at the same time, they reinforced the army's heroic memory of defeating the conquered. With militarism comes the culture of hypermasculinity embodied in the state, which spilled over into Maya peasants' local systems of power. Conversely, it is important to highlight those socioeconomic, ideological, and religious factors accounting for resistance to militarization within "red," or pro-URNG communities, which I discuss in Chapters Four and Five.

Propaganda is defined as "a form of mass communication and persuasion" controlling people's minds with the goal of "guaranteeing a popular response as desired by the propagandists."[81] In Latin America, with the notable exception of Nina Schneider's examination of different types of propaganda used by the state to legitimize itself in Brazil during the dictatorship and how they were received,[82] few studies have explored how the Cold War's grandiloquent rhetoric of national security and development ideology was used to fabricate war mythology that cast the army as the savior of poverty-stricken communities. In the *Ethics of Memory,* Avishai Margalit claims, "A myth lives within a community when members of the community believe the myth as a literal truth."[83] In Guatemala, Cold War myths interacted with local histories and layers of silence, ultimately leading groups of ex-patrols and their families to cover up the war's unpalatable truths in ways that went beyond criminal complicity to silence their neocolonial relations to the nearest military outpost.

As I discuss in "Impossible Memory and Postcolonial Silences," the commission "did not quite reveal the war myths,"[84] such as the army's rhetoric glorifying the patrols for their service, internalized by co-opted patrols. This is displayed in a rather hidden memorial that Remijnse found in the Joyabaj municipality with the text "Their memory lives on in our hearts, as an example of the duty and glory to our free and sovereign fatherland."[85] Above all, these were the systematic lies, the made-up stories the army used to build its mass-based support in the countryside, relying on a fascist propaganda containing false promises of security and development as a means of recruitment into the patrol system.

Memmi asserted that "fervent feelings of belonging" to the nation, corresponding to a "mob psychology appealing to passionate motives,"[86] created the conditions of internal colonialism that were fertile ground for nationalistic propaganda to find compelling reasons for peasants to join the patrols, in the context of fear not just of military violence but also of further uprootedness, as sociologist Manuel Antonio Garretón notes regarding the Chilean experience with right-wing dictatorship.[87]

My emphasis on ideological resonance allows me to revise my earlier view that overly stressed the NSD mindset the army had "imposed" upon Maya groups.[88] Instead, I now examine how people received and incorporated war propaganda, transmitting alienating ideologies, as determined by Siniša Malešević, who argues that for effective war propaganda to resonate, a preexisting process must unravel. This involves the "ideologization of the 'masses,' or centrifugal ideologization."[89] Similarly, the Khmer Rouge, Alex Hinton notes, set up its ideological model through radio broadcasts, songs, and slogans to encourage peasants to seek revenge against "the capitalist and reactionary classes."[90] Examining the 1972 Burundi situation, René Lemarchand argues that the state misrepresented the origins of the violence through what he terms an "inverted discourse," or false metanarrative.[91] Similarly, in Guatemala, the army created an inverted discourse that proved central in mobilizing patrol platoons against the country's "internal enemy."

In the volatile early aftermath, a military mindset, understood as a "cluster of attitudes … the various elements … related to the nature of military expertise,"[92] remained deeply embedded within pro-army communities' everyday lives. Yet, there has been little discussion about its revival and how it continued to perpetuate loyalty to the army that was rooted in blurry binary identities. In fact, the Cold War patrol system is a quintessential example of a subaltern group exhibiting overlapping identities under extreme life and death situations: between victims and perpetrators and between civilians and soldiers. Dirk Moses suggests that it is important to move beyond binaries in order to view war and genocide roles in less rigid terms, and he warns us of the danger of representing "passive victims, wicked perpetrators, and craven bystanders."[93] This is an approach that echoes Tzvetan Todorov's remark that "mutually exclusive categories of angels and demons cannot explain how ideology shapes multiple roles."[94]

Similarly, Omer Bartov observes that lumping together war identities "produce[s] tremendous social, political, and psychological tensions," obscuring the complexity of bloodshed.[95] In Brazil, sociologist Martha Huggins suggests that victims also can take on the role of perpetrators under extreme duress, denoting a complex gray zone.[96] For Guatemala, peace and conflict scholar Lieselotte Viaene has argued that genocidal violence created more gray areas than the "clear victim-perpetrator dichotomy,"[97] further accentuating the contradictory war and genocide roles of Maya peasants. As Nelson suggests, participation in the patrol system at the village level made "the line between victim and perpetrator difficult to see."[98] A second binary, that of the civilian identity, has been challenged since civilians have become "irregular combatants,"[99] according to Martin Shaw.

On 26 January 2012, I found the picture below (Fig. 0.2) of Gilberto Reyes lying outside of the supreme court building. Proving conscription, it shows these overlapping binaries. On this day, a lower-court judge was hearing allegations of crimes against humanity of Ríos Montt. Reyes's photograph vividly

Figure 0.2. Outside of the Guatemala City Supreme Court Building. © Author, 26 January 2012.

parallels portrayals of victims dressed in camouflage uniforms hanging on the bare walls of homes when I was collecting testimonies for the commission. Often, these photos were some of the only ones families had of their relatives. The rest were taken by the army when their son, brother, father, grandfather, cousin, or uncle either had been conscripted into military service or had "volunteered" to serve.

This mindset is one of the pillars sustaining community-level militarism found within pro-army groups and communities. As Zygmunt Bauman notes, "Old habits of thought die hard,"[100] concurring with Leo Kuper's assertion that ideologies are not easily taken apart.[101] Writing about Rwanda's perpetrators, Omar McDoom argues that such a mindset was required to mobilize Hutu perpetrators. Once beliefs defining the war in cultural terms were activated, the escalation "into genocidal violence [became] the product of a complex interaction of other motives ranging from coercion, opportunism, habituation, conformity, racism, and ideological indoctrination."[102] Similarly, Helen Fein remarks that asking what leads people to kill requires a theory that explains "how structural, situational and cultural forces" can account for mass atrocities.[103] By focusing on the type of perpetrators, Fein notes, we can begin unveiling genocidal ideologies and how—I hope to show in this book—they were reenacted in the war's unsettled aftermath by the internally oppressed themselves.[104]

Sociologists have examined different levels of collaboration, relying on different terms—accommodation, collaboration, and cooperation—to differentiate between involuntary and voluntary cooperation.[105] In Nazi Germany, Hannah Arendt accused the Judenräte, the Jewish councils, of collaboration with the Nazis, a thesis refuted by Bauman's groundbreaking studies.[106] Andrew Rigby has also distinguished between five types of collaboration during World War II involving local populations and their occupiers.[107] Historian Timothy Brook's *Collaboration: Japanese Agents and Local Elites in Wartime China* emphasizes collaboration between the invaders and local Chinese elites in the first year of the occupation that began at the bottom, in the towns, rather than at the top, as in the case of France's Vichy regime collaboration with Nazi Germany.[108]

Studies of collaboration with the army during genocides are lacking in Latin America. Nelson insightfully has observed, "We must be alert to the contradictory ways militarized power also incites, induces, and seduces Guatemalans, including the Maya," a seduction linked to addictive power.[109] Manz concurs in her analysis of postwar ongoing violence.[110] This was particularly the case in the poorest Chichicastenango communities that failed to testify before the Truth Commission. From a critical postcolonial point of view, these findings are important, since they suggest that the army targeted the poorest communities for mobilization as belligerent groups in support of its patrol system. Far from recognizing their collaboration, however, the post-Peace Accords administrations sought to systematically undermine their amigos' grievances as war veterans, or what I term "subjugated allies," which I discuss in Chapters Six, Seven and Eight, particularly.[111]

Enduring Social Silence

Elucidating the interplay between the failed demilitarization of the patrol system and the reproduction of constructed social silence as one more element shaping the war's wake can shed light on the relentless military control over local populations elsewhere in South Asia and Africa. In Latin America, since the late 1990s, scholars have examined official memories justifying or denying past crimes against humanity and the rise of human rights groups promoting the historical memory of victims targeted for their political views.[112] Social silences have a specific purpose as people codify and enforce norms within the "inner space of the circle of silence."[113] In "Courageous Soldiers," I explore "pacts of silence" in the Chilean experience in which impunity regarding human rights crimes showed that both current and former military officers, and their civilian collaborators, do not "just" refuse to speak. Rather, they engage in an "active silence," one that reveals their unbroken loyalty to the military, long after the 1990 demise of the Pinochet regime.[114]

Jay Winter and others have argued that silences are social practices, and in the context of war and genocide, he highlights one particular silence, a "political" or "strategic silence," which refers to a chosen mechanism to avoid further conflict. An example of this type of silence took place in Spain after the end of the Franco regime, when a "transition" led to the denial of a state-led inquiry about past atrocities.[115] In *Shadows of War*, sociologist Efrat Ben-Ze'ev argues that silences constructed regarding wars were tacitly agreed to and maintained over the years by Israeli soldiers. Yet, they began breaking as veterans grew older. In the same volume, Eviatar Zerubavel suggests that social silence is "more than simply absence of sound."[116] Rather, it implies a consensual denial and deliberate avoidance of taboo themes. Similarly, I emphasize how postwar militarism facilitated the reproduction of these silences, and the issues they denied, to reveal instead the lies the army told Maya peasants about the origins of the war.

For the case of El Salvador, Robin Maria DeLugan, in *Reimagining National Belonging*, observes how museums and monuments initiated by civil society grappled with the unpalatable truths of the 1981 El Mozote Massacre, which otherwise have been silenced by the state.[117] Focusing on Africa, historian Ruth Ginio suggests that silences are selective, especially regarding "the ugliness of a colonial past in which black soldiers broke the protest of black men and women struggling against their French masters."[118] Ginio observes that the oppressed betrayed decolonizing struggles, exemplified in the *tirailleurs sénégalais* being ordered to repress the Malagasy revolt in 1947 or the loyalist Taitai allying with colonial settlers against the revolutionary Mau Mau seeking independence (1952–1960).

In Guatemala, pro-army peasants resembled an Indian informer in his betrayal of the Maya K'ichés that led to their defeat during the Conquest[119] as well as the "Ayaconas," the Mapuche term assigned to those who sell out to the Chilean state. Those communities where a military ethos is most entrenched, which I define as "garrison communities," are analyzed in Chapter Eight. In this type of community, the prolonged coerciveness of military control and economic deprivation nurtured interconnected cultures of "fear," "violence," and "silence."[120] In Chapter Nine, to illustrate how military-like violence was used as reprisal against those denouncing human rights crimes, I examine *La Cadena* (the Chain) in the 2000 Xalbaquiej lynching, which enabled the legacies of genocide to continue in the form of public executions.

In the initial chapters, I offer background to this book. On a continuum of postwar militarization and militarism, I then divide this book into two comparative parts. In Part I (Chapters Four and Five) I examine the unfolding polarization process affecting some sixteen outlying communities in the east, particularly from the Chupol area, which is identified by the army as "red," or "pink." In Part II (Chapters 6-9) through the unique voices of ex-patrollers, ex-military commissioners, reserves, and civil affairs specialists (S-5) I focus on a cluster of western communities most likely defined by the military as "white" or pro-army communities (Mactzul, Paxot, and Saquillá), which are located on the northwestern corner of Chichi.

Notes

1. Feierstein, "National Security Doctrine in Latin America," 489–490.
2. Quoted in Esparza, "Globalizing Latin American Studies," 8.
3. CEH, Conclusions, 18.
4. The term "Ladino" indicates people of mixed Indigenous and Spanish heritage.
5. CEH, Conclusions, 38, 39; Also see Victoria Sanford for a quantitative discussion of how during La Violencia, under the General José Efrain Ríos Montt regime, there was "a 25 percent increase in the number of massacre victims …" Sanford, *Buried Secrets,* 158.
6. Geographically, the township is characterized by steep hills forming part of a volcanic ridge, with altitudes ranging from 1,900 to 2,500 m (6,233–8,202 ft).
7. Also written as *Wuj.* See the translation by ethnologist Dennis Tedlock.
8. Bunzel, *Chichicastenango,* 236.
9. Remijnse, 254.
10. Also known as "ACODER." At the community level, I will use hamlet, village, community, and canton interchangeably.
11. Author interview, Rigoberto.
12. REHMI 1998, II.119.
13. CEH, II.234.
14. Schneider and Esparza, "Whose Transition? Whose Voices," xi–xxviii.
15. Biess, *Homecomings,* 1.
16. Calero, *Chiefdoms under Siege;* Vinson, "Race and Badge"; Archer, "Bourbon Finances and Military Policy."
17. Matthew and Oudijk, *Indian Conquistadors,* 14–15.
18. Powell, *Soldiers, Indians, and Silver,* 158.
19. Perera, *Unfinished Conquest.*
20. Reichardt, "Fascist Movements," 457.
21. Alvarez, *Genocidal Crimes,* 4, 12. The crime, Helen Fein and others have noted, is executed by a bureaucratic apparatus characteristic of modernity and it happens regardless of the surrender or lack of threat offered by the victim. Fein, *Genocide Watch,* 3.
22. Bartov, *Mirrors of Destruction,* 5.
23. See particularly Fanon, *Wretched of the Earth,* 97–144.
24. Smith, *Guatemalan Indians and the State,* Kindle locations 1041–42.
25. Browning, *Ordinary Men,* xx; see also Sluka, *Death Squad,* 27.
26. Stoll, *Between Two Armies,* 6.
27. Kobrak, "Long War in Colotenango," 222, 233.
28. Sáenz de Tejeda, *Victimas o Vencedores?*
29. Reisz, "High and Popular Culture."
30. Paige, 56.

31. Ibid., 67–69.
32. Memmi, *Dominated Man*, 46.
33. Pebley and Goldman, "Social Inequality and Children's Growth."
34. "Guatemala Squeezed," 5.
35. Hristov, *Paramilitarism and Neoliberalism*, 8.
36. CEH 1999, Conclusions, 86; CEH, 1999, Vol. II, 227.
37. Memmi, *Dominated Man*, 45.
38. Memmi, *Colonizer and the Colonized*, 93, 90.
39. Theidon, "Intimate Enemies," 97.
40. Arens, *Genocide in Paraguay*, 31.
41. Memmi, *Colonizer and the Colonized*, 88.
42. Fanon, *Wretched of the Earth*, 2.
43. Wood and Schmink. "Military and the Environment," 92.
44. Little and Smith, *Mayas in Postwar Guatemala*, 2.
45. See also Schirmer, "Prospects for Compliance."
46. Ross, "Dimensions of Militarization," 562–64. See also the definition by Enloe, *Maneuvers*, 3.
47. Ross, "Dimensions of Militarization," 563–64; Vagts, *History of Militarism*, 13.
48. Vagts, *History of Militarism*, 17.
49. Pion-Berlin, *Civil-Military Relations*, 2, 3.
50. *Genocide Studies and Prevention: An International Journal. (GSP) Special Volume Genocide Studies: Debates from the Latin American Margin*, 8, no. 1 (2013).
51. Remijnse, *Memories of Violence*, 140.
52. Browning, *Ordinary Men*, 4.
53. Lang, *Military Institutions*, 11, 12. Huntington identifies civilian-military relations as an aspect of national security (*Soldier and the State*, 1).
54. Huntington, *Soldier and the State*, 84.
55. Janowitz, *Professional Soldier*, 343.
56. Loveman and Davies, *Politics of Antipolitics*, 3.
57. McCoy, "Trained to Torture," 26.
58. I am grateful to Jenny Escobar for her insightful comment on the power dynamics between the United States and Latin America's armies formation.
59. Adams, *Crucifixion by Power*, Kindle locations 4012–13.
60. Ibid., 4027.
61. Fanon, *Wretched of the Earth*, 3.
62. Ibid., 141–42.
63. Pion-Berlin, *Civil-Military Relations*, 10, 2.
64. Ibid., 9.
65. Quoted in Pion-Berlin, *Civil-Military Relations* 7, 9.
66. Pion-Berlin, *Civil-Military Relations*, 11.
67. Kees Koonings in Silva, *Soldier and the State*, 9.
68. Akçam, *Shameful Act*, 161; Lemarchand, *Burundi*, 70–71.
69. Mechbal, "Los Moros."
70. Engel, *Historia de las Divisiones*, 208.
71. LaDuke and Cruz, *Militarization of Indian Country*.
72. Smith, "Militarization of Civil Society," 10.
73. Carey, "Who's Using Whom?" 174.
74. Carey, *Our Elders Teach Us*, 179.
75. Ibid., 185–86.
76. Kobrak, "Long War in Colotenango," 222.

77. Fanon, *Black Skin, White Masks,* 85.
78. Manz, *Paradise in Ashes,* 159.
79. Nelson, *Finger in the Wound,* Kindle location 1260.
80. Alvarez, *Genocidal Crimes,* 49, 161.
81. Aristotle A. Kallis, quoted in Luckert and Bachrach, *State of Deception,* 1–2.
82. Crucial aspects in the propaganda were "the goal of national unity, and the realization of the 'common good.'" Schneider, *Brazilian Propaganda,* 6.
83. Margalit, *Ethics of Memory,* 65.
84. Esparza, "Impossible Memory," 172.
85. Remijnse, *Memories of Violence,* 286–87.
86. Memmi, *Colonizer and the Colonized,* 96.
87. Garretón, "Fear in Military Regimes."
88. Esparza, "Post-war Guatemala," 383.
89. Malešević, *Sociology of War and Violence,* Kindle location 192.
90. Hinton, *Why Did They Kill?* 27.
91. Lemarchand, *Forgotten Genocides,* 42.
92. Lang, *Military Institutions,* 10.
93. Moses, *Empire, Colony, Genocide,* Kindle location 217–19.
94. Todorov and Bellos, *Hope and Memory,* 180.
95. Bartov, *Mirrors of Destruction,* 93.
96. Huggins, Haritos-Fatouros, and Zimbardo, *Violence Workers.* See also Payne, *Unsettling Accounts.* Regarding Africa, see Foster, Haupt, and de Beer, *Theater of Violence,* 4.
97. Viaene, "Dealing with the Legacy," 1161.
98. Nelson, *Finger in the Wound,* Kindle location 5752.
99. Shaw, *What Is Genocide?,* 119.
100. Bauman, *Modernity and the Holocaust,* 152.
101. Kuper, *Genocide,* 84–100.
102. McDoom finds that 57 percent of respondents attributed their participation to obedience to authority, followed by an ideological mindset of war (33 percent), which meant fighting for their country or defending themselves against the enemy. The third most popular answer was coercion (20 percent). McDoom, "Rwanda's Ordinary Killers," 14.
103. Fein, *Genocide: A Sociological Perspective,* 44.
104. Fein, *Accounting for Genocide,* 30.
105. Helen Fein notes that collaboration is motivated by reward, incentive, or a desire to retain one's status as well as mutuality of goals." Fein, *Accounting for Genocide,* 34.
106. Jewish councils and elders collaborated because they believed they "could avert consequences more serious than those which resulted." Arendt, *Eichmann in Jerusalem,* 91; Bauman, *Modernity and the Holocaust,* 117–50.
107. They are political, military, horizontal, social, and economic collaboration. Rigby, *Justice and Reconciliation,* 19.
108. Brook, *Collaboration,* 2.
109. Nelson, *Finger in the Wound,* Kindle location 1270–71
110. Manz, "Continuum of Violence," 153.
111. Chuchiak, "Forgotten Allies," 175–76.
112. The field of memory studies in English is quite rich. For Argentina, see Jelin, *State Repression* and Feierstein, *Genocide as Social Practice.* For Chile, see Stern, *Memory Box of Pinochet's Chile* and Gómez-Barris, *Where Memory Dwells.*
113. Winter, "Thinking about Silence," 4.
114. Esparza, "Courageous Soldiers," 196–208.

115. Winter, "Thinking about Silence," 5.
116. Zerubavel, "Social Sound of Silence," 33.
117. DeLugan, *Reimagining National Belonging,* 18.
118. Ginio, "African Silences," 138–52.
119. Perera, *Unfinished Conquest,* 3–4.
120. REMHI 1998, I.107.

1

The Methodological Crisis Revisited

Chichi is well developed now, it has tourism, hotels, this, and that, but only a few benefit from that, the vast majority of my people … we suffer, we are very poor.
—Author Interview, Andrea

Westernized human rights categories used in large-scale investigations, such as the Truth Commission and the Proyecto Interdiocesano de Recuperación de la Memoria Histórica, or REHMI Report, often fell short of capturing the lived experience of the Maya victims of Cold War counterinsurgency campaigns. For example, the REHMI staff was confronted with the unexpected task of categorizing deaths resulting from crimes not inscribed under international law, such as to "die of fear" or to "die of hunger." The REHMI referred to these theoretical and methodological challenges as its "methodological crisis."[1] Similarly, in this study I also faced fieldwork challenges that prompted me to revisit methodologies in my attempts to uncover the ongoing military control still impacting Chichicastenango communities.

I argue that a decolonizing, self-critical ethnography was best suited to reveal deeply unequal power relations because it allowed the building of short, but trustful, relations with pro-army allies as well as both low-level and high-ranking military officers. I discuss how this type of ethnography can inform a postcolonial military sociology in designing a safe and empowering approach to uncover the legacies of prolonged military control at the local level and Maya peasant-military relations. As Māori scholar Linda Tuhiwai Smith points out in her benchmark *Decolonizing Methodologies,* a methodology that moves away from reiterating oppression should "take apart a history of Western imperialism claiming to 'know' Indigenous experience."[2] To examine people's experience with long-term ramifications of militarization and militarism in Chichicastenango's two halves, I draw from ethnographers carrying out their fieldwork on terror and violence,[3] venturing into "male-dominated settings" and violent institutions.[4]

The latter arrangements refer to "sites where social relationships and cultural realities are critically modified by the pervasion of fear, threat of force or (ir)regular application of violence."[5] I address the methodological dilemmas and risks involved when gaining access to human rights organizations in the east and communities' authorities, ex-civil patrols and ex-military commissioners, under the army's control in the west. Why would still-active ex-patrols and ex-military commissioners open up to a Chilean-born, light-skinned Latina, a working-class immigrant to the United States, a doctoral candidate? How did my ethnic, class, and gender status inform my attempts at building a trustful rapport in both sides of Chichicastenango? How had pro-army authorities asserted their "male superiority"? Did they take charge of the interview process?

As opposed to conventional and status quo ethnography, critical ethnography interrogates assumptions and gives authority to participants' voices to use this knowledge for social change. This type of ethnography can be a compelling tool for uncovering grassroots' subordination to military control that quantitative inquiry is ill-equipped to reveal. Complemented by historical archival research, it can yield unique oral histories that illustrate the experience of the oppressed with militarization and militarism, racism, and extreme conditions of intolerable poverty.[6]

While it is best applied with "vulnerable," easily wounded, and traumatized populations, as well as with people whose autonomy is diminished and whose lives are marginalized, such as Indigenous peoples, it also is suited when reaching out to "hidden" or "hard to reach" populations, such as military personnel, whose voices are often difficult to record due to the secrecy engulfing security institutions. Critical fieldwork is used, as Jim Thomas observes, with the ultimate goal of contributing to social change by taking into account the viewpoint of participants on the researcher.[7]

Complementing my approach to learning about Maya peasant-military relations—the latter the workers of violence, to paraphrase Martha K. Huggins[8]—I rely on feminist theory, offering critical insights about the personal dimensions of political power, questioning gender roles, patriarchy, and masculinity "in ways that do not re-inscribe interests of the privileged."[9] From this view, accessing both populations (human rights victims and pro-army groups) required me to remain aware of the impact of my own identity in the local communities. Relying on C.W. Mills's classic "sociological imagination"[10] linking the internally oppressed situation to the status quo to challenge them, I was able to scale the walls of silence. I have avoided the use of the term "informers," a concept that eerily invokes the word "infiltrator," applied to those denouncing their neighbors to the army during the war.

Participants from both halves of Chichicastenango representing the voices of the aggrieved and the army consented to be interviewed on the condition of complete anonymity to guarantee confidentiality. Disclosure of their identity would have meant possible reprisals from the army if found providing war secrets, and if these became public. Pro-army interviewees feared that legal proceedings could be used against them. "It had happened," Rigoberto, from Patzibal, once told me. However, being upfront about the fact that no material gain was attached to their participation in the study was difficult. It highlighted my privileged position in relation to most participants. However, transportation funds and meals were provided.

Fieldwork Before The Truth Commission (1990–1997)

By the time I gained entry into Chichi's two regions in mid-2000, I drew on extensive prior fieldwork analyzing human rights crimes in Guatemala. I had been introduced to the country's bloodbath in 1992 when I was an undergraduate at Hunter College and interning at the Unitary Representation of the Guatemalan Opposition (RUOG). Later, in 1994, I visited the refugee camps set up by the Mexican Refugees Aid Commission (COMAR) in Chiapas. After a few days, I crossed the border through Huehuetenango and eagerly headed to Guatemala City.

From 1996 to 1997, I made two more visits to the capital in the context of my dissertation research, during which I established long-term relationships with grassroots groups' leaders that eventually proved pivotal for my later fieldwork in the war's early aftermath. In 1996, my interest in human rights led me to apply to the United Nations in Guatemala City, hoping I could intern with them. To my surprise, a year later, I was successfully interviewed by the UN to join the Truth Commission as a field researcher. Little did I know that when I arrived at the commission's headquarters in Guatemala City in late August 1997, I would be assigned to collect testimonies in southern El Quiché, an area contested by both the state and the rebels.

At that time, I now realize, I naïvely thought that this international endeavor could eventually contribute to bringing enduring "peace and reconciliation" to war-torn Maya communities. It is a view that resonated (and resonates) with the modernizing bias of international law embodied in the westernized UN's human rights practices.[11] This emotional reflexivity to examining implications, as noted by Huggins and Marie-Louise Glebbeek, is "epistemologically relevant for understanding research outcomes."[12]

The Historical Clarification Commission (1997–1999)

On 1 September 1997, the commission opened its offices in the capital, and in more than ten departments, including El Quiché, Huehuetenango, and the Verapaces. Through posters, fliers, radio, and television ads—mostly in Spanish but also in the Indigenous languages Maya-K'iché and Maya-Kachiquel—it launched a nationwide campaign to persuade the population to tell their war testimonies in confidence, *en confianza*. The flier below (Fig. 1.1) illustrates these efforts.

Figure 1.1. "It is time to tell the truth!" The commission urged all Guatemalans to come forward and share their war testimonies with us. © ÇIRMA, Archivo Histórico. Colección 57, Personal Collection, Marcie Mersky.

At least one radio announcement specifically targeted human rights per-petrators, but few came forward. At our Santa Cruz office, two former patrols involved in the horrendous Chijtinimit massacre came forward—only a few weeks earlier I had taken the testimony of the parents of one of the victims. The CEH guaranteed the "confidentiality of the sources and witnesses" and asserted the "need to break the walls of fear and silence"[13] to achieve reconcil-iation. As a representative of the commission in El Quiché, I bear witness to the harrowing atrocities, told in chilling detail, that Maya peasants suffered at the hands of the army.

Encountering the "Internal Colonial Situation"

In what became a life-shaping epiphany, I also painfully witnessed the wretch-edness Maya peasant families are forced to endure after centuries of exploita-tion and looting of their communities. In retrospect, no historical account could have prepared me to confront the scourge of internal colonialism I found in El Quiché: families of six or more living in dark, dirt floor huts made out of corrugated metal lean-tos (*laminas*), children shoeless and undernourished, pale-skinned children running to hide from strangers—like myself—asking sensible questions about their war experiences.

Being a witness to their precarious lives, I learned to tell the difference among the children from different communities based on my observation of their tooth deformities, how pale they were, and their swollen stomachs, all maladies due to insufficient nourishment. As a result, I became quite con-scious of my privileged life in New York City but also of my own working-class roots living under General Pinochet's regime (1973–1990). This meant I was familiar not only with firsthand stories of atrocities but also with resistance to military rule, and thus I found shared ground with survivors in their grief and their hope for justice. Significantly, survivors' extreme poverty was starkly contrasted with the salaries made by UN staffers (including myself), as also noted by Alexander Hinton in his field trips to postgenocide Cambodia in the early 1990s.[14]

Under a Tree: Learning to Laugh with Sorrow

Unlike the public nature of the South African Truth and Reconciliation Com-mission, CEH witnesses' interviews were not broadcast on TV. Rather, they took place in the privacy of communities' oratory or school building or sitting on the grass under a tree. Along with other fellow staffers, I trekked up, down, and across mountains to reach isolated settlements, and once I even traveled by helicopter to interview survivors living in the steep mountains in northern El Quiché, in the Ixil Triangle. At first, following the semi-open-ended questionnaire designed by the commission, I asked individual survivors questions related to the acts of violence they had witnessed or knew about. Over time, however, mothers, grandparents, uncles, *compadres* (godfathers), cousins, and neighbors' testimonies would spontaneously evolve into collective interviews as family members stood around and asked others to help them reconstruct the events, transforming an individual testimony into a communal endeavor, pretty much in line with community life.

Showing their strong sense of solidarity, women's groups such as the National Coordination of Widows of Guatemala (CONAVIGUA), the Peasant Unity Committee (CUC), and the K'amalb'e Rech Tinamit Ixim Ulew warmly offered us hot coffee and boiled eggs—and even made jokes about their war experiences.[15] Hinton, reports a similar experience from Cambodia: despite the suffering they had endured, most people "were extremely friendly and warm."[16] From this participatory research experience, I learned that relying on survivors' rather dark sense of humor also could connect me with them to elicit war narratives. I relied on a "sympathetic understanding," or Verstehen, when interviewing war and genocide survivors, victims, perpetrators, rescuers, and bystanders alike.[17] Not only does this type of sociological empathy involve cultural understanding of people's belief and value systems, but it also needs to tackle their underprivileged underpinnings.

The Power of a Ticket out: The Importance of Timing

When interviewing survivors whose voices had been silenced and unrecognized, I was quite aware of what I term "the power of a ticket out"—as well as the diplomatic immunity granted by the commission. This meant the ability to go back to New York, guaranteeing my safety from violent reprisals by perpetrators and their collaborators hoping to disturb our truth-telling investigation. This power, as in the case of foreign war anthropologists working in Guatemala, presupposes an acknowledgement of one's power in the field. Unlike Guatemalan researchers, who for the most part face deadly threats—exemplified by anthropologist Myrna Mack's stabbing to death by a military death squad on 11 September 1990—foreign scholars are less likely to encounter deadly risks in their studies.

Occasionally, while conducting fieldwork for the commission, my fears of being targeted for taking war testimonies increased. This happened, I remember vividly, on 2 April 1998, when Bishop Juan José Gerardi Conedera, who pioneered the REHMI project, was bludgeoned to death in his house. Yet, I rarely felt that the team or I was seriously threatened, as far as I can recall.[18] Conducting fieldwork in poverty-stricken communities proved to be a lasting learning experience that would prepare me for my postcommission research in Chichicastenango. It showed me ethnographic practices I could not have learned otherwise—such as to keep silent, to attentively listen, and to, at the very least, say *maltiosh,* "thank you," in Maya-K'iché.

I now realize that when I was told in early 1997 that I was going to work for the Truth Commission, I was full of idealism and felt that I "could make a difference," as expressed by Beatriz Manz.[19] It was with this enthusiasm and naïveté that I entered the early aftermath of the war in Chichicastenango to learn about the lingering effects of militarization and militarism.

Field Working A Local Context: A Case Study

A few months before ending my tenure with the commission, I was assigned to explore in-depth a particular municipality's experience with the war. I chose Chichicastenango because of my love for craft markets and for a rather pragmatic reason: back then I did not know how to drive, and Chichi was conveniently located, only some twenty minutes away by a "chicken bus" that would take me to the urban center, the pueblo. I made trips particularly during market days, when hardworking neighbors and community authorities converged to run small shops and sell their crafts and goods in the local market. I also made trips to the Chupol area when invited by organized groups during community events, such as voter registration efforts or Maya ceremonies.

I obtained a map of communities and marked the interview locations with different colors (without knowing it, I was doing what armies routinely do when charting their intelligence operations). It was then that I noticed the striking disparities in the number of human rights crimes identified by the CEH, as I discussed in the Introduction. Adding to this puzzle was the western area's lack of human rights organizations, which had prevented me from gaining access to eyewitness testimonies. Once my obligations to the CEH were over, I went back to Chichi to delve deeper into the history of both regions to explain why some communities testified, while others did not. Defining all of the seventy-nine communities that existed in Chichi in 2000 as either "militarized" or "nonmilitarized" would ignore each community's singular histories. So, I identified these villages along a continuum of militarization and militarism, accounting for shared patterns of experiencing the failed demilitarization of the patrol system in the early aftermath in the west, as opposed to the more collective, heroic resistance to the patrol system manifested in the east.[20] (For a socioeconomic profile of these communities, see Appendix 1).[21]

A total of seventy individual and collective taped and nontaped interviews were collected in Chichicastenango, Santa Cruz (capital of El Quiché) and Guatemala City. Accounting for the west, I carried out twenty individual and collective interviews with former patrols and military commissioners in positions of authority in their communities, such as auxiliary mayors, health promoters, leaders of betterment committees, and army officers. As in the case of Huggins's study of former torturers in Brazil,[22] in a short period of time I only carried out, with some exceptions, one interview with each participant.

In the east, I carried out fifty interviews with the director of the local health center, Catholic clergy and lay people, municipal firefighters, founders from the local Peasant League, betterment committees, and Maya priests, members of the state and Indigenous municipalities, and representatives from human rights groups and local nongovernmental organizations (NGOs). The NGOs included ASDECO (Asociación de Desarrollo Integral Comunitario), FUNDADESE (Asociación Cooperación para el Desarrollo Integral), CASODI (Coordinadora de Asociaciones de Desarrollo Integral), the European Community Program, the United Nations Mission to Guatemala (MINUGUA) overseeing the Peace Accords, the Comisión Presidencial de Derechos Humanos (COPREDEH), and the Municipal Planning Office (OMP). Most of the participants were males ranging in age from twenty to seventy. When speaking with Maya peasants, simultaneous translations were used. Men tended to speak Spanish, or *castilla,* more frequently than women.

The East: a Collaborative Research Approach

Spending time in the field opened doors for both rewarding and disappointing research experiences. This is illustrated in my collaboration with Miguel, Juan, and Marcos, representatives of the Association for the Progress of All (APA) from Chicuá II, which was located alongside the interdepartmental road in the east. In the collaborative approach, "research methods are jointly chosen, objectives are identified and the researched assists in interpreting data."[23] APA leadership, Miguel, Juan, and Marcos, all Maya-K'iché peasants and former patrols themselves, were in the process of recruiting families into a microcredit entrepreneurship aimed at the trading of apples, plums, and avocados produced in their communities. They possessed unique, intimate knowledge of the political and military strategies the army had used to corral support for its patrol system, their implications, the township's war and genocide history, in general, and its traditional system of authority.

The leadership also included Fabiola, but only the men agreed to collaborate with the study, with a mutually agreed upon schedule to carry out interviews. They soon became "knowledge brokers," "cultural brokers," or "gatekeepers,"[24] defined as qualified, grassroots intellectuals who have special knowledge of the larger cultural and historical context.[25] As we ran errands and set up appointments together, I do not recall encountering any kind of sexual advances such as other women researchers have faced in the field, though sometimes they offered flirtatious remarks.[26]

APA members carried out several other tasks: (1) developed a snowball sampling, a recruitment technique in which one participant suggests another one, along with local authorities and human rights groups from eastern communities; (2) set up and collected interviews; and (3) carried out the interviews in Maya-K'iché, which they or other Maya-K'iché assistants later translated. The APA representatives' participation in this study was essential in deciphering cultural codes I could not otherwise understand.[27] In their view, for example, the army had taken advantage of the administrative divisions separating communities into microregions to impose various, targeted strategies to gain each population's support. In their interviews, APA members raised questions about feelings of "guilt," a cultural value deeply ingrained, for having the belief that people had brought the violence upon themselves or for not serving their communities, itself a cultural understanding rooted in traditions based on mutual reciprocity. Juan, for example, often would ask participants, "Why did the army treat you like this? Do you feel you did something wrong?" Feelings of defeat also abound in postwar testimonies from organized communities: "We failed; we lived through all this for nothing [*por gusto*]. We don't want anything. We were in the mountains, and what did we gain? Nothing, we are in worse conditions," a peasant told Andrés, a priest from Santa Cruz.[28]

To gain APA trust, I was asked by its leadership to organize a one-day "orientation" workshop (*taller*) about microlending resources with Pietro Vitteri, a representative I knew from the European Union working in the design and implementation of sustainable development projects in El Quiché. I also helped them draft a proposal for a three-year economic project. My collaboration with APA illustrates my awareness of my responsibility to give back concrete and symbolic resources to vulnerable populations who lacked access to the information and networks I possessed.

When I asked Miguel about their experiences trying to gain membership to western communities, he explained: "We have tried to enter, but, we as well as institutions are repelled (*rebotamos*)." APA's main perception was that community authorities in western communities were "under the spell of the army," or in the *Hands of the Army*, the title they suggested for my doctoral dissertation. Their efforts to expand their membership in western communities, however, were often largely rejected by village authorities.

In APA's eyes, this rejection occurred because the army manipulated the authorities and, therefore, "People do not want to talk to strangers" or "Unknown outsiders are not welcome." Despite casting themselves as a neutral, apolitical association, membership was not growing within families in the Saquillá, Paxot, and the Mactzul cluster presumed to be under the army's control. I was told by Miguel to avoid using the term "organization," a word evoking the war's most violent years, when being organized into peasant groups was criminalized by the military. Even the slightest enunciation of *organización* was synonymous with trouble and could bring suspicions from the army's collaborators.

Instead, we agreed that I would use "survey" (*encuesta*). Thanks to APA's support, I reconnected with human rights groups mobilizing in the Lacamá and Chontolá communities in the east. Soon after, leaders began inviting me to their homes, where I carried out mostly, but not only, collective open-ended interviews on families' doorsteps and in their backyards. My visits to the Chupol area took place during the day, after which I went back to Posada Conchita—the conveniently located inn I had rented a room in next to the municipal and Indigenous municipal buildings—often by public transportation or my car, since by then I finally had learned how to drive.

An unexpected outcome was that APA eventually became a focus of my study. To my disbelief, after a year of repeatedly discussing the army's crimes perpetrated in their communities, Juan asked me to serve as a bridge between APA and El Quiché's Army's Civil Affairs Unit, whose officers were known during the war as S-5 and were responsible for military-civil relations with community authorities. He explained their request regarding the need to acquire fruit containers. In Chicuá I, he told me, the army had brought material to build the elementary school where "the community had contributed [to the joint project] with one day of work." Maybe this time the army also could help APA get what they needed to trade beyond Chichi, in El Salvador and Honduras.

Politicized Contexts: The Myth of Neutrality

Challenging positivistic studies, Jeffrey Sluka suggests discarding the illusion of "observer's neutrality" that scholars often are taught to assume. Quite the contrary, Sluka poignantly asserts, "Whether or not you take sides," those around you "actively involved in the situation are going to define whose side they think you are on." This definition will take place, "regardless of your professions of neutrality."[29] In my case, when reaching out to communities in the east, my attempts at neutrality soon faded away as people close to the study began to call me a "nun." They associated me with Esteban, a clergy from the Marista Brotherhood who had been living in Guatemala since the early 1970s and was well known among parishes as a caring, religious man. I explain this assigned identity as a sociological "halo effect," or biased effect defined as the unconscious, global evaluation used to assign attributes to people about whom we know little.[30]

This perception of me being "a nun" and identifying with people's leftwing politics helped me gain the trust of leaders and authorities opposing the army. When I visited the Chontolá and Chupol communities, for example, authorities, unlike in the west, showed fewer suspicions about my presence in their communities. As a result, I also felt more comfortable disclosing my leftist political views, and I engaged with people based on my gendered experience with rightwing military dictatorship. By admitting my own biases, my own experience growing up under General Pinochet resonated with survivors. As Manz, herself born in Chile, reports, "Peasants' knowledge of the gross human rights violations in Chile sparks curiosity that gives ways to conversations."[31]

Some of my efforts for keeping apparent neutrality involved renting an affordable room at Posada Conchita, a cozy inn located on 8th Avenue, Zone 1, across from the sixteenth-century white stucco Catholic church in the center of the market plaza. I soon made the Posada's second floor my "headquarters" for conducting interviews with pro-army community authorities in particular, since efforts to interview them in their communities flatly failed, as I discuss below. This contrasts with Richard Wilson's study of changes in Q'eqchi identity in the early 1990s as well as Victoria Sanford's multisite approach examining communities' participation in exhumations.[32] Instead, my study approach mirrors that of Hinton in postwar Cambodia, when he settled in one city, from which he visited communities, due to high security concerns for himself and those involved in his study.[33]

Despite the Guatemalan Institute of Tourism (INGUAT)'s claims of the township being a "Mecca of tourism," as colorful, religious, and cultural manifestations are frozen in time in postcards to attract revenue from tourism,[34] the town's urban center lacks adequate services and accommodations, except for the pricey Maya Inn Hotel (even today, twenty years after the war ended). Over time, store and restaurant owners, market merchants, storekeepers, waitresses, and representatives from Catholic, human rights, and popular organizations as well as civil affairs personnel from the nearest military outpost all became accustomed to seeing me beyond the Thursday and Sunday market days, when tourists were gone. The rest of the week, the center goes back to its normal routine. Its main streets, that now can be seen without the improvised, nylon-covered stalls, are flooded with locals going about their business, taking children to the health post and soliciting birth and death certificates at the Ladino and Indigenous municipalities.

Interviewing War Survivors

I followed Ann Oakley's strategy of engaging in the type of "progressive friendship" with human rights leaders and groups that enabled me to develop a nonhierarchical relationship with research participants.[35] I tape-recorded most interviews, with participants' permission granted to me on the basis that I would tell others about the tragedy that had besieged them. In a context where participants felt at ease, I asked questions that could generate personal views, instead of asking specific questions about the war. For example, when I accompanied the daughter of a close friend of mine, and a key cultural broker, from the Chontolá community, I asked about women's views on marriage and motherhood as I disclosed my own marital status. By using this biographical approach, I gradually obtained insights into this community's capacity to organize and the role of women in facilitating the emergence of grassroots groups before and after the genocide.

Progressively, questions shifted to discussions of their war histories and their perceptions about the war's lasting repercussions. I realized that to feel safe before they told me their views on sensitive themes, survivors needed time to reconstruct war memories to a stranger. For the most part, however, organized survivors were ready to give their testimonies on this side, since they belonged to human rights networks informing them of the different local and international efforts undertaken to keep their memories alive.

The West: A Unique Entry (1999–2000)

Critical ethnography questioning deeply unequal military-Maya relations was pivotal for gaining entry to and establishing a trustful rapport with militarized authorities in the west. This happened despite their initial suspicions, illustrated by community authorities barring my visits to meet with them in their communities. Roughly, this was the area of the Mactzules (4,000 people in six communities), Paxot (a population of 3,650 in three communities with similar names), and Saquillá (a population of 1,000 in two communities). This area is characterized by infertile mountains and higher levels of poverty, as "higher altitude is associated with land scarcity, poorer agricultural conditions, and greater remoteness from transport networks and other public services."[36] (See Appendix 1.)

I based my strategy for interviewing pro-army communities' representatives on (1) the unfolding of a snowball strategy, (2) attempts to occasionally visit communities, (3) talks with leaders and members of the Association of Friends of the Army (Asociación Amigos del Ejército), and (4) traveling with the army to plant seedlings in the Chulumal I community (discussed in Chapter Three).

Unlike in the east, where developing a "progressive friendship" with survivors worked well with leaders from the Chupol area, I was quite certain I could not develop the same kind of close relations with militarized authorities from the western region. Yet, could I achieve a reliable rapport if I befriended former patrols whose allegiance to the army had remained unchanged? Anthropologist Aldo Civico has presented similar questions in his study of Colombian paramilitaries: Can—or should—researchers have "benevolent" feelings for people whose beliefs and actions they utterly despise?[37] Is displaying a political view possible, or even desirable, when cultivating relationships with alleged human rights perpetrators or collaborators participating in our studies? This was the case when I attempted to collect interviews with community authorities from the west, since my disclosure would, most likely, have endangered those around me. I was concerned that military collaborators could brand me a sympathizer of the URNG, which could have brought retaliation upon those providing me with information.

My efforts at keeping an apparent political neutrality proved pivotal when gaining access to pro-army groups because claims of being "neutral," and therefore "apolitical" soundly resonated with the military's own assertions of being uninterested in political power, as examined in Brian Loveman and Thomas M. Davies's *The Politics of Antipolitics*. I relied on a "neutral" device to persuade authorities from the west that I was not "ideologically" tainted against their pro-army political stance. Thus, I seized every opportunity to appear as neutral as possible, and not to openly judge former patrols' past or current collaborations with the military. Over time, and unexpectedly, among pro-army peasants I met, my identification with the military was such that once an amigo gave me a folder addressed to me as the "military's lawyer."

When seeking access to the Mactzules, Paxot, and Saquillá areas, pro-army group representatives—former patrols in their posts as auxiliary mayors, principals (the community's highest authority), presidents of ad hoc planning committees, betterment committees, and pro-development (*comités de promejoramiento*), variously named—systematically ignored my requests to visit them. After waiting for three excruciating months, I had not successfully secured even one interview with authorities from the west. Was something terribly wrong with my research strategy? APA leadership assured me otherwise: for them, this time was normal when gaining trust with more closed authorities, such as those in the western area. "Do not despair," *no te desesperes*, was often their encouraging advice.[38]

Tea and Cookies at the Military Zone: The Importance of Timing

Anthropologist Ruth Behar notes that the deep emotional encounter with atrocities calls for the "engaged observer" to connect with people whose actions and ideology one is seeking to understand, "without actually going native."[39] In Behar's views, in order to accomplish this epistemological task, researchers are required to disclose their own class, ethnic, religious, and political backgrounds to empathize with research participants. But the full disclosure of my biography became a difficult endeavor when seeking to elicit information from militarized populations.

Ricardo Falla, the prominent Jesuit anthropologist documenting massacres and the plight of internal refugees from the Ixcán region, explains in *Quiché*

Rebelde why he "only" appeared as a Catholic priest to the internally displaced, organized into the Communities in Resistance (CPR). "I did not say anything about being an anthropologist," he writes. "I could have kept my identity as priest and passed as someone who wanted to study their traditions … But this was impossible … because [Guatemala] is a small country and my identity was public."[40] Cultural criminologists examining the immediacy of crime have also argued that withholding information is sometimes necessary to establish the rapport necessary to interview members of vulnerable populations.[41]

In late June 2000, I decided to reach out to high-ranking officers from Military Zone No. 20 without the direct help of APA. Our shared concern was that the army would associate them with my study, which eventually could subject them to the repercussions that I was less likely to suffer because of the aforementioned power of my ticket out of the country. My entry into the world of amigos and the Civil Affairs and Local Development (S-5) officers in mid-2000 was through Manuel Pinzón, a former United Nations colleague, who in 1999 was the director of the Government Office for Human Rights (COPREDEH).

My goal was to request his help to get access to representatives from pro-army communities through the Army Zone. Pinzón immediately admitted that the "Army's Civil Affairs Unit was overseeing the reconversion of the PACs into Peace Committees," [42] and he facilitated my introduction to the civil affairs director of the army general staff, Colonel Manuel Jesús Chávez. Chávez, after disclosing that the Army Zone kept anthropological studies of communities (which I actually never had access to), referred me to Infantry Colonels José Samayoa and Edgar Noel Palacios. Within a couple of weeks, I was on my way to the fortified military zone, and I paid my first official visit to Colonel Samayoa to introduce the study. Before I headed there, I alerted close friends about my meeting at the zone in the event that they did not hear from me that evening—my tactic of self-protection.[43] After all, I was about to meet with members of the institution responsible for the slaughter.

To my surprise, I was welcomed with coffee and cookies, a reception I interpreted as the type of paternalism female researchers experience when attempting to gain entry into predominantly male institutions. I told Colonel Samayoa up front about my prior fieldwork collecting testimonies for the Truth Commission, but I did not disclose my own political views regarding the role of the army in the early 1980s. As our conversation unfolded, I dropped the name of General Pinochet and asked if I could interview the army's followers from Chichicastenango, a spontaneous occurrence Kovats-Bernat has called "strategies of improvisation."[44]

Colonel Samayoa appeared delighted as he expressed his profound admiration for the Chilean dictator. He ordered his assistant, Major Portillo, to make a personal phone call to solicit the collaboration of the Chichicastenango municipal mayor, Manuel Sut Lucas, who was elected on a FRG platform, and his general secretary. Because they learned that I was not a human rights lawyer representing any aggrieved group seeking criminal accountability and because of the supremacy of the army's male-dominated values system, I was not perceived as representing a real threat to the military. Clearly, the postwar climate of impunity had emboldened the army and Ríos Montt's followers to feel they could express their views to a foreigner without repercussions.

From then on, relying on a "snowball" technique, I negotiated my entry into western communities. Undoubtedly, this particular entry points to critical challenges in assessing respondents' narratives: Did they give truthful accounts? To what extent did they follow the army's anticommunist script, or "mantra," as observed by Paul Kobrak?[45] Were ex-patrols and pro-army authorities' narratives tainted by the fact that it was the army that had initially sanctioned the interviews?

Interviewing the Army's Subjugated Allies: Amigos

This network of sanctioned participants eventually led me to interview authorities, ex-military commissioners, and former patrols. The amigos working out of the Army Zone had more education, and at least one even had some basic English skills following his claimed military training at Fort Benning in the United States (whether or not this was the case I was not able to verify). Yet, even when considering that my entry was through the local S-5, pro-military community authorities showed great distrust and repeatedly requested a full disclosure of this study's aims. They demanded reassurance that I would not reveal their identities, and only a few allowed me to tape-record the interview. As long as I avoided pointed questions about their role during the war, they were willing to talk to me about their ongoing relations with the army. The mayor, Sut Lucas, went as far as to offer me an office inside the municipal building to carry out interviews! I declined his offer, however, to avoid raising confusion about my research goals among human rights participants from the Chupol area.

Instead, I relied upon a large kitchen table and close friends stopping by to help me greet participants with hot chocolate or coffee and *tamalitos* or *chuchitos* (typical Guatemalan food) to encourage interviewees (*para animar a la gente*). Even though I gained entry into militarized groups, spending time with families in their communities was highly restricted by authorities— thus my choice to rent a room at Posada Conchita to carry out interviews. As a result, I was prevented from attending ceremonies, making keen day-to-day observations of activities, or interviewing the community elders who possessed knowledge about the years anteceding the 1980s genocide. Most of all, authorities kept me from observing interactions between army members and the community—except when I went to the Chulumal I community.

I was concerned primarily for the safety of this study's participants, whom I saw as vulnerable to the military's reprisals. This fear led me to conduct most of my interviews with pro-army authorities within two months, July and August, echoing the similar time frame that Huggins used to collect her interviews with police officers accused of torture in Brazil. I reasoned that respondents soon could talk to each other and realize they perhaps had given me crucial war information that could bring harsh retaliation from the army upon them and their families. After all, the amigos were telling me in their own words about their unbroken relations with the military, which not only amounted to a clear violation of the 1996 Peace Accords but also provided strong evidence that the army had prevailed in their efforts to promote military-Maya peasant relations.

What Does This Study Bring to Us?

The following chapters will show the complicated negotiations community authorities entered into with the army as they extended to negotiations I encountered in this study. Peasants I sought to interview often asked me what kinds of benefits this study would bring to them. Why should they take time off from their hard work on their *milpa* (corn field) to travel to Posada Conchita to meet with me? People I spoke to often remarked, "The community wants more information [*quiere datos*] because between 1981 and 1982 they were tricked [*engañados*], and now they are fearful." The term "research" is seen as being "inextricably linked to European imperialism and colonialism" and one of the "dirtiest words," Tuhiwai Smith points out.[46] A large amount of patience on my part proved to be a valuable requisite to gaining *la confianza*, as I encountered a wall of silence and secrecy around the subject of the recent past.

Once I began interviewing, I understood authorities' reluctance to speak to me: in their eyes, my visit could "quickly raise suspicions" among former patrols, ex-military commissioners, their families, and all those who did not want to get involved in any initiative not sanctioned by the army, which could result in repercussions.

To my questions about their relations with the army, some answered, "a saber" or "Who knows?" But others were more forthcoming. Jacinto, from Pajuliboy, for example, once told me, "We might create a big mess. Later you can visit the community and ask questions about culture and that sort of thing, but not about what happened during the war."[47] Army loyalists did not like to see peasants convening private meetings: "The way that people are now gathered together, the military does not like it."[48] Yolanda, from Chupol, remarked on how being organized into human rights groups divided families. "This family has four brothers, and the last child, who is a daughter, is organized, but her brothers disapprove [of] it."[49] Scaling the walls of silence maintained by neighbors, families, and communities suspicious of a foreigner asking questions about their relations with the army was one of the most challenging obstacles. Obtaining the blessing of the Auxiliatura Indígena proved pivotal.

"One of Us": *The Auxiliatura Indígena*

I often dropped by the Auxiliatura Indígena to chitchat with the secretary, who was from the community of Chijtinimit, the scene of two gruesome massacres in the early 1980s of patrols disobeying the army's orders to enlist (Chapter Six).[50] For the most part, conversations with representatives from the Council of Elders were stifled when I raised questions about the past violence and the military. Still, they lent their aid to this study by writing a letter of support requesting community authorities to facilitate interviews! The Auxiliatura also facilitated my contacts with authorities during a Sunday meeting held between a group of about fifty community' authorities, auxiliary mayors, betterment committees, health promoters, and principals.

On this occasion, showing the rapport I had painstakingly established with the highest Maya authorities, the secretary told the convened authorities I was "one of them," an acceptance I assumed I had gained by virtue of living and spending time in Chichi for about a year. A few minutes later, I was asked by the authorities to stand up on a chair to be seen by the group standing in the dark and crowded room. From the back, I heard voices from the group asking if lunches would be served. I replied they would, as members from the APA translated the exchange. I felt integrated, albeit momentarily, into the rather hermetic Auxiliatura Indígena.

On at least four occasions, I had the opportunity to travel to communities in the west to meet with authorities and families, efforts that ultimately failed. Once, I went along with a rural health promoter (*promotor rural de salud*) to the Mactzul II community, but once again, when we arrived, there were no organized groups or authorities expecting us—only the mountain's cold silence witnessed our efforts. Yet another time, I went along with local European Community representatives to Paxot III. This time, I was allowed by authorities to conduct a brief survey, asking demographic questions and about development projects brought by the army. However, the low response rate, coupled with glaring inconsistencies, does not allow a thorough interpretation.

Military Scripts, Talking Point Interview List, Informed Consent

To elicit responses from former militiamen and S-5 officers, I relied on a "topic list," used also by Simone Remijnse, with open-ended questions related to authorities' relations with the army and the army's security and development projects in their communities.[51] Questions posed to the S-5 included the goals of the program, the relationship between the army and community authority, and the meaning of progress and development. In his study of Argentina's political violence, Antonious Robben warns of the dangers of "ethnographic seduction," defined as participants' attempts to move away from a deeper understanding of the war.[52] To avoid drifting away from my central topic, I adjusted, readjusted, and reframed interviews and tried them—sometimes successfully, sometimes unsuccessfully—depending on my interviewees' identity. As Kimberly Theidon argues, "In methodological terms, the utility of questionnaires is limited when studying sensitive topics and subjective processes in a climate of distrust," such as that which characterizes the legacy of fratricidal war in Guatemala.[53]

I did not raise questions about their involvement in war or postwar criminal activities because I feared that by doing so I would push them away from the study. Were pro-army authorities' narratives part of a larger military narrative, or were they sincere in their views of the army? Most interviews show a similar script they all knew too well when I asked questions such as: "Can you tell me about the public work the army has brought into your community?" Although a few told me they witnessed the massacring of their neighbors, such as in Saquillá II, my interviewees explicitly avoided accounting for their own role in the killings.

But to what extent were self-reported narratives from militarized and colonized Indigenous groups mediated by the fear of army reprisals if caught disclosing any incriminating war secrets? Were they seeking to manipulate the interview to appear favorable to the military in case the interview fell into the hands of the S-5 officers and collaborators? Past studies have suggested the hidden nature of peasants' true feelings against the army. A survivor, Emiliano, told Manz that people who had been under military control "were angry at the army. Yet, they do not express what is in the bottom of their thinking."[54] Similarly, a Maya activist who was forced to lead the civil patrol in his rural community during the war told Diane M. Nelson, "I have two faces. One I showed to the army. One I showed to my people."[55] This paradox may have led to the fact that, most of the time, I interviewed them in the company of another fellow authority, who was keeping a close watch on what was said, suspecting war secrets could be revealed to me.

Presuming that ex-patrols told me what they believed the army would approve of them saying, there is clearly an ideological script emerging from the narratives, which largely resonates with the military's Cold War rhetoric. In short, while at the individual level there was diversity among the ex-patrols with whom I interacted, rightwing community authorities had a common militarized mindset. Few ex-patrols spoke about their religious views in this study. In fact, obstacles to interviewing professedly Evangelical active and former patrols proved largely insurmountable, and thus, their voices as members of Evangelical Protestant churches, such as Iglesia de Dios, Príncipe de Paz, and Jesucristo de los Últimos Días, are largely absent in this study.

Finding the Right Name

One challenge with written material has to do with inconsistencies in the names of communities as recorded in newspapers and official documents. Name confusion emerges from different spellings of the same name, "Chaquijyá" instead of "Saquillá," for example. This makes it difficult, if not almost impossible, to obtain an accurate demographic profile or historical account. This confusion can point the researcher to locate the community either in Chichicastenango or in another department where a similarly spelled community exists. This unreliability calls for ethnographers to carry out their own socioeconomic surveys to account for more precise demographic profiles, if resources permit.

In fact, learning about the pregenocide history and socioeconomic profile of western communities was, along with getting access to militarized authorities, one of the most challenging efforts in this study because so little has been written about each individual community or cluster thereof. I chose not to use pseudonyms when identifying communities in order to corroborate information with archival material and for future scholars to validate findings.

Sustained Relationships (2000–2015)

Soon after the Xalbaquiej lynching (Chapter Nine) in July 2000, I was advised by a schoolteacher who feared for my safety to leave the township for a few days because, while riding a bus to Guatemala City, my name was overheard whispered in the context of my interviews with Xalbaquiej representatives. I found this incident daunting for my safety and for all those who trusted me enough to tell me about their views of the army and who had shared with me possibly incriminating information. I was paralyzed by fear at the thought of being burnt alive for asking questions about the army's relations with communities. Relying on the power of my ticket out, I soon decided to return to the United States in late August 2000.

But how does one leave the people one has become close to and developed trusting relationships with? Tuhiwai Smith argues that "reporting back" or sustaining relationships with the people involved is "never a task that can be signed off" once fieldwork is over and that one aspect of a decolonizing methodology is to share knowledge produced. From this view, the relationship with the community is not a short endeavor for intellectual gain but is ongoing, because "sharing knowledge is a long-term commitment."[56]

Following Tuhiwai Smith's approach, I did not quite leave the field completely in 2000. Before leaving, I disclosed the main findings of this research, which did not prove difficult with APA members, since they were well aware of this fact. For nearly twenty years now, I have kept in close contact with friends and APA members in the east. In fact, in 2015, during one of my short visits to Chichicastenango, I met with Juan, whom I contacted through common friends. But sharing my findings with pro-army authorities was a challenging task: how does one tell Maya authorities that their loyalty to the army proved devastating for their own communities?

Access to the Municipal Firefighters Department

As I recount in *Remembering the Rescuers,* my unique access to the bundle of administrative logs neatly kept by the second commander of the Chichicastenango Municipal Firefighter Branch reveals the urgent need to preserve local war archives.[57] Like the World War I ambulance drivers in Europe, *bomberos* played a critical humanitarian role.[58] The trucks traveled daily into remote areas to pick up corpses and the wounded. With very few resources, and with only basic training in first aid, a team cleaned up massacres, helping others voluntarily.

On countless occasions, after being summoned by families, neighbors, or the police, two full-time firefighters and at least five volunteers risked their lives to aid the wounded and to transport the deceased to Santa Elena, the nearest and only hospital morgue. Due to the area's lack of drivable roads, team members often were forced to hike through rugged mountains to reach communities located far from any paved roads—or even trails—and then carry the wounded or dead literally on their backs. Given that there are few archival written records of the violence, the *bomberos'* registry offers an unrivalled source of information on the causes of death of genocide victims. I built a database with twenty-two variables, including the date and hour the truck left its station, the type of weapon used, and who had paid for the gasoline used.

Communities' Local Archives

Another source of war and genocide material is written petitions to the El Quiché Public Ministry from peasants denoting their legal approach to contesting oppression.[59] Across the highlands, organized neighbors, despite the chilling fear of reprisals from the army, wrote to denounce intimidation from civil patrols because of their participation in human rights groups (Chapter Five). I also attempted to secure, with limited success, public records, for example, from the Good Samaritan Hospital in Santa Cruz to evaluate narratives.

At the municipal administration, birth and death records were inaccessible, largely because boxes I could see stacked to the ceiling were in complete disarray and I figured they would require a large amount of time to clean and organize. By comparison, access to archives on the Armenian genocide also proved critical, as forcefully noted by Taner Akçam.[60]

Updating a Decade-Old Manuscript

Two very important factors helped me complete this manuscript. First, I repeatedly went back to the original interviews translated into Spanish and field notes to corroborate or dispute theoretical assumptions. Second, I went back to Guatemala to conduct archival research in 2011–2012. By 2000, when I returned to New York City, my fieldwork was far from over, as the question about the postcolonial knots tying Rigoberto's "military soul" to the army continued to haunt me. My return was followed by a long, self-imposed absence resulting from my closeness to communities involved in the Xalbaquiej lynching.

Ten years later, in August 2010, I returned to Guatemala to reestablish my networks. In Guatemala City, I learned that the Army's Instituto de Prevision (IPM, the army's retirement department) kept databases of the demobilized patrols obtaining payments for their war services. I met with an army representative who showed me a room containing the files of the ex-patrols with information about who their immediate supervisors were in the army's chain of command as indicated in war patrols' ID. I was told to write a letter to government authorities, a suggestion I could not follow up on because I could not easily find an NGO to support my securing the database. In 2011, I went back to southern El Quiché as an electoral observer for the Organization of American States (OAS), certifying the first "fair" postwar elections and used this opportunity to reconnect with former local human rights leaders from the east. I tried establishing some new relations with army officers, but these attempts proved unsuccessful due to my short stay in the country—I needed more time to gain their trust.

Conducting historical research proved pivotal because it allowed me to corroborate the tight relationships the army historically has forged, and continues to forge, with Maya peasants across the countryside. This is why, between 2011 and 2012, I spent five months at CIRMA's (the Mesoamerican Center for Research) archives in the colonial city of Antigua. There I reviewed military journals going back to the late nineteenth century, such as *Memorial de la Escuela Militar, Revista de la Brigada Militar Guardia de Honor,* and *Anales de la Escuela Politécnica;* newspaper articles from *El Gráfico* and *El Imparcial;* political and military pamphlets; fliers, posters, and photographs found in *Prensa Libre, Siglo XXI*; and archives from private human rights organizations.

In 2013, I again visited Chichi on a short visit to friends and organizations. In June 2015, along with Stephanie Alfaro, a former student of mine, I filmed and interviewed the firefighter commander to record his rescue role at the height of the genocidal violence. My last trip took place in February 2017, when I traveled back to complete this book.

Notes

1. REHMI II. xxi.
2. Tuhiwai Smith, *Decolonizing Methodologies*, 4.
3. See Sluka, *Death Squad*; Nordstrom, *Different Kind of War Story*; Hinton, *Genocide*; Scheper-Hughes and Bourgois, *Violence in War and Peace*.
4. Gurney, "Not One of the Guys"; Huggins and Glebbeek, *Women Fielding Danger*; McSherry, *Incomplete Transition*; Payne, *Unsettling Accounts*.
5. Kovats-Bernat, "Negotiating Dangerous Fields," 1.
6. Thomas, *Doing Critical Ethnography*, 5.
7. Thomas, *Doing Critical Ethnography*.
8. Huggins, Haritos-Fatouros, and Zimbardo, *Violence Workers*.
9. Nagar and Geiger, "Reflexivity and Positionality," 267–78.
10. Mills, *Sociological Imagination*, 5.
11. Ekern, "Modernizing Bias of Human Rights."
12. Huggins and Glebbeek, "Women Studying Violent Male Institutions," 363–64.
13. CEH, I.35.
14. Hinton, *Why Did They Kill?*, 7.
15. On one occasion, a woman laughingly told me about her "half-dead" victim. When I asked her what she meant, she told me that her husband was in a wheelchair.
16. Hinton, *Why Did They Kill?*, 7.
17. Ferrell describes the term as a "process … whereby the researcher comes to share, in part, the situated meanings and experiences of those under scrutiny" ("Criminological Verstehen," 27).
18. Every team of field researchers across the country was assigned to military personnel from, for instance, Spain or Uruguay.
19. Manz, *Paradise in Ashes*, 5.
20. The communities clustered in microregions identified in this study are the following. In the west: Micro region 1 (Chijtinimit); Micro region 2 (Mactzul I, II, II, IV, V, VI); Micro region 3 (Patulup, Patzibal; Paxot I, II, III, Saquillá I, II, III, Xalbaquiej); Micro region 7 (Pocohil Segundo Centro). In the east: Micro region 5 (Chuchipacá II, Chutzorop, Lacamá I, Lacamá II, Lacamá III, Panquiac, Tzanimacabaj, Xabiyaguach, Xecalibal, Xecoja); Micro region 6 (Agua Escondida, Agua Viva; Chuguexa I, Chuguexa II A, Chuguexa II B, Chuguexa II, Chunima, Chujulimul I, Chujulimul II, Chupol, Pajuliboy, Sacpulub, Xepol, Chontolá, Sacpulub, Lacamá, Pajuliboy, Chicuá, Xabiawach, Panquiac, Chipacá).
21. By 1932, Ruth Bunzel had reported, "Hamlets are grouped in five areas, each under the jurisdiction of a principal whose roles are similar to the principal found in each community" (*Chichicastenango*, 234).

22. In comparison, twenty-three police officers were interviewed by Huggins, Haritos-Fatouros, and Zimbardo for *Violence Workers*, 7. As with this study, Huggins also spent three months conducting interviews. Huggins and Glebbeek, "Women Studying Violent Male Institutions," 375.
23. Huggins and Glebbeek, "Studying Violent Male Institutions," 364.
24. Brotherton, *Youth Street Gangs.*
25. Lieselotte Viaene, in her work about Q'eqchi responses to war legacies, highlights the "involvement of other mainly local knowledge brokers, such as local peasant intellectuals" ("Voices from the Shadows," 267).
26. See a useful discussion about how ethnographers report little about the "erotic equation," the sexual interest between fieldworker and informant. Newton, "My Best Informant's Dress," 4.
27. APA was formed in 1998 and was composed of twelve cantons. It was created as a not-for-profit, apolitical, nonreligious organization aimed at the integration of communities to foster agriculture, textile, craft, and trading.
28. Author interview, Father Andrés, Santa Cruz.
29. Sluka, "Reflections on Managing Danger," 287.
30. Nisbett and Wilson, "Halo Effect."
31. Manz, *Paradise in Ashes,* 5.
32. Wilson, *Maya Resurgence in Guatemala,* 5; Sanford, *Buried Secrets,* 17.
33. Hinton, *Why Did They Kill?,* 16.
34. The town included thirty-four stores, four restaurants, and approximately 3,000 informal stall stands. Organizaciones de la Sociedad Civil, "Hacía El Siglo XXI," 22, 23.
35. Oakley, "Interviewing Women."
36. Pebley and Goldman, "Social Inequality and Children's Growth," 17.
37. Civico, "Portrait of a Paramilitary."
38. To compare, restricted access to communities also was reported in Sololá. "Not even MINUGUA can go there, because the PACs do not permit it," Bonifacio Diego, mayor of Santa Catarina, Sololá, said. HNG, *Prensa Libre,* "Aldea de Sololá," 15.
39. Behar, *Vulnerable Observer,* 5.
40. Falla, *Quiché Rebelde,* 2. Falla also acknowledges that he passed as an ordinary person when conducting fieldwork with the Yaruros of Venezuela.
41. Tunnell, "Honesty, Secrecy and Deception," 207–8.
42 Author interview, Pinzón.
43. Kovats-Bernat, "Negotiating Dangerous Fields," 213.
44. Ibid., 209.
45. Kobrak, "Long War in Colotenango," 222.
46. Tuhiwai Smith, *Decolonizing Methodologies,* 1.
47. APA interview, Jacinto.
48. Collective interview, Margarita, Chupol.
49. Collective interview, Yolanda, Chupol.
50. Marie-Louise Glebbeek's postwar study of the reconversion of the Guatemalan National Police into a civilian force relied on a flexible approach to gain trust, which was almost spontaneously dependent "upon the situation" afforded. For example, she suggests some chitchat often was used to elicit information. Huggins and Glebbeek, "Women Studying Violent Male Institutions," 374.
51. Remijnse, *Memories of Violence,* 45.
52. Robben, "Politics of Truth and Emotion," 83.
53. Theidon, "Reconstructing Masculinities," 13.
54. Manz, *Paradise in Ashes,* 133.

55. Nelson, "Means and End/s."
56. Tuhiwai Smith, *Decolonizing Methodologies,* 15, 16.
57. Esparza and DeYcaza, *Remembering the Rescuers.*
58. See Hansen, *Gentlemen Volunteers.*
59. To see more of this legal undertaking, see David Carey (*I Ask for Justice*) in his account of judicial battles undertaken by poor Maya peasants.
60. Akçam, *Shameful Act,* 3.

2

A Postcolonial Reenactment
The Cold War Civil Self-Defense Patrol System

The Indigenous soul has been broken since colonial times.
— Author interview, Staff, Justice Program, USAID-El Quiché

In this chapter, I give an overview of the preexisting militarization that led up to the Cold War Civil Self-Defense Patrol (PACs) system conscripting Maya peasants. I follow the approach of Martin Shaw, who has emphasized the urgent need to acknowledge that "studies of war and militarism have often developed in the fringes, rather than at the centre" of sociological inquiry.[1] Shaw recommends building a historical sociology of war, examining local contexts impacted by prolonged military control. In Guatemala, this context is pervaded by the scourge of internal colonialism, where past political history of military dictatorships, militias, battalions, and military control has shaped institutions of the elites as well as the oppressed, with far-reaching implications for marginalized populations.

Understanding the PACs system and genocide requires understanding this local context. As Richard N. Adams has noted, the genocide was a "logical extension of preexisting Indigenous-Ladino relations."[2] Among other scholars, Guatemalan sociologist Carlos Figueroa Ibarra has remarked that the Ladino leadership held unabashed racist and classist views of peasants as less than human, which were used to justify violence in controlling the population.[3]

I argue that the PACs were not a "paramilitary" defense group,[4] which is often both the scholarly and popularly held view. Just as with "death squads" and "militias,"[5] the term "paramilitary" has varied meanings that can be broadly defined as a semi-independent armed group protecting the status quo. Chris Alden et al., for example, define militias as a "military force composed of civilians outside of a state's formal military structure."[6] In this study, PACs can be considered a militia group only in the sense that they reiterated colonial practices of enlisting part-time groups up until the creation of the army in the late nineteenth century.

Distinguishing PACs from paramilitary groups is pivotal because it reveals Maya peasant subordination to the army, despite claims of the so-called voluntariness of service into the military. A central argument in this book is that this presumed voluntariness ignores the underlying coercive internal colonialism compelling peasants to join military battalions or PACs. In fact, historically, there is a long legacy of "voluntary" enlistment, from the Spanish conquest to the present day. As sociologist Jasmin Hristov argues regarding Colombian paramilitary groups, PACs were "created and funded ... with military and logistical support provided unofficially by the state."[7] However, in contrast to Colombia, where, as Kimberly Theidon notes, paramilitary groups were "transformed into an economic, social and political force,"[8] service into PACs did not transform peasants' power structure.

Just after the accords were signed—except for a few elite groups of ex-patrols and former military commissioners who improved their personal lot—most ex-patrols stayed as poor as they had been during their service to the army. In short, the military-oligarchy elite will not tolerate armed Maya groups that can turn against them; armed groups are prohibited by the constitution. Thus, I define the patrol system as a state-sponsored Indigenous irregular force, a branch of the military that involved communities' oaths of allegiance to a military culture profoundly nationalistic and tied to a strict chain of command.[9]

Some scholars, like Jennifer Schirmer, rely on a rather limited historical view by tracing the patrols back to only 1966, when civilians were mobilized into part-time militias to defeat the leftwing guerrilla group, MR-13 (Movimiento Revolucionario 13 Noviembre).[10] Others, such as historian Michael McClintock, recount that in 1983 an army spokesman described the patrols as reminiscent of the 1880s programs that ousted the original population from potential coffee-growing lands "while keeping them on hand as a captive labor force."[11] My point of departure is the colonial era to tackle (as in the case of Guerrero, Mexico) the military's role "in the construction of subjectivities and social memories" of Indigenous peoples.[12]

This postcolonial view will show that prior to the Cold War's patrol system, Indigenous peoples already had a long and complicated history binding them to the military in their capacity as auxiliary forces, militias, and battalions (the last is explored in Chapter Six). These preexisting ties were forged in a context in which, as Albert Memmi suggests, the colonized has been made feel "in no way a subject of history."[13] As Frantz Fanon has asked, "Isn't the colonial status the organized enslavement of a whole population?"[14] An account of preexisting community-level relations with the army shows, in the words of Cynthia Enloe, that some groups "relate to the larger whole, not as participants who belong, but as resources to be exploited" and are, therefore, "mobilized as cannon fodder."[15]

Colonial and Liberal Continuities

During colonial times, native populations were incorporated into armed militias as circumstances required, repressing revolts and later maintaining the Liberal order. In light of the colonizer's racial fear of arming the Indians, who could turn against them, their collaboration had conditions: the use of weapons and riding horses was prohibited, as stated in the seventeenth-century Laws of the Indies, except when given to the "Indian amigos," such as in the case of Tlaxcala, Mexico.[16] To get them to collaborate, Spanish settlers co-opted local power structures, authorities, and nobles as "loyal Indian chiefs were ... rewarded by the Crown."[17] Known as the caciques, these authorities received, by decree, "coats of arms, [while] their sons were offered superior Spanish schooling,"[18] privileges normally denied to Indians.[19] Those empowered, as historian Marc Drouin has observed, were called to ensure law and order as "the dignified ... nobles of times past ... became 'pathetic sycophants,' acting ... as agents of social control among their own people" and allied with the Church.[20]

Despite the repeated attempts to modify Indigenous communities' internal organization and traditions, however, some institutions and authorities necessary to maintain order were preserved. One such local institution was the rural police force known as the "lieutenants," which was made up of wealthy merchants who would become the military commissioners on 9 July 1938.[21] This militarized authority was added to a complex hierarchy of politicoreligious leaders who came to constitute the power base in each community: members of the Cofradía, *alcaldes auxiliares* (auxiliary mayors), and principals (see front diagram).

The Liberal regimes of the nineteenth century's efforts to strengthen state control over the land and workforce have been analyzed extensively elsewhere.[22] My point here is to emphasize that to reproduce a subjugated workforce, liberal regimes reenacted the colonial practice of recruitment into militia service to secure control over the production of coffee in the countryside that began in 1871. At the beginning of the twentieth century, imposing constraints on Indigenous labor and land tenure was the US United Fruit Company (UFCO; nicknamed the "octopus" because of its widespread exploitation of natural resources across Central America), which took possession of the most fertile landholdings producing and selling bananas and was given a railroad and port facilities in Puerto Barrios.

As Adams points out, with the creation of the army in 1873 under President Justo Rufino Barrios, militia members had to respond to a centralized government instead of the local garrison. David Carey argues that starting in the early twentieth century, the army "came to depend on Mayans to comprise the majority of their troops" through conscription.[23] Also around this time, local military commissioners organized a market day, when officers would arrive in communities and forcibly press young men into service.[24] Reliance on militias to repress Indigenous resistance prevailed under General Jorge Ubico Castañeda's dictatorship (1931–1944).[25]

In addition, new laws, such as the 1934 Law against Vagrancy and the Law of Public Work, replaced earlier forms of coerced labor with a law "that was almost equally coercive," Jim Handy says.[26] Peasants revolted to resist these compulsory work laws but were easily repressed, as military control tightened its grip on the country.[27] At the same time, volunteer companies and conscription were part of Ubico's attempts to incorporate Maya into the army and national life. As Carey asserts, "Ubico designed volunteer companies to ensure military participation of all men in the community." However, this type of company was a "misnomer because Ubico required everyone to contribute their time and effort. He wanted to have prepared soldiers."[28]

The Cold War's Counterinsurgency Campaigns

As Daniel Feierstein has remarked, Cold War era Latin America was brimming with the mobilization of popular movements composed of workers, students, teachers, peasants, Indigenous peoples, and shantytown dwellers protesting exploitation and U.S. intervention in the region, particularly after the 1959 Cuban revolution.[29] In response, states became national security states promoting the doctrine of national security (NSD), launching callous counterinsurgency campaigns to squelch revolts, bringing a renewed form of bloody militarization and militarism to the region.[30] Political scientist J. Patrice McSherry defines a national security state as "a specific type of capitalist state associated with a dependent and internationalized development model" that engaged in the systematic violation of human rights in societies increasingly polarized by class and ethnic differences.[31]

As I have argued elsewhere, the doctrine's lynchpin was its anticommunist "internal enemy" rhetoric, which largely transformed leftwing opposition "into targets of military campaigns where the enemy was not a foreigner but a fellow countryman."[32] The NSD was transmitted to Latin American officer corps at the notorious School of the Americas in Panama and at Fort Bragg, North Carolina—now renamed the Western Hemisphere Institute for Security Cooperation. In his studies of El Salvador, Ignacio Martín-Baró notes that to frighten people, psychological warfare must "penetrate their primary frame of reference," such as beliefs and values.[33] This type of state displayed fascist ideology when it assumed that, in the words of Guatemalan scholar Ricardo Falla, it "was the source of truth and the source of right."[34]

The demise of the "Democratic Spring," the ten-year reprieve from repression against the poor under Juan José Arevalo (1945–1951) and Jacobo Árbenz (1951–1954), has been examined in-depth elsewhere.[35] Therefore, my aims here are twofold: first, to highlight that Árbenz was himself a member of the officer corps that led a faction of the army against the tradition of military hegemony and, second, to highlight that the U.S. Central Intelligence Agency "directly intervened and overthrew the revolutionary government"[36] to protect the landholdings of UFCO, forcing Árbenz into exile. Colonel Carlos Castillo Armas's rise to power marked a turning point in the launching of bloody military efforts to eradicate the 13 November 1960 insurgent movement, the first left-leaning group led by military officers, which was defeated in 1966–1967 in eastern Guatemala.[37]

Rural Police: Military Commissioners

Beginning in the late 1930s, working ad honorem, military commissioners, a type of rural police, were given the authority to recruit troops, arrest petty criminals, and convene neighbors when requested by the army; they generally were empowered in all issues related to the control of the rural population.[38] On 10 September 1954, through Decree No. 79, the state created the Department of Organization, Instruction and Training of the Military Reserves, which ordered military commissioners to act as a "bridge between the population and the military."[39] Patrick Ball, Paul Kobrak, and Herbert Spirer argue that in the 1960s, under the Julio César Méndez Montenegro administration, as the United States increased military aid, the army activated military commissioners in "almost every village … in the country," initiating "a widespread, active spy network,"[40] as commissioners became "privileged local representatives of the counterinsurgency," authorized to "detain suspects and carry guns … charged with reporting on the presence of insurgents as well as political organizers."[41]

In 1966, the Méndez Montenegro presidency reactivated some 3,000 to 5,000 commissioners "to repress political opponents of the Partido Revolucionario."[42] According to their legal mandate, "commissioners and their auxiliaries are members of the army when they are assigned with military missions."[43] Beginning with President Colonel Arana Osorio, increased power was granted to commissioners, who received *fuero militar,* or legal immunities, in 1973, as members of militias were given during colonial times.[44] The REHMI notes that many military commissioners were participants in the extreme rightwing National Liberation Movement (MLN), which was created in the post-1954 coup d'état to represent the interests of the coffee plantations and cotton and sugar exporters in connivance with the Democratic Institutional party (PID).[45] The MLN's secretary-general, Mario Sandoval Alarcón, was known for sponsoring death squads such as la Mano Blanca, which killed thousands of political opponents, particularly in the countryside.[46]

Strategies during the War: Beans and Bullets Massacres

Following the 1980s National Plan of Security and Development, the military devised a multilevel pacification plan that would, ironically, ensure a transition into democracy though a "twenty-five-year program," which would extend beyond the years of bloodshed.[47] There are two defining moments within the counterinsurgency campaigns. The first was characterized by the decimation of leadership cadres in the late 1970s. Selective killings began in Ixcan under President General Kjell Eugenio Laugerud García, but they did little to eliminate rebel activities. In late 1981, a second phase began in which the army moved its troops to the northwestern highlands under the leadership of President General Fernando Romeo Lucas García, launching attacks against villages presumed to be under rebel control. These were identified as "red," "pink," or "yellow," depending on their levels of collaboration, in the San Marcos, Huehuetenango, Alta Verapaz, El Quiché, and Petén departments.[48]

Because the military had come to its own assessment that in light of "the nation's inflexible traditional agro-export production model" and its maldistribution of wealth, the country "was in the throes of a strong Marxist-Leninist insurgency."[49] For the military, development was (and continues to be) "regarded as the province of the military state." As a result, it realized that more emphasis had to be given to economic concerns versus merely destroying the enemy.[50] A total of eleven counterinsurgency plans were launched. Among them were Victory 82, Firmness 83, Firmness 83-I, and Institutional Re-encounter 84. After the state's launching of counterinsurgency campaigns, a new guerrilla movement made up of four groups came together in 1982 as the National Revolutionary Unity (URNG), awakening the longstanding elites' fear of Indigenous revolt that could threaten the class and racial divides upholding their entrenched racial ideologies and privileges.[51]

On 1 October 1981, General Benedicto Lucas García launched a callous offensive in southern El Quiché, assaulting the Chupol area, which had moved to support the rebels after undergoing a process of consciousness awakening, informed by liberation theology, as I discuss in Chapter Four. For the state, the insurgency was like a cancer: it could not be stopped; it had to be extirpated.[52] Trained at France's famous St.-Cyr military academy, General Lucas García, chief of staff and brother of President Lucas García, directed the slaughter against the insurgency. The rebels, as Susanne Jonas has observed, were "not simply those who have taken up arms, but also the unseen hundreds of thousands among Guatemala's 87 percent majority who have refused to accept a fate of poverty and discrimination."[53] Different levels of collaboration between the URNG and supporters involved the noncombatants, the Irregular Local Forces (FIL), and the Local Clandestine Committees (CCL), which were composed of unarmed *campesinos* (peasants) providing food and medical supplies to other equally poverty-stricken peasant rebels.

By 1981 this process had integrated an estimated 250,000 people participating in the guerilla fronts or as their mass support.[54] To break the solidarity links between organized rural communities and the rebels, the army needed to gain the collaboration of Maya communities it belittled, reenacting a colonial/postcolonial paradox: pitting the oppressed against each other. From the army's perspective, the growing incorporation of communities into FIL and CCL required them to "drain the water where the fish swim," reminiscent of military strategies used by the British in Malaysia and the French and the United States in Vietnam.[55]

General José Efrain Ríos Montt's Years

Following the 23 March 1982 coup d'état, General José Efrain Ríos Montt gave continuity to the Lucas García scorched earth policy. The PACs system, already in place beginning in 1981 in Uspantan, El Quiché, also was further institutionalized. A born-again Christian, active in the El Verbo Church, Ríos Montt was trained at the School of the Americas.[56] At this time, Evangelical churches sprouted everywhere, proselytizing their conservative brand of Christianity, as reported by David Stoll and others.[57] Because of the army's record of human rights abuses, President Jimmy Carter cut off all military support to Ríos Montt in 1977. Yet, the military circumvented the ban and bought 15,000 Galil rifles between 1970 and 1981 from Israel, in addition to Uzi submachine guns and M-79 grenade launchers, among other weapons. To secure arms, the Ministry of Defense, via the state enterprise Guatemalan Military Industries (IMG), set up the "only substantial domestic arms industry in Central America ... in the department of Alta Verapaz, which also assembled Israeli Galil assault rifles under license."[58]

In the highlands—and particularly in Huehuetenango, El Quiché, and the Verapaces, where the URNG was suspected of having active mass-based support[59]—Ríos Montt ruthlessly ordered massive military attacks against "red zones," or *matazonas* (killing zones).[60] Ríos Montt unleashed the worst years of the counterinsurgency campaigns, decimating communities. The commission concluded that "from 1978 to 1984 ... 91 percent of the violations documented by the CEH were committed." Under General Ríos Montt's regime, 249 massacres were carried out, costing nearly 7,000 lives.[61] Episodes of mass killings were "followed by other stages of 'control' and 'development,'" mainly through the formation of the patrol system.[62]

The Civil Self-Defense Patrol System: A Cold War Militia

After asserting the active support peasants gave to the URNG rebels, the army realized the need to activate its old strategy of recruitment of the poor into auxiliary forces and created the Civil Self-Defense Patrol system. By relying on preexisting community power-based structures, networks, and trustworthy authorities (such as auxiliary mayors, military commissioners, and betterment committees), the army first called up its reserves.[63] In this sense, at least the first patrollers were not lacking military experience; they were not all strictly civilians. Rather, they had preexisting relations with the army. On 3 November 1981, *Prensa Libre* reported that General Lucas García had criticized vice-presidential candidate Leonel Sisniega Otero, a cofounder of the MLN, for suggesting the peasants be organized into militias.

This, General Lucas García observed, was a clear violation of the constitution, which prohibited the arming of civilians,[64] unless they were under the strict control of the army. García claimed that campesinos from Nebaj, Joyabaj, and Chichicastenango had requested arms from the army to defend themselves from subversives (*facciosos*).[65] As a way to circumvent this legal hurdle, the general "gave instructions to peasants to join the patrols, who would then become part of the permanent reserves of the army, and that at any moment they would receive the necessary equipment."[66] From then on, the army spokesperson and the government-controlled reporting of the patrols recast PACs as a "paramilitary" force, which helped the army disguise that patrollers had become part of the army's reserves force.[67] To increase militarized defense forces, some "2,000 reservists were recalled to active duty for six-month tours" on 1 July 1982. Peasants who did not respond to the military's call to active duty were "forced to join the military ranks" through perks and by force, according to General Alejandro Gramajo Morales.[68]

Carol Smith suggests that by the early 1980s there were "some 7,000 to 8,000 new recruits each year ... between 10 and 20 percent of the rural male population between the ages of 18 and 24, to serve two-year hitches."[69] According to Yvon Le Bot, the forced recruitment of young males through the *agarraderas* (abductions) lasted between eighteen and thirty months, depending on the circumstances. The best soldiers were offered a chance to continue as part of the Policia Militar Ambulante (PMA), or G-2, *confidenciales,* and military commissioners.[70]

The army used different counterinsurgency strategies to co-opt the population into collaborating with the patrol system. Among these was the army's

1960s civic action strategy that metamorphosed into the early 1980s Civil Affairs and Local Development Division (AA.CC & D.L) D-5, under the coordination of the Joint Operations Center of the Army General Staff.[71] Also used by militaries in Bolivia, Puerto Rico, the Philippines, South Korea, and Vietnam, civic action efforts delivering aid in the countryside were psychological operations (PSYOPs). These were initiatives aimed at propagating the myth of the internal enemy to persuade peasants to collaborate, similar to deceptive narratives used in the Holocaust such as "having only one truth," in Primo Levi's words.[72]

Through leaflets, the army demonized the rebels and claimed that peasant families' safety was its national priority (Chapter Six). At the local level, civic action units were called S-5. In the Ixil area in northern El Quiché, the army developed Operation Ixil and established Development Poles, military colonies (which Diane Nielson and others have analyzed) such as the Choatalúm community.[73] Simultaneously, the military put strict censorship on radio stations, television stations, and newspapers in place, further restricting the already scant information available to the illiterate population.

Called Up to Serve Guatemala: Conscription into the Patrols

The organization of peasants into the patrol system was framed within the logic of "low-intensity warfare" (LIC) enshrined in the Firmness 83 plan aiming at achieving the "highest degree of cohesion within the army."[74] Firmness 83 also delegated the security of families and communities to patrol groups, which meant the coordinated integration of economic aid with PSYOPs and security measures. On 14 April 1983, through Decree 222-83, the patrol system was officially recognized.[75] Under Decree 160-83, the PACs system was formalized with the creation of the Military Fund for the Protection of the Patrols to assist families after the death of family members serving in the patrols.[76] Though the military persistently claimed that service in the patrols was voluntary, and systematically denied its institutional relations to the patrols, PACs constituted compulsory army service. Illustrating peasants' reluctance to join the patrol system in remote areas were the military's repeated attempts to get peasants to join: "The army on at least four occasions instructed local men that patrolling was obligatory."[77]

In June 1982, claiming to act in the spirit of encouraging national unity, Ríos Montt called for an armistice by giving peasants an "opportunity" to resettle in the Development Poles and join the patrols.[78] Many hungry, tired, and internally displaced persons hiding from the army in the mountains for days and months accepted the armistice. According to historian Maribel Rivas Vasconcelos, there were at least four types of patrols, with those closely identifying with the army most likely to become human rights violators.[79] According to the REHMI, those who were more pro-army received favors and services, such as access to community property.[80]

Amilcar Méndez Urízar, leader of the Runujel Junam Council of Ethnic Communities, (We Are All Equal [CERJ], a human rights group), noted that some 2 percent of the PACs, their leaders, and commanders were implicated in human rights abuses.[81] There were PACs known as the "specials" that were "like the army itself" and used by the military to attack rebel forces. Systematically, the military told its commanders to encourage the patrols to "recover or keep the loyalty and to induce its active participation in favor of the government."[82]

Military Tasks and Hierarchical Structure

Military commissioners and their auxiliaries—themselves reservists—or those perceived as trustworthy were assigned as PACs' chiefs and commanders, selected by the army for one or two years.[83] By 1984, more than 1 million peasants, or 25 percent of the population, had been incorporated into the patrol system.[84] Military commissioners became the lowest-ranked military officials, yet they exercised almost unlimited power at the local level. By the early 1980s, commissioners and other army spies provided an important rural intelligence service (known in the countryside as S-2 when operating within military zones and D-2 at the state level) for the army because they had the capacity to infiltrate organized families in their own or nearby villages.

Patrols were given an identity card, and military plans regulated their "war conduct." Below each patrol's photograph "The civil patrol is a man who cares about the peace and tranquility of his land and participates to achieve it" was printed and the signature of each local military zone commander appeared. Initially, the patrols in each village were under the direct control of the Military Reserve Command, and later, in 1983, they were subordinated to the Civil Affairs and Development Companies (D-5) responsible for military-Maya relations. Following the neocolonial practice of legalizing exploitation, the army renamed the patrols twice over the years to disguise their institutional links with the army. First, upon return to electoral democracy in 1986, patrols were renamed Voluntary Self-Defense Patrols (CVDC), and later they were nominally converted into Peace and Development Committees through Decree Law 19-86.[85]

Similar to the organization of military intelligence, Civil Affairs was vertically organized.[86] Intelligence informants, known as the "eyes and ears," included military commissioners, PAC chiefs, and commanders.[87] Many commissioners went far beyond reporting on local political activity and became involved in torture, murder, and disappearance, as illustrated by the 1982 Massacres at Rio Negro during which military commissioners accused peasants of stealing food from workers of the National Electricity Institute (INDE).

Yet others—illustrating the diverse community responses as well as individual proclivity—sought to hide their allegiances with the rebels. Meanwhile, guerrillas tried either to co-opt or eliminate those commissioners politically favoring the army.

Training the Patrols

Patrols were used by the army for their knowledge of communities' footpaths and terrain and to force the complicity of the larger population in securing their plots of land from the rebels.[88] REHMI concluded that training "became a collective practice session involving the entire community."[89] Kobrak asserts that "indoctrination sessions" misrepresented the origins of the violence, claiming that it had been started by the URNG guerrillas.[90] Like the long-term experience with discrimination and racism that leads to a process of depersonalization, psychological drilling to make the transition from civilian to soldier involves instilling what Jacques Sémelin calls the "fantasy myth."[91] Soldiers were trained to suspend judgments, were always under threat of punishment, and had to follow orders. As REHMI points out, military drilling that led them to become "inured to suffering was the first step in training for violent acts … built into military training in the form of total disregard for the dignity and lives of the soldiers."[92]

Quite telling is the story that a former militiaman, Mateo, told Victoria Sanford about this type of drilling: "We were taught to use weapons and practice with live munitions … they taught us how to beat campesinos and how to capture them. We practice with each other … After three months, I was a very different person, I felt like a soldier."[93] The army considered eating dogs for a meal a transformative event in which men lost their fears and allowed hatred to be implanted. In his study of U.S. veterans, psychologist Robert A. Clark argues that the sociological imagination of soldiers includes "ideals of patriotism and conventional stereotypes of masculine behavior."[94] To achieve this imagery the army inculcated patriarchal values by teaching PAC members the "Hymn to the Macho Patrol."[95]

Patrols became victims when they were used as human shields against insurgent attacks or when those who objected to patrolling were informed on by their neighbors, other patrollers. If patrols did not obey, they were required to pay other patrols to replace them or else pay a fine, be jailed, or be thrown into pits and callously killed by other patrollers.[96] Two of the most horrifying massacres, those of Plan de Sanchez and Dos Erres, took place when "Indian communities refusing to join the Patrols, the military responded by teaching them a lesson."[97] These punishments were inflicted by the patrols both at the direction of the army and of their own accord, yet they were always sanctioned by the larger military control. The army's Corps of Engineers victimized the patrols by forcing patrollers to provide unpaid labor in the construction of roads and community buildings,[98] echoing the experience of starving Irish people forced by the British to build roads in the mid-nineteenth century.

The army also victimized the patrollers when, "Already poor, they were ordered to patrol from 12 to 24 unpaid hours, or when they were forced to purchase weapons and uniform shirts from the army."[99] Patrols were also compelled to carry firewood to the Army Zone and to military commissioners' homes. Desertion was punishable under the military code by two month's to one year's imprisonment and a death sentence during wartime.[100] Though unreliable statistics prevent us from learning how many patrols became victims at the hands of other patrols, a government report indicates that by 2003, there were 12,836 widows of patrollers.[101]

According to REHMI, patrols became human rights perpetrators when they committed 12.76 percent of all human rights violations, compared to 7.44 percent for military commissioners. Patrols are identified as the perpetrators in one in five massacres (18.12 percent) and military commissioners in one in twenty (5.38 percent).[102] Of all human rights violations PACs committed between 1981 and 1996, 94 percent were committed between 1981 and 1983.[103]

Illustrating the different responses to conscription, the pictures below show patrollers during talks given by the army in a relaxed setting. According to David Stoll, in the Ixil area, Chajul women translated such political talks.[104]

Figure 2.1. Unknown location. Soldiers giving talks to civil self-defense patrols (PACs), 1984–1990 © CIRMA, Fototeca Guatemala, Archivo Fotográfico del Comité Holandés de Solidaridad con el Pueblo de Guatemala.

In 1993, just three years before the formal ceasefire, the army continued pressuring peasants to join the patrols, resulting in the emergence of some "1,276 Committees of Peace and Development, consisting of 92,971 unarmed adult men."[105] The Kennedy Center for Human Rights reported that of 393,132 members of PACs, 127,633 had been incorporated into the newly conceived Peace and Development Committees (CPDs), as renamed under President Ramiro de León Carpio, by late 1996.

Military Celebrations: A Pledge of Loyalty

Studies analyzing the patrol system have overlooked the role played by oath ceremonies used to seal this Cold War pact of collaboration between rightwing peasants and the army. The army-organized ceremonies compelled the patrollers to swear their loyalty through a public pledge of allegiance, as depicted in the photographs below. This type of ceremony, Memmi suggests, is often employed by the colonizer to impress the oppressed, encouraging a form of militaristic authority over the rest of the community. Memmi writes, "The military ... has the advantage of being able to impress the crowds with their uniforms, their weapons, their medals."[106] With each ceremony, the army nationalistically claimed the imperative need to forge unity between the military and the illiterate Maya peasant population. This picture shows patrols marching against the background of the national anthem and the raising of the Guatemalan flag as they took the oath of allegiance, while the Ladino soldier on the left salutes Maya peasants.

Figure 2.2. © HNG, Prensa Libre, "Juramentan a Más Patrulleros." 18 April 1983, 4.[107]

A group of 1,500 peasants from diverse communities took the oath and walked under the flag in Santa Catárina Ixtahuacan, Sololá, swearing to combat the "enemies of Guatemala threatening to harm their families and communities."[108] The photograph below depicts patrols giving the patrols' sash to a Maya woman as their godmother, while observers look on.

Figure 2.3. Members of the civil patrols, armed with rifles, adorning the Queen of Beauty of the PACs in Huehuetenango during a demonstration in support of the government and protesting the war in 1993. © CIRMA, Fototeca Guatemala, Juan Rolando González Díaz.

To get peasants to pledge their loyalty to them, the military construed the Cold War mythology of itself as being on the side of the people against the feared incursion of "international communism." The army's fascist ideology is illustrated in the message given by Brigadier General Héctor Mario López Fuentes to the population at the inauguration of Military Zone No. 3 in Chimaltenango: "We Guatemalans need to be united in order to repel the enemies of the fatherland, because we face the historic challenge of making Guatemala a strong nation to leave as a legacy to future generations."[109]

Ending the War: The August 1996 Supporting Peace Plan

Since the beginning of the patrol system, patrol groups in some areas sought to break ties with the army. According to the Kennedy Center's report, "Some patrollers were able to leave the PAC system with great difficulty and danger … while others lost their lives, and yet others were able to stop serving without problem."[110] Officially, and following the Army's August 1996 Supporting Peace Plan (Plan de Operaciones Apoyando la Paz) overseen by President Álvaro Enrique Arzú Yrigoyen (1996–2000), still-active patrol groups were disbanded in disarming ceremonies. Military commissioners were disbanded in 1995 through Decree Law No. 79-95. Simultaneously, and in an effort to attract foreign capital and jump-start the Guatemalan economy, the Arzú administration privatized "the energy sector and devise[d] a new Mining Law … within the framework of neo-liberal Structural Adjustment Programs imposed by the World Bank and International Monetary Fund."[111]

Throughout 1995 and 1996, disbanding ceremonies gathered thousands to honor the patrols. Asserting the paradoxical nature of the colonized celebrating the colonizer's festivities, Memmi writes, "It is the colonizer's armies which parade, the very ones which crushed the colonized and keep him in his place."[112] The army established a three-color system for demobilization, the same classification system it used to assess their war allegiances: white was reserved for areas of low intensity in the armed conflict (Izabal, Jalapa, Chiquimula, Jutiapa), while pink was reserved for the departments with medium intensity of rebel presence (Baja Verapaz, Chimaltenango, Santa Rosa, Escuintla, Sololá, Suchitepéquez y Quetzaltenango), and red for areas the army identified as high conflict (San Marcos, Huehuetenango, Alta Verapaz, Quiché and Petén).[113] As with the pledges of allegiance of the early 1980s genocide, the military relied on its grandiose ceremonies.

The first official demobilization of some 800 patrollers took place on 9 August 1996 in Barrancas, Xemal, and Colotenango, Huehuetenango, when they returned fifty-eight Mauser rifles the army had given them fourteen years before. On that occasion, General Otto Pérez Molina (president 2012–2015, ousted on charges of corruption) hailed the patrols for their historical contribution to defeating the rebels.[114] However, the army gave conflicting narratives about the disarmament and demobilization of patrols and failed to produce an accurate number.[115] By December 1996, a total of 270,906 patrols had, on paper, been deactivated by the army in compliance with the Peace Accords, as monitored by the United Nations' Mission to Guatemala (MINUGUA).[116] By the army's own admission 24 percent of the guns have not been turned in.

At these ceremonies, patrols were encouraged to remember fallen patrols. For example, on 6 September 1996, Colonel Cecilio Peláez Morales told a group of demobilized patrollers as their names were read, "It is time to store the rifles and remember those killed in combat."[117] Furthermore, ex-patrols were praised "for their participation in the struggle to safeguard national sovereignty."[118] By conflating former patrollers' identities with national security and development, the military elevated former patrols to patriotic symbols, which ultimately served either to cement or to encourage a mutual, but highly unequal, pact of silence with the military—kept to this day. The picture below shows patrols proudly handing over their rifles after years of service and waving flags. Such photographs filled the pages of the country's newspapers.

Figure 2.4. Solemn disbanding ceremonies, during which patrols gave back their arms, took place on August 9 1996 in Colotenango, Huehuetenango © CIRMA, Fototeca Guatemala, Araminta Gálvez García. Archivo of the United Nation's Observer Mission in Guatemala (MINUGUA).

Figure 2.5. One of the first official army ceremonies that, with the participation of representatives from local government, the United Nations, and the Catholic Church, disbanded the patrols. © CIRMA, Fototeca Guatemala, Araminta Gálvez García. Archivo MINUGUA.

However, this formal demilitarization was largely symbolic; it was used by the army to encourage, renew, or instill ideological dependency. During the disbanding of the Colotenango communities on 9 August 1996, Méndez Urízar accused the army of manipulating a "political show" by claiming disarmament.[119] Far from abandoning the old national security doctrine, this praetorian mindset was reincarnated in the early aftermath of the war in some authorities, practices, and structures in communities across the highlands.

Although President Arzú decreased the size and resources of the armed forces significantly, he left their institutional autonomy intact, giving continuity to their claimed role as protectors of the poor.[120] In compliance with the Peace Accords, military personnel, troops, specialists, zones, detachments, and recruiting centers were allegedly reduced by 33 percent by the end of 1997. Yet by 1998, as Schirmer notes, the army gave conflicting numbers of the base number of military forces. She asks, "33 percent reduction of exactly what exactly?"[121] Schirmer concludes, "Reducing these personnel and installations has been uneven at best. Only two out of a total of twenty-three military zones … actually closed, eight detachments reopened and six new ones established" to combat delinquency, in the name of public security.[122]

Soon after, Arzú's successor, Alfonso Portillo, increased the armed forces' missions and budget. According to observers, "During the four years under … Portillo, the army's budget grew to Q3.75 billion (U.S.$500 million) in addition to Q906 million (U.S.$120.8 million) in anomalous transfers that [he] ordered."[123] Disguised by a façade of democracy, a year before the signing of the Peace Accords, the Treaty of Democratic Security was passed by Central American governments to ensure the penetration of the military in the state and in the countryside.[124] At the local level, ex-patrols' threats of assassinations and the lynching of human rights defenders, church workers, judges, witnesses, journalists, and labor unionists continued in the war's wake as the army continued to praise former patrollers as the "country's heroes."[125]

Notes

1. Shaw, *Post-Military Society,* 5, 8.
2. Adams, "What Can We Know?" 283–84.
3. Figueroa Ibarra, "Culture of Terror."
4. McAllister and Nelson write that the PAC was "a paramilitary force organized by the army" (*War by Other Means,* 3).
5. The United States has acknowledged the use of militias to defeat insurgency in, among other cases, Algeria (1992–2004), El Salvador (1979–1992), Guatemala (1960–1996), Indonesia (1976–2005), and Peru (1980–1992). Jones, "Strategic Logic of Militia."
6. Alden, Thakur, and Arnold, *Militias and the Challenges,* 4.
7. Hristov, *Paramilitarism and Neoliberalism,* 4.
8. Theidon, "Reconstructing Masculinities," 5.
9. Nelson, *Finger in the Wound,* Kindle locations 5751–52.
10. Schirmer, *Guatemalan Military Project,* 83.
11. McClintock, *American Connection,* 253.
12. Orraca Corona, "Ejército, Subjetividades y Memoria Colectiva," 107.
13. Memmi, *Colonizer and the Colonized,* 93.
14. Fanon, *Wretched of the Earth,* 48, fn7.
15. Enloe, *Ethnic Soldiers,* 13.
16. Del Carmen Velázquez, "Los Indios Flecheros," 237.
17. Asselberg, "Conquest in Images," 79; see also Handy, *Gift of the Devil,* 18–19.
18. Drouin, "To the Last Seed," 14.
19. Handy, *Gift of the Devil,* 28; see also Pollack, "Levantamiento K'iché," 38.
20. Drouin, "To the Last Seed," 14.
21. CEH 1999, II.158.
22. See McCreery, "State Power, Indigenous Communities."
23. Carey, *Our Elders Teach Us,* 178–79.
24. Ibid., 179
25. Martínez Pelaez, *Motines de Indios,* 133.
26. Handy, *Revolution in the Countryside,* 10, 52.
27. Handy, *Gift of the Devil,* 72.
28. Carey, *Our Elders Teach Us,* 183.
29. Feierstein, "National Security Doctrine," 492.
30. Hanhimaki and Westad, *Cold War,* 380.

31. McSherry, "National Security State," 122.
32. Esparza, "Globalizing Latin American Studies," 8.
33. Martín-Baró, *Writings for a Liberation Psychology*, 139.
34. Falla, "We Charge Genocide," 84.
35. Schlesinger and Kinser, *Bitter Fruit*; Hanhimaki and Westad, *Cold War*.
36. Heller, *Cold War*, 145.
37. For a history of this early guerrilla movement, see Aguilera Peralta.
38. REHMI 1998, III.5; CEH, II.158, 159.
39. CEH, I.158, 159.
40. Adams, *Development of the Guatemalan Military*, 106.
41. Ball, Kobrak, and Spirer, *State Violence in Guatemala*, 99.
42. CEH, II.159; Schirmer, *Guatemalan Military Project*, 18.
43. CEH, II.162.
44. CEH, II.160, fn. 378. In February 1973, Decree Law 4-73 established that military commissioners and their auxiliaries were members of the army and they were, as such, protected. CEH, II.164.
45. REHMI 1999, 206; CEH, II.159-60.
46. Black et al., *Garrison Guatemala*, 124. CEH, II.160.
47. Schirmer, *Guatemalan Military Project*, 235.
48. Ibid., 48. See also the map of the army's task forces, xiv; CEH, II.185.
49. Gramajo Morales, "Political Transition in Guatemala," 111-12.
50. McSherry, "National Security State," 127.
51. Schirmer, *Guatemalan Military Project*, 22; Ball, Kobrak, and Spirer, *State Violence in Guatemala*, 90.
52. CEH, II.281.
53. Jonas, *Battle for Guatemala*, 6.
54. According to RHEMI, "During the time of its greatest organizational peak, the EGP spanned almost 80 percent of national territory, whether armed combatants or members of support bases." REHMI 1998, III.198. The State Department indicated fewer combatants and supporters, no more than 60,000. Black, Jamail, and Chinchilla, *Garrison Guatemala*, 111.
55. Hess, *Explaining America's Lost War*; Carruthers, *Winning Hearts and Minds*.
56. Garrard-Burnett, *Protestantism in Guatemala*; see also Gill, *School of the Americas*.
57. Stoll, *Is Latin America Turning Protestant?*
58. Godnik et al., "Stray Bullets," 5.
59. Ball, Kobrak, and Spirer have noted, "The top five years for rural killings and disappearances are all between 1980 and 1984 ... [when the state] committed fully 82 percent of rural murders for the entire 36 years of armed conflict." *State Violence in Guatemala*, 49.
60. Schirmer, *Guatemalan Military Project*, 45.
61. The departments most affected by crimes committed by military commissioners (1962-1996) were El Quiché, 42 percent; Alta Verapaz, 17 percent; Baja Verapaz, 15 percent. CEH, II.181.
62. Hale, "Consciousness, Violence," 818.
63. REHMI 1998, II.122.
64. HNG, *Prensa Libre*, "Benedicto Lucas García crítica," 4; Schirmer notes the initial date of the patrols as being September 1981 in Chimaltenango and Huehuetenango (*Guatemalan Military Project*, 83).
65. HNG, *Prensa Libre*, "El Ejército dará armas," 2.
66. CEH, II.183.

67. In 1993, for example, Ombudsman Jorge Mario Garcia Laguardia asserted that PACs were a "paramilitary force."
68. Schirmer, *Guatemalan Military Project*, 47, 87.
69. Smith, "Militarization," 10.
70. Le Bot, *La Guerra en Tierras Mayas*, 81.
71. CEH, II.36.
72. Levi, "Primo Levi's Heartbreaking."
73. Jonas, "Guatemala: Acts of Genocide," 385.
74. HMP, Ejército de Guatemala, "Plan de Campaña Firmeza 83."
75. Similar to death squads, Jeffrey Sluka suggests, "While death squads operate outside the law, they effectively do so with impunity and are generally and secretly fully integrated into the state's regular security network" (*Death Squad*, 5).
76. CEH, II.182–87.
77. Jay, *Persecution by Proxy*, 35.
78. Schirmer, *Guatemalan Military Project*, 83.
79. The other three types were "1) those who collaborated with the rebels and at the same time participated in the PACs, 2) those who sought to protect their communities through their participation into PACs, and 3) those who obeyed orders and attacked their communities." Rivas Vasconcelos, "La Guerra Fría," 159.
80. REMHI 1998, II.126.
81. CIRMA, Infostelle 84, Zubieta, "Guatemala, Dudas ante Desmovilización."
82. HMP, Ejército de Guatemala, "Manual de Guerra Contrasubversiva."
83. CEH, II.191.
84. CIEN, "Informe sobre el Aporte."
85. REHMI 1998, II.118.
86. Civil affairs followed a hierarchy similar to that of the army's intelligence. For a diagram of the army's intelligence hierarchy, see Schirmer, *Guatemalan Military Project*, 160.
87. See Figure 0.1 for an illustration of the military structure.
88. CEH, II.201.
89. REHMI 1998, II.122.
90. Kobrak, "Long War in Colotenango," 222.
91. Semelin, *Purify and Destroy*, 13–22.
92. REHMI 1999, 131.
93. Sanford, "Gendered Observations," 126–27.
94. Clark, "Aggressiveness and Military Training," 423.
95. REMHI 1998, I.212.
96. OAS, "Los Comités Voluntarios"; CEH 1999, II.208–9.
97. Schirmer, *Guatemalan Military Project*, 116.
98. CEH 1999, II.196; REMHI 1998, II.119.
99. Ewen and Goldman, "Civil Patrols."
100. War Resisters' International, "Country Report and Updates."
101. CIEN, *Informe Sobre el Aporte de Capital*.
102. For a breakdown of participation in human rights crimes, see REHMI 1999, 120.
103. CEH 1999, II.229.
104. Stoll, *Between Two Armies*, 140.
105. Schirmer, *Guatemalan Military Project*, 101.
106. Memmi, *Decolonization and the Decolonized*, 16.
107. My gratitude to Daniele Volpe for taking this picture at the Hemeroteca Nacional.
108. HNG, *Prensa Libre*, "Juramentan a Más Patrulleros," 4.

109. Foreign Broadcast Information Service, "Military Zone No. 3 Inaugurated," 42–43.
110. Solomon, *Institutional Violence*, 25. Patrols from the Xecoja community from Chichi-castenango disbanded their platoons because "patrolling for 24 hours caused a hard economic burden for their families." CIRMA, Fondo Infostelle, Signatura 84; CDHG, "320 Campesinos Renuncian."
111. Van de Sandt, "Mining Conflicts," 11.
112. Memmi, *Colonizer and the Decolonized*, 103.
113. CIRMA, Fondo Infostelle, Signatura 84; CDHG, Informe Diario, "Gobierno Fija Fecha."
114. CIRMA, Fondo Infostelle, Signatura 84; CDHG, Informe Diario, "PAC de Colote-nango." On 1 August 1996, the minister of defense General Julio Balconi declared that PACs would be disarmed starting in mid-July, removing 15,000 weapons from the hands of some 350,000 patrollers. CIRMA, Fondo Infostelle, Signatura 84, Cerigua, "Date Set for PAC Disarming."
115. According to General Vásquez, about 20,000 arms, mostly old M1 rifles, had been dispersed to PACs until 1994. Solomon, "Institutional Violence," 11.
116. CIRMA, Infostelle 83, Cerigua, "Civil Patrols Pass into History."
117. CIRMA, Infostelle 83, Informe Diario, "Se Desmovilizan PAC."
118. CIRMA, Infostelle 83, Cerigua, "PACs Glorified."
119. CIRMA, Infostelle 83, Cerigua, "PACs Disarm."
120. MINUGUA reports, "Army representatives agreed to a ... reduction in numbers, from 45,000 to 30,820 personnel. The army also claimed that the actual size was 35,000 personnel, making reduction to 31,000 a minor adjustment" ("Promise and Reality").
121. Schirmer, "Prospects for Compliance," 23.
122. Ibid., 22–25.
123. Guatemala Human Rights Commission, "Army Has Disproportionate Budget," 7.
124. Klepak, Rojas Aravena, and David Mares, "Relaciones Hemisféricas."
125. MINUGUA, "Thirteenth Report."

3

A Chameleonlike Army
Civic Action, a Postcolonial Strategy

Civil Affairs does not tell people what they have to do. We mainly help them in case
of natural disaster, reforestation, construction of bridges, and excavation of trenches.
—Author interview, Colonel Samayoa

In this chapter, I examine those local, complex militaristic arrangements that were already in place, enabling the genocide in the countryside in the early 1980s, by the time the army imposed its patrol system. One such militaristic arrangement was the civic action strategy brought to Latin America by the 1960s U.S. Alliance for Progress, a mix of economic and military assistance set up under President John F. Kennedy's Special Group to advance the "doctrine of Military Civic Action."[1] Willard F. Barber and C. Neale Ronning have conceptualized civic action as "the use of preponderantly indigenous military forces on projects useful to the local populations at all levels ... education ... public work, agriculture, [and] transportation" to improve the "standing of the military forces with the population."[2] From the army's perspective, "civic action assistance projects can advance the interest of the [United States] in supporting democracy throughout [the] Third World."[3]

Apologists for the kind of development delivered by the army will justify it on the basis of the dire conditions of poverty. Undoubtedly, there was (and still is) a desperate need for basic infrastructure in this region, but civic action, rather than bringing development, increased opportunities for the neocolonial military to cast itself as the "protector of communities" to gain their support. This type of counterinsurgency strategy profoundly recolonized community-level power structures by co-opting the support of Maya authorities, families, and communities. In the process, the army brought with it its racist view of peasants disguised in humanitarian development and advanced a Ladino identity built upon the "humiliation of the Maya."[4]

Although the pervasive involvement of the army in Maya community affairs can be traced back to the late nineteenth century,[5] for reasons of space in this chapter I will take General Jorge Ubico Castañeda's regime (1931–1944) as a point of departure for army-led projects camouflaged as bringing progress to impoverished communities. In the early aftermath, by delivering poverty aid, the military continued to bolster sympathy for its civil affairs (S-5) specialists rehearsing the image of the army's supremacy in peasants' mentalities and social practices. Civil affairs, responsible for liaising with communities, gave continuity to civic action.

A historical sociology approach will reveal that, like a chameleon changing its colors, the military has successfully adapted to different historical circumstances over the years to subvert civilian authority and keep control over rural areas by gaining the support of poverty-stricken communities. Additionally, this analysis will allow us to interrogate, in the words of Jennifer Schirmer, "the habits of the minds of the Guatemalan … a complex task since the military is the least researched and understood institution in Guatemala."[6] This approach follows a trend in the region examining preexisting mechanisms present by the time state terrorism and genocidal processes were unleashed.

Maria Alicia Divinzenso, for example, points out that a study of civic action in Argentina allows us to examine the wide range of activities in which the army was involved with international, state, and local educational, cultural, and recreational activities.[7] Globally, as with the case of the Air Force Civic Action in Southeast Asia, in the words of Captain Betty Barton Christiansen, the army's goal has been that, "military civic action could thus become both a preventive and a curative weapon for communist-inspired insurrection and an additional American tool with which to fight the cold war."[8]

Public Works Predating Civic Action

A former minister of war under the ruthless dictatorship of Manuel Estrada Cabrera (1898–1920), General Jorge Ubico Castañeda was known as the "Tata president"[9]; he ruled with a mixture of authoritarianism and public works to gain popular support. His militaristic missions of public surveillance, cartography, and administration in rural areas exemplified his regime. Greg Grandin aptly notes that Ubico "assum[ed] the role of benevolent father … who would arrive yearly in indigenous communities to attend to assorted complaints, often acting against local elites."[10] These were the years known as the *tacita de plata* (little silver cup), a nickname "that communicated the era's reputation of charm and security." [11]This alleged security, however, was imposed by the brutality of the regime and disguised by grandiose public works, constructed under Ubico's architect, Rafael Pérez de León: the National Post Office, the National Palace of Culture, and the National Police Headquarters, among others.

Efforts were made by Ubico's administration to extend literacy programs to Indigenous conscripts to produce a "good Maya" stripped of "laziness." For example, in 1935 *Revista Militar* reported that educating conscripts meant "that the military service has also become a means of effective cooperation with civil education and for the upbringing of upstanding citizens."[12] Yet, in another issue, Colonel Enrique C. Valladares L. describes the "natural qualities" of the Indian as being "hard working, [possessing] resistance, and [possessing] love for the land," all patriotic elements, in the army's view, that needed to be coopted by the military's "civilizing" mission,[13] as colonizing projects often cast themselves to be.[14]

Despite the army's assessment of Ubico's development initiatives, observers like Richard Adams have pointed out that his administration did "nothing to alleviate the economic and social repression of the Indian,"[15] as the underlying coercive structures of the country's peasant economy remained unchanged.[16] Michael D. Kirkpatrick also notes how "Ubico used the roads to boost his public persona and to point to the palpable results accomplished by his regime despite the economic woes facing the country."[17]

Following a postcolonial mindset, the dictator maintained that the military was the only institution that upheld the moral and cultural values of the nation justifying his continuous reliance on "massive road building efforts," which reinforced the army's self-assigned role in the "development" of peasant families and communities. As Kirkpatrick asserts, "Ubico was credited for successfully uniting Guatemala via an extensive network of roads. And he did so through taxation and forced labor directed towards public ends."[18] Ubico's condescendingly "direct contact" with the population involved attending to their personal needs, as reported by the army in its *Military Journal,* by visiting municipalities, schools, and even jails. Acting as a protecting father with the *inditos* (little Indians), often he would order the release of those who, in his view, were unjustly detained.

During one of General Ubico's motorcycle-riding administrative expeditions into Nahuala in Sololá, the 1937 *Revista Militar* noticed that neighbors were reluctant to join the militias. This refusal contrasted with militias in Chichicastenango. During General Ubico's visit to the township, Ubico was struck by the discipline and precision displayed by the militias proudly marching in front of his committee. "What is the secret to get them to march in this manner?" Ubico asked. The answer, he was told, was that its instructor, Major Jesús Ramírez Monta, spoke the K'iché language fluently and therefore could convey orders to reserves.[19] The militaristic description of militias as apt for marching, points to the army's paternalistic narrative. As Albert Memmi has pointed out, a condescending view of the oppressed, "occupies an important place in the dialectics exalting the colonizer and humbling the colonized."[20] Despite the oppression endured by Indigenous peoples, which denoted their blurry identities, Mayan militias clad in uniform were often displayed during festivities marching to honor the general.

A Prelude to Genocide: Forging a Fascist National Unity

Starting in the late 1950s, the United States funded and trained anticommunist civic action initiatives in Central America to be carried out by the local military with the participation of the U.S. Navy and Air Force. In his unique ethnographic account of Bolivia's civic action programs in the early 1960s, William Handford Brill asserts, "Civic action is based on the [army's] awareness that good, grassroots civil-military relations are a requisite for an effective counterinsurgency program."[21] The underlying assumption was (and continues to be) that the military possesses the best organization and manpower that, in theory, can contribute to economic and social progress in rural areas. This military capacity involved the construction of bridges, roads, school buildings, highways, sewer systems, communications networks, medical clinics, and potable water wells. Civic action was legalized in amendments made to the U.S. 1959 Mutual Security Act.

Locally, civic action in the region was the result of the coming together of various armed forces from El Salvador, Costa Rica, Guatemala, Honduras, Nicaragua, and Panama creating the Central American Defense Council (CONDECA).[22] According to Adams, "The Inter-American Defense Board approved a resolution to use military personnel and equipment for purposes of economic development, education, and highway settlement work."[23] In convening with the goal of bringing security and development to the region, CONDECA ended up reproducing the Cold War ideology in Central America. The army's pervasive influence in the region was part of what Alan McPherson has described as a process of "increasing North-South intimacies ... a conflict in which not just state violence, but the Liberal logic of modernization ... was pivotal."[24]

As in the rest of Latin America, in Guatemala civic action involved direct collaboration with the U.S. Embassy and the U.S. Agency for International Development (USAID), among other foreign institutions, to supply the means for civic action to successfully deliver "humanitarian" infrastructure to the poor and illiterate in the countryside. Thus, aiding the unfolding process of genocide there was a host of global and local institutions militarizing development by facilitating the logistics that equipped the army's different branches.

The Alliance for Progress and USAID

To combat the rapid spread of revolutionary upheavals in Latin America following the Cuban Revolution in 1959, Kennedy's Alliance for Progress provided some U.S.$20 billion in public and private aid to the region. The aim was to bolster the middle-class merchants, industrialists, and farmers, whose economic growth could, according to historian Henry Heller, "raise the whole of the population of Latin America out of poverty."[25] Critics have emphasized how, while initially praised as a pivotal effort, the Alliance for Progress "soon ran into difficulties ... it served only to perpetuate the hold on power of Latin American military governments and oligarchies,"[26] while socioeconomic indicators, such as education, barely grew.

Against this backdrop, on 17 August 1961 the Cultural Service and Civic Action was established in Guatemala, preceding the army's D-5 division that organized the local Civil Affairs and Local Development Division (AA.CC & D.L) to liaise with communities, beginning in the early 1980s.[27] Through civic action initiatives, the armed forces brought the myth of "benevolent development initiatives" and psychological operations, and fabricated nationalistic propaganda telling peasants that they and their families needed the security only the army could provide and exposing them to lies and half-truths to compel them to collaborate with the local outpost.

With the close technical advice of USAID, the "progress" of otherwise forgotten communities tied the local village with the broader global humanitarian institutions. Since then, programs have been funded in Bolivia, Guatemala, El Salvador, Nicaragua, and Honduras—to be carried out by national armies with the participation of the United States military. In fact, in the 1960s, the USAID and American Cooperative of Remittances (CARE) funded and actively participated in several health care campaigns, delivering aid "from the American People." In late 1961, at the request of U.S. advisers from Fort Georgia, a delegation from Peru arrived in the country to monitor its progress.[28]

Programs aided by help and technical advice from the U.S. Army involved the construction and repair of school buildings, roads, bridges, and houses; reforestation; breakfasts for children; transportation to remote areas for dentists and doctors offering preventative care; and supplies. Adams also asserts that the army printing press received "strong support" from USAID.[29] Often, as literacy material was sent to the countryside in El Petén, Baja Verapaz, and Chimaltenango, military commissioners were responsible for the attendance of the people enrolled.[30] Economic "progress," the army reasoned, would prevent peasants from allying with communist groups, cannily converting a poverty issue affecting Maya communities into, eventually, a national security one. But paternalistic poverty aid, note liberation theologians Leonardo Boff and

Clodovis Boff, increases dependency on the oppressor "not enabling them [Indigenous, the poor] to become their own liberators."[31]

A Blitzkrieg of Civic Action:
The United States and Local Specialists

Though it is commonly believed that civic action projects were delivered mostly in Zacapa in the 1960s, where the first guerrilla rebels mobilized, provisions and civic work also reached the western highlands, the departments of Huehuetenango, El Quiché, Sololá, San Marcos, the Verapaces, and El Petén. To gain peasants' approval for its projects, the army disingenuously told them its aims were to improve their social conditions and to bring progress to their communities. Civic action, however, did not just deliver collective services to rural communities. To penetrate and recolonize their communities, the military also provided health and literacy services to its own troops and reserves, echoing the programs delivered to Bolivian troops.

The direct, active involvement of U.S. specialists is illustrated by the 1969 arrival of Infantry Major José L. Morales, a Puerto Rican military instructor and Vietnam War veteran trained at U.S. military schools.[32] Morales defined civic action as the use of armed forces during peacetime to bring social and economic progress to the population—and hence provide security against the communist threat.

Echoing Samuel P. Huntington's "part-time citizen-soldier," Morales asserted, "Every individual, before becoming a soldier, has been and continues to be a citizen. Every citizen has the moral obligation to collaborate with the development of his or her nation."[33] Huntington defines the citizen-soldier as the soldier inspired by the duty to serve but not necessarily to "perfect himself in the management of violence."[34] By endowing Indigenous soldiers with civic action tasks in remote areas they knew well, the military accomplished its goal by reaching down to the lowest levels of the community: their families. But to do so, it needed to coordinate with community representatives. This was done by training specialists who were members of the local population, were specifically recruited for this purpose, and spoke the local Mayan language. As a result, seemingly harmless development projects introducing x-rays and health campaigns brought militarism to communities' doorsteps.

The underlying assumption was that local soldiers trained as nurses and teachers could easily penetrate families and communities to spread the army's material provisions—and its national security rhetoric. Military doctors provided the only medical aid available, and troop units stationed in sparsely populated areas were often the only tangible manifestation of national authority.

And whereas Adams has argued, "Whether it profoundly changes the traditional suspicion of the Campesino toward the military is an open question,"[35] I want to suggest that civic action successfully penetrated deep into the collective memory of the most vulnerable communities, as I show in Part II.

In early 1970, the army realized the need to select soldiers who would eventually become, as Schirmer notes, "force multipliers" and "excellent intelligence sources."[36] Indigenous reserves and recruits trained as health practitioners were seen by the army as pivotal for making liaisons with village authorities. The graphic shown below demonstrates the hierarchical approach to development that civic action efforts promoted.

Plan for Health Activities in Communities

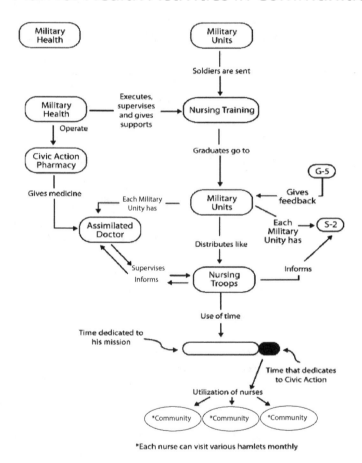

Figure 3.1. © CIRMA, Archivo Histórico, Colección de Documentos y Publicaciones del Ejército, Document #65.

First, at military bases, low-ranking Indigenous soldiers were selected for training as medical specialists. After graduating, they returned to their military posts. These peasant-soldiers ultimately dedicated a quarter of their time to visiting communities to encourage the widespread participation of families in local civic action committees.[37] These soldiers-specialists fed intelligence units (S-2) and civic action with detailed information drawn from demographic surveys about rural communities, while USAID and CARE provided medicine to the civic action pharmacy along with a *medico asimilado,* a uniformed assimilated civilian professional who oversaw the role of the "Indigenous peasant-soldier-nurse."[38]

Civic action was considered to be a "very, very effective weapon" for winning the hearts and minds of the desperately impoverished peasants.[39] In Quetzaltenango, civic action personnel transported equipment donated by USAID for the Trade Schools (ACEN), which included typewriters, desks, calculators, and more.[40] According to Adams, the army made great use of its printing press, again with strong foreign support from USAID. Some "2,000,000 sets of a first reader series were provided, together with workbooks, teaching aids, charts and so forth, during the 1963–1965 period," following a story line similar to the one of the newspaper advertisement for the army's literacy projects I discuss in Chapter Six.[41] Characterizing the military's role in improving social conditions and being financially responsible, Colonel Enrique Peralta Azurdia claimed in 1963 that the civic action was actually concerned with the welfare of Guatemalan children, linking poor educational performance to malnutrition and hunger.

To provide palliative aid, civic action programs provided 300 light meals to the students of the Instituto Nacional para Señoritas de Centro America (INCA), which petitioned to publicly recognize the army's work on behalf of schoolchildren. As in previous projects, such as that in Zacapa that benefitted 1,755 students, breakfast and lunches were funded by CARE and benefitted five schools in the area. To inaugurate its nutritional program, the army used an air force C-47 to transport local and U.S. officers.[42]

Sustained popularity allowed the military to justify the buildup of war machinery, despite—or maybe because of—the fact that the large majority of rural communities lived in extreme poverty. Locals' acceptance of the army is illustrated by the request of the Construction Committee of the Tecún Umán statue in Guatemala City that the Defense Ministry administer its finances because "things are being done with honesty."[43] Tecún Umán was the king of the K'iché who fiercely fought against the infamous Captain Pedro de Alvarado. This example shows that the army's efforts to gain control not only over the country's finances but also in administering military Maya cultural symbols helped it gain popularity within rural communities. As one officer put it in the 1960s, "The military is no longer despised. Our people are noble and the military is the product of the same people."[44]

To entice Indigenous peasants to accept civic action and to reduce the local population's resistance to and skepticism of the military, the army relied on Mayan languages. For example, in 1970, during a civic action mission to the eastern region, the military presented themselves in Maya-Q'eqchi: *Lao cuanco anajcuan sali Ejército, la essmescolaj* (We are from the army; do not worry). The editorial condescendingly notes, "After the translations, there were times when the report was somehow funny, just like when a peasant put the mike inside his mouth as far as he could in order to talk."[45] By choosing to highlight this incident, the *Revista Militar* shows the institutional view of Maya peasants as having no intellectual capacities and portrays them as childlike, needing to be taught how to behave in public.

Educating Maya Troops: "Taming" Indigenous Subjectivity

The Guatemalan army was formed in 1871 as a permanent and stable institution, and the Polytechnic School (Escuela Politécnica) was established 1 September 1873. Since then, a small cadre of aspiring high-ranking officer cadets, the *señores cadetes*, drawn from the middle and lower classes have received instruction on performing public projects. These projects bring relief to impoverished communities, similar to that provided by the civic action projects implemented during the Cold War years.[46] Following the positivism of Westernized military sociologists, Adams alleges that "by the turn of the century [the military] had developed a strong esprit de corps," producing, in his view, a highly organized and professionalized force.[47]

Through its officer cadets, low-ranking Indigenous reservists received training and were inculcated with the army's institutional memory, values, and mindset, including dehumanizing views of Maya peasants. This is poignantly expressed by Maya scholar Demetrio Cojtí Cuxil: "Oppressing the Indians is not the same as oppressing a people. It is oppressing a degenerate race of disorganized groups incapable of self-government ... [This is] a hidden thought of the colonialists."[48]

By the early 1960s, the class and ethnic cleavages were evident within the armed forces between the enlisted or conscripted Maya soldiers and the officer corps. Statistics are not readily available on the officer corps who entered the Polytechnic School, but we do know that "all the members ha[d] at least secondary school education" and that those who entered the permanent force and military reserves were 62.50 percent illiterate and 57.13 percent belonged to the "Indian race," in Adams's words. Of these, 13.71 percent did not speak Spanish and only 31.00 percent had Spanish as their first language.[49]

Rather than seeking to empower their reservists, the military's aim was to transmit its nationalistic values to prepare conscripted low-ranking soldiers to serve the Ladino state and to convince them that their individual sacrifice was required to defend Guatemala. According to a military essay, "We do not believe that the task of educating them is futile, even inculcating a little bit of culture ... Once stripped from his *primitive state,* the army teaches [the Indigenous soldier] how to read, write, and [perform] military service techniques."[50] The aim was (and continuous to be) to Ladinize Maya peasants, to strip them of their ethnic identity, and, during war and genocide, to integrate them into nationalistic projects as "part of the army." The story of subjugated allies, of patrols and former patrols collaborating with the army, shows that Indigenous peasants gained, as Robert Carmack has noted, some advantage in society vis-à-vis Ladino power, as I discussed in the Introduction.

The Army's Corps of Engineers: Building Bridges and Roads

As seen, roads were viewed as instruments of progress, promising to link Guatemala to the rest of the world. By 1962, the year the Corps of Engineers was founded, the army was providing rural villages with specialized personnel, engineers, and construction workers, as it remained strategically concerned with repairing main and hinterland roads (*caminos vecinales*) and bridges connecting municipalities. Analyzing train construction in India, Ravi Ahuja has pointed out that engineering imperialism comprises "visible symbols of superiority," characterizing Eurocentric male patriarchy.[51]

Similarly in Guatemala, the army saw its role as vital for community development. Roads, it was said, could contribute to modernizing their *cultivos,* crops. By opening new roads into isolated communities, the Corps of Engineers gave the illusion of progress in the eyes of the poor, while at the same time, it created spaces to be used by the military to reenact deeply unequal social relations for its own gain. In reality, the military was driven by its Cold War colonizing mission; building these roads was part of the strategy for facilitating the movement of military equipment and personnel to colonize new areas and for gaining control over the population's hearts and minds.

Referring to the fact that "progress" is used as a political smokescreen to justify the conquest of lands, people, and mindsets, Aimé Césaire writes that the colonizer likes to "throw facts at my head, statistics, mileages of roads, canals, and railroad tracks."[52] A similar situation was found in Cambodia, where "French colonial authorities, while building roads, cities, and schools, did little to modernize the Cambodian economy." Rather, they produced "rubber and other agricultural commodities, which they exported."[53] A 1970s *Revista Militar* reports on how the army saw its role as vital for community development.

Quietly, but surely, the civic action's machinery for road construction has been *penetrating* the heart of the jungle, demolishing hills or filling in abysses to open up the way to the material advancement of isolated communities, the development of which was being blocked by the lack of an access route.[54]

Officers specialized in more than the techniques of construction: importantly, projects and the training of the officer corps and reservists also included notions of attack and defense of public spaces like squares and plazas.[55]

Following Bourdieu's "sociological gaze," suggesting the importance of the photographic archive for denouncing the unequal power relations upheld by French colonialism in Algeria, I explore photographs depicting the army's civic action. These reveal the army's underlying logic for strengthening its postcolonial ties with the illiterate population. Through its Corps of Engineers, as shown in Fig. 3.2, with its heavy military vehicles on a forest road, the military promoted its own institutional memory as the "savior" of the people by bringing "progress" to their communities in the mid 1960s. By reorganizing spatial infrastructure through a very ubiquitous process of road and other kinds of construction, the army created space for the kind of social breakdown that can be used by

Figure 3.2. © CIRMA, Archivo Histórico, Colección Familia Figueroa Ibarra. Memoria de Labores del Gobierno Militar 1964–1965, 27.

the oppressor to recreate military-Maya relationships for their own purposes.[56] Fig. 3.3 shows uniformed soldiers serving bread to Indigenous children. This illustrates the army's goal of promoting the paternalistic notion that its presence brings nothing but caring support for rural families' well-being.

These images provide unusual insight into peasants' acceptance of the delivery of health and roadwork projects. Hidden from these photographs is the larger context of the army's entrenched racism against Indigenous peasants. For Pablo González Casanova, "Racism and discrimination correspond to the psychology and politics characterizing colonialism."[57] By providing these much-needed basic services, the army intentionally deepened the dependency of peasant families on its services and created a favorable image of itself as a provider of social justice. As economist Gary Anders suggests, the colonizer strangles and co-opts the colonized into accepting dependency and underdevelopment: "They are," in his words, "prisoners of an internal colonial system which uses their very presence as a resource for the benefit of the white dominated external economy."[58]

Figure 3.3. © CIRMA, Archivo Hisstórico, Colección Familia Figueroa Ibarra. Memoria de Labores del Gobierno Militar 1964–1965, 43.

Role of Reservists: Maya Patriotism

Reserves, drawn from the Maya peasantry in the highlands, played an important part in the strategy of civic action during this prelude to genocide. According to one military journal, reserves were critical in providing "abilities or skills [that] can be taken advantage of to protect the country and their own families. Reserves play a patriotic role in alphabetizing the population in municipalities and cantons."[59] These actions generated local support for the military and encouraged a close relationship between soldiers and the Maya population in which, "the soldier, in addition to being the [local population's] guardian, is its brother."[60]

Beginning in April 1969, the Comandancia de Reservas Militares (Military Reserve Command) carried out a vast program of projects benefiting the population in rural municipalities and villages in Huehuetenango. Not only did they maintain and improve roads and bridges originally built poorly by the army itself, but they also brought potable water, sports, and cultural events to highland villages. During this time the illiteracy rate in Chichicastenango was 93 percent in a population of 36,036 people, indicating the larger context in which the Maya peasantry was encouraged to join the reserves to serve an anticommunist, non-Indigenous military.[61]

A *Revista Militar* article from 1970 defined civic action as a technique capable of effectively using the military's resources to aid a particular population, who would, over time, spontaneously participate in its own social and economic prosperity. By providing orientation and technical assistance to the poor, the military surreptitiously intended to increase dependence on the military by making the peasantry feel that development was their project and that it was their responsibility and not that of the military. The army's involvement in public works continued throughout the 1970s. On 15 June 1975, General Kjell Eugenio Laugerud praised the army for providing 158,000 citizens with basic literacy, and 5,262 with basic education since 1946. He also proudly acknowledged the preventive nature of the medical and dental campaigns: since April 1970 "760,000 people have been vaccinated and another 315,000 received curative treatment."[62]

On the occasion of the fifteenth celebration of officer promotion by the Dirección de Estudios Militares (DEM), Colonel Boris Rebbio Porta España, subdirector of the Center for the Study of the Military (CEM; later renamed Centro de Estudios Superiores de la Defensa Nacional [CESDENA]), stressed that development and security complement each other. "Development," the colonel noted, "becomes social when its fruits take a social form. With this in mind, our studies also include sociology, constitutional law, international law … in order to educate military professionals with a broader view of national and international realities."[63] First Captain of Infantry Otto Fernando Pérez

Molina, awarded with distinction for his service, is an example of this education. Marking the continued presence of the peasant soldier reserve in the political sphere, the same Pérez Molina, having reached the military rank of general,
was sworn in as president of Guatemala on 14 January 2012 (Chapter Ten).

The recognition of the military as the most powerful institution was later
used to justify its involvement in developing infrastructure in the countryside,
even as the bloodshed was spreading in the early 1980s. Another army goal
was to "Foster the population's own will to contribute to its own progress,"[64]
automatically assuming Indigenous families were not interested in participating in their own progress. However, as I show in Chapters Four and Five, the
collective participation of sectors of the peasantry in Maya-led grassroots organizations since the 1960s attests to Indigenous communities' determination
and resilience to take control of their own socio-economic, political, and cultural development.

By the time the army assaulted communities to destroy the "seeds of communism" in the early 1980s, the military had already established civic work
programs in rural communities, supplying them with health, educational,
or microeconomic services. While performing the roles of builders, doctors,
dentists, and agricultural technicians, the military maintained its national,
non-Indigenous, Ladino character, belittling the people they saw and objec-
tified as "resources."

As the Genocide Unfolded

Beginning in the early 1980s, the army modeled its Civil Affairs and Local
Development Companies (or S-5 division) after the civic action of previous
decades and continued to supply rural communities with basic infrastructure,
education, health, housing, sports, agricultural, and cultural projects. As genocidal violence accelerated, war through minimum force—the penetration of
specialists into the local population—was the central concept of civil affairs.[65]
Eleven civil affairs companies were set up by the military, and at each regional
military base, specialists brought to communities a message aimed at promoting "solidarity with the army and to encourage peasants to willingly join the
patrols."[66]

Each S-5 unit was composed of seventy-three soldiers, who would give mo-
tivational talks to patrols.[67] According to the 1982 Victory, or Beans and Bullets military campaign, "Every military zone will include one officer with S-5
tasks, this will also involve rural promoters, teachers or nutritional auxiliaries
included to coordinate the control of all governmental entities working in the
development of the rural area."[68] In 2000, Mateo, a member from the president
of the COPREDEH (the Presidential Commission to Coordinate Executive

Policy in Human Rights), discussed the patrols' "approval" of the army in exchange for rewards:

> Civil Affairs was like a complement of the war … People were not going to become allies of the military without getting anything in return, that is to say, finding themselves in a situation of exploitation and poverty, the army would bring programs to deceptively improve the quality of their lives.[69]

At least three central elements of civil affairs work gave continuity to the army's civic action role: (1) services for the development of the population, (2) local participation in these efforts, and (3) the strengthening of the military's relationship with the Maya peasants. In the process, the army maintained its institutional relations and forged alliances, thus facilitating S-5 companies' rapport with locals. In this civil affairs incarnation, the military not only continued to supply communities with palliative projects but even extended its support in the distribution of land titles to rural communities.

Beginning in the early 1980s, as the heavily equipped army laid siege to unarmed peasant communities, the army's high command relied on a well-planned strategy to model its Civil Affairs Division after the successful civic action of the 1950s.[70] For example, according to Victory 82, an additional construction unit was added to the military task force, operating in southern El Quiché.[71]

At the same time that the state's security forces were mercilessly slaughtering peasant families, civil affairs work continued with help from USAID, as local S-5 specialists became the institutional knot tying the nearest military outpost to pro-army communities' structures of power. S-5 personnel continued to promote and execute the long-term project of social development for the sake of perceived threats to national security, a strategy aimed at fostering military-minded development and relief to poverty-stricken families who welcomed the military into their communities. According to Schirmer, "Local Civil Affairs and Development Companies demand[ed] the local population [participate] in local development projects and security apparatuses."[72] By portraying itself as the army of and for the people, the Corps of Engineers incarnated civic action's goals: to forge unity with rural communities.

Pablo, a human rights lawyer, explained how the army high command's mindset reached all the way down to the village level through its civil affairs officers,

> The general staff had a G5, [who] reproduces, at the departmental level, the structure of the army. They are the ones in charge of departmental policy. Each G5 has detachments, inside there is an S5 in charge of organizing, and who has, under his charge, all the community action at the level of this structure. The essential ones are the D2 [intelligence] and the D5; the former has the information, and the latter is in charge of the psychological profiles and of the entire political organization.[73]

Keeping Families Content and Healthy

As the anticommunist counterinsurgency violence rapidly escalated in the countryside, civil affairs attempted to distract the peasantry and gain their continued loyalty and positive regard during the winter holidays. Through the Ministry of National Defense, the military delivered toys in various communities to children between one and seven years old, who received the presents with their families. Candies and piñatas were offered in the capital to school-aged children. The parents were thankful to the army for bringing their families the magic of Santa Claus, complete with free soft drinks.[74]

But all this "aid" took place in the context of deeply embedded ethnic and class discrimination against Maya peasants. The Massacre of Cuarto Pueblo on Sunday 14 March 1982 in the Ixcán in northern El Quiché provides a further glimpse into the army's deep-seated hatred for Indigenous groups. On that Sunday morning, after a five-month absence from the area in the aftermath of the first Cuarto Pueblo Massacre that took place on April 30, 1981, soldiers returned to the Cuarto Pueblo community. The local military commissioner, Santos Velásquez, had asked them not to run from the army, because it was a crime and that he could handle the army if the need arose. Through afraid, many of his neighbors trusted him and waited for further instructions. Immediately, Santos Velásquez walked from the market's main square to the road; he stopped on a stone and saluted men he thought were his fellow soldiers: "Comrades, we had meetings every other week with you. I am a commissioner." The soldiers, without saying a word, shot the commissioner in the chest. He died right then and there. An army officer holding a two-way radio said as the event was happening: "We had meetings with this clown?"[75] The second Cuarto Pueblo Massacre had began.

Showing their ambiguous ties with military commissioners, on other occasions, the military would carry out fundraising efforts to aid. An example of this is Deomedes Pérez Ramirez, an impoverished assistant to a commissioner who had lost all his material belongings to a fire in Jutiapa on 10 March 1965, as reported at least once in an edition of *Ejército*.

The Early Aftermath of War: A "New" Doctrine

Amid suspicions of corruption and bribery in the early aftermath of war, as it had done in the past, the army disingenuously claimed a new "military metaphysics," a term used by C.W. Mills in his critical appraisal of the preponderance of the U.S. military at the onset of the Cold War.[76] Guatemalan civil-military relations scholar Bernardo Arevalo de León argues that with the signing of the Peace Accords, "The Military initiated a process that led to its own institutional transformation, well beyond its original intentions."[77] Yet, nothing could be further from the truth. Instead, showing its characteristic Janus faces, the army once again reconverted its old structures into military-like security groups, which were composed of ex-civil patrols, and increased its budget, as I discussed in Chapter Two.

Proof of this is the army's "new doctrine of security and peace" in the postaccords years enshrined in the 2003 *Libro de la Defensa Nacional de la República de Guatemala,* or *Libro Blanco.* "For the first time in the history of the state," the army claims, "the military recognizes its subordination to civil power, and emphasizes the integration of the National Defense in the State's General Policy." Most importantly, it also makes claims of recognizing the army's self-assigned role in maintaining the internal security.[78] Supporting the army's self-appraisal as an agent of peace, President-elect Alfonso Portillo Cabrera (2000–2004) remarked, "This [was] a necessary step towards the consolidation of the armed forces, professionalization in the new environment arising from peace and international changes."[79]

While simultaneously acknowledging the role of the United Nations and the OAS in providing advice, Portillo proudly noted, "The Libro Blanco is another example of a renovated state and country." A close reading, however, suggests that the ideology of national security criminalizing social protest and human rights activists continued to gird the army's military doctrine even seven years after the signing of the Peace Accords. This internal security doctrine identifies "the nation and state as one, with the military as the main instrument for the realization of national goals."[80]

Considering the prevailing militarization in the early aftermath, it is truly remarkable that in 2003 human rights organizations pressed the congress to pass the Civil Service Act, which provides a social alternative to mandatory military service.[81] Indeed, this was one of the few successful steps toward the full, long-term demilitarization of civil society.

Ironically, in the context of a USAID-financed TV advertisement to promote the work of the Truth Commission, a former staff member for the commission, Elizabeth Oglesby, notes, "From the same folks who helped deliver counterinsurgency … now we have human rights and peace projects."[82]

In Action: Photographing Civil Affairs

Back in 2000, during one of my visits to Military Base No. 20, I observed how representatives of the community of Xatinap, Santa Cruz, capital of El Quiché, requested a truck to transport construction materials into their community. When I asked Lieutenant Estuardo Duarte whether community authorities usually made such direct requests to civil affairs, the officer proudly echoed the pregenocide army's doctrine, explaining that, in fact, this was often the case because the military possessed the technical and human resources that were nonexistent in poverty-stricken communities.[83]

According to the El Quiché army commander, in "peaceful times," "Civil affairs seeks the support of the population through local development and psychological operations such as help in disaster emergencies, reforestation, bridges, making ditches ... they also participate in vaccination and educational campaign[s]."[84] The army continued to persistently make systematic efforts to recast itself as the agent of progress, publishing photographs of soldiers actively participating in the construction of bridges in national newspapers. These images, along with conciliatory propaganda, helped the army renew old ties or reinforce its already strong ones with co-opted village authorities, who welcomed S-5 officers in pro-army communities.

Visit to Chulumal I: Reforestation with the Army

By socializing children at a very early age, the military creates the idea that men can and should be part of the army, a pivotal part of militarization. Officially, civil affairs units were deactivated in 2002, when they were once again renamed and nominally restructured; they are now linked to the *escuelas de paz*.[85] But civil affairs personnel continued to liaise with former patrols, ex-military commissioners, and reserves, though officers told me that G-5 and S-5 were no longer used. On 4 July 2000, playing the role of participant-observer, I accompanied Lieutenant Duarte in a military truck to plant seeds with schoolchildren in the community of Chulumal I, a community only four kilometers away from Santa Cruz, with 800 people at the time of my fieldwork. Colonel Samayoa told me on that occasion, "In Chichi, the Corps of Engineers is opening roads for the commercialization of apples and avocados."[86]

As I walked through the guard post to meet the lieutenant at the military zone, I noticed this rather hypocritical slogan written on the external walls of the military base: "We are afraid of God and our Mission is based on the country's Political Constitution. We adhere to the fulfillment of human rights." Upon our arrival in Chulumal, the representative of the National Forest Institute (Instituto Nacional de Bosques, INAB), a schoolteacher, and a throng of second and third grade students greeted us, enthusiastically helping to unload the seedlings. The reforestation goal was to plant 2,000 trees, covering twenty-seven hectares. According to Lieutenant Duarte:

> Many people think that, in peacetime, the army has no real reason to exist, but that is not the case, because we offer help against forest fires ... the goal is to raise awareness ... the military does not harm people, but, rather, it trains them; they are discharged with an education.[87]

As Luis, the INAB representative, remarked, "The participation of the army, at least with their human resources … in projects of small social impact changes the mentality" about the role of the military. Tellingly, Luis responded with an energetic "Yes, my lieutenant" to every instruction from Duarte. Further indicating its close connection with the army, INAB coordinated with S-5 to control the outbreak of fires. On the surface, the long-term goal of the reforestation activity was to plant 2,000 trees to cover twenty-seven hectares. But the intention of the army was not to protect the environment of Maya communities. Rather, its goal was to shape itself in the social imagination as the benefactor of impoverished rural families.

The activity closed with a communal lunch provided by the hosting school and the S-5. Soldiers in camouflage enthusiastically played basketball with the schoolchildren, some of whom announced at the end of the event that they would also like to become soldiers. However eager the military was to impact Indigenous communities, the military mindset prevailed that the Maya were not capable of organizing themselves and needed the military's intervention and influence. These aspirations to join the military pointed to the effectiveness of the military's social campaigns in infiltrating the communities they penetrated.

These compelling images of peasants' acceptance of infrastructure projects delivered by the military show the success of the army's paternalistic discourses and practices in co-opting authorities, families, and communities. In this picture, the schoolchildren from Chulumal I boarded the military truck carrying their seeds. Their relaxed demeanor showed the children's familiarity with uni-

Figure 3.4. July 2000, Chulumal I, Chichicastenango. © Author.

formed soldiers and plainclothes army sympathizers (in the extreme left). The army's institutional memory maintained its national, Ladino character, belittling Indigenous men, whom they saw merely as human resources. By providing trucks and gasoline and planting trees, the military continued to represent itself as a peace-building institution. An army specialist told Schirmer in the wake of the genocide, "My job was to brainwash the people. My work consisted first in erasing the cassette that the subversion had recorded onto the people, and later record[ing] onto them a new cassette."[88]

Figure 3.5. July 2000, Chulumal I, Chichicastenango. © Author.

This picture shows Maya schoolgirls interacting with the young uniformed soldier plowing the seeds, indicative of the normalized presence of the army in rural communities, bringing civil affairs programs to communities four years after signing the Peace Accords, in 2000. The schoolteacher, a young woman, soldiers, and children came together to help out in the task of reforesting the area during a sunny day.

Visit to the Tzocomaj Stadium: A "Dormant Dinosaur"

On 23 July 2000, Rigoberto, the president of the Friends of the Army Association, invited me to greet a group of reserves and former patrollers and to introduce this study to reservists during their weekly Sunday meeting with an S-5 officer. This meeting took place at the Tzocomaj football stadium, where the army had celebrated the patrols' alleged dissolution in 1996. After assuring them that their identities would remain confidential if they agreed to be interviewed, to my surprise, the reservists applauded my intervention telling them I was there to understand their relations with the army. As I watched the leader of the group take the attendance of the roughly thirty reservists gathered around, Lieutenant José García, from the army's reserve unit, made remarks with racist tinges, pointing to peasants' likely contribution to the country's progress—if they could only snap out of their "lethargy."

By comparing them to a "dormant dinosaur that could be awakened," this officer downplayed peasants' agency, reducing them to an animalistic state. In his words, "They are an important human resource that is important to organize. We must create attractive projects to integrate them."[89] As a result, thwarted images of the colonized continued to justify sustained exploitation. Describing the oppressed as lazy is useful, Memmi asserted long ago, because "it is economically fruitful."[90]

Ironically, by characterizing Maya reserves as a physically strong and powerful "creature," the officer betrayed the army's condescending view, from which it delivered a host of militaristic development projects designed to both erase the military's bloody, recent past and promote its false image as guardians of poverty-stricken communities. As a result, the pernicious aftereffects of civic action promoted by civil affairs enabled the rearticulation of bellicose ideologies. In some communities, such as the Chupol area I analyze in the next chapter, however, Cold War ideology competed with liberation theology prior to the genocide, allowing peasants to confront the army's propaganda.

Notes

1. Gaillard, *Civic Action versus Counterinsurgency*, 3.
2. Barber and Ronning, *Internal Security and Military Power*, 6.
3. Colonel Karl W. Robinson, director, Strategic Studies Institute. Quoted in Gaillard, *Civic Action versus Counterinsurgency*.
4. Handy, "Democratizing What?" 46.
5. See, for example, the various issues of the *Memorial de la Escuela Militar*, 31 January 1891.
6. Schirmer, "From the Horse's Mouth," 29.
7. Divinzenso, "La transformación de las relaciones cívico-militares."
8. Christiansen, "United States Air Force," 4.
9. Translated as "father president."
10. Grandin, *Last Colonial Massacre*, 49.
11. Kirkpatrick, "Optics," 307–8.
12. HNG, *Revista Militar*, "Guatemala Renace," 5.
13. HNG, *Revista Militar*, "La Función del Ejército," 473.
14. Ahuja notes that in India, the "colonial engineer … was celebrated as the incarnation of Britain's 'civilizing mission'" ("Bridge-Builders," 96).
15. Adams, "Ethnic Images and Strategies," 1.
16. Handy, *Revolution in the Countryside*, 10.

17. Kirkpatrick, "Optics," 314.
18. Ibid., 289.
19. HNG, *Revista Militar*, "Expedición Administrativa," 69; Maxeños's military skills are also noted in a local El Quiché Magazine: "heirs of Tecun Uman, they are addicted to a military career. "El Heroe Indiano."
20. Memmi, *Colonizer and the Colonized*, 79.
21. Brill, "Military Civic Action in Bolivia," 2.
22. Seckinger, "Central American Militaries," 247.
23. Adams, *Crucifixion by Power*, Kindle Locations 4504–5.
24. Cited in Purcell, "Connecting Realities," 131.
25. Heller, *Cold War*, 158.
26. Hanhimaki and Westad, *Cold War*, 380.
27. CEH, II.36.
28. CIRMA, *El Imparcial*, "Acción Civica del Ejército Observada."
29. Adams has said, "Perhaps the strongest arm of the civic action program has been literacy" (*Crucifixion by Power*, Kindle location 4516).
30. CIRMA, *El Imparcial*, "85 Centros de Alfabetización."
31. Boff and Boff, *Introducing Liberation Theology*, 5.
32. HNG, *Revista Militar*, "Acción Civica, El Desarrollo," 17–22.
33. Ibid., 51.
34. Huntington, *Soldier and the State*, 15.
35. Adams, *Crucifixion by Power*, Kindle locations 4525–26.
36. Schirmer, *Guatemalan Military Project*, 81, 91.
37. Huntington, *Soldier and the State*, 12.
38. Ejército de Guatemala, "Army General Order." See also Ejército de Guatemala, "Ley Constitutivo del Ejército."
39. HNG, *Revista Militar*, "Acción Civica un Arma," 51–55.
40. CIRMA, *El Imparcial*, "Acción Civica del Ejército."
41. Adams, *Development of the Guatemalan Military*, 107.
42. CIRMA, *El Imparcial*, "Ministro de la Defensa."
43. Ibid.
44. HNG, *Revista Militar*, Navarino, "Que Es y Como Nació," 86.
45. HNG, *Revista Militar*, García C., "Una Experiencia Involvidable," 41.
46. Keberlein Gutiérrez, "Guatemalan Liberal Revolution," 145.
47. See Adams, *Crucifixion by Power*, Kindle locations 4006–13.
48. Cojtí Cuxil, "Politics of Maya Reivindication," 19.
49. Adams, "Development of the Guatemalan Military," 95.
50. HNG, *Revista Militar*, "La Función del Ejército," 472. My emphasis.
51. Ahuja, "Bridge-Builders," 96.
52. Césaire, *Discourse on Colonialism*, 43.
53. Gottesman, *Cambodia*, 15.
54. HNG, *Revista Militar*, "Contribución del Ejército al Progreso," 51. My emphasis.
55. In 1986, Diane M. Nelson spent time visiting Development Poles. Here, she says, "Army engineers were building wide roads and bridges to connect the new consolidated villages that were sprouting up … Progress in this case meant running water, a school, a Civil Patrol post, and housing" (*Finger in the Wound*, Kindle locations 1279–81).
56. I am thankful to Lydia Shestopalova for her insights on this particular point.
57. González Casanova, *Sociología de la Explotación*, 195.
58. Anders, "Internal Colonization," 43.
59. HNG, *Revista Militar*, "Una Experiencia Involvidable," 35.

60. CIRMA, *El Imparcial,* "Acción Civica Militar en Actividades."
61. CIRMA, Publicaciones *Revista Gumarcaah,* 1969.
62. CIRMA, Colección de la Morgue, *Prensa Libre,* "El Ejército es un Agente," 6.
63. CIRMA, *El Imparcial,* "Vinculación de la Seguridad."
64. HNG, *Revista Militar,* "Acción Civica," 51–55.
65. Schirmer, *Guatemalan Military Project,* 103–23.
66. Ejército de Guatemala, "Plan de Campaña Firmeza 83-1," Annex "F."
67. Ejército de Guatemala, "Plan de Campaña Firmeza 83-1."
68. Ejército de Guatemala, "Plan de Campaña Victory 82."
69. Author interview, Mateo.
70. "Each Commander will appoint, out of his own cadres, one (1) S-5 Officer, until the titleholder is appointed." Ejército de Guatemala, "Plan de Campaña Victory 82," 16.
71. Ibid., 2.
72. Schirmer, *Guatemalan Military Project,* 103. "As Gramajo recounts, 'We recalled Reservists to active duty and all the doctors, teachers, civil engineers, people working for the Government in Cobán [Alta Verapaz], Huehuetenango, [and] Quiché had to spend time in the areas of conflict. If they refused to go, they would be forced to join the military ranks.'" Schirmer, *Guatemalan Military Project,* 47.
73. Author interview, Pablo.
74. CIRMA, *El Imparcial,* "Ejército en Reparto de Navidades."
75. CEH, VII.104.
76. Mills, *Power Elite,* 205.
77. Arevalo de León, "Civil-Military Relations," 70.
78. RESDAL, *Libro Blanco.*
79. Ibid.
80. Crahan, *Human Rights and Basic Needs,* 7.
81. WRI, "Country Report and Updates: Guatemala."
82. Oglesby further writes, "Examples of these AID-funded activities included … a traveling photo exhibit of exhumations sponsored by one of Guatemala's forensic anthropology groups" ("Historical Memory and the Limits," 24, fn29).
83. Author interview, Lieutenant Duarte.
84. Author interview, Colonel Samayoa.
85. Ejército de Guatemala, "Seguridad."
86. Author interview, Colonel Samayoa.
87. Author interview, Lieutenant Duarte.
88. Schirmer, *Guatemalan Military Project,* 111.
89. Author interview, Lieutenant José Garcia.
90. Memmi, *Colonizer and the Colonized,* 79.

4

The Beheading of a Popular
Maya Uprising in a "Red Community"

I am the daughter of misery and social inequality ...
I have survived the genocide and cruelty.
—Rigoberta Menchú, winner of the 1992 Peace Nobel Prize

Leo Kuper's pioneering studies in Africa have shown that polarization processes "by which members of the same society are ranged against each other in deadly enmity" precede genocide.[1] This ensuing antagonism is shaped, Kuper asserts, by "ideologies circulating which encourage the commission of genocide."[2] Similarly, in this chapter, I argue that by the time the army ordered peasants and reservists to join the Civil Self-Defense Patrol (PAC) system, competing ideologies embedded in liberation theology and national security doctrine (NSD) along a multilayered political and religious process had internally divided communities and families in nearly all Maya-K'iché, Chupol, and outlying villages in the early 1980s. Divisions arose between the traditionalists, or *costumbristas* (the *principales,* who guide the *cofradías,* or religious brotherhoods), and those espousing a process of Catholic religious conversion, those pledging their loyalty to the army, and those supporting the URNG rebels.

What external factors led to the rise of this ideological process of class and ethnic consciousness awakening? Postcolonial scholar Arturo Arias notes that two factors fashioned the birth of the new Maya revolutionary consciousness: Catholic Action promoting the gospel of liberation theology, and the ability to form a new cadre of Indigenous leadership in the 1970s.[3] In theologians Leonardo Boff and Clodovis Boff's compelling assertion, "Liberation theology was born when faith confronted the injustice done to the poor" and soon spread across Latin America, challenging the status quo.[4] As a result, lay catechists were the first to join the leftwing rebel forces seeking to decolonize their communities, as also observed by anthropologist Richard Wilson when analyzing the participation of the Q'eqchi in the war.[5] In the Chupol village and outlying communities, geography was also a pivotal factor.

I define as "literate communities" those Chupol communities that were better prepared to consciously unmask the true goals of the army's civic action and psychological campaigns (PSYOPs) disseminating the internal enemy propaganda designed to compel peasants to join the patrol system. Bordering the Chimaltenango and Sololá departments, where intense rebel activities were occurring, the Chupol area was typified in military cartography by the army's intelligence reports as a "red" *matazona*, or conflict zone.[6]

Because of its geographical distance from the town's urban area, el pueblo, Chupol is considered an administrative center, with a health post, schools, and a market providing service to seventeen outlying hamlets that belong to microregions five and six (see Map 2). Itself stretching along six kilometers, and centered on the 110-kilometer marker of the Interamerican (or Panamerican) Highway, Chupol is 125 kilometers away from Guatemala City and 20 kilometers from Chichicastenango's urban center. It is also near Los Encuentros, a busy intersection that was highly contested in the early 1980s by state soldiers and the URNG insurgency due to its strategic location connecting the departments of Huehuetenango, Totonicapán, and Quetzaltenango and the lowlands plantations.

Anthropologist Carlota McAllister notes not only that Chupol is geographically one of the farthest, southernmost cantons from the center but that this distance from Chichicastenango's urban center also makes it more independent of influence from both the Indigenous and the Ladino municipalities. Like the rest of the rural communities, Chupol is bounded by two or three generations of family networks dating back to the sixteenth century, when Chichicastenango was founded. In Chupol, by the late 1990s, most families survived in less than two *cuerdas* (almost two acres), compared to their ancestors' 5.9 cuerdas, anthropologist Carlotta McAllister has shown.[7]

First Polarization: Liberation Theology and *Costumbristas*

Liberation Theology resonated with Chupol communities lying off the Interamerican Highway. Prior to the arrival of the first Maryknoll missionaries in 1943, the Catholic Church and its socioeconomic, political, and religious program known as "Catholic Action" were introduced in the highlands, shaping radical social changes and creating internal divisions within communities.[8] In early 1955, "Spanish Sacred Heart Missionary priests arrived to take charge of pastoral work for the entire department of El Quiché," initiating intracommunity religious divisions.[9] Initially, foreign Catholic missionaries followed anticommunist views, but once they were confronted with the appalling poverty affecting rural communities, they radically changed their views and adopted the new gospel of liberation theology, transforming a postcolonial institution into one supporting the internally oppressed.[10]

Like elsewhere in Latin America, foregrounded in the unfolding religious conversion was the organization of illiterate peasants into ecclesiastical base communities (CEBs) or rural Christian base communities, cooperatives, and peasant leagues (farmer's syndicates), or Ligas Campesinas. In some communities, these new grassroots organizations became the "instruments of struggle," raising class and ethnic consciousness against oppression. To understand this process, social psychologist Ignacio Martin-Baró argues that it is pivotal to include the role of ideology, to grapple with its political effects, rather than just individual experience with emancipation.[11] Local catechists used the structures made available to them by the Catholic Church and encouraged a "horizontal religiosity" that strongly resonated with the resilient Mayan cultural value system characterized by collectively pursuing projects for survival. This horizontal belief contrasted with the "vertical religiosity" embodied in the Evangelical Pentecostal belief that salvation lies beyond this world.[12]

At local Bible study groups, for example, "participants learn[ed] new values and practices."[13] CEB members, organized into local directives, met in villages and introduced a radical interpretation of the Bible, benefiting families with critical political discussions.[14] In the words of Sebastián Morales, a peasant unity community (CUC) founder from Chuguexa I, Catholic Action raised political awareness: "Missionaries told the Indigenous people: you are equal, you have the same rights."[15] Aiding in the transmission of new ideas was Maya peasants' lived experienced with strong solidarity links between family and social networks.

Ideological and religious hostilities, however, soon arose between those who embraced the radical liberation theology challenging the political authority vested in the traditionalists,[16] often associated with the fascist National Liberation Movement (MLN), which wielded significant power in their communities. Conflicts arose "between relatives and neighbors, even between parents and children."[17] In the case of San Antonio Ilotenango, El Quiché, anthropologist Ricardo Falla argues that the traditionalists accused Catholic Action of being "'witch doctors,' that processions were being prevented, and in general that the Tradition was being changed."[18] In Chupol, McAllister asserts, "In overthrowing the spiritual authority of the cofradías ... Catholic Action also lent authority to political and economic behaviors quite foreign to those sanctioned by costumbre, radically transforming the grounds on which Indigenous identity was constructed."[19]

Expansion of Roads: Hopes for a Dignified Life

For communities lying off the main road, facilitating the introduction of the new liberation theology gospel was the expansion of the Interamerican Highway in 1956.[20] Chupolenses used the highway to increase their economic, social, and political networks throughout El Quiché. The Interamerican High-way "definitively freed Chupolenses from hated plantation work," as McAllis-ter suggests. "By virtue of lying in the highway's path," McAllister continues, Chupolenses "suddenly gained access to a means of transport for their goods other than their own backs," a considerable improvement further accentuated "when third-class bus lines began to run on the highway in the mid-1960s."[21] As their geographical isolation was now reduced by easier access to el pueblo and other adjacent townships, and particularly to Guatemala City, merchants both traveled to meet and were visited by outside institutions: rural Catholic Action catechists and Spanish and North American missionaries.

Across El Quiché, Catholic Action resonated with "people with a profound spiritual and mystical outlook of life."[22] Julio, a former peasant league member, remarked on the arrival of Catholic Action to convert peasants in his home-town: "Well, not all the people attended the priest workshops. People practiced their customs, they prayed to God, they respected God but they did not ac-cept the Catholic religion."[23] Julio later acknowledged the role played by close family networks in convincing him to convert: "In my own case, a brother of mine told me that there is a God. I went with my brother and took part in the workshops."[24] To aid in the spreading of the new ideas, radio programming in Maya-K'iché, the Emisora Diocesana, was set up in 1965 that helped raise new awareness of their capacity to create their own grassroots organizations to rise above their wretchedness.[25]

In Chupol, "by the late 1960s, priests in many communities were deeply in-volved in parishioners' efforts to set up agricultural cooperatives, savings and loans institutions, Betterment Committees, peasant leagues, and rural schools and markets."[26] Sebastián, a former president of Catholic Action from Chu-guexa I, remarked on how the Chupol community became not only a com-mercial but also a political center for nearby and dispersed settlements when the church building and the open-air markets were founded in 1969: "Father Felipe told us he would look for a piece of land in Chupol to establish the local parish. His desire was to build an oratory and a market. Soon after, the call was out to attract vendors."[27] McAllister notes that by the 1970s, most of the authorities, such as auxiliary mayors and elders, who had converted to Catholicism were young, low-scale producers and underprivileged in terms of landownership; these even included some *costumbristas* and traditionalists.[28]

By setting up "a physical market in which to engage one another," farmers could finally begin to participate in "proper market relations at home as well as on the road."[29] Falla notes that by the mid-1960s, from a total population of 249,704, an estimated 70,000 persons had aligned with Catholic Action in El Quiché.[30] The rapid spread of this new doctrine and the capacity of Maya com-munities to transmit it to their networks helped create a new Indigenous lead-ership, facilitating the emergence of literacy efforts, rural cooperatives, and grassroots peasant organizations. This incipient social change triggered the rise of what Barrington Moore has termed "revolutionary petty middle-class peasantry."[31]

Empowerment through Literacy: New Mayan Leadership

Brazilian theologian Paulo Freire's analysis of critical literacy observes that learning to read and write is a subversive action because it involves a "self-transformation producing a stance of intervention in one's context."[32] Peasants from Chupol, Chuguexa, Agua Escondida, Las Trampas, Chucalibal, Semeja, and the more hinterland Chontolá communities had acquired the needed information telling peasants that the demoralization instilled by the everyday racism permeating their communities was not their fault. Over time, to be a Chupolense "was to have consciousness," McAllister poignantly asserts.[33]

Acquiring the Spanish language was a pivotal transformative experience for Chupolenses and nearby communities. Learning how to read and write in Spanish had a multiplying effect that ultimately proved very efficient, since entire families joined literacy workshops, which encouraged the active participation of Maya women—who until then had been subordinated by a hierarchical structure—into Catholic Action projects.[34] By the 1970s only 7 percent of the population qualified as literate (see Appendix 1 for a comparative socioeconomic profile of "red" and "white" communities, the latter I discuss in Chapter Six).[35] Catechists began to read and became community and local committee leaders, building schools and getting drinking water. Those who knew how to read and write in Spanish, "went out in pairs visiting hamlets. We would work throughout the day and at night, we would give our talk."[36]

Candelario from Chuchipacá recalled how critical literacy allowed catechists to participate in meetings and workshops where they acquired leadership skills: "People in charge had to attend meetings and trainings; the first ones to participate were the members of the Catholic Church. One of the first ones was my father," he proudly concluded.[37] From as far as the Quiejel community and from Saquillá, a western community, neighbors went to Chontolá and Chupol to participate in Catholic Action projects. During this time, a wide range of newly organized peasant groups sprang up as peasants took advantage of what was being offered to them: all-Indigenous *alfabetizadores* (literacy promoters) had participated within the Accion Católica Rural Obrera (JARO), and in 1970, the women's branch was constituted into the Juventud de Accion Católica Rural Obrera Femenina (JACROF).[38]

Teaching methods informed by liberation theology involved the use of words that could eventually generate political discussion, such as "fertilizer."[39] This word is part of peasant's vocabulary and was used to help them understand why access to it was not easily available in rural areas. In the process, young catechists formed and led grassroots organizations, seeking aid from outside institutions to finance the construction of school buildings or road expansion.[40] One crucial source was the United States Agency for International Development (USAID), which had funded rural cooperatives, agriculture, health, education, and infrastructure since the Mutual Security Act of 1953, formally channeling some "$750 million in development assistance, food aid, and economic support,"[41] in addition to, as I explore in Chapter Three, funding counterinsurgency campaigns.

This type of critical literacy, aimed at uncovering the roots of social injustice, clashed with the literacy programs promoted by the administration of General Fernando Romeo Lucas García (1978–1982), which fostered the status quo. In newspaper advertisements published, for instance, by *El Imparcial* on Wednesday 6 December 1981, the Ministry of Education instructed students to read the word "stone" (*piedra*) in order to acquaint themselves with the words "mortar" and "pestle," tools peasants used (and use) to process their daily staple, corn. While important, the army's literacy plan showed little intention of promoting critical understanding of the larger oppression. To compare, groups opposing the army disseminated fliers in 1983 raising awareness of the army's manipulation of beauty contests of Indigenous women while simultaneously bombing their ranches.[42]

Driven by the historical fear of Indigenous uprisings, high-ranking officers expressed their concern over empowering the subaltern through literacy. Sources note that Colonel Gonzáles Rivera (nicknamed "Colonel Poison"), governor of El Quiché during the Colonel Alfredo Enrique Peralta Azurdia administration (1963–1966), used to cynically brag that it was urgent to stop all educational activities led by the Church because the "day that the Indians rise above their ignorance, it would be our end."[43]

Cooperativism and New Pesticides

Across Latin America, as part of their involvement with the U.S. Alliance for Progress, states promoted cooperativism with the aim of pacifying revolting communities in the late 1950s and the 1960s. By 1967, 27,000 rural *campesinos,* distributed through fifteen cooperatives, had joined the movement. A similar finding is reported in Roger Plant's *Guatemala: Unnatural Disaster,* in which Plant argues that by March 1976, there were 510 agricultural, artisan, savings and loan, and consumer cooperatives in Guatemala, with 290 (57 percent) in areas populated by Indigenous peoples.[44] This participation in cooperatives spoke to a sea change in peasants' political attitudes.

Encouraged by the spread of self-run cooperatives and literacy programs, peasants understood they could produce social change. As Esteban recalled,

"The answer to [peasant] poverty had to be found within the people them-selves ... so they began to enforce, micro-credit and chemical fertilizers ... cooperatives operated in Chichicastenango."[45] An array of new technical re-sources and training were made available to peasants through savings and loans institutions and training on farming with pesticides to produce low-scale commercialization of new products, like apples.

Locals also participated in the founding of the Instituto Indígena in the early 1960s, where courses where given to "bilingual promoters of educa-tion."[46] Since 1967, the Sindicato de Trabajadores Agricola Independientes—forerunner of the CUC—had organized and recruited members in the com-munity of Chutzorop and Chupol.[47] Although scattered, only a few families' memberships were drawn from western communities like Saquillá, Paxot, and Xeabaj. Over time, participating in cooperatives and literacy projects led to further political and religious divisions between the orthodox traditionalists and Catholic Action followers, which was aggravated by the outgrowth of peasants' organizations demanding changes in the oppressive structures after the 1976 earthquake.

A Thirty-Three-Second Revelation

With the 1976 earthquake, solidarity links were established with the urban social movement in Guatemala City. The powerful seism left a dreadful toll: 25,000 people dead, countless others wounded, and 1.2 million people home-less nationwide.[48] At least 140 people died in Chichicastenango, as peasants' humble ranches were flattened by the intensity of the natural disaster.[49] Frank M. Afflito defines it as a "class earthquake" because it directly affected the most vulnerable in the countryside. Sebastián, from Chuguexa I, also a CUC founder, explained why the earthquake rapidly brought down their homes: "The houses were made of sun-dried-brick adobes, one adobe on top of an-other, and they did not have any reinforcement on the corners."[50]

For many observers, the "class and ethnic" earthquake not only unveiled peasants' vulnerability to natural disasters but also served to encourage rela-tions with the leftwing, radicalized, Ladino urban sectors of students, trade unions, professionals, and lawyers from Guatemala City. These liaisons further validated the Maya-K'iché's demands and reinforced solidarity across Indige-nous and non-Indigenous divides. Sebastián noted the earthquake's political impact in the evolving process of consciousness raising: "Before the earthquake, I did not know anything" about organizations.[51] In the army's eyes, the negative perception was that the earthquake had served to unite the poor through the "communal spirit that Catholic Action had encouraged for many years."[52]

Candelario from Chuchipacá also described the formation of new committees that brought awareness of the need to work together: "After the 1976 earthquake, committees for improvement were created: members from the communities were summoned to the provincial governor's offices. Initially, people did not know what a committee was, and what purpose would it serve."[53] Chupolenses quickly recovered and founded the Cooperativa Agricola,[54] in addition to establishing peasant leagues to demand the protection of the rights of all peasants, Indigenous and non-Indigenous, from state abuses. The Maya peasant uprising was crystallizing—but so was an unfolding ideological and religious polarization process.

Second Polarizing Layer: The Peasant Unity Committee

In the mid-1970s, a new cadre of Maya leadership emerged, founding branches of peasant leagues and adding yet another division in Indigenous communities between those siding with the new leadership and those siding with the status quo, and even within emerging Indigenous grassroots groups. Among the last was the Peasant Unity Committee (CUC), born on 15 April 1978 in El Quiché, in la Estancia in Santa Cruz with representatives from Uspantán, and the Sololá Department, under the political slogan, "clear head, heart in solidarity, and clenched fist."[55]

CUC represented Indigenous as well as non-Indigenous day laborers in the fincas (estates) and addressed the injustice of forcibly recruiting young males into the army, known as *las agarraderas*. Nationally,

> on the coastal plantations and modernized Highland fincas, a new federation of rural laborers … [the CUC] successfully mobilized both Indians and Ladinos in strikes and marchers—such as the National strike of March 1980, when 80,000 laborers paralyzed fourteen sugar refineries and seventy large fincas—and negotiated better working conditions, in spite of constant aggressions from the military and vigilante groups.[56]

For Robert Carmack, the CUC was "more ideological than any previous Indian organization had been."[57]

In Chichicastenango, the CUC first was organized in Chuguexa I (26 kilometers or 16 miles from the township center) in the early 1970s. McAllister notes that within a few months of its formation in Chupol, "almost every household in the village had joined."[58] Sebastián, CUC cofounder from the area, noted its gradual emergence: "The CUC was founded in 1978, but its *concientización* [consciousness raising] work had begun in 1972."[59] On the relationship between his own religious conversion and the CUC, Sebastián noted:

I followed Mayan religion, I would also go to church, but I did not know about the suffering of the people. I remember they [CUC] talked about giving water to the thirsty and clothes to the poor. So I analyzed: If I myself do not have food or water, what was I supposed to give to the people? So, I realized that the solution was to empower ourselves.[60]

Like other peasants from Chupol, Sebastián's class and ethnic analysis shows how CUC discussions about their own marginalization led him into a critical self-questioning of his community's experience with conditions of extreme poverty and exploitation. He further added, "The CUC was formed by Indigenous, peasants, poor Ladinos, Catholic Action, some evangelicals. CUC did not hide their people; CUC was there to orient the people, to work with them, and we would take the opinion of the people into consideration."[61]

Christian Democratic Party and Peasant Leagues

Aiding in the unfolding process of promoting peasant leagues was the work of the Christian Democratic Party (DC), which successfully recruited membership "against the exploitation of migrant plantation work, conscription, prohibitions against cutting down trees, delinquency, land and water expropriation, and cultural discrimination."[62] Since the early 1960s, the party had had strong ties with the Catholic Church and promoted similar economic developments as those sponsored by the Church because "it was often the only political platform speaking peasants' languages, interpreting its culture, and respecting their cultural makeup."[63]

In 1974, Tomás Tiniguar from the Chuabaj community, a DC candidate, became the first Indigenous elected municipal mayor known for his involvement in the Catholic Action. Miguel, a schoolteacher, remarked that postearthquake efforts focused mostly on "reconstructing the torn areas, particularly in the Chupol area because in that area, people were better organized, thanks to the Catholic Church. From that moment on, roads started being built everywhere."

Miguel further reminisced that the Tiniguar administration "built streets and brought several potable water projects to the municipality during his tenure." Miguel concluded about Tiniguar's leadership, "He was always a DC leader; he wanted to help the population in the poorest areas because they did not receive a lot of help."[64] Later, in 1978, Domingo Morales, from Chuguexa II B, became the second consecutive Christian Democrat Indigenous mayor. He favored grassroots development by bringing potable water, rural schools, and a new health center into remote villages.[65] DC mayors implementing grassroots development was not, however, welcome by those who sided with the status quo. Tomás, a former peasant league founder from Chicuá I, explained that some neighbors and families "were ready to understand what was happening while others did not get it."[66] This highlights political divisions between those who thought the option was armed confrontation, like the CUC, the peasant leagues who advocated nonconfrontational means, and those who sided with orthodox traditionalists.

Sebastián further explained this ideological division between CUC and Liga Campesina: "I was also one of the first in organizing with the peasant league. Unlike the CUC, Liga Campesina said that we had to work to change people's mentality to raise their consciousness." "The CUC disagreed," Sebastián remarked, "and wanted to begin the revolution. So there was a contradiction between them, because the CUC wanted to eat the food because it was hungry, but Liga Campesina said, no it is better that the food gets really cooked."[67] Tomás also explained the ensuing polarization: "The conflict was about whether to follow the armed struggle as espoused by the CUC or with the application of the law."[68] On 14 February 1981, the CUC assembled and called on the Maya to rebel, a historical political act sealed in the Iximché Declaration.[69]

Military Commissioners and Reserves

Increased levels of peasant class and ethnic consciousness shaped the formation of what the army later identified as red villages in its Victory 82 Counterinsurgency Plan, laying out the national security ideological and operational details identifying pro-rebel villages. This profiling was based on the military's in-depth understanding of communities' geography, their organizational structures, and their systems of authority. In this context, the role of military commissioners in policing their communities proved pivotal. Pedro describes how security was trusted to the commissioners: "Before the violence came [in the early 1980s], we did not know any soldiers. The only person we knew was the military commissioner ... He was responsible for securing order when the community celebrated a holiday. He was in charge of capturing any thief."[70]

McAllister asserts, "Very few people in Chupol do military service. I know of three families with sons in the military who recently returned to their communities, and I know of two men who served in the early 1970s."[71] The activation of military reserves and military commissioners and the organization of the PACs in the early 1980s again split communities ideologically, as the army used its informers to threaten those who stood up against injustice: young Catholic catechists, CUC members, and peasant leagues leaders.

McAllister notes that women felt that the army's racist indoctrination techniques shaping their children's identity made it difficult for men to return to their communities because it also "disposed them to be abusive toward their families." Macario, from Chupol, noted how the military commissioners deliberately manipulated families' poverty for their own personal gain: "The military commissioner took away our children. Sometimes when a mother or father says to them, 'Please do not take my son,' they said 'they must go, they are men, but if you give me some money, I will not take them.'"[72] But Chupolense women fiercely resisted militarization, and on at least one occasion, armed with machetes, even chased down commissioners.

A local, Antonio, told McAllister, "The Chupolenses did not allow themselves to be taken away: mothers and children defended the young with sticks and stones, and the military commissioners had to leave with their tails between their legs. Right then and there began the quarrel between the army and the general population."[73] During this time, José Algua Tecum, a military commissioner, was allegedly disappeared by the rebels.[74]

Showing how CUC empowered its members to resist militarization, Fernando, an ex-peasant league leader, a former patrol and ex-military commissioner from Chupol, and, at the time of the interview, a human rights leader, told me about when he challenged the army:

> [When I quit the army] I threw my identification to the captain, because I knew that organizations like the CUC were supporting me. If I was arrested, [the organization] will get me out because the law does not allow work without pay. I was a military commissioner for five years. Who can survive five years, without money for the bus, or for food?[75]

Fernando's bold response that he would not join the army to be further exploited shows the extent to which he had been empowered by knowing the law, thanks to his participation in popular groups, like the CUC. In contradictory terms, showing the overlapping of binaries, Fernando took great pride in telling me he had served as a patrol chief in Chupol. By resisting the forced recruitment of their children into the army, McAllister shows, many Chupol families collaborated with the URNG rebels.

The Siege of Chupol: The Beheading of an Uprising

The growing participation of families in organized peasant leagues, along with the CUC lending their support to the URNG rebels, led the military to identify the Chupol as a red, or communist, community in the mid-1970s. To an army that perceived Indigenous peasants as "simple, ignorant, and in a state of nature,"[76] the rebellion of Chupolenses was unacceptable. There are two distinguishable moments when the military assaulted communities it had identified as collaborating with rebel groups. The first was between 1978 and 1980, when state violence targeted the newly emerged Maya leadership—Catholic cate-chists, the CUC and peasant leagues, cooperativists, teachers, and organized young Maya peasants—by systematically kidnapping, torturing, and murder-ing them.

During a second phase, between 1981 and 1983, when 81 percent of human rights violations were registered,[77] the army launched its brutal counterinsur-gency campaigns, beginning with the 1981 Ashes and 1982 Beans and Bullets scorched earth operations. For the largely unarmed peasant population along the Interamerican Highway, this meant the ground and aerial bombing of their ranches and the slaughtering of peasants inside schools and oratories as Indig-enous troops gang-raped women and girls and smashed babies' heads against walls and burned and looted their communities. High-ranking officers gave orders to destroy the milpas (cornfield) to eliminate the source of food for guerrillas.[78] These tactics, Beatriz Manz notes, were "reminiscent of the Span-iards' arrival in Hispaniola centuries ago … [when] Europeans introduced 'ar-tifice famine' by destroying the cultivated fields to subjugate the population and starve 'the rebellious.'"[79]

The aim of the genocidal violence was twofold. First, the army sought to iso-late the URNG rebels' social base from their collaborators and sympathizers, the defenseless and unarmed population. Second, the army's aim was to instill fear within the population to annihilate their will to organize independently from the army. At the end of 1981, the military moved to occupy the boarding school Marista, next to the Tzocomaj football field, a pivotal step leading up to the siege of the population in the administrative center. Following the army's strategy of total control, it set up a permanent outpost of "six companies, each with 160 soldiers"[80] off the Interamerican Highway in 1981; it was later moved next to the Catholic Church in 1985. From here, the army gained a panoramic view of the Chupol area.

Selective Killing: Targeting Maya Leadership (1978–1981)

As Zygmunt Bauman has aptly noted, "It is hoped that the marked group, once deprived of leadership and centers of authority, will lose its cohesiveness and the ability to sustain its own identity, and consequently its defensive poten-tial."[81] Over time, the group will devolve into a collection of disaggregated in-dividuals who will then be assimilated into the new structure and "policed directly by the managers of the new order."[82] In Guatemala, this translated into military operations targeting Maya elders and traditional authorities, whose influence could mobilize families either into collaborating with or joining the guerrillas (or the army, I show in Chapter Six). By destroying the elders, the army sought to break down communities' identities and altered the transmis-sion of ancestral knowledge,[83] a genocidal process also present in other cases of extreme forms of violence, targeting "cultural bearers, such as the intelligentsia and priestly class."[84]

An eyewitness told of an army officer's blatant racism debasing Maya elders in 1982: "You must tell me who are the sorcerers who practice the *costumbre* because they must be killed. We do not want sorcerers doing rituals against the army."[85] Yet, among these so-called sorcerers were those who abetted the military, which shows the ambivalent ties the military encouraged with communities by killing their own "amigos" (Chapters Eight and Nine).

Killing of Catholic Action Catechists and CUC members

Unsurprisingly, priests and lay catechists became targeted by counterinsurgency campaigns to eliminate red communities.[86] Military assaults against the Catholic Church forced its clergy to make the unprecedented decision to close all the parishes in El Quiché from 1980 until 1985.[87] Among the first renowned Catholic casualties in Quiché were Father Faustino Villanueva, who was assassinated in Joyabaj on 10 July 1980, and Juan Alonso, tortured and murdered on 15 February 1981.[88] Both had actively pioneered the establishment of cooperatives by securing fertilizer. In Chichi, the Truth Commission documented the killing and disappearance of at least eight confirmed Catholic catechists. Yet another source reports that over fifty catechists were murdered within the Chupol area.[89]

Sebastián commented on the army's opposition to the Catholic Church: "When the army arrived, they said that [catechists, priests, and nurses] spoke '*babosadas*,' silly things, and went after every Catholic Action catechist."[90] Demonstrating the military's ire against those who challenged its power, in Santa Cruz, El Quiché, soldiers "crowned" Antonio Hernández, a Maya CUC leader, with a berry plant, and with this "crown of thorns, they gave him a Bible, pulled down his pants, and nailed him to a cross."[91] The overall impunity of such criminal acts eerily echoes Bartolomé de Las Casas's description of "Indians being thrown into the holes they had dug."[92] All in all, according to REHMI, 51.63 percent of the victims belonged to a religious group, 18.70 percent belonged to a Betterment Committee, and 5.79 percent were cooperative leaders.[93]

Killing of Municipal Authority: Tomás Tiniguar and Domingo Morales

Indigenous mayors Tomás Tiniguar and Domingo Morales were selectively assassinated. Tiniguar was killed in 1978, only a year after his term was over. Jesús, a former URNG member, told me, "When his brother was kidnapped, Tomás went to the military base to ask for his whereabouts. As he returned, he was killed in the Sepela Bridge."[94] Morales was assassinated on 18 June 1981.[95]

The Municipal Fire Department log notes that the mayor and his bodyguard, Gregorio Chicay Ceballos, were found in the street, full of bullets, near Escuela Flavio Rodas.

Witnesses also told the commission that alleged army personnel had fired on the victims from a car without a license plate, which was a common practice during the war.[96] According to Miguel, leader of the Fire Department, at that time, Morales' opposition to the evaluation of property projects in El Quiché appears to have caused his assassination. In the 1980s, with the closing of political spaces and the indiscriminate attacks against real or suspected army opponents, many Catholic Action, CUC, peasant leagues, and cooperativist leaders and their families were forced to go underground, particularly after the Massacre of the Spanish Embassy on 31 January 1980, which "radicalized a significant number of young Mayas." CUC members joined the armed struggle and continued to denounce the bloodbath in the highlands.[97]

Killing The Rebels' Collaborators

In the late 1970s the Augusto César Sandino Front (FGACS) rallied supporters in the southern tip of Chichicastenango. In the Chupol area, the EGP rebels found active, mass-based support and mobilized them into the Irregular Local Forces (FIL) and the local clandestine committees (CCL), consisting of sympathizers and collaborators.[98] These were small, unarmed groups of between eighty and ninety people, aiding in securing provisions. According to an eyewitness, the hinterland area of Lacamá served as a hospital for the rebels. In San Martin Jilotepeque, in the Chimaltenango Department, "the fourteen-year-old kids were the messengers since they were able to walk fast and make announcements."[99] Defying the military, peasants from literate communities used sentinels and prearranged loud signals to alert the community of the soldiers' incursions.

Pedro, a former URNG member, explained how his sense of socioeconomic injustice about the lack of decent wages convinced him to join the FIL: "The main problem that existed in Guatemala would be poverty, inequality, lack of jobs, no salaries … Through a friend I realized the need to stand up and fight."[100] Pedro's response reflects the dynamics of empowerment fostered by his involvement in sweeping cooperative and literacy projects.[101] Like peasants in India, they made sense of revolutionary change "by translating it into their codes."[102] As a result, CUC leaders from Chupol, Chuguexa, Las Trampas, Agua Escondida, Chontolá, and Xabiyaguach collaborating with the URNG became part of a broad category of "internal enemies" that were targeted for human rights crimes. By the time the PSYOPs reached the Chupol area in the early 1980s, entire families and communities had participated in profound class and ethnic consciousness processes that had empowered them to decipher the half-truths told by the army.

Peasants Ambushing the Oppressor: Drawing the Army's Ire

Given the military superiority of the Guatemalan Army, the insurgency naïvely harbored hopes of claiming southern El Quiché and its bordering Chimaltenango Department as a "liberated territory." Control of Los Encuentros by the URNG insurgency would have jeopardized the mobilization of troops further north into the Ixil area, where the carnage against communities rapidly escalated.

Around this time, on 20 July 1981, *Prensa Libre* reports some 500 rebels taking over el pueblo and setting the Chichicastenango municipal building on fire, burning to the ground the secretary and treasury units and historical documents. Foreign tourists made their way to the capital as the mayor lamented the loss of revenues.[103] A few days later, it reported that Alvaro Arzu, then INGUAT director, asserted that, as a result of the fire, some 30,000 people were unable to work, damaging tourism.[104]

On 1 October 1981, General Benedicto Lucas García touched down in a helicopter along the highway to personally lead an offensive under its Iximché task force against the EGP front and the FGACS, who were seeking to establish, in the words of observer George Black, "at least a no-go area for government troops."[105] By 1981, as a large number of families and communities were lending their support to the EGP, the "military concentrated its troops in the western highlands and terrorized the guerrillas' potential civilian base of support."[106] To encourage collaboration from this area, the army kidnapped Emeterio Toj, a founding CUC member whose voice on the radio was familiar to peasants. From a helicopter flying over the Chupol area, the army pressured him to say, "This is Emeterio ... Don't be afraid. The army won't do anything."[107] The rebels were unable to sustain their gains in the area, and their offensive was, ultimately, a failure.

In Xepol, Chichicastenango, on 17 December 1981, a battle took place between EGP forces and soldiers, leaving seventeen rebels dead. Repeatedly, the army spokesperson told the press that it had found considerable armaments, submachine guns, claymore mines, and grenades made in the United States and in the Soviet Union. By claiming that "communist terrorist bands" had attacked residents, the military deliberately deceived the peasants it claimed to save from the hands of the rebels: the offensive had "rescued families."[108] A Runujel Junam Council of Ethnic Communities "We Are All Equal," (CERJ) member described the massive intensity of the attacks and heavy aerial bombing that drove neighbors into hiding: "We all left the canton and hid in the ravines under the trees. They threw bombs at us from Chupol, and the bombs reached us and destroyed our houses. They burnt and killed people, the cows, the calves, the roosters, all the animals."[109]

This massive assault on communities off the highway led to the internal displacement of Chupolense families into hinterland villages, like Lacamá II. Fernando, from Chupol, lamented, "Even I went away to another place, to another village. I went to Panimache II … when the army got stronger and bombed those places … As a result [of the displacement], my wife got sick and died."[110] One witness described foot soldiers' assaults: "They burst with bullets everywhere and people got really scared."[111] In El Quiché 70 percent of the population was displaced out of fear, according to Schirmer, under extreme physical and psychological conditions hiding from state troops.[112]

Terrified by the scorched earth campaigns, many families joined the EGP rebels, who offered them protection, but whose weakened military force left them utterly defenseless. While families sought shelter in the area of Lacamá, many did not believe that the state soldiers could hurt them and therefore stayed, only to be pitilessly executed in their homes. This trust that the army would not hurt them suggests that the population had close ties with the army through conscription, civic actions, or the army's public works during the Ubico years.

As David Maybury-Lewis has asserted, "The massacre of indigenous peoples was routinely practiced and routinely accepted in the heyday of imperialism."[113] The impaling of victims, for example, was not a new act in Guatemala. In fact, it is a practice that has been used since colonial times to subdue Indigenous leaders, such as Tupac Amaru in Peru.[114] At the Chupol outpost, after more than 100 people were kidnapped in broad daylight from Chichi's market, reportedly taken to the Chupol outpost and never seen again, eyewitness reported that soldiers used heavy equipment to excavate and create "space" to dump corpses of those "disappeared."[115]

A Utopian Leftwing Project: Defenseless Population and Deception

Blind triumphalism led the rebel forces to encourage participation. In addition, the Truth Commission concluded that lack of weapons was the single most important reason for the EGP's failure to undertake higher combat levels during the uprising's peak in the early 1980s. Chupolenses who joined the EGP found that there were few weapons with which to defend themselves. Sebastián regretted their lack of arms and blamed the guerrillas for lying about providing them with weapons, "If you killed me with a machete, and I only have my hands. That's the difference. If we both had a machete, then we will see who wins."[116] In his study of Chiantla, a military bastion in Huehuetenango, Paul Kobrak bitterly blames the rebels for failing to anticipate the army's responses to peasants' collaboration with the guerrilla.[117]

These feelings of having been deceived by the rebels are further illustrated in a written document given to me from the Chutzorop I and Xecalibal communities: "The rebels told communities that they already had gained control over the country. They told us it was necessary to take [up] arms to defend our rights and promised to give us arms. But it turned out that these were lies."[118] Richard Wilson has also noted that in the Verapaces, "there were too few arms for the people, and too few revolutionaries to coordinate the civilian mass-based support."[119]

On one occasion in July 1981 alongside the Interamerican Highway, the EGP front and the FGACS ambushed the army, relying on the detonation of claymore mines and peasants' enthusiastic support. The military discovered traps two or three meters deep with pointed sticks as rebels collaborators built defenses against military assaults. In 1982, clashes took place between the EGP forces and soldiers in Tzanimacabaj and Sacpulub, where a two-day confrontation left eight rebels dead. Undoubtedly, the brutal response to ambushes by peasants hailing the rebels along the highway was the military's implicit recognition of the threat posed by the involvement of entire communities, such as Chontolá and Chuguexa. Also in Santa Maria Tzeja in 1983, Manz explains, peasants collaborated with the rebels by setting up *buzones,* or bunkers—a strategy that infuriated the military.[120]

Further acts of resistance by the peasants continued to draw the ire of the armed forces to the region. For example, on 25 July 1981, soldiers arrived shooting frenziedly and throwing grenades at the community of Chucalibal (located off the highway). As residents Isabel Macario Calel and her daughter Isabela Jucaran Macario fled their ranch, army soldiers pitilessly gunned them down.[121] The next step in the counterinsurgency plan was to consolidate the long-term military control over rural areas by calling up reserves and ordering all men aged between fifteen and fifty to patrol in each community. In this context, PSYOPs fabricated an "inverted discourse," making half-true claims that frightened peasant families into seeking protection at the Chupol military outpost, which the army then falsely claimed to be an indication of peasants' "voluntary request" for weapons and the organization of self-defense patrols to protect their families and communities.

Third Polarization: Civil Self-Defense Patrol System

With the creation of the patrol system, new ideological conflicts exacerbated preexisting ideological cleavages, dividing families between those who supported and those who did not support the army's patrol project. From the community Xabiawach, patrols hunted those internally displaced in Chupol, Chuguexa II B, and Lacamá.[122] To seal them off from contact with URNG rebels, the army grouped various communities in one area and established a military outpost by ordering families to bring their own corrugated tin sheets to build it. In Pajuliboy, patrollers were organized in 1983 and stayed for fifteen years. A peasant told me, "I participated some nine years because it was obligatory, but later I left and joined the CERJ [the group that organized the resistance against the patrollers]" (Chapter Five). In Chontolá, some wanted to enlist in the patrol because it gave them power and took advantage to settle old personal affairs with neighbors. In Lacamá I, a human rights organizer from K'amalbe told me in 1997:

> We were together for around three months and in Lacamá II, for around four months. The patrollers constantly went to the army to get information ... the patrol along with the army started to look for things the guerrilla fighters had buried like bunkers [*buzones*]. Soon, even ex-guerrilla leaders, now patrols, started to patrol even if in reality they didn't do anything. José Riquiac Tecúm was the mere commander of the patrol of all of the cantons, he is in contact with the local bosses and patrols ... He had a list and one by one, he looked for them. The men who accepted stayed in the patrol and everything was OK, while otherwise they were killed, and if they accepted there were still harsh conditions. They paid a large amount of 2,000 to 3,000 Quetzales to be set free.[123]

As I show in the next chapter, eyewitness testimonies presented by families from this area to the commission show that in 1982, patrols from Chupol either obeyed the army's orders or, on their own accord, with the military power invested upon them, captured Manuel Perez along with twenty-one other victims.[124] Similar to other cases of enforced disappearance, victims were taken to the nearest army outpost and were never seen again. Violence by patrollers against other patrollers also took place in Chupol, as shown when, in 1982, soldiers captured sixteen-year-old Juan Toj Morales, a patrol chief.[125]

Municipal Firefighters' Department Log

In *Remembering the Rescuers* I discuss the rescuer role the Chichicastenango municipal firefighters took in the municipality by recording in administrative logs, in chilling detail, the victims' injuries.[126] In 1981, in 12 percent of the cases, more than one cause of death was recorded. In 37 percent of the cases, the bodies presented gunshot wounds, while in 42 percent, victims died in their most productive years (between twenty-one and thirty years old) and were mostly male, a finding that concurs with the commission's results regarding the age of most war victims.[127]

Children were callously killed by soldiers' bullets and beatings. This was the case of Miguel Panjoj Conoz, who was only five years old when the firefighters found him with a bullet in his left side and took him to the Santa Cruz Hospital. Also in Lacamá I, the cadavers of children riddled with bullets were picked up. In 2000, Miguel, the second firefighter commander, reminisced about children's corpses in the mountains: "It was of great impact. We were used to picking up bodies resulting from car accidents or due to alcohol accidents. But these were bullets killing people."[128] As past studies have shown, the patrols' violence left communities internally fragmented between those who pledged their allegiance to the army and survivors who had participated in a vibrant uprising, with enormous consequences for Indigenous peoples' historical memory and human rights activism demanding justice for the bloodshed.[129]

Notes

1. Kuper, *Pity of It All,* 9.
2. Kuper, *Genocide: Its Political Use,* 85.
3. Arias, "El Movimiento Indígena," 70–95.
4. Boff and Boff, *Introducing Liberation Theology,* 3–4.
5. Wilson, *Maya Resurgence in Guatemala,* 212–13.
6. The township of Santiago Atitlán in Sololá was also considered a red community. Sosa Velásquez, *Rupturas y Construcción,* 75.
7. FAO.org, "Guatemala: Agricultural Census." Even three acres is a very, very small plot of land—too small for a family of five or six people to survive on. CIRMA, CGD, McAllister, "Chupol," 22.
8. Maryknoll Catholic clergy also established missions in Peru. Behrens, "Confronting Colonialism," 1. For a more detailed account of the Maryknoll in Latin America, and in Guatemala in particular, see Melville, *Through a Glass Darkly.*
9. Handy, *Revolution in the Countryside,* 142–43.
10. Handy notes that the Second Vatican Council, in the early 1960s, declared a preference for the poor. Handy, *Gift of the Devil,* 239. According to observers, "Between the 1940s and the 1960s the number of priests in Guatemala swelled from 114 to 494." Levenson-Estrada, *Trade Unionists against Terror,* 64.
11. Martín-Baró, *Writings for a Liberation Psychology,* 137–38.
12. Ibid., 143.
13. Boff and Boff, *Introducing Liberation Theology,* 6; Arrabure, Vieto, and Schugurensky, "New Cooperativism."
14. Composed of a president, vice-president, secretary, and treasurer. Catholic Church, *El Quiché,* 53.
15. Author interview, Morales.
16. For the experience of the township of Joyabaj with power struggles in the municipality between traditionalists and Catholic Church leadership, see Remijnse, *Memories of Violence,* 149.
17. Falla, *Quiché Rebelde,* 18. See also Schirmer, *Guatemalan Military Project,* 39.
18. Falla, *Quiché Rebelde,* 194.
19. McAllister, "Rural Markets, Revolutionary Souls," 8.
20. Later, on 16 August 1968, a second stage of the expansion of a new twenty kilometers of paved road from Los Encuentros to Chichi's town center introduced further social change for Chupolenses. CIRMA, *El Imparcial,* "Carretera: Encuentros Chichicastenango," 1, 4.

21. McAllister, "Rural Markets, Revolutionary Souls," 10. By 1944, thirty-four out of seventy-five men reported being merchants. CIRMA, CGD, McAllister, "Chupol," 15.
22. Catholic Church, *El Quiché,* 39.
23. Author interview, Julio.
24. Ibid.
25. Catholic Church, *El Quiché,* 67. It ran first under the name of Radio Santa Cruz, and later under Radio K'iché beginning in 1965, and was run by priests. Falla, *Quiché Rebelde,* 459.
26. McAllister, "Rural Markets, Revolutionary Souls," 8.
27. Author interview, Sebastián; CIRMA, CGD, McAllister, "Chupol," 55.
28. CIRMA, CGD, McAllister, "Chupol," 47.
29. McAllister, "Rural Markets, Revolutionary Souls," 11.
30. Falla, *Quiché Rebelde,* 27. Other observers also note that by 1968, there were more "than 80,000 members ... over half the youth and adult population of the department participated in the movement." Konefal, "May All Rise Up," 78.
31. Moore, *Social Origins.*
32. Freire, *Education for Critical Consciousness,* 48.
33. CIRMA, CGD, McAllister, "Chupol," 2.
34. Catholic Church, *El Quiché,* 69–72. As Greg Grandin notes, "Throughout the late 1960s and early 1970s, female members for the most part were expected to do little more than to organize other women into support committees" (*Last Colonial Massacre,* 133).
35. INE, *Census 1973.*
36. Catholic Church, *El Quiché,* 43.
37. Author interview, Candelario.
38. Arias, "El Movimiento Indígena," 76.
39. Ibid., 75.
40. According to Mario Enrique Sosa Velásquez, security and development committees from Santiago, Atitlán, played a pivotal role in the reconstruction of local Indigenous power (*Rupturas y Construcción,* 160–62).
41. For a summary of funding given for development covering the genocide years, see Smith, *Forty Years in the Altiplano,* 9. USAID had also funded seventy-four Catholic Action members to lead "interests groups," McAllister, "Rural Markets," 8.
42. See Konefal, *For Every Indio,* 110.
43. Catholic Church, *El Quiché,* 59.
44. Plant, *Guatemala: Unnatural Disaster,* 87; Marc Drouin, "1982 Guatemalan Genocide," 84.
45. Author interview, Esteban.
46. Catholic Church, *El Quiché,* 65, fn74.
47. According to Grandin, "While it did not take its name until 1978, the CUC has roots that go back to the 1967 creation of the Sindicato de Trabajadores Agricolas Independientes in Chichicastenango" (*Last Colonial Massacre,* 268).
48. Bastos and Camus, *Quebrando el Silencio,* 29.
49. From a total population of 45,733. See Asturias Montenegro and Gática Trejo, *Terremoto 76,* 118. On the Richter scale, the earthquake registered 7.5. Nationwide, official casualty figures reported about 23,000 people killed, 77,000 injured, and 1.2 million left homeless. See also Arias, "El Movimiento Indígena," 83–85.
50. Author interview, Morales.
51. Ibid.

52. Catholic Church, *El Quiché*, 109.
53. Author interview, Candelario.
54. CIRMA, CGD, McAllister, "Chupol," 26.
55. *Cabeza clara, corazón solidario, puño combativo.* See CUC, "Lucha, Resistencia e Historia."
56. Bethell, *Latin America: Politics and Society*, 364.
57. Carmack, "Story of Santa Cruz Quiché," 51.
58. CIRMA, CGD, McAllister, "Chupol," 14.
59. Author interview, Sebastián.
60. Author interview, Morales.
61. Ibid.
62. Rene de Leon Schlotter, of German origin, a member of congress representing El Quiché and with strong links with Santa Cruz clergy was one of the ideological founders of the Democracia Cristina Guatemalteca (DCG). Catholic Church, *El Quiché*, 72, fn77.
63. Catholic Church, *El Quiché*, 73.
64. Author interview, Miguel.
65. CIRMA, CGD, McAllister, "Chupol," 30.
66. Author interview, Tomás.
67. Author interview, Sebastián.
68. Author interview, Tomás.
69. For the Iximché Declaration, see Vela Castañeda, *Masas, Armas y Elites*, 83–84.
70. Author interview, Pedro.
71. CIRMA, CGD, McAllister, "Chupol," 51.
72. Author interview, Sebastián.
73. CIRMA, CGD, McAllister, "Chupol," 51–52.
74. Author interview, Domingo.
75. Author interview, Fernando.
76. See Chapter Three.
77. CEH, II.320.
78. Ejército de Guatemala, "Plan de Campaña Firmeza 83-1."
79. Manz, *Paradise in Ashes*, 143.
80. CEH, VII.79–88.
81. Bauman, *Modernity and the Holocaust*, 119.
82. Ibid.
83. CEH, IV.191.
84. Moses, *Empire, Colony, Genocide.*
85. CEH, III.334.
86. Between 1976 and 1978, 168 community leaders, mostly Indigenous, from El Quiché were murdered. Handy, "Rights in Guatemala," 10.
87. CIRMA, CGD, McAllister, "Chupol," 56.
88. Catholic Church, "Y Dieron la Vida," 89, 95–101.
89. HMP, CERJ Archive.
90. Author interview, Morales.
91. CEH, II.362.
92. Mader, "Dracula," 185.
93. REHMI 1998, IV.486.
94. Author interview, Jesús.
95. Author interview, Miguel.

96. CEH, X.873; According to the 1981 fire department log, the body of the mayor showed a bullet wound on the left side of the chest, another bullet wound on the right side of the back, and still another bullet wound on the chin.

97. Konefal, *For Every Indio,* 111.

98. Estimates of the number of Indigenous guerrillas range from just 3,500 to as much as half a million. Adams, "What Can We Know?" 286.

99. García, "Herederos de la Guerra," 22.

100. Author interview, Pedro.

101. Chatterjee, "Nation and Its Peasants."

102. Ibid., 10.

103. HNG, *Prensa Libre,* "Municipalidad de Chichicastenango Quemada." All in all, the damage was estimated at 2 million quetzales. HNG, *Prensa Libre,* "Acciónes Terroristas."

104. HNG, *Prensa Libre,* "Paro Turistico Afecta."

105. Black et al., *Garrison Guatemala,* 111. Some observers have noted, "The people cut telegraph wires and used nails, barricades, fallen trees … to block the roadways for dozen of miles in both directions in an effort to impede the army's overland access to the occupied areas. Once the occupation was over, the people thronged to Los Encuentros … shouting the victory cry '*Hasta la victoria siempre.*'" Arias, "El Movimiento Indígena," 103–4.

106. Ball, Kobrak, and Spirer, *State Violence in Guatemala,* 49.

107. Konefal, "May All Rise Up," 206.

108. CIRMA, *El Gráfico,* "17 Facciosos mueren en Enfrentamiento," 17 December 1981, 5.

109. HMP, CERJ Archive.

110. Author interview, Fernando.

111. CIRMA, Infostelle, Signatura 82, "Noticias de Guatemala," 6.

112. Schirmer, *Guatemalan Military Project,* 56. See also Manz, *Paradise in Ashes,* 124.

113. Maybury-Lewis, "From Elimination," 324.

114. Higonnet, *Quiet Genocide,* 117, fn60. See also, Garrard-Burnett, *Terror in the Land,* xi.

115. CEH, II.79–88.

116. Author interview, Morales.

117. Kobrak, *Huehuetenango,* 37–60, particularly.

118. HMP, Chutzorop, Chichicastenango Archive.

119. Wilson, *Maya Resurgence in Guatemala,* 26.

120. Manz, *Paradise in Ashes,* 116.

121. CEH, X. 836.

122. Collective interview, Mutual Support Group, GAM.

123. Author interview, Human Rights Organizer (Anonymous).

124. CEH, X.1181.

125. CEH, X.1187.

126. Esparza and et al, "Santo Tomás Chichicastenango's Municipal Firefighters," 57–78.

127. CEH, II.322–23.

128. Author interview, Miguel. For a detailed sample list of wounds as registered in the log, see Esparza and et al., "Santo Tomás Chichicastenango's Municipal Firefighters," 75–77.

129. For patrollers collaborating with the guerrilla, see Sáenz de Tejeda, *Victimas o Vencedores?* 70, fn26.

5

Early Disbanding, Postgenocide Resistance, and *Na'tab'al* (Memory)

Well, for me, militarization affects us greatly because we aren't soldiers, we are civilians, but more than anything, militarization is what is here for the time being. We are a country under pressure from militarism.
—Collective interview, Raúl

Soon after the carnage of the early 1980s was over, the "literate" communities I discussed in the previous chapter became what I call "mnemonic" communities, showing the different temporalities of aftermaths. Mnemonic communities are, according to Eviatar Zerubavel, "the family, the workplace, the ethnic group, the nation" seeking to break the entrenched silence over past human rights crimes.[1] As Roddy Brett and others have pointed out, it was the courageous mobilization of Guatemalan human rights grassroots groups that emerged under the human rights framework demanding truth, memory, and justice in the mid 1980s, well before the end of the war in 1996, that helped scale the walls of silence.[2]

Throughout Latin America, women have played a pivotal role in the struggle to break the silence over the past. Zerubavel notes that in Argentina, "The Mothers of the Plaza de Mayo … exemplify such group silence-breaking."[3] Since their emergence, the iconic human rights group has defied long-held traditional values keeping women out of politics. In Guatemala, in many areas of the western highlands, this type of community-based organization made up of survivors courageously emerged by overcoming lingering and renewed fear of reprisals.

In spite of past political allegiances and religious affiliations that still fragmented communities, they not only contested the state's efforts at denying the slaughter but also called for the demobilization of the patrol system. Though past studies have emphasized how these groups advocated truth, memory, and justice, few have emphasized how they also challenged the widespread military control over their communities and their villages' extreme levels of poverty, which were rooted in their class and ethnic oppression. Unlike past anthropological research focusing on organizations identified with Maya cultural politics—such as the Coordination of Organizations of the Pueblo Maya of Guatemala (COPMAGUA) and Majawil Q'ij, as identified by Diane Nelson and others—I concentrate on human rights groups contesting militarization and militarism.[4]

The army was considered a thorn in the side, *una piedra en el zapato*, of mnemonic communities.[5] The Chupol was such a community, where former Catholic catechists, CUC and Peasant League members, or their survivors led human rights groups to contest the army's power in their communities. Unlike in the west—where ex-militiamen expressed their admiration for the non-Indigenous army (Chapter Seven)—Maya groups on this side sought to dismantle the patrols and their legacy as early as 1984. Human rights leaders showed great disdain for the military in the aftermath of the Peace Accords: "What does the army bring to us? Nothing."[6]

Subaltern Resistance: Against Lost Memories

Tzvetan Todorov argues, "The totalitarian regimes of the twentieth century sought to achieve total control of memory … Among the techniques was to intimidate people and to forbid them to seek information or to pass it on."[7] This was certainly the case in mnemonic communities, as human rights groups not only resisted the state's efforts to clamp down on information regarding human rights crimes but also resisted the resurgence of the civil self-defense patrols.

As early as 1984, poor Maya widows from Chupol, Chontolá, Chunimá, Agua Escondida, and Las Trampas joined the Comité Nacional de Viudas de Guatemala (National Coordination of Widows of Guatemala [CONAVIGUA]), the Grupo de Apoyo Mutuo (Mutual Support Group [GAM]), and the Rujunel Junam Council of Ethnic Communities (CERJ). These groups challenged ongoing military control embodied in former state security forces: ex-patrols, undisbanded military commissioners, their former auxiliaries, reservists, and foot soldiers. In the early 1990s, these organizations mobilized under the umbrella organization the Sectores Surgidos por la Represión (Sectors Emerging out of Repression).[8]

The mobilization of human rights groups accomplished two goals. First, it helped dismantle the military litany of lies about its unbroken institutional relations with the ex-PACs under the pretext of an internal menace threatening their own and nearby villages. By then, groups of survivors from Chupol had attained a new level of collective consciousness through their involvement with liberation theology, literacy, and cooperative projects. Carrying the photographs of the disappeared, human rights activists successfully brought international attention, challenged official denial, and criticized the laws of amnesty extinguishing criminal responsibility except for crimes against humanity, as enshrined in so-called Reconciliation Law No. 145-1996. Second, their actions gave continuity to their past political activism: engaging in memorials presented by human rights groups, paying visits to congress, staging demonstrations, blocking roads, and leveling complaints at the international level.

Human rights organizations became sites of remembrance, recalling Pierre Nora's *lieux de memoire,* the notion that "there is no spontaneous memory," so groups create archives, museums, and anniversaries to materialize these memories.[9] By mobilizing into local human rights groups, Chupolenses found support among each other and found the courage to publicly denounce the state's genocidal acts. This illustrates the solidarity traits of Maya peasants' resilient culture that is noted in the postcolonial scholarship focusing on Latin America. Violent confrontations followed their emergence, however, as ex-militiamen accused human rights groups of being an armed wing of the former URNG rebels. Often, human rights groups coordinated the support provided by international peace brigades (PBI) to accompany their leaders and give them some protection.[10]

In Chupol, reorganizing into new organizations presented various challenges. Ideological antagonism, for instance, between former Catholic catechists, Peasant League members, and cooperativists—who blamed each other as being the source of the early 1980s violence that besieged them—continued in the war's prolonged aftermath, as did ideological and religious antagonism between these and militaristic groups. "Neighbors who are not organized, they tell us that we are 'bad people, *mala gente,*' when we arrive at meetings," lamented Fernando.[11] Denoting the overlapping identities left by the war in internally polarized communities, Fernando had been a Peasant League organizer, Catholic catechist, ex-military commissioner, and former patrol chief. About his community's capacity to self-organize, Fernando observed, "It is hard, because people do not want to accept organizations, because they say that it is for the guerrilla rebels."[12]

Chupolense leaders that had previously participated in CUC also complained of their community's internal divisions, "These groups are divided. Some of the neighbors support the FRG [Guatemalan Republican Front] because they believe they have the courage to combat the assailants, the thieves."[13] In the early aftermath of the mass killing in Chupol, there was some significant organized resistance. Fernando poignantly summarized it: "In this area, we denounce, we stand up, we do not fight within the same groups."[14]

The Mutual Support Group (Gam): Donde Estan?

One of the first organizations to publicly emerge demanding accountability for the war's over 50,000 people disappeared was GAM on 4 June 1984. GAM "was founded by a group of women who met time after time during their visits to the city morgues, in search of their loved ones,"[15] Mario Polanco, a cofounder, told me in 1994. "This struggle," Mario continued, "goes from the individual to the collective demanding the appearance of family members, the alive appearance of all the people who have disappeared, and not only Fernando, not only Héctor … but of all the people who have disappeared."[16] Collectively, human rights activists refused to subordinate to the overarching fear of death caused by the killing of their founding members. Fernando Garcia, husband of Nineth Montenegro, the original founder of GAM, was kidnapped on 18 February 1984. Later, in early 1985, another cofounder, Rosario Godoy de Cuevas, was brutally murdered with her 21-year-old brother Augusto and her two-year-old son.[17]

On 27 July 1988, GAM members accused the army of forcing neighbors, students, and teachers to join a protest against Father Ventura Lux Herrera, a beloved priest in Chichi. The army told neighbors that Ventura Lux "no longer announces the words of God, but rather he was praying in support of the rebels." In the protest, soldiers dressed as civilians participated but were recognized because of their close-cropped hairstyles. Those inciting attacks against the priest (who survived on that day) were patrols from Chicuá I and representatives from the Auxiliatura Indígena, among them, Sebastián Yacon, Geronimo Antonio Aj, Manuel Pol, and Sebastián Panjoj. Four years later Ventura Lux died in an alleged car accident.[18]

Chupolenses were among the first to join GAM, Carlota McAllister asserts.[19] Peasants from this area described the needed level of consciousness that informed their human rights work in the organization:

> In these communities, like Chupol, Chuguexa, people are more conscientious about the war experiences, they know why the struggle began, which was because our rights were violated, we did not have freedom … Back in those days people were more aware; this is why they got organized. But the military saw people with more consciousness and assaulted their communities, and people who were dominated came to attack us, because we demanded our rights.[20]

Nicolás, a GAM member, reflected about the postwar military control percolating through their day-to-day lives and how activists continued to resist the army's attempts to co-opt them: "Militarization is a policy to see how to put this idea in the minds of the population through military commissioners, even though, in fact, nowadays there are not any military commissioners, but they have used a similar strategy to maintain it hidden like this."[21] Nicolás further added about the aftermath of the war:

> I see that that which was promised is not being delivered, because all the agreements, which were signed [between] the government, the army, and the URNG [say] we have to be at peace, but there definitely is not peace; why is that? Because

there are the people who participated with the army or the G2 [army intelligence], and right now they are acting in the same way, and therefore there have not been changes. Also, the police are now a civilian police group, but it is the same thing and it acts in the same [militarized] way.[22]

The ongoing criminalization of political opposition to the army did not end in the mid-1980s in the wake of the genocide. On Friday, 2 March 1990, approximately 200 members and GAM sympathizers were attacked by 300–400 stone-throwing members of the civil patrols of seventeen different communities from Chupol, mobilized by Manuel Perebal Ajtzalam, patrol chief from Chunimá.[23] Moreover, in the postwar years, according to GAM members from Chupol, loyalist ex-patrols remained in positions of authority. "They listened, they controlled our organizations and made decisions about what to do with their neighbors," noted Juan, a "cultural broker" who had facilitated my entry into eastern communities (Chapter One).

"Do you know if there are military commissioners?" I asked Nicolás. "No, there is no news if they still exist, but in communities where there are no human rights committees, there is always news that they are hidden."[24] On another occasion, he described how the military had continued to harass them: "We do not have the threat of war weapons but we do have the political war of the army; this always exists within communities." Nicolás recognized that those who had remained tied to the army continued to have a militaristic mind since, "Even if they contact the army as civilians, their mentality continues to have the idea of the military."[25] By 2010, GAM was continuing its human rights work by exhuming the remains of patrollers Apolinario Urízar Cifuentes, Esteban Yuja Quip, and Esteban Tello Cifuentes in San Miguel Uspantán, who were allegedly killed by the rebels.[26]

Rujunel Junam Council of Ethnic Communities "We Are All Equal" (Cerj): Resistance to the Patrol System

While it clandestinely began to organize in 1983, CERJ publicly emerged on 31 July 1988 to demand the end of forced conscription into the patrol system and respect for the human rights of the oppressed and the marginalized. Quickly, its membership grew to 6,000 peasants refusing to join the patrols.[27] CERJ's main goal was to provide those refusing to patrol with legal assistance, particularly in El Quiché and Sololá. From its initial stages, the CERJ claimed that the patrols system violated Article 34 of the 1985 constitution prohibiting compulsory participation: "to join nor to belong to self-defense groups or associations or similar groups."

As REHMI concluded, "Beginning in 1986 … CERJ epitomized the resistance to the PACs."[28] According to CERJ records, despite the ongoing pressure from the army to keep its PAC structure alive, groups of patrollers had managed to break ties with the military as early as 1987 and became conscientious objectors, leaving some political space for the reorganization of grassroots resistance. Those Chichicastenango communities where a few or most of the patrol groups voluntarily broke away from the army in 1988, nearly ten years before their official disarmament, included Chuguexa I, Chuguexa II B, Chupol, Lacamá II, Quiejel, and Sacpulub, all from the eastern region.[29]

Also in 1995, 320 members from the Xecoja community wrote a legal document[30] that they sent to the president of the country in which they stated peasants' refusal to provide security for their communities, since patrolling brought them "illnesses and economic hardships."[31] In an interview, the founder of the CERJ, Amilcar Méndez Urízar, a Ladino schoolteacher from San Andrés Sajcabajá and former congressman for the New Guatemala Democratic Front (FDNG), explained that those ex-patrols implicated in human rights crimes remained tight to the power they derived from their closeness to the army. Amilcar recounted how families slowly began to mobilize to collectively overcome the war's psychosocial scars:

> Families that had their husbands killed or kidnapped started to move and these families started to unite and the only mechanism that they looked for to psychologically confront the war was the organization. The people who remained alone had to go on the army's side against their will by doing patrol service.[32]

In 1996 Méndez Urízar publicly protested that the army was recycling the patrols' structure into solidarity peace committees and other military-led groups allowing for the state-sponsored violence to continue in rural communities.[33] The army ensured that Méndez Urízar and CERJ members paid the price for challenging the military's stronghold over the patrol system as human rights groups repeatedly denounced the acts of intimidation against him and his family. These included death threats that forced them into exile, the kidnapping of family members in 1993, and—most likely linked to his human rights work—the death of his son, José Emanuel "Pepe" Méndez Dardón, also an active supporter of CERJ, in 2007.[34]

Ignacio, a CERJ coordinator, reminisced, "Little by little we organized in CERJ and we helped each other. Not everybody, however, just a group."[35] Méndez Urízar noted, "There were a few families organizing, these were families of victims that refused to patrol ... they believed that the best way to overcome fear was by organizing."[36] In 1990 Méndez Urízar was awarded with the Robert F. Kennedy Human Rights Award for his courageous efforts to protect the lives of patrols refusing to serve in the army.

Anibal, a CERJ member, summarized in a written document what it meant to take part in a human rights organization before the war was over:

In the years 1993, 1994, and 1995, they have not done more damage to us because we are organized, three organizations are helping us, the GAM, CONAVIGUA and CERJ, any threat or problem which we have, the organization helps us, even though they say that we are guerrilla fighters and bad people, we get together to help each other and defend each other from this; we get together and we are not afraid, we are more confident in the organizations because they tell us our rights, and that there are laws which defend us.[37]

Collective memory also served in the fight against impunity for the killing of those who dissented against patrolling. Under the Serrano Elias administration (1991–1994), twenty-five CERJ members were killed.[38] CERJ helped its members file numerous writs of habeas corpus nationally, subsequently presented as evidence in human rights cases brought before international mechanisms such as the Interamerican Court of the OAS in Costa Rica. One such case is illustrated by the 29 October 1994 abduction of José Sucunú Panjoj, from the Quiejel community, who was fifty-nine years old and the father of eleven children. A CERJ member since 1988, Sucunú Panjoj had led parents' accusation against a patrol chief, Sebastián Macario Ventura, of sexually assaulting a woman in front of 100 students in 1993 while working as a schoolteacher. CERJ also brought the 27 February 1991 killing of peasants for refusing to reintegrate the patrols into the community of Chunimá to the attention of the international human rights system.[39]

Since he became a CERJ member, Sucunú Panjoj had been harassed by patrols accusing him of belonging to the URNG rebels. Witnesses declared before the Inter-American Commission of Human Rights that Macario Ventura, accused of abducting Panjoj, had offered this menace to his victims: "I have already eliminated his son, I am only missing the father."[40] In 1999, an amicable settlement was achieved, including reparations given to survivors in "the sum of Q 2,048.25[41] as seed capital for raising and fattening pigs."[42] Also in September 1996, CERJ, along with the Coordinadora de Trabajadores Quichelenses (CTQ), accused the army of manipulating patrols into marching against their demobilization in Chichi.

This recognition of the enduring effects of militarism speaks to peasants' awareness of the army's democratic façade. Fernando, from CERJ, described the military's continuous practice of exploiting peasants' extreme poverty to recruit them:

There are two soldiers who are giving advice to young people 18 years of age and older, they said to offer services, there in the area are bakeries, and so many jobs for young people … So I told them, look, I have a question, would a young person with his family, his expenses, his clothing, his toothpaste, and his families be able to reach those 620 quetzales?[43]

But the army did not like that Fernando complained, and soldiers began following him. "I went to the plaza and was watching who was following me, I hid in my house and I changed my clothes and I went again, and in the end they were looking for me in the plaza," Fernando recalled.[44] Luckily for him, he turned to CERJ for advice: "But because I am in the CERJ organization, I consulted with them, and we went to the detachment and went to advise the commander, and I asked him, 'Why are you harassing me?'"[45]

In the immediate aftermath of massacres, the army found resistance to its attempts to gain control over Chupol since families reorganized. "Some fifty houses in CERJ are organized (out of 600 families)," a peasant told me during a collective interview.[46]According to Reginaldo, conflicts between CERJ and pro-army groups supporting the army's alleged development projects continued unabated in Chupol: "The mere truth that the army is there now, they do not do any harm, and that they even help with a potable water project. But CERJ members do not like the military."[47] Reginaldo also told me, "Notice that here with us, male heads of families, September 15th comes around, the army offers piñatas, music, and they even provide a truck for the kids' street parade."[48]

CERJ members continued to be targets of political repression by former patrols organized, for example, into the FRG. On 27 September 2003, the Chichicastenango candidate for municipal major, José Tiriquiz, allegedly killed Eusebio Macario Chicoj, one of the founding members of CERJ, in his Chulumal IV community. Macario had been promoting compensation for victims of the conflict and had criticized Tiriquiz for his involvement in alleged corruption.[49]

Up until 2000, CERJ continued to provide workshops on reparations to victims and sought to execute development programs and to strengthen local power. "What CERJ wants is to save people's lives; if there are death threats, then CERJ denounces [them] to authorities."[50] This leader summarized the postwar goals of the organization: "The objective of CERJ is demilitarization but we have not changed this yet, because [militarization] still exists today."[51] CERJ challenged President Alfonso Portillo's claims of demilitarization of the state and society by claiming that the presidential general staff, charged with human rights crimes, had remained intact.[52] Campaigns of harassment, threat, and selective murder were directed at CERJ activists.[53]

The Coordination of Widows of Guatemala (CONAVIGUA)

As had been the case with the Argentinean mothers, motherhood within Indigenous communities traditionally was restricted to duties performed within the private sphere. For example, McAllister notes that in Chupol, "women work[ed] in the home, while men cultivate the corn their family eats ..."[54] In the years following the genocide, however, Maya women—widows, sisters, nieces, daughters, and cousins—stepped into the public realm, organizing into the Coordination of Widows of Guatemala (CONAVIGUA). They demanded justice, truth, and reparations for the damage done to their families and communities and pressed for the full demobilization of the patrol system. According to the Truth Commission, the war left between 30,000 and 50,000 widows and 200,000 orphans.[55] Carrying out self-help activities in communities, members mobilized, demanding their right to be conscientious objectors.

Unlike the top-down, militaristic civil patrol structure, CONAVIGUA was, and still is, a grassroots approach against militarism and militarization and for social justice for families and communities. Maya widows' participation in human rights groups defies notions of victimhood understood as self-pity, challenging transitional justice notions that "victims are too preoccupied with their own distress to develop firm views on how to reach justice and reconciliation."[56] Studies focusing on Latin America also show that survivors collectively organize despite the lingering trauma, challenging "victimhood" notions embedded in the literature of the past decades.[57]

Since its early beginning on 13 September 1988, CONAVIGUA has addressed human rights crimes and the encroaching conditions of extreme poverty. "We offered workshops (*cursillos*) to promote the participation of women [in politics]. We explain what the laws and the Constitution are, to teach them about human rights and how to protect them through our organization."[58] By July 1989, there were some 6,000 participating women.[59] "We organize to bring relief to the most urgent food, health, and housing needs for our children and our family and to demand the government to ensure education for our children ... with school supplies," a CONAVIGUA document reads.[60] "What we want," it concludes, "is the respect to our dignity as women and as widows opposing human rights abuses."[61]

Discussing acts of dignity, Todorov comes to the following conclusion:

> No power can ... deprive a human being of ... the very freedom that defines his humanity and that permits him to remain human ... that decision must give rise to an act that is visible to others (even if they are not actually there to see it). This can be one definition of dignity.[62]

There are various examples of widows' mobilization to contest their subordination to military rule that occurred before the end of the war in 1996. In May 1989, some 200 widows from Zacualpa, El Quiché, convened in front of the local municipal building to protest against the municipal mayor, who was accused of discriminating in the distribution of aid sent by the European Community to war-torn areas. As a result, CONAVIGUA leadership and activists received death threats, were thrown in jail, and were killed by former patrols in their communities.[63] In 1990, a military commissioner accusing Maria Mejia of opposing the civil patrols system shot her to death in her Parraxut village in El Quiché.[64] Also in 1990, CONAVIGUA leaders demanded that the Ministry of Defense return the hundreds of youths who were forcibly recruited for military service by armed men in civilian clothes in the capital on 28 April.[65]

The organization's leadership also directly addressed a high-ranking military officer who had ordered the slaughter. In July 1991, General Manuel Benedicto Lucas García, who had led the vicious military assault against villages in Chupol in late 1981, rejected accusations from CONAVIGUA blaming him for the past genocidal violence. "I was a combatant, not a *genocidaire*," the general is reported to have defiantly replied in a *Prensa Libre* interview.[66] On another occasion, Rosario Pu, then the leader of the CUC, continued to criticize Alvaro Arzú's government's rhetoric of reconciliation. In a speech in December 1997, Arzú asked for forgiveness. But he only spoke in Spanish, without a translator, and for Pu the speech was "a sham" for "external consumption."[67]

CONAVIGUA's strategy of resistance also drew the international community's attention. For instance, on 27 October 1993, CONAVIGUA and CUC members occupied the OAS Office in Guatemala City for a few hours to protest the resurgence of the PACs system in their villages.[68] In 1996, María Canil of CONAVIGUA stressed the importance of dismantling the patrol structure:

> No groups of this type may remain. For this to be total, no group may remain, because they might want to use them on other jobs, or as a way in with military commissioners, who remain armed in some places, even though their dissolution has been decreed ... We believe that the former PACs should not be part of the local development councils.[69]

The group's cornerstone goal has been to achieve the rights of Maya youth to be conscientious objectors. In various testimonies, young Maya males gathered by CONAVIGUA in 1995 attest that "soldiers only know how to kill, and accuse their neighbors of being *guerrilleros*, and to steal."[70] For CONAVIGUA, the effects of long-term military control over their communities had devastating implications, "We can attest that through military service, the military has sought to annihilate our culture, and our cosmology ... the lack of respect for nature and life are Westernized values that highly contrast with the indigenous way of life." In addition, impoverished women recognized the psychological changes in young males owing to the military's indoctrination: "Military service inculcates in the minds of soldiers values that are *machista*, violent, selfish, bullying, individualistic, and engaging in consumerism."[71]

Ignacio's recognition speaks to the legacy of the civil patrols: "The army has its roots in communities, what the army is doing right now is forming groups in communities."[72] CONAVIGUA members commented on the bitter statements made by pro-army groups, "They say to us, 'It is better that you look for a job and make some money to buy your things.' They think I cannot work."[73] This idea that members "do not work" echoes the army's perception of Indigenous families: those who are organized are bad people, *mala gente.* In May 2000, CONAVIGUA activists marched through the capital city's streets warning of the perils involved in reactivating former army collaborators.[74] By 2004, CONAVIGUA's demands for human rights trials remained unchanged: to bring to court those responsible for the massacres is the only desire of victims.[75]

After the War: You Can Tell Others

As I argue elsewhere, it is important to dispel the notion that "everyone testifies to truth commissions."[76] Rather than being "paralyzed," by trauma, organized survivors from the Chupol area were ready to testify to the commission by mid-1997.[77] The mobilization of human rights groups led to the emergence of "cultural resistance in Latin America," Schirmer suggests, as survivors sought to collectively preserve the memory of their victims as prominent leaders in their communities fighting for social justice.[78]

As Jean Franco argues, "The massive repression … was indeed motivated by this strategy of extermination that would remove all traces of the militants' ideals, motives, and passions from the national memory."[79] Organized, they shared fears, hopes, and dreams—but also oral projects, firm goals for change, and claims against authorities that aimed to systematically destroy rural Indigenous communities and their way of life. As scholars have asserted, "Remembering is never a quiet act of introspection or retrospection. It is a painful remembering, a putting together of the dismembered past to make sense of the trauma of the present."[80]

Against a hostile socioeconomic and political environment, grief-stricken Maya widows, orphans, and Catholic Action catechists were convinced of their duty to remember: that only by telling about the tragedy that besieged them could they dignify their missing, tortured, killed, and raped family members whom the state wrongly labeled as "terrorist delinquents." In the words of Lieselotte Viaene, they were ready to "push forward the thorny issues of justice, truth and reparations on the political and judicial agenda."[81]

Without these groups, the work of the commission would not have successfully collected over 7,000 testimonies. Like the Mexican Zapatista Movement, they "stand as a symbol of the active subaltern," because they epitomize the remarkable resilience of Indigenous collective action.[82] Through locally based organizations, survivors with a past history with the politics of empowerment of the 1970s and 1980s were mobilized to provide information. To many, this was the first time they would share the horrors they experienced through the genocidal violence. Based on this information reported to the commission, I built a data set from the commission's recall period (1962–1996) showing that in 100 percent of cases eyewitnesses identified security forces, the patrollers, and military commissioners as the perpetrators.

From 1962 to 1996, the recall period covered by the CEH, 953 people of the reported 107 cases were victims of human rights crimes. This represents 2.4 percent of the estimated total population of 40,000 in Chichicastenango during 1980 and 1981. Of all the victims in Guatemala, 46 percent were from El Quiché. Of all the victims in El Quiché, 5 percent were from Chichicastenango. Between 1962 and 1996, the CEH documented 953 victims of human rights crimes in Chichi, of which only 285 (30 percent) could be identified (166 men, 53 women, and 66 children), leaving 70 percent (668 victims) unidentified.[83] Forensic investigation reports also exist for these massacres, confirming their occurrence.

The fact that testifying survivors told what happened to the 668 unnamed victims is worth considering. On the social character of collective memory, Zerubavel remarks, "Consider, for example, the role of others as witnesses whose memories help corroborate our own."[84] By remembering their neighbors who suffered the atrocities, survivors contributed to the collective remembrance of otherwise forgotten Cold War victims, other fellow community neighbors, as they remembered them as people with a shared historical experience. To compare, in South Africa, anthropologist Fiona Ross recalls that "women first and foremost told about the suffering of their partners, husbands, sons, and brothers and not about themselves and the atrocities they had suffered."[85]

Mnemonic communities stand in stark contrast with the more militarized "garrison" communities (Chapter Eight). Postwar Santa Maria Tzejá, extensively analyzed by Beatriz Manz, can also be typified as a mnemonic community coming together to recover the historical memory.[86] Remembering the past is one of the crucial efforts states undertake to forge national identity, scholars have long pointed out.[87] In *The Social Frameworks of Memory,* Maurice Halbwachs suggests that all memory is a social process, shaped by the various groups—family, religious, geographical—to which individuals belong.[88]

From this view, those who gave their testimony became representatives of other voices and other stories. Above all, what drove Maya men and women to testify was their profound conviction of the need to assert their dignity through moral and economic reparation: "We were treated like animals. But we are people" was repeatedly voiced in testimonies received by the commission as eyewitnesses provided lists with material losses.[89] From the individual to the collective, human rights groups acted as witnesses to their lives, reaffirming their engagement in the "labors of memory," to paraphrase sociologist Elizabeth Jelin.[90]

Figure 5.1. Chupol area, Chichicastenango, 2000. Photo © the author.

This photograph shows resilient Indigenous women from the Chupol area. Their courageous stance to break the silence, rather than deny the postcolonial role of the military in the genocidal assault, involved publicly denouncing how soldiers, military commissioners, and patrols attacked their communities and stole from them their few material possessions. To a large extent, their mobilization addressing collective grievances points to manifestations of goodness, or heroic values, which, as in the case of Polish survivors during the Holocaust, "acted as a kind of drug … that helped them withstand even the most difficult ordeals."[91] Remarkably, despite the larger context of military control over their villages, nearly a thousand testimonies were received from the Chupol area by the Truth Commission, which suggests that without the participation of Chupolenses the truth effort could not have reconstructed the collective memory of the state violence in the area.

Yet Chupol's abundance of testimonies is surprisingly overlooked by McAllister when she asserts, "The REHMI and CEH include little information on Chichicastenango because the same Chichicastecos did not come forward before these initiatives."[92] This assertion leaves unexplored the role of organized groups in bearing witness and the efforts undertaken to break the silence over the violence and to keep alive the historical memory of their communities. Furthermore, McAllister argues that patrols from communities remote from Chupol did not participate in massacres and that Chupolenses refused to turn in lists of names to the military outpost.[93] Yet, testimonies received by the commission show that, despite efforts to avoid participating, local patrols were accused of human rights crimes.

As Told by Human Rights Groups

Rosalina Tuyuc, CONAVIGUA leader and director of the Programa de Resarcimiento, noted in 2003, "The toll is enormous, so the process should be done well. Seventy percent of the people we interviewed had never given their testimony and are not included in the report of the CEH."[94] The commission received over 7,000 testimonies nationwide that told of acts of cannibalism, the raping of children and women, and the dismembering of bodies as well as of the acts of military celebrations that took place in the carnage's aftermath and the pillage of communities. As mentioned earlier, I built a data set drawn from the commission's report. Though these numbers must be viewed cautiously, since not all victims and family members testified, they nonetheless provide us with a baseline to evaluate the war and genocidal violence in the township, as told by groups of widows from the Chupol area.

The commission shows that 91 percent of the 107 human rights cases represent casualties from either Chupol or other more inland communities, such as Lacamá I and Tzanimacabaj. A total of 953 victims were found in these cases. The fact that the majority of the victims, 724 people (76 percent), were killed in twenty-one reported massacres (20 percent) underscores the magnitude of the counterinsurgency campaign in Chupol and its vicinity. The army bears responsibility for fourteen of the massacres.[95] Following the national pattern of state-sponsored violence, the army alone was responsible for 81 percent of the 107 Chichicastenango human rights cases (against 803 victims). The second most frequent perpetrator was reported to be the PACs, who were responsible for 8.41 percent of the cases, resulting in 103 victims. The communities with the greatest number of victims were those located along or near the Interamerican Highway in the Chupol area: Chontolá (39), Chupol (84), Agua Escondida (88), Chuguexa and Chuguexa I and II (127), and Lacamá I, II, and III (350).

The crimes against most of the human rights victims took place in Lacamá I, II, and III. This is one hinterland area where peasants took refuge from the army's persecution and the burning of their families, ranches, livestock, and cooperatives. The highest number of human rights crimes, out of a total of 107, were 35 and 40 in 1981 and 1982, respectively, coinciding with the highest number of human rights crimes that took place during the peak of the genocide (1981–1983). Most human rights crimes correspond to violations to the right of life: extrajudicial killings (38.32 percent), forced disappearances (33.64 percent), and massacres (19.63 percent).[96] The CEH concluded that the practice of forced disappearances was meant to dissuade peasants from organizing into groups to oppose the military.[97]

The Lacamá II Turnikaja Massacre

The Lacamá II, Chuguexa, and Chontolá massacres are examples of the army's need to reaffirm its superiority in the eyes of its victims. On 2 August 1982, a platoon of forty to fifty soldiers launched its offensive against the hinterland Lacamá II community. Back in 1997, during a visit to the ravines known as the Waterfalls (Las Cataratas in Spanish and Turnikaja in Maya-K'iché), I trekked with some survivors down the mountain to the site of the mass grave.[98]

Eyewitnesses told me that soldiers relied on an ex-rebel wearing a hood to show them the way to where families from various communities hid from the bombing, the raping of young girls, and the pillaging of their homes.[99] Most families ran against the waterfalls as soldiers chased them down, fatally shooting some 200 men and women, including the elderly, and children. Some of the victims were tortured, asphyxiated, or beaten to death. Children's eyes were removed as bodies remained in the ravines and were eaten by animals.[100] As with other large-scale extrajudicial killings, the Turnikaja Massacre left a trail of violent memories imprinted on the social fabric and the collective consciousness of Maya communities in the area.

The Chuguexa Massacres

Widows from the community of Chuguexa recounted that the EGP gathered them in 1980 and encouraged families to resist military control by joining the irregular local forces (FIL) and the local clandestine committees (CCL)— self-defense groups. In response, state soldiers came to warn neighbors against the incursion of "*guerrilleros* badly advising communities."[101] Soon after, soldiers killed over 100 people in at least three massacres in Chuguexa, Chuguexa I, and Chuguexa II.[102]

The first massacre took place in Chuguexa II when soldiers fired on twenty-five peasants, at least two of them children, in 1980.[103] In August 1981, soldiers performed a second massacre in Chuguexa I and II by killing twenty-five people, at least four of them children, and leaving only one survivor. Later, in July 1982, soldiers entered the village in a frenzy, killing at least fifty-seven peasants in Chuguexa I. Among the victims was Anastasia Pixcar Mejia, murdered as she was giving birth.[104] In this massacre, Tomása and Juana Morales Sen, two young girls, were raped and decapitated, and Tomása Morales Sen, an elderly woman, was mercilessly beaten to death.[105] This sequence of massacres, and their victims' profiles, shows the army's larger pattern of systematic violence against villages identified as "red" or pro-URNG rebel communities.

The Chontolá Massacre

Soldiers and patrols entered the Chontolá community, only three kilometers from the Highway, on 6 November 1981; soon after, eight identified victims and approximately sixteen unidentified victims were captured. They were all brought to the oratory, where they were tortured and burned alive. Soon after, the PACs brought all the neighbors together in one place and, calling it a "temporary military detachment," the people in the communities were ordered to take the roof sheets and things that could be used to construct a patrol post in the center of the community.[106]

Candelaria Pixcar, shown below, is a CONAVIGUA leader from Chontolá who, in 2012, still traveled, organizing widows and women in general in the eastern side.[107] Not all survivors from Chontolá, however, followed Candelaria's activism; others adhered to Evangelical sects promoting forgetfulness and helping to perpetuate collective silence. Candelaria's husband Tomas Calel Pantoj, a Peasant League organizer, had been killed during the genocide.

When she joined CONAVIGUA in the late 1980s, she was, like many other Maya-K'iché women, illiterate in Spanish. In the larger context where war survivors received "no social validation" from the successive rightwing

Figure 5.2. Santo Tomás Chichicastenango, 28 January 2012. Photo © Pierre-Yves Linot.

administrations, CONAVIGUA offered widows support.[108] Candelaria's activism convinced her that only by organizing could widows find some protection from the state and its Maya authorities' allies and gain respect for their human rights. Throughout my initial fieldwork in 1997, Candelaria denounced former patrol chief José Riquiac Tecum before MINUGUA in Santa Cruz for threatening her. When I returned in 2012, she repeatedly told me that her past experience organizing Peasant League's committees had given her the knowledge and courage to move on, so she could provide for her family. Even today, she still experiences the psychological scars of fear: "Neighbors have information, but they are afraid to give it. Just by encountering the military they are afraid. When I think about [*la violencia*] I get very nervous."[109]

In 2000, Rosa Tuis Guarcax denounced the rape of a twelve-year-old girl by an ex-military commissioner, who was at that time assistant mayor for a community in San Pedro Yepocapa, Chimaltenango.[110] Rosa suffered from retaliatory attacks by former patrols. Between military control and resistance, survivors of scorched earth campaigns kept on demanding truth, memory, and justice, for both their own cases and those of their neighbors, even at great personal risk. As Kerwin Lee Klein suggests, "Memory is not a property of individual minds, but a diverse and shifting collection of material artifacts and social practices" and actions that CONAVIGUA members courageously engaged in.[111] As Victoria Sanford notes, the forced recruitment into civilian patrols also silenced, "but could not do away with, human agency."[112] The organization succeeded in passing legislation (Decree Law 20-2003) to create a new civic service law providing a civilian alternative to compulsory military service (Ley de Servicio Civico Nacional) in 2003.[113]

Exhuming the Past: Clandestine Cemeteries

Sanford's research has shown that the public nature of grieving and exhumations helps create open spaces for healing and reconciliation—unlike secrecy and silence. In the Chupol area, few burials followed the slaughter and grief. Grassroots efforts to exhume war remains took place in the context of renewed ties between former patrols chiefs and the military and the installation of new checkpoints along highways in Huehuetenango, Chimaltenango, and Chichicastenango. In addition, soldiers were seen searching buses and their passengers, and the military operated checkpoints near three villages in Chichi early in 1997. Defensoria Maya, another Indigenous rights group, protested, "For indigenous peoples, military activities have historically been linked to massacres, repression, terror and intimidation … The army's presence alone inhibits organization by the population and the construction of peace."[114]

That human rights organizations were (and are) demanding exhumations is evidence of the impact of organized groups mobilized in the Chupol area. As fear from patrols and army's reprisals crippled families' attempts to search for victims of massacres, only 50 percent of survivors providing testimonies to REHMI knew where remains were, and only 34 percent could give them proper burial.[115] Thus, mass graves are widespread in El Quiché, including in tourist-friendly Chichicastenango.

Human rights groups, CONAVIGUA, CERJ, and FAMDEGUA (Families of the Disappeared of Guatemala) actively organized, demanding resources and technical assistance to exhume their victims. The Guatemalan Forensic Anthropology Foundation (FAFG) had exhumed a total of 174 remains by 2004. Communities with the highest number of exhumations were Panimache (35), Chupol (28), Chuguexa II B (26), Sacpulub (24), Chuguexa II A (16), and Lacamá I and II (10). Significantly, the Panimache community, with the highest number of exhumed remains, has only one human rights case of enforced disappearance reported by the CEH. This lack of testimonies to the commission of crimes in this particular community might be due to the pervasive fear of testifying in the late 1990s. Maya peasants—men, women, and children—became martyrs for the Maya uprising, suffering gruesome deaths at the hands of the army.

Families' ties to cultural and spiritual practices were being systematically undermined through the ongoing and pervasive role of ex-militiamen now in positions of authority. However, by keeping the collective memory of their victims alive, survivors from Chupol contested the army and the patrol-like system, as acts of remembrance became an indicator of commitment to the memory of human rights victims.

Notes

1. Zerubavel, "Social Memories," 283.
2. Brett, *Social Movements, Indigenous Politics.*
3. Zerubavel, "Social Sound of Silence," 41. Since 1977, the Mothers successfully challenged the state's denial over the 30,000 of forcibly disappeared by state security forces (1976–1983).
4. Nelson, *Finger in the Wound.*
5. Literally, "a rock in the shoe."
6. Collective interview, Nicolás.
7. Todorov and Bellos, *Hope and Memory,* 113.
8. Bastos and Camus, *Quebrando el Silencio,* 93.
9. Nora, "Between Memory and History," 12.
10. PBI spent, for instance, four years accompanying Amilcar Méndez and other leaders. S. González, "Guatemalans Refuse."
11. Collective interview, Fernando.
12. Ibid.

13. Author interview, Reginaldo.
14. Collective interview, Fernando.
15. CONADEGUA, "Violencia y Represión."
16. Author interview, Polanco.
17. The victims were found dead inside their car at the bottom of a ravine known at the time to be a body dump near Amatitlán. Americas Watch Committee, "Group of Mutual Support."
18. CIRMA, Inforpress, No. 561.
19. McAllister and Nelson, *War by Other Means,* 100.
20. Collective interview, Nicolás.
21. Ibid.
22. Ibid.
23. CIRMA, Inforpress, No. 1903.
24. Collective interview, Nicolás.
25. Ibid.
26. Acan-Efe, "Exhumarán restos," 15 March 2010.
27. Simon, "Eterna Primavera, Eterna Tiranía."
28. REHMI, II.141.
29. The record covers the period from 31 July to October 1988. CIRMA, Infostelle, Signatura 84; CERJ "Presentación Primer Informe." Patrols from Santiago Atitlán had also demobilized after four years (Sosa Velásquez, *Rupturas y Construcción,* 80). According to observers, "In three months of activity, 78 villages were resisting service in the patrols. But by mid-1989 at least 7,000 Mayans refused PAC service. Méndez … distributed copies of Article 34 among residents so they could campaign effectively." S. González, "Guatemalans Refuse."
30. This type of document, known as "memorials," is testimony of the many strategies peasants resort to in order to petition, demand, and denounce injustices. They are often notarized.
31. CIRMA, Infostelle, Signatura 84; CIRMA, CDHG, "Campesinos Renuncian."
32. Author interview, Méndez.
33. CIRMA, Infostelle, Signatura 84; CERIGUA, "PACs Disarm."
34. Defamatory pamphlets left in Washington, D.C. during a luncheon honoring Méndez Urízar on 15 October 1991. Jay, *Persecution by Proxy,* 47.
35. Author interview, Ignacio.
36. Author interview, Méndez.
37. HMP, CERJ Archive, "Historia Chichicastenango."
38. Jay, *Persecution by Proxy,* 27.
39. Pasqualucci, "Medidas Provisionales."
40. The petitioners further reported that on 2 February 1995, the victim's spouse had filed a formal complaint with the district attorney, accusing Macario Ventura of responsibility for the disappearance of her husband and the death of their son. OAS, Report No. 21/98 Case 11.435.
41. About U.S.$273. OANDA.com, "Historical Exchange Rates."
42. OAS, Report No. 19/00 Case 11.435.
43 Collective interview, Fernando.
44. Ibid.
45. Ibid.
46. Ibid.
47. Author interview, Reginaldo.
48. Ibid.

49. Peacock and Beltran, "Hidden Powers," 12; see also, Amnesty International, "Fear for Safety."
50. Collective interview, Fernando.
51. Author interview, Ignacio.
52. "Cinco Grupos Clandestinos," *Noti Mundo.*
53. Remijnse, *Memories of Violence,* 182.
54. McAllister, "Rural Markets, Revolutionary Souls," 15.
55. CEH, IV.205, fn500.
56. Huyse, "Tradition-Based Approaches," 18.
57. Merry, *Human Rights and Gender Violence;* Madlingozi, "On Transitional Justice Entrepreneurs"; Escobar, "Memoria Viva."
58. CIRMA, CONAVIGUA, Guatemala, Introducción, August 1993.
59. CIRMA, CONAVIGUA 60, "Viudas o Guerrilleras."
60. CIRMA, CONAVIGUA 60, "Qué es CONAVIGUA." See also Associaió d'Amistat, *Guatemala a Grandes Trazos,* 42.
61. CIRMA, CONAVIGUA 60, "Qué es CONAVIGUA."
62. Todorov, *Facing the Extreme,* 61.
63. CIRMA, CONAVIGUA 60, Qué es CONAVIGUA,21.
64. CEH, VII.175–84. Even before 1988, when Maria joined CONAVIGUA, patrols and military commissioners accused her of bringing food to guerillas and later organizing widows in her community.
65. CONADEGUA, "Security Forces."
66. CIRMA, CONAVIGUA 60, "Fui Combatiente no Genocida."
67. Rosario Pu poignantly asserted, "The wounds will remain open until the government specifically admits it was the Army that [did the killing]." "To talk about forgiveness is easy, but moral and economic reparations are necessary if we are to begin to forget these sad histories." Jeffrey, "Restorative Justice Worldwide," 23.
68. CIRMA, CONAVIGUA 58, "Resolver la Problematica."
69. CIRMA, Infostelle, Signatura 84, "Disolución de Grupos."
70. CIRMA, CONAVIGUA 60, Guatemala, 15 May 1995.
71. CONAVIGUA, "El Reclutamiento Militar."
72. Author interview, Ignacio.
73. Collective interview, Yolanda; CONAVIGUA.
74. HNG, *Prensa Libre,* 16 May 2000.
75. HNG, *Prensa Libre,* Seijo, "Víctimas a Resarcir."
76. Esparza, "Impossible Memory," 175.
77. For fieldwork among Guatemalan Coca-Cola workers offering a detailed account of trade unionism's struggle to overcome the paralyzing effects of fear and fight against state terror, see Levenson-Estrada, *Trade Unionists against Terror.*
78. Schirmer, "Those Who Die for Life," 57.
79. Franco, *Cruel Modernity,* 20.
80. Bhabha, "Foreword," xxxv.
81. Viaene, *Voices from the Shadows,* 16.
82. Nora, "Between Memory and History," 7.
83. According to the commission, 15 percent of the total human rights victims registered are people whose identity is unknown. CEH, II.318.
84. Zerubavel, "Social Memories," 285.
85. Hydle, "Anthropological Contribution," 261.
86. Manz, *Paradise in Ashes.*
87. Zerubavel, "Social Memories"; Anderson, *Imagined Communities.*

88. Halbwachs, *Social Frameworks of Memory.*
89. Author interview, Tomás.
90. Jelin, *State Repression.*
91. Todorov, *Facing the Extreme,* 5.
92. CIRMA, CGD, McAllister, "Chupol," 6.
93. Ibid., 9.
94. HNG, *Prensa Libre,* Seijo, "Víctimas a Resarcir."
95. Nationwide, the CEH found that 626 massacres were attributed to state security forces: 69 percent of extrajudicial executions, 41 percent of sexual violence, and 45 percent of torture. In 63 percent of the massacres the army acted alone, while in 27 percent it acted in collaboration with PACs or military commissioners. Three percent were only PACs, and 1 percent only military commissioners. CEH, III.256.
96. Six percent of the cases correspond to torture and 3 percent to sexual violence.
97. CEH, II. 412–15.
98. CEH, X.1084. Case 2899, August 1982, 200 people, Lacamá II.
99. "At home we had two engines of light, speakers, amplifiers . . . Everything was stolen, my blouses *huipiles,*" declared a witness to the commission (CEH Internal Memorandum, HMP).
100. CEH, X.1084. Case 2899.
101. Collective interview, CONAVIGUA, Chuguexa.
102. CEH, X. 1016, 1027, 1087. Case 15043, 1980, twenty-five people; Case 16255, August 1981, twenty-six people; Case 2854, July 1982, fifty people.
103. CEH, X, 1016. Case 15043, 15 August 1980.
104. Survivors said, "Half of the baby was in and half out." CEH, X, 1087. Case 2854,
105. CEH, X, 1087. Case 2854.
106. Author interview, Pixcar.
107. Schirmer, "Seeking of Truth."
108. Lykes, "Children in the Storm," 154.
109. Author interview, Pixcar.
110. Amnesty International, "Further Information."
111. Klein, "On the Emergence of Memory," 130.
112. Sanford, *Buried Secrets,* 70.
113. RESDAL, *Libro Blanco.*
114. CONADEGUA, "Security Forces."
115. REHMI, I.23.

6

"Inverted Discourse"
Collaboration in "White Communities"

The people in rags do not revolt.
—Primo Levi

There, hanging on the walls, are the portraits of our military presidents: we saw
Ubico . . . Peralta Azurdia . . . Arana. Father Casas, who has an in-depth knowledge
of Indigenous psychology, tells us: "This is how our Indigenous people are, the
ancestral idea of their kings makes them identify with supreme military authority."
—Hermana Cortez Ruiz

Encouraged by civic action, propaganda, and military strategies forced upon them, sectors of the population collaborated with the army. According to intelligence reports, communities considered under military control were identified as "white," "pink," or "green," depending on their socioeconomic and cultural traits. In Chichicastenango, these communities were most likely the off-the-path Mactzul, Saquillá, and Paxot cluster of communities, along with some adjacent cantons (see Map 0.2). By the time that scorched earth campaigns were launched in the early 1980s, I argue in this chapter, this area had a preexisting historical, ideological, and geographical affinity for the military.[1] What role did the national security doctrine play in facilitating this collaboration? Why did the Guatemalan National Revolutionary Unity (URNG) rebels fail to receive active support from this area?

To encourage or renew allegiances, the army effectively reinterpreted Maya history, exploited the grinding poverty of populations targeted for co-optation, and infantilized the population. From the army's standpoint, Maxeños' (as Chichicastenango locals are called) previous war experience was endowed with their pre-Hispanic "disciplined spirit" and "warriorhood," a view that facilitated their co-optation. To achieve its goals, the military relied on callous terror campaigns used in connivance with the Army's Civil Affairs and Local Development Division (AA.CC & D.L in Spanish) or the S-5 branch and psychological operations (PSYOPs) and the Army Corps of Engineers, among other divisions. Much like the practice of the Gendarmerie aiding local militias in Poland during the Holocaust,[2] the un-uniformed patrol system, including the military commissioners, was a crucial anticommunist strategy that allowed the Guatemalan army to finally get the upper hand over the URNG rebels.

Five key factors led to the development of a collaborative community disposition in the far Western Chichicastenango communities. First, a preexisting militarization and militarism in this area probably had shaped military control over white communities through peasant participation in the Chichicastenango Historical Battalion. Second, the internal colonial situation affected the northwestern corner of Chichicastenango—particularly those most isolated from the Interamerican Highway, even though they were closer geographically from el pueblo, the urban center. Third, I also suggest that the process of *concientización* that had unfolded in the Chupol area in the late 1970s and promoted solidarity communities did not take place, leaving families more open to accepting the "internal enemy" discourse propagated by the military. This fed into peasants' false ethnic consciousness and class and rendered them more vulnerable to co-optation.

Instead, the new layer of militarization and militarism imposed upon these communities via the patrol system and the new roles assigned to military commissioners as chiefs of PACs acted as a cohesive force uniting families and communities to support the military project. As Katharine E. McGregor observes in the case of Indonesia, polarization "is a significant threat to the power of political militaries," and therefore armies hope to ensure "unity," across the population and, as I argue, across its potential local-level collaborators.[3] Fourth, the army's reliance on an "inverted discourse," as discussed by René Lemarchand in the context of the 1972 Burundi genocide. Fabricating the "internal enemy" war mythology provided false information to illiterate communities, thus constructing the idea that the army was protecting them rather than assaulting them. Fifth, massacres committed by the military against its own "amigos" reenacted the callousness of the conquistadors massacring their own allies.

Traces of Colonialism: The Chichicastenango Historical Battalion

Military control engulfed northwestern white communities bordering Totonicapán in two separate time frames, 1813 and the early 1980s (see Map 0.2). In 1813, border disputes were fueled by a need to preserve community boundaries. Conflict over land resulted in the uprising of neighbors from Mactzul against Ladino authority. When asked by the mayor of Totonicapán to "convene in the community of Mactsul to resolve land litigations over a bordering terrain, neighbors protested and threw rocks at official representatives." The incident resulted in nearby militia groups being told to garrison in Lemoa, an adjacent area connected to Santa Cruz, El Quiché's capital.[4]

During the early 1960s, the same northwestern communities bordering Totonicapán became militarized again when Army Zone No. 6, known as Mariscal Gregorio Solares, was established in Santa Cruz, El Quiché. Later, Army Zone No. 20 was set up near Lemoa.[5] Though there is scant evidence to indicate the level of Indigenous participation from these communities in the 1877 Chichicastenango Historical Battalion, their geographical proximity to the Lemoa area—unlike that of the Chupol community and neighboring villages—suggests that neighbors from these communities most likely served in the battalion.[6]

Sixty years after the Mactzul (Mactsul) incident, under the Liberal government of Justo Rufino Barrios (1873–1885), the army organized the 1877 Chichicastenango Historical Battalion, which may have participated in the campaign of the Central American Union in 1886.[7] As discussed in Chapter Two, the use of auxiliary forces is a colonial and postcolonial practice found throughout Latin America. In 2000, Luis, a schoolteacher and an army ally, provided the following written excerpt about the battalion:

> The Historical Chichicastenango Battalion dates back to the incorporation of the Maya population into militias, which was a policy of Liberal Governments. Males between the ages 15 and 50 could join. In the municipality of Santo Tomas Chichicastenango, militias were formed in 1877 to crush a K'iché uprising over land conflicts. Throughout the years, the Battalion developed as any other organization, according to circumstances. Today it is known as a symbolic torch of Chichicastenango's soldiers. The Sut (or Tzut) wrapped around their heads, a symbol of authority to follow, and their complexion tanned by their hard work under difficult weather conditions makes the Historical Battalion unique in El Quiché.[8]

This account of the origins of the Chichi battalion highlights some of the continuity between participation of sectors of Maxeños and the iteration of colonial practices in the form of rural militias. Driven by a dominant military memory of past wars, the excerpt also notes, "Our ancestors tell us that when the country was in danger and required the patriotism of all citizens, the Battalion said: 'here we are.'"[9] This nationalistic sentiment—evoking militaristic values shown repeatedly in military journals, such as strength, patriotism, courage, and sacrifice when serving the fatherland, *la patria*—is entrenched with extreme, paternalistic notions of masculinity recasting peasant men as guardians of families and communities against URNG rebels. Māori cultural scholar Brendan Hokowhitu suggests that European-style masculinity in New Zealand's Māori communities is rooted in colonization, allocating "disciplinary and authoritative power through notions of tradition and authenticity."[10]

This view often excludes other forms of Indigenous leadership in the name of constructed traditions, which in turn "reifies a focus on the past."[11] At the township level, Chichicastenango's conservative leadership and members of *cofradías* fit this description since they rely on authoritarian values to perpetuate their power while they simultaneously pledge their allegiance to the army. As I mentioned in the Introduction, the Auxiliatura is the highest Maya authority. Diane M. Nelson has summarized this, "Elders and *principales* [community leaders] are very powerful and there is a deep mysticism they will not share with us [researchers]."[12] In this 1960 *Revista Militar*, the battalion reserves are shown marching and proudly carrying floral arrangements (Fig. 6.1[13]):

Reserves' esprit de corps is embodied in the traditional head wrap—known as the *sut, tzut,* or *tzute*—which was worn for battalion recruits' military ceremonies. This garb tellingly shows the "liminal position, half way between the subjugated and the subjugators," in the words of historian Ruth Ginio when examining the case of the *tirailleurs sénégalais*.[14] Likewise, the military identities of Maya peasants have been long shaped by divided loyalties exalted by the non-Indigenous state when they are required to serve the country—even when without uniform, as in the case of the civil self-defense patrols (PACs). Highlighting the notion that Maya cultural identity is trapped in ambiguity, Indigenous scholar Demetrio Cojtí Cuxil has remarked that it is "flexible, fluid and elastic … [but] also an ambivalent identity, one identity by tradition, the other by allocation through coercive means."[15]

Figure 6.1. © HNG, *Revista Militar.* April–June 1960, Reservas Militares, 81.

Framing Collaboration: The "Internal Colonial Situation"

Among the poorest and those isolated from the Interamerican Highway, the army found a captive, obedient, and easily controlled support base to become complicit in the bloodshed, the REHMI Report concluded.[16] Though rebel forces had not established a solid presence and had failed to build their mass-based support, the military managed to manipulate people's fear of further uprootedness, exalted their masculinity, and seduced them with incentives and rewards, ultimately driving rightwing militiamen to collaborate. Patrols on this side thus reenacted a long-standing colonial paradox: sectors of the internally colonized turned against their own neighbors and left behind a trail of secrecy and ethnic and class betrayals.

White communities average about eleven kilometers from the main urban center of Chichicastenango, but by the late 1970s they had nearly no access to asphalt roads.[17] Access to Mactzul and Paxot from the urban center was only possible by trekking through broken terrain, despite the fact that only seventeen kilometers of dirt road separated these villages from the urban center. Even short distances to white communities were quite difficult to travel by car, particularly during the rainy seasons, when dirt roads become rivers of mud. Lack of transportation infrastructure characterized these communities' geographical and socioeconomic isolation.

According to the World Bank, in rural areas, geographical location is highly intertwined with ethnic exclusion, poverty, and employment opportunities, in addition to limited social and commercial networks.[18] Richard N. Adams situates these isolated communities at one extreme of a continuum of communities: as the traditionalist retaining the symbols of their Maya identity, languages, community organization, clothing, religious practices, those least assimilated into the Ladino-dominant society and ultimately doomed to vanish.[19]

These dire conditions are asserted by the World Bank in Guatemala: poverty and vulnerability are chronic, resulting from the peasantry's precarious life rooted in tiny plots of land due to unequal land ownership.[20] As Beatriz Manz suggests, between 1950 and 1964 the highlands population grew 41.3 percent, fragmenting already small plots and leading to even more intense use.[21] According to a 1960s USAID report, "In 1950, 76 percent of all farms were under 3.5 hectares while in 1979 this figure had risen to 78 percent." Most tellingly, in 1970, 88 percent of the country's farms were too small to feed a family.[22]

Faulty statistics (see Chapter One) make charting the political economy of individual households a daunting task, leaving important gaps about the mean household and the types of revenue-bringing economic activities performed by families. Nevertheless, since the 1970s, basic numbers illustrate troubling levels of illiteracy, unemployment, and poor health. The 1973 census reveals, for instance, a literacy rate below 13 percent and nearly 70 percent unemployment in the Mactzul community. Families lived without potable water, latrines, or electricity, which contributed to poor health conditions.

Large portions of the Mactzul population were also impacted by stunted growth, a condition linked to poor maternal nutrition, poor food quality, and frequent infections, in turn tied to "community infrastructures, national policies, and [globalized] economic conditions."[23] In Appendix 1, I illustrate incredibly high levels of peasants in rural communities reporting not working and similarly poor literacy rates. The most salient observation is that the greater total population in the white communities posed a greater burden on the 1,125 who were economically active in Mactzul, Paxot, and Saquillá in 1973. In contrast, within red communities the total population was smaller and higher percentages were employed, lowering dependency on a slightly higher pool of breadwinners.

Extreme poverty and disenfranchisement was (and is) also rehearsed in the collective memory of peasants from white communities. Manuel, a former patrol chief and reservist from Saquillá I, painfully described his precarious life and the "choices" presented to him when he was seven years old:

> I remember that if I left for school for a whole week, my dad would give me five cents to buy some candy ... So, I realized that if I studied, I did not have money, and if I went to work with my dad, I had money. I was more worried about the money. It was much better if I did not go to school, because it was a big job that we did on the land, so I decided to go with my father. I was about seven when I quit school.[24]

Showing the link between extreme poverty and conscription, like many young Maya males, Manuel had later on "voluntarily" joined the army to escape the dire conditions of poverty and to serve the country. He further recounted, "We were ashamed to ask my father for things because he was the only one supporting us. He made his living as a bus driver's assistant ... for 12 years ... If he had had any studies, he would have been concerned about our education."[25]

Prelude to Genocide: Far from Liberation Theology

Compounded with preexisting militarization and centuries of mistrust of outsiders, poverty-ridden families from white communities refused to participate in the process of class and ethnic awakening led by Catholic Action, which encouraged participation in literacy projects and the use of new fertilizers and farming equipment (see Chapter Four). By the 1970s, the *cofradía* had become a tool of oppression, with "one layer of indigenous peoples exploited by another," points out Arturo Arias.[26]

The *cofradías* are linked to the municipal center through rituals, ceremonies, and festivities keeping the traditional Maya culture alive. But unlike in the more geographically accessible Chupol area, by the late 1970s, hinterland northwestern communities remained largely untouched by sociopolitical changes that led other areas to eventually support the EGP rebels. A similar outcome was found by Richard Wilson in the context of the Department of Alta Verapaz about which he points out that international poverty relief agencies often ignored remote communities, "pass[ing] over the isolated Q'eqchi territory in favor of groups with better access to major roads and markets."[27]

To experiment with new, revolutionary ideologies and with new crops simply seemed too risky for families on this side. Used to the old ways and far from the main highway that could open up possibilities to connect them with the outside world, they were wary of anything that could threaten the only thing under their immediate control—their subsistence. Tragically, the class and ethnic alienation of peasants constructed by centuries of oppression led them to reject new seeds that could have ameliorated their plight, in the short term. This conservatism, in the words of George Lovell, has "meant minimal cultural change at the community level."[28] As long as the most "essential value, because it is the most meaningful, the land," is kept, Fanon has argued, the colonized will refuse social change.[29]

Collaborating with the Oppressor

Far from the process of religious conversion and grassroots organizing that brought hopes for a better future in the east, white communities were located strategically closer to current military posts, including a garrison from the Liberal years (discussed above), shaping their conservative outlook.[30] In the case of Peru, sociologist Ivan Degregori notes that starting in the early 1980s, the army called up its reserves and grouped peasants from villages within populated nuclei close to barracks and organized them into civil self-defense committees.[31] He also notes that rebels' "greatest problems occurred in the poorest regions that were at the same time the most traditional."[32] By the late 1970s, white communities were most likely aligned with ultra-rightwing political parties, such as the MLN. The MLN was the "party of organized violence," as MLN members themselves called it, a "quasi-fascist organization," corralling votes and organizing death squad violence by appropriating anticommunist Cold War discourse since the 1950s.[33]

The actions of at least some community authority figures demonstrate support for the army. While counterinsurgency campaigns beheaded the revolutionary and popular movement in the Chupol area, members of Chichicastenango's *cofradía* Virgen Maria de la Cruz, depicted in the photograph below (Fig. 6.2),[34] participated in an army-led inauguration of a water pipe project funded by the Interamerican and Development Bank (BID, in Spanish), in collaboration with the local Auxiliatura Indígena, the Instituto de Fomento Municipal (INFOM), and the government of El Quiché Department. Though I could not confirm whether these particular *cofradías* members belonged to white communities—Mactzul, Paxot, or Saquillá—the picture suggests that Maya religious authorities from Chichicastenango supported the army's civic action projects.

By validating their "humanitarian" development projects, Maya authorities helped disguise the co-optation of local authorities. In order to guarantee default "agreement with the government's political foundations and policies"[35] and to keep the important flow of revenues from the "boom of tourism," the *cofradías* were at once co-opted and contained by militarization made desirable by folklorizing "the Maya."[36] Silvia Rivera Cusicanqui notes that in Bolivia Aymara and Quechua were also folklorized in her critical discussion of the betrayal of masculinized Ayllus—the traditional form of Andean community. Rivera Cusicanqui argues that Indigenous authorities turn their backs on their communities by making political compromises with the state.[37]

Figure 6.2. Coronel Carlos Pozuelos of the Gumaracaj Task Force with members from the *cofradía*. © HNG, *Prensa Libre*, "Chichicastenango: Iniciada Construcción," 19 December 1982, 16.

"Inverted Discourse": Civic Action and the PSYOPS

In the early 1980s, S-5 civic action strategies—after programs were adjusted to exploit the value of the civil affairs and PSYOPs component—resonated most profoundly with the poorest communities. Siniša Malešević suggests that a process involving a "centrifugal ideologization of the 'masses'" needs to unfold for war misinformation and national stereotyping to resonate. This refers to the spread of nationalistic rhetoric to the larger population, in which people "become both objects and subjects of full-fledged ideological action."[38] Acknowledging this process, Malešević argues, helps us understand people's willingness to kill for the nation.[39] As Jacques Sémelin has asserted, "Propaganda ... contributes to the creation of a sort of *semantic matrix* that gives meaning to the increased force of a dynamic of violence that then works as a 'launching pad' for massacre."[40] Ideology is employed by leaders to "channel anxiety on to an easily identifiable enemy"[41] and provide the population with "an explanation of the source of the threat."[42]

To achieve this goal, in the early 1980s, the military created civil affairs and fabricated the "inverted discourse" strategy disseminated through PSYOPs. This type of discourse consists of making false accusations, shifting blame, and using scapegoats, just as they were used in the 1972 Burundi genocide to entice perpetrators to slaughter some 200,000 to 300,000 Hutus. According to Lemarchand, this type of discourse in Burundi refers to when "the insurgents [were] portrayed as having committed a monstrous act of genocide directed against the Tutsi as a group."[43] In Guatemala, in General Héctor Alejandro Gramajo Morales's words, this was a project of "reorganized truth" drilled into peasant minds through leaflets dropped from airplanes, radio and television discussions, and local civil affairs specialists responsible for giving "ideological talks" to orient patrols, military commissioners, and reserves in a specific direction.[44] From 1982 to 1983, Gramajo, educated at the School of the Americas, was the army vice chief of staff and director of the army general staff.

The PSYOPs campaign functioned as the backbone of a widespread process of ideologizing the peasant masses. Through flyers the army provided different information to communities depending on their identified political allegiances. Observers have noted that war information "was not disseminated to reach the entire population"; instead, it was directed to "either different groups of military personnel, or select groups of civilians."[45] PSYOPs officers infused rumors with half-truths, such as the "voluntariness" of the patrol system and hate speech demonizing the rebels and propagating the army's "internal enemy" myth.

An analysis of the 1980s iconography, visually defining the war for remote communities, sheds light on how the military used imagery to actively mobilize segments of the peasantry and gain their collaboration. Tragically, despite the absence of EGP rebels in the western area of Chichicastenango (with the possible of Saquillá II, where it appears that rebels may have made initial contacts with individual families according to some interviews), the army deliberately told peasant men that bands of "subversive delinquents" were ready to attack their communities and rape their wives at any time. This narrative imposed on peasants a distorted representation of the origins of the violence, leading some patrol groups to collaborate with their own oppressors.

In one flyer, the army depicted guerillas as common delinquents, indiscriminately assaulting ranches and raping women. In another leaflet (Fig. 6.3), this one announcing the arrival of "subversive terrorists," the rebels were illustrated as having devil tails and horns. Dropping those flyers suggests the army knew all too well that the warrior Maya narrative was a myth. Alex Hinton points out that, often, genocidal regimes "co-opt preexisting cultural knowledge, dressing it up in new ideological guises" that help keep "compelling resonances while legitimating new structures of domination" over victim groups.[46] This iconography demonstrates that the army's goal was to position itself as a guardian institution, even going so far as to contradict its own claim of the "brave Maya." This reveals that the army was not interested in protecting communities, as it publicly claimed, but rather in bolstering their collaboration with the PAC system at the cost of the very same communities it allegedly intended to protect.

Figure 6.3. Flyer illustrating the evil nature of rebels as opposed to the valiance of the patrols. © HMP Ejército de Guatemala Collection.

In analyzing violence in Germany, the former Yugoslavia, and Rwanda, Sémelin concludes, "The most extreme discourses present these enemy figures as necessarily frightening, even diabolical, for the purpose of 'othering' and 'dehumanizing.'"[47] In white communities, this dehumanizing process was shaped by families' lack of access to solidarity networks and reliable information about what was happening nearby were particularly susceptible to manipulation by PSYOPs. Replacing the warriorization of these communities, the army now infantilized peasants, representing itself as working on their behalf, rather than with them, toward "security" and the "benevolent progress" brought by the Army's Corps of Engineers (see Chapter Three). Yet, painting Indigenous people as warriors seemingly contradicted the army's long-standing belittlement of Indigenous peoples: it was part of the overall coercion and manipulation to get them to collaborate. As PSYOPs fabricated the internal enemy, the army sought to manipulate the symbols of pre-Hispanic and war virtues to build its support base by shaping historical memory and cultivating a military ethos. Manipulation of the cultural notion of guilt and values like peasants' service to their community was at the core of these efforts.[48]

Failure to protect their families and communities from an alleged internal enemy seeking to "destroy the country" made them "bad" Guatemalans—at least for those peasants who felt like a "Guatemalan" to begin with. Was this the national identity felt by pro-army groups in western communities? While this question is difficult to answer in light of the absence of historical studies on Maya nationalism in this particular area, what remains clear is that in the absence of organized groups opposing the army and the lack of accurate information about government policy, personal and collective choices were made by those who, called to serve, reenacted a postcolonial legacy: Indigenous collaboration with their own oppressors.

Explaining the "tame" Aches' malign identification with his persecutors in the genocide in Paraguay, Richard Arens asserts, "The loss of identity experienced by the Indians ... accounts for the emergence of the 'tame' Indian. It is he who may be found to aid and abet the white persecutors in their onslaught against his people."[49] Similarly, this identification with the *genocidaires* in the case of some patrol groups was achieved by PSYOPs reenactment of a racist rhetoric designed to construct a "homogenous Indigenous culture" that could be used to restructure society.[50] Jennifer Schirmer suggests that PSYOPs helped the army shape a new, homogenized Maya identity.

As Jim Handy has pointed out, "It didn't matter where Polin Polaina [the fictional character used in the army's flyers] originated from, he was marked by the homogenous character traits" of the "good Maya" or, as asserted by Staffan Löfving, the "neutral Maya," particularly analyzed in the context of development poles.[51] Polin Polaina, as discussed by Schirmer, was depicted wearing *traje* (traditional dress), plowing the land, taking care of family, and living a harsh, but nevertheless peaceful life. This type of peasant accepted the dictates of the internal enemy discourse that portrayed the patrol system as a "voluntary" organization required by communities themselves, rather than imposed upon them by the army.

The 1982 Victory Plan gave the following instructions to civil affairs when organizing the plainclothes patrols: "It must appear to be wanted by them."[52] Against this background, to gain peasants' goodwill, the army called for the national unity of "all" Guatemalans, conflating Ladinos and Maya, from all social classes to defeat the alleged communist threat, which means that the "othering" process was not rooted in ethnic differences but rather on ideological terms. As past studies have shown, the internal enemy myth also loosely conflated Catholic and cooperative groups with "bands of delinquents" robbing and burning peasants' subsistence crops and raping their wives—and thus equating Maya women with property.

In El Quiché, the military made systematic efforts to convince peasants to join the patrol system. One such effort was to identify the local population's experience of rural poverty with high-ranking officers. For example, in 1981 in the township of Joyabaj, General Benedicto Lucas García, chief of the army general staff, told patrols that he understood peasants' poverty. He himself came from a rural background, and he commented that "the man with a straw hat is loyal and honest. He does not lie and is used to behaving truthfully."[53]

The army misrepresented the origins of violence arriving from outside village borders, leading patrols to attack Catholic or peasants' groups actively supporting the rebels in the Chupol area or those families in their own communities suspected of individual participation in revolutionary groups. By portraying the war's events "upside down," illiterate peasants were made to feel beholden to the army, the institution with which they were most familiar in their capacity as servicemen, conscripts, reserves, military commissioners, and their auxiliaries, and were now promoted to commanding positions, as patrollers and patrol chiefs and commanders.[54]

A Recolonizing Strategy: Civic Action Delivering Provisions

Under extreme systems of coercion and pressure from the military, there were very limited choices for patrols. Yet, unlike Stoll's "caught between two armies" thesis, which strips Maya peasants of their political and moral agency, white communities—from a position of powerlessness—naïvely sought to negotiate with the army to leave them alone. In exchange, they would collaborate with the army and accept its civic action projects.[55]

Civic action was brought to Guatemala and the rest of Latin America in the early 1950s to provide a sort of militaristic "development" to establish the current government as a source of prosperity while fighting real or imagined communists. Also used in Malaysia and in Vietnam, civic action's system of economic rewards and incentives were designed to encourage support for the military. The underlying aim was to co-opt local authorities and leaders by delivering projects, roadwork, health and education campaigns, and improve basic infrastructure with the active participation of the community. By paternalistically providing communities with palliative development, the military aimed to distract them from the fear raised by growing awareness of slaughter and to gain community support for the patrol system allegedly bringing security in the midst of war chaos and bloodshed, betrayals, and complicity among the oppressed.[56]

A health center director, Luis, a military sympathizer, described how S-5 officers delivered projects and patrols executed them:

> What I do remember is that the army would come with several bags of potatoes … with seeds for planting; if you own a small piece of land, potatoes are profitable … When the school was built, it was the patrol officers themselves who got down to work during the day.[57]

Linking aid provided through the 1982 Beans and Bullets counterinsurgency plan to patrol service, Governor Oscar David Méndez Girón of the Sololá Department announced in 1983, "Men are paid in food and commodities for work on roads, schools, or other projects needed in the community."[58] By the army's own admission, the patrols received monetary compensation during the war as they were incorporated into the nation's reserve units as members, showing the army's awareness that to gain peasants' collaboration it needed to exploit their poverty.

Falling Prey to Cold War Militarism

Despite the absence of rebels in white communities, peasants blamed guerrillas for bringing the bloodshed into their communities and sought training and weapons from the very same army that victimized them.[59] "Even if we have to mourn our dead, we will defend Guatemala, our families, and our food," a patrol from El Quiché reported in 1982.[60] General Lucas García indicated that the army was supporting the patrols and that arms were being delivered to ensure "effectiveness."[61] Vicente, former patroller and an S-5 collaborator, describes being galvanized by the alleged menace of terrorist delinquents: "It's not that the military forced us; we organized into civil patrols because the need arose … to protect our communities from the criminals. When we organized civil patrols, the war stopped. If the war continued, where would we be?"[62]

The false perception of security, that it was the mobilization of the patrols that stopped the violence, indicates the success of the army's psychological warfare tactic in shaping a militarized Maya. Whether fearing for their lives or the lives of their family members, compelled by extreme poverty, or benefitting from the extension of the army's power, patrols obeyed military commands. In discussing the role of patrols in protecting their communities, Vicente revealed:

> The patrols were groups of collaborating people, well organized. Without organization, nothing worked to preserve the neighbors' goods ... to provide security, and there's nothing wrong with that. I can be a patrol at my home and organize my children because most of the population asked for it. Why? Because there was a lot of delinquency, that's it, for safety reasons.[63]

In one of the few nationwide studies examining patrols and former patrols who had voluntarily disbanded, the Human Rights Ombudsman Office (PHD) interviewed 10,000 patrollers in 1994, showing that in most cases, patrols had never been in an emergency situation, nor had they confronted the "enemy."[64] It also concluded that groups of patrols had internalized the army's rhetoric of a pervasive threat of delinquents, exposing the overall peasant misperception that patrolling brought security and peace to their communities.[65]

Military Commissioners and Patrols Chiefs: Historical Ties to the Army

By the early 1980s, military commissioners were already rooted in community affairs as spies (*orejas*) providing an important rural intelligence service for the army. Commissioners and their auxiliaries were usually ex-soldiers answerable to the army's' chief of reserves. In many communities, commissioners went far beyond reporting on local political activity as they joined in the state violence, becoming involved in torture, sexual violence, murder, and enforced disappearance.

Commissioners became the Cold War's caciques against everyone "questioning the existing system of indebtedness, of compulsory work as marshals, of unpaid community service, and of authoritarianism and abuse of power."[66] Guerrillas, meanwhile, tried to either co-opt or eliminate the commissioners, the most exposed local members of the military intelligence hierarchy. In historian Matilde González's study of San Bartolomé, Jocotenango, El Quiché, military commissioners were perceived as the real leaders of the village, considered the "moneylenders, the shop and bar owners, the contractors or financial backers who guaranteed the forced or semi-forced recruitment of the people in their villages for seasonal labour on the coffee and cotton farms on the south coast of Guatemala."[67]

The duties of patrol chiefs involved overseeing patrol shifts and providing lists with the names of neighbors accused of being guerrilla members, or "bad people" (*mala gente*). Doroteo, from the Pocohil community, explained, "The heads themselves [gave the orders] that it was [the community's] duty to patrol when they initiated the patrol, it was fifteen people per day."[68] Carol Smith observes, "Once released from direct military service, many recruits become military commissioners in their local areas, paid to assist in further recruitment and the local intelligence gathering."[69] Just how many peasants were "ready to serve" as reserves is difficult to tell, as the army refuses to disclose this type of information, or if it does it is utterly misleading, as shown in the census. For example, according to the 2002 census, there were only 467 members of the armed forces in El Quiché.

Pedro, a military expert in Guatemala, described how the army kept a captive pool of peasants ready to serve the country for any unexpected "emergency":

> At that time, the military commissioners were those who depended on a reserve squad. Because these people … besides recruiting, had as their mission, once the military service of their recruits was over and they had returned to their villages, to keep them somehow under surveillance … so that they could call them back in times of emergency during mobilization.[70]

The patrol system was organized around a military-style hierarchy in which certain types of peasants were included at the expense of others. For example, patrol meetings were closed to outsiders: "When they had their talks, or meetings, they told us: please leave us alone, only the chiefs will discuss," Emilio from Saquillá II recounted.[71] For some patrol groups, proximity to the army also meant expressing an enhanced masculinity. "When the army came, they also became courageous: they were already side by side with the army. They were already 'super machos,' they used to say."[72] The military drew from populations that took the opportunities offered in the context of war to gain prestige and status from their perceived proximity to the military, while shaping their masculinity.

An anonymous former president illustrated this enhanced militaristic masculinity to the CEH in 1999: "This is the first time in the history of Guatemala that the Indigenous feels useful and important before the masters because they were the ones blocking the mobilization of the rebels. And they did it with a rifle in their hands." Highlighting the importance of holding a rifle, he told the story of a patroller who proclaimed, "'Ah! What is important is to carry a rifle, it doesn't matter if we do it on the right or left shoulder.'"[73]

Relying on intelligence reports gathered by local amigo informants, the army identified communities it could trust to provide with arms, usually old rifles, since arming the peasantry was the military's greatest war challenge. Indeed, even in communities whose members the military was most certain would remain loyal, the military gave few and antiquated weapons. The military's deliberate decision to "under-arm" these groups revealed not only the army's deep-seated suspicion of rural communities that, if armed, could turn against it, but also recognition of the power held by the country's majority. The REHMI Report notes the "patrols that were more in tune with the army were given weapons. The delivery of weapons depended on several factors [among them] the background of the communities; a certain level of certainty on the part of the army that the armed communities were not working for the guerrillas; and that the heads of the patrols, or commissioners, would be personally responsible, even with their lives, for the weapons they delivered."[74]

Pascual, a health promoter from Saquillá II, recounted the army's criteria for the provision of arms: "They had squads with .38 guns ... Because they were the army's allies, the military gave the guns to them ... On the other hand, a civilian would not get even a gun."[75] The army also encouraged peasants to procure their own weapons, contributing to the step-by-step process of militarizing everyday life, as rightwing peasants came to glamorize the possession of guns. A witness from Chichi told the CEH about the collection of funds to buy weapons "the army did their talks and people were scared of the arrival of the guerrilla ... but because we did not have arms we collected funds to buy some ... Never did I think they would be used to kill our own people."[76]

General Victor Augusto Vásquez conceded in 1994 that patrols were organized even in areas free of *guerrilleros*. In fact, an interview in Chichicastenango with patrols chiefs by the Robert F. Kennedy Memorial Center for Human Rights also found that patrols had never caught a single thief.[77] Still, in those white or pink communities where the guerrilla threat was not present, persistent PYSOPs campaigns effectively spread rumors of menacing delinquents and heightened feelings of vulnerability.[78] Exemplifying how militarism is a family affair, transmitting values through generations,[79] Maya women were also encouraged to provide intelligence to support patrols. "The woman should help her husband, and she can do this by informing her husband of what she hears in the market so subversion will not return," a senior commanding officer in El Quiché told the press.[80]

As late as December 1993, three years before the signing of the Peace Accords, soldiers entered Chichicastenango and demanded that peasants enlist in patrols. If peasants refused to patrol, they were severely punished and, often, thrown into pits to die. Pascual from Saquillá II recounted how refusing to patrol turned his own friends into enemies:

> I was threatened by acquaintances and friends who belonged to the same community. [But I told them], "Look, I am here working voluntarily with the patrols, because, as far as the patrol is concerned, nobody is forcing me, I am doing it wholeheartedly, and if you do not agree with the way I am doing it, then, I will just quit, and that's the end of it" ... I resigned, and the mob almost beat me up with sticks.[81]

Military rules and collective punishment were not only harshly imposed against disobedient patrols but also brutally extended to women. In Pocohil, a survivor recounted, "It was terrible what happened here, because not only the men were affected by this violence, they also made the women 'disappear' and, later on, they tortured several women ... I remember, the authorities ... the patrolmen flogged them."[82]

Subaltern Resistance to PACs

Showing the cross-community dynamics of resistance to the patrols even in those communities where the patrol system penetrated in the absence of a real guerrilla threat, legal action against the army was initiated in white communities. In Paxot III widows petitioned on behalf of their husbands who were wrongly accused by the army of belonging to rebel groups. Maria Canil Lastor and Micaela Saquic Ajanel brought charges against military authorities that their husbands, Antonio Marroquín Cuin and Manuel Marroquín Bernal, respectively, had been falsely accused of being guerrillas and unjustly arrested by the patrols of Paxot III on 10 June 1983.

Ironically, the two women publicly denounced the harassment to General José Efraín Ríos Montt, the very same general who had ordered the bloodshed, and bravely requested an investigation of their hamlet's patrol chiefs.[83] About a decade later, on 12 March 1992, Pedro Marroquín, Sebastián Marroquín, and Miguel Cuin Marroquín, also from Paxot III and who may have been relatives of the above victims, filed a complaint with the PDH (the Human Rights Ombudsman Office) in Santa Cruz, El Quiché, against former civil patrols as well as past and present military commissioners from their community for accusing them of being guerrillas and threatening to murder them.[84]

The Reenactment of Colonial Brutality

On this side of Chichicastenango, violence began with the patrol system. Without rebels effectively challenging its dominance, why did the army sanction massacres against its own supporters? While past studies claim that the military only attacked communities typified as pro-rebel, or "red," villages, the army also assaulted its own allies.[85] Rape, mutilation, torture, murder, massacres, beatings, arson, looting, abduction, forced disappearance, enslavement, and internment were the war's trademarks, even in white and pink communities.[86] However, in this type of community "more selective killings and torture were carried out, sometimes without the destruction of crops or buildings."[87]

As the REHMI notes, "Although the massacres will never be fully explained, the army offensive, the progression of massacres, and their internal structure, obeyed a certain logic … They were not merely a spontaneous reaction."[88] Out of twenty-one total massacres committed in Chichicastenango, only two were reported by witnesses to the CEH from the cluster of northwestern communities: Chijtinimit and Mactzul II.[89] Even though the army identified these white communities as its allies, it sanctioned patrol-on-patrol attacks.

The Chijtinimit and Mactzul II Massacres

Testimonies provided to the CEH report that regular state soldiers, military commissioners, and patrols from the six Mactzules went to the village of Mactzul II on 10 August 1982. There, they tortured a group of approximately thirty local patrollers.[90] On the next day, they blindfolded their victims and transferred them to a nearby ravine, where they were executed. Weeping, the village's women asked why their husbands were so viciously tortured. The attackers—their own neighbors—coldly responded that they were purging their community of delinquents and that the women should go home if they wanted to save their lives. For most, the internal enemy myth was enough to justify the massacre.

One eyewitness told the commission, "I did not have the courage to see them being killed, but many did. I said to myself, if they are guilty, they should go to jail."[91] Though most crimes committed by soldiers and patrollers in the area of Mactzul were underreported to the CEH, their traces are found in the log of the municipal firefighters. Between 1981 and 1983, thirteen bodies, showing bruises, machete cuts, and gunshot wounds, were recovered. Most victims belonged to Mactzul II.

A second massacre took place on 23 July 1983. Patrollers from the six neighboring villages, relying on their intimate knowledge of the paths between communities, massacred twenty-five peasants in the Chijtinimit community for refusing to enlist in the patrols.[92] By earmarking the non-patrollers as disobedient, the military recast them as the internal enemy. A week later, according to the *New York Times,* another eleven on-duty patrollers suspected of being subversives were killed by other patrols.[93]

These two massacres are not unrelated. Rather, the attacks illustrate a pattern of reenacting colonial atrocities against those who refused to serve the army or were considered traitors. For example, historian John F. Chuchiak IV reports in "Forgotten Allies" that Francisco de Montejo in late 1538 used "brutal methods to procure allies and porters from among the Lenca Indians."[94] As the REHMI asserts, "When the commander's expectations were not met by his subordinates, or when 'specialists' got out of control or knew too much, they were killed."[95]

The public execution of non-patrollers by patrols from nearby communities left an ongoing legacy that affected the capacity of peasant families and communities to self-organize. For many army allies, crossing the threshold into violence was robbing and looting their neighbors' homes and raping their wives. In some cases, surviving women were forced to marry the military commissioners. As Victoria Sanford notes, military commissioners, "used their ill-gotten power to steal the lands of neighbors, rob livestock, extort money, rape women and commit other crimes."[96]

War ties and divided loyalties, mediated by class and ethnic oppression, continued to be encouraged by, for instance, the continuation of the 1877 Chichicastenango Historical Battalion, as shown below. Like in the 1950s, reserves clad in traditional dress, marching and carrying floral arrangements, participated in military celebrations. On 30 June 1996, only six months prior to the end of the war, on National Army Day, the battalion once again proudly marched through the streets of Guatemala City, carrying the automatic weapons acquired for their own ethnic destruction. The seemingly contradictory identities of Maya-K'iché and the Guatemalan military were on dramatic display (Fig. 6.4).

In the years following the war, the plainclothes patrols emerged embodying values such as loyalty, discipline, and heroism—as told by the army. Unlike in the Chupol area, for white communities, a renewed layer of dependency upon the army contributed to silencing the dark past, as illustrated in the lack of eyewitness testimonies provided to the Truth Commission from this area.

Figure 6.4. Army Day. Photo © Vince Heptig, 30 June 1996, Chichicastenango Historical Battalion.

The uniformed patrols' violence left communities tied to the army, with enormous consequences for communities' historical memory and the fostering of social silences. This lasting legacy took place in the context of the Guatemalan Republican Front (FRG) reinforcing the ideological justification of "internal security" for ongoing militarization and militarism, thus silencing dialogue regarding the country's shameful past of human rights crimes.

Notes

1. Though pro-army communities were also located in the western highlands, the army claimed that white villages were located within the country's northeast: Izabal, Jalapa, Chiquimula, and Jutiapa, mostly, except for the Chorti, non-Mayan departments. CIRMA, Infostelle, Signatura 84; CDHG, 13 August 1996. See also Schirmer, *Guatemalan Military Project*, 48.
2. Zbikowski, "Night Guard"; Engelking, "Murdering and Denouncing Jews," 443.
3. McGregor, *History in Uniform*, 111.
4. AHG, Leticia González, "Revueltas Indígenas," 163–76; see also Pollack, *Levantamiento K'iché*, 104–5. I am assuming that this Macsul community corresponds to, at the time of this study in early 2000, one of the six Mactzules.
5. For a history of the garrison, see Ejército de Guatemala, "Mariscal Gregorio Solares."
6. Rivas Vasconcelos also mentions that these green or white communities were located close to urban centers. Rivas Vasconcelos, "La Guerra Fría," 120; see also Schirmer, *Guatemalan Military Project*, 48.
7. "Historia" Feria Departamental de Quiché: Fiestas Elenas.
8. "Historical Batallion." HMP.
9. Ibid.
10. Hokowhitu, "Producing Elite Indigenous Masculinities," 23.
11. Ibid., 30.
12. Nelson, *Finger in the Wound*, Kindle location 3397.
13. My gratitude to Daniele Volpe for taking this picture at the Hemeroteca Nacional.
14. African soldiers conscripted by the French to participate in the repression of the Malagasy revolt in 1947. Ginio, "African Silences," 139.
15. Cojtí Cuxil, *Configuracion del Pensamiento*, 2.29.
16. REHMI, II.162–77.
17. Except in Saquillá, which was accessible by truck.
18. World Bank, *Poverty in Guatemala*, 6.
19. On the other extreme, are the "Ladinized," the most integrated into the larger society. Adams, *Integración Social en Guatemala*, 219, 220.
20. World Bank, *Poverty in Guatemala*, 2.
21. Manz, *Paradise in Ashes*, 37.
22. Hough et al., "Land and Labor in Guatemala," 7.
23. UNICEF, "Chronic Malnutrition."
24. Author interview, Manuel.
25. Ibid.
26. Arias, "El Movimiento Indígena," 86.
27. Wilson, *Maya Resurgence*, 209–10.
28. Lovell, *Beauty That Hurts*, 127.
29. Fanon, *Wretched of the Earth*, 9.

30. Coinciding with Schirmer's studies. Schirmer, *Guatemalan Military Project*, 55.
31. Degregori, *Las Rondas Campesinas*, 24–25.
32. Ibid., 67.
33. Grandin, *Who Is Rigoberta Menchu?* 115, fn13.
34. I am grateful to Daniele Volpe for taking this picture at the Hemeroteca Nacional.
35. Holm, "Militarization of Native America," 472.
36. According to Esteban, a Catholic clergyman/priest, Chichicastenango's tourism grew in the 1970s as a result of the wave of cooperatives that improved the socioeconomic standing of some merchant peasant families I discuss in Chapter Four.
37. Rivera Cusicanqui, *Oprimidos pero no Vencidos*, 19.
38. Malešević, *Sociology of War*, 192.
39. Ibid., 190.
40. Semelin, "Towards a Vocabulary of Massacres," 199.
41. Semelin, *Purify and Destroy*, 16.
42. Malešević, *Sociology of War*, 92.
43. Lemarchand, *Forgotten Genocides*, 42.
44. Schirmer, *Guatemalan Military Project*, 113. See Americas Watch, *Civil Patrols in Guatemala*, 17.
45. Smyth, *Painting the Maya Red*, 2–3.
46. Hinton, *Why Did They Kill?* 29.
47. Semelin, *Purify and Destroy*, 16.
48. Wilson explains how the army utilized the concepts of sin and culpability to construct an imaginary threat (*Maya Resurgence*, 241).
49. Arens, *Genocide in Paraguay*, 31–32.
50. Handy, "Democratizing What?" 52.
51. Löfving, "Silence and the Politics." The "good" or "neutral" Maya adds to a long list of types of Indigenous peoples found in mostly anthropological literature; see Stoll, "Obligatory Indian"; Handy, "Democratizing What?" 52.
52. Ejército de Guatemala, "Plan de Campaña Firmeza 83," 97–98.
53. CIRMA, *El Imparcial*, "Ofensiva Anti-Guerrillera."
54. "Most Kachiquel men served as conscripts in the Guatemalan military." Carey, "Who's Using Whom?" 174.
55. To compare, civic action was ineffective in Ixcán. See Falla, *Massacres in the Jungle*, 42.
56. Ejército de Guatemala, Appendix No. 3, "Plan de Campaña Firmeza 83."
57. Author interview, Luis A.
58. Wright, "Guatemala's Civilian Patrols"; *Prensa Libre* reports that a total of 3,000 bushels of corn, 2,000 bushels of flour, 2,000 bushels of milk, and 2,000 boxes of oil were dispersed by Reserve Commander Waldemar Castellanos. HNG, *Prensa Libre*, "Integrantes de Patrullas," 8.
59. CEH, II.205–8.
60. HNG, *Prensa Libre*, "Más de 40 Muertos," 6.
61. HNG, *Prensa Libre*, "800 Peteneros," 8.
62. Author interview, Vicente.
63. Ibid.
64. PHD, "Actuación de los Patrulleros," 46.
65. The study also found that some 72 percent were less than forty years old and had family responsibilities; about 80 percent were married. PHD, "Actuación de los Patrulleros," 39.
66. González, "Man Who Brought the Danger," 320–21.
67. Ibid, 320.

68. Collective interview, Doroteo.
69. Smith, "Militarization of Civil Society," 11.
70. Author interview, Pedro.
71. Author interview, Emilio.
72. Ibid.
73. CEH, II.190.
74. HNG, *Prensa Libre,* "Campesinos Quieren Armas," 2.
75. Author interview, Pascual.
76. CEH, II.208.
77. Solomon, *Institutional Violence,* 20.
78. Taner Akçam also notes the role of rumors in warning peasants of the impending massacres against Christian minorities during the Armenian genocide (*Shameful Act,* 150).
79. Legree et al., "Military Enlistment and Family Dynamics," 46.
80. Wright, "Guatemala's Civilian Patrols."
81. Author interview, Pascual.
82. Collective interview, Emanuel.
83. HNG, *Prensa Libre,* "Denuncian Abusos," 8.
84. HMP, CERJ Archive.
85. Frank Smyth has suggested that the military only targeted those specific villages that authorities deemed to be supportive, or potentially supportive, of Marxist insurgency (Smyth, *Painting the Maya Red,* 2).
86. For belligerent communities implicated in human rights crimes, see REHMI, II.122. For the killing of patrols against other patrols in Zacualpa, El Quiché, see, for example, CEH, VII, Illustrative Case No. 53, 163–68.
87. Schirmer, *Guatemalan Military Project,* 55.
88. REHMI, 133.
89. CEH, X, Mactzul II (Case 2990) and Chijtinimit (Case 15379), 1076, 1098.
90. Juan Macario Tzoc, Juan Macario Pacajoj, Petronila Salvador, Tomás Macario Salvador, Juan Ordóñez Set, Francisco Ajanel, Tomás Canil.
91. CEH, II.218. Eighteen people, Mactzul.
92. Unlike the Mactzul area, Chijtinimit is located near the urban center.
93. Chavez, "Guatemala Mobilizes."
94. Chuchiak, "Forgotten Allies," 182.
95. REHMI, 132.
96. Sanford, "'Grey Zone' of Justice," 403.

Nationalistic Mythology Revival

Failure to Dismantle the Internal Enemy Myth

If one takes the time to investigate, there have been very few civilian governments throughout history; for the past five hundred years, the mentality has been military-oriented. No wonder many people still show that characteristic. And that's the reason why our grandparents were forced to get haircuts and to behave like military men. We are suddenly behaving, unconsciously under the influence of militarism.

—CEDFOG

Daniel Feierstein and others have noted that genocide does not end with the deaths it causes but, rather, begins with them.[1] Fueling its enduring legacies is a shared military mindset and militaristic culture, a discussion largely absent in genocide studies focusing on Latin America. Regarding post–World War II Germany, Charles S. Maier has argued that failure to disarticulate the Third Reich led collaborators to be reintegrated into the new Cold War state.[2] Frank Biess's study of prisoners of war's (POW's) returning to postwar German society demonstrates that war legacies comprised "the social and emotional context for the postwar confrontation with fascism, war, and genocide," where the thorny issues of national guilt, responsibility, and betrayal took center stage in the minds of Germans.[3]

It is revealing to consider the failed policy of denazification (*Entnazifizierung*)[4] when examining the continuity of the patrol system in the early postwar years (2000–2004) in Chichicastenango. Denazification refers to the long process of removing and disarticulating the cultural symbols of the Nazi regime, judicial prosecution, and war propaganda.[5] Looking at the return of POWs to divided Germany in the wake of World War II, Biess shows that legacies are not easily mastered because they are "multifaceted," assuming "different temporalities that have made it difficult to proclaim an end to the 'postwar' period."[6] In fact, each atrocity and each benchmark, such as the 1996 Peace Accords, has multiple aftermaths.

There are also striking parallels between the failed demilitarization of the patrol system and the unsuccessful purge from power of former Nazi officers and party members.[7] Failure to punish perpetrators led pro-army ex-patrollers and ex-military commissioners to perpetuate the political authority given to them by the military during the peak of the genocide. Over the years, they became their municipal and community representatives: municipal and Indigenous elected officials, auxiliary mayors, and leaders of community-based development projects.[8]

Similarly, in Chile, former collaborators with the General Augusto Pinochet regime remained in positions of authority in their roles as, for example, municipal mayors, as in the case of Cristián Labbé.[9] Second, with an effect similar to that of the 1945 Potsdam Agreement on postwar Germany, the signing of the Peace Agreements between the URNG rebels and the state in 1996 "did not constitute a break with the past."[10] Quite the contrary, the years following the war were characterized by the revival of "internal enemy" ideology that justified the criminalization of human rights groups, while discussions of reconciliation were co-opted by the various administrations, leaving the national security state nearly intact.

Despite official disbanding of patrols, the ties binding groups of ex-patrols and their communities to the army remained largely intact in some sectors of rural areas.[11] This cadre of what I term post-Cold War "subjugated allies" composed of loyalist ex-patrol chiefs and ex-military commissioners refers to those who, by 2000, continued to support the military. They did so by keeping their mutual but unequal relations with the local army outpost, mediated by class and ethnic oppression based on the false belief that the army continued to visit their communities for the welfare of their families and communities.

What was sustaining the ongoing bonds between Maxeño authorities and the postwar military outposts? As before and during the genocide, subjugated allies continued to gain from incentives the army offered them, their families, and their communities. Quite telling of this subjugation is the fact that the highest Maya traditional authority, the Auxiliatura Indígena, also kept its tight ties with the army by their traditional rituals, such as the flying pole (*palo volador*), at army celebrations—though sometimes they refused to do it because the army had not provided them with the right truck to carry the pole.[12]

The resurgence of the ex-patrols in the early aftermath challenges the "extreme fear" theory as the most dominant coercive factor accounting for the 1 million patrollers mobilized during the genocide. Rather, ex-patrols and ex-military commissioners' loyalty can be explained through an examination of three crucial socioeconomic, political, cultural, and ideological pillars that sustained patrol survival and fostered the highly complicated ties binding sectors of Chichicastenango communities to a postwar, entrenched status quo army. These are (1) a system of socioeconomic incentives and rewards given to communities supporting the army; (2) a military, praetorian mindset indifferent to claims of civil control; and (3) co-opted local power structures. Before delving into these pillars sustaining unbroken ties between ex-patrollers and the army, I contextualize the immediate background in which ex-patrols and former military commissioners made claims to the army for their "war services," all the while a renewed militarization was under way.

Renewed Militarization: The Country's "Heroes"

By 2000 the United Nations' Observer Mission in Guatemala (MINUGUA) had systematically recorded the continuity of human rights crimes against the organized sectors of rural areas that had revolted in the late 1970s. In contradictory terms, MINUGUA claimed, "Ex-patrols have not changed their discourse or methods." Simultaneously, however, it argued that "thirteen agreements and more than 300 commitments constituted a broad and comprehensive blueprint for change."[13]

Peace and conflict scholars have faulted the Agreement on the Strengthening of Civilian Power and on the Role of the Armed Forces in a Democratic Society (AFPC) Peace Accords for giving patrollers a mere thirty days to demobilize and excluding them from the Disarmament, Demobilization, and Reintegration (DDR) program, land titles, and other provisions given to demobilize URNG rebels.[14] DDR programs are known to be short-lived security initiatives dealing with demobilized soldiers by providing initial socioeconomic assistance and disarming cantonment sites, particularly used in Africa with mixed results.[15] Despite their goal of keeping initial peace when armed groups' militaristic structures are being disarticulated, these programs fail to address the pervasive nature of militarization and militarism embedded in social practices and military cultures internalized by the oppressed.

Following the dominant narrative, on 24 June 1996, Defense Minister General Julio Balconi misleadingly announced a DDR plan for patrollers by telling reporters that a first phase of *concientización,* which consisted of "explaining to PAC members why civil patrols were no longer necessary; a second phase in disarming the PACs; and a third phase in which patrollers would be presented with the option of remaining organized, for other ends."[16]

The evidence suggests, however, that patrollers were not included in DDR programs, and even if ex-patrols had been included, DDR programs fall short in severing deeply rooted ties between the ex-patrols and the nearest army outpost because civil-Maya relations are bound by deeply unchanged conditions of internal colonialism, rendering the DDR human rights framework used by the UN utterly ill equipped to reckon with the ongoing militarization in the context of a failed "democratic transition." According to DDR scholarship examining former warring groups' demobilization, patrols became the "spoilers," undermining the peace agreements.[17] In the case of the ex-patrols, this view excludes the larger context in which these demobilized militias have been pressured to maintain unbroken ties with the military to this day.

Demanding Wartime Payment

By 2000, against a broader postwar context of sustained state-sponsored militarization and ongoing economic pressures, it is important to highlight what sociologist Carlos Figueroa Ibarra calls the army's "recovery of 'lost political terrain' ... by reiterating its nationalistic ideology, reminding peasants that their families' security and development depended on their support to [José Efraín] Ríos Montt."[18] In years following the Peace Accords, President-elect Alfonso Portillo called the ex-patrols "the country's heroes" when asked about payment for their wartime service.[19] To encourage this view, the army continued to portray itself as an army of peace and the protagonists of a new school of thought. In the eyes of those communities that had been heavily targeted by PSYOPs and civic action programs, the military's rebirth meant "peace and progress," as top Ladino politicians advocated the reestablishment of the PAC system.

Already in 1997, ex-militiamen from El Petén Department were demanding payments and in-kind benefits, such as land and housing, for their war services, not only for themselves but also for the widows and orphans of the patrollers killed during the war. According to a study funded by USAID, there were some 12,836 widows and, specifically in El Quiché, 3,847, the highest number of the country's twenty-two departments.[20] In August 1996, Rosalina Tuyuc, human rights activist of the Coordination of Widows of Guatemala (CONAVIGUA) and legislator for the New Guatemala Democratic Front (FDNG), denounced the army for organizing the wives of ex-military commissioners in the Ixil region. Tuyuc warned, "These women still have a counterinsurgency mentality," which in her eyes, "was no longer valid."[21]

By 2002, over 70,000 ex-patrollers had, with the support of the Association of Guatemalan Military Veterans (AVEMILGUA), reorganized into twelve departments demanding war compensation.[22] While not officially recognized as war veterans by the state, ex-militiamen and their families blocked highways and occupied oil refineries in Petén and threatened to reactivate their militaristic structures if the FRG administration did not respond to their demands.[23] Responding to their mobilization, police forces were sent to break up protests, on one occasion killing an ex-patroller, José Interiano Lopez, in the department of Izabal.[24] CERJ (Rujunel Junam Council of Ethnic Communities "We Are All Equal") leaders advocating a meaningful demilitarization of the PAC system accused the state of betraying the patrols by abandoning them once they had been mobilized against their own neighbors.[25]

By May 2003, more than 160,000 ex-patrollers had received U.S.$221 (Q1,747), the first of three payments.[26] Beginning in 2005, reenacting their subordination to the army, ex-patrols were required to reforest land to justify these payments through a program known as the Árboles de Paz (Trees of Peace). Human rights groups, such as the Mutual Support Group (GAM), CERJ, and the Myrna Mack and the Rigoberta Menchú Foundations, contested the payment. To a large extent, this demand to plant trees reiterated the conquistadores' response to their "amigos": ignoring their demands for compensation for participating in Spanish military campaigns as they became, in the words of historian John F. Chuchiak, the "forgotten allies."[27]

A System of Incentives: Civil Affairs Division S-5

Conditions of internal colonialism continued to pressure ex-patrols and ex-military commissioners to pledge their loyalty to the army. In Chichicastenango, by 2001, of 3,625 schoolchildren examined in 2001, 72.5 percent were found to be impacted by malnutrition. That same year, some 44.0 percent of children under five were stunted and 60.2 percent of children between six and nine years were physically underdeveloped.[28] By 2004, 38.0 percent of the rural population survived on less than one dollar a day.[29]

As during the war and genocide, the army's Civil Affairs Division, or (S-5), continued to exploit communities' pervasive conditions of internal colonialism by bringing palliative poverty aid to families, thereby gaining the support of former patrols for the army's internal security mission. Meanwhile, a sea of potential conscripts and enlistees were encouraged to see military service as a viable escape from their poverty.

As Father Andrés, from the El Quiché Archdiocese, once told me, "I have seen that even after the patrols were [formally] disbanded, [the army] still gathers people together. They still have patrols in Saquillá I." He further mentioned the military exercises taking place every weekend in open air at the Tzocoma stadium, "There are former military commissioners, reserves and some demobilized patrols who continued to assemble every Sunday morning with the S-5."[30] The army kept providing in-kind and concrete provisions as part of the S-5 public relations campaign linked to the lingering rhetoric of facilitating larger infrastructure projects such as the much-needed road improvements to remote communities.

What did the ex-patrols gain from their continuous loyalty to the army in the early aftermath? When asked about the type of army-led projects his community received, a representative of the Betterment Committee in Saquillá I, Pablo, replied, "The army once repaired our roads ... It also seems that they once went to a nearby community and they helped putting out a fire in a forest … that is the support that the military has given to our communities."[31]

For "white" communities suffering a precarious existence, the repair of roads connecting them to the nearest town was perceived as substantial progress. The unpaved roads were often washed out during the rainy season, making commutes of short distances difficult and time consuming.[32] The army's Corps of Engineers continued to bring similar projects to communities, filling in potholes and bolstering the image of the army in otherwise forgotten or neglected communities (Chapter Three). In Chunimá, in the east, Carlota McAllister also reports the delivery of economic assistance and a literacy project by the army through the local Improvement Committee.[33]

An army intelligence collaborator, Salvador, justified the army's postwar involvement in communities: "The state, through the Ministry of Education and, in turn, through their district representatives, does not have the financial resources to pay a bricklayer to build a wall. They [the teachers] would have to foot the bill, but they do not do it because their salaries are extremely low."[34] Ultimately, the perception of S-5 as "agents of change" remained deeply entrenched in communities seeking military assistance for the much-needed socioeconomic services and projects. Salvador showed awareness that the army was seen in a negative light, but, nonetheless, he expressed confidence that this situation could be reversed. In fact, by his own admission, the civil affairs unit was there to revert the army's negative image through the delivery of civic action projects.

The postwar army continued to reinforce the idea that the patrol system had left peasants with important life lessons. Pablo, from Saquillá, reminisced about army-led development projects, given the military's broad expertise in rural economy: "Yes, because the army can give us training as bakers … because before the violence, when the PACs had not yet been organized, we lacked projects. But as soon as the patrols were organized, we obtained many things, roads, bridges, schools."[35]

Education and Poverty Aid Programs: Buying Loyalties

Soon after the war ended, the army continued to reward the support of former patrollers and their families with material and social rewards for embracing military culture and values.[36] In-kind and palliative poverty aid programs normalized the army's ongoing presence in the war's wake. Repeatedly, former patrollers expressed their appreciation for the system of rewards the military provided them. Rigoberto, from Patzibal, where the patrol system lasted twelve years, explains that enlistment and military service gave him an education:

The military helps you study from first to sixth grade. By fulfilling your duty as a citizen, you get an occupation, which you did not have. More than anything else, education and respect for people. You will find that some people, who do not belong to the military anymore, think differently, but that is personal. In my case, and for the majority, it is because of [the military] that I started working, I can speak Spanish and I also learned other Indigenous languages.[37]

Rigoberto concluded our interview by proudly admitting that his community was quite open to receiving help from the army: "What the community wants is help from the military. In that case, Military Zone No. 20 is approached and it provides for the transportation of construction materials for the community. Above all, it provides security."[38] Rigoberto's remarks took place in the context of President Portillo's call for the reconversion from old intelligence structures to give "security to people," proclaimed during Army Day celebrations.[39] But not only were ex-PACs co-opted by political campaigns, they were also used as security agents and offered compensation. In the central park of Cobán, Alta Verapaz, for example, ex-patrollers "were offer[ed] jobs with good salary and all benefits ... Many former PACs accepted because there is much poverty."[40]

In Exchange for Votes: Building Rightwing Platforms

Peace scholar Marek Thee argues that the phenomenon of ongoing militarism "needs to be defined in clear socio-political terms," a view that helps elucidate the importance of the intimate link between the country's internal colonial situation and the renewal of the militia system.[41] For many observers, the resurgence of the patrol system in areas later controlled by the FRG was not at all happenstance. Rather, the history of mutual support between the military and sectors of ex-patrols was highly effective in corralling votes for FRG candidates. For Rosalina Tuyuc, those who sided with the army were "the opportunists," who exploited their ties with the army for their own selfish benefits. Exchanging votes for material benefits during election campaigns continued relentlessly and the FRG was able to win more than 70 percent of all the municipalities in El Quiché in 2000, allowing General Ríos Montt to become president of the congress in 2001 and then run for reelection in 2002.[42]

In his study of ex-patrols in Sacatepéquez, Suchitepéquez, and Petén, sociologist Ricardo Sáenz Tejeda states, "By 2001 the ex-PAC comprised a political force of some 500 thousand to one million people, in addition to their wives and eldest sons exploited by the FRG to corral votes who guarantee[d] the triumph of the party."[43] During his presidential campaign, Portillo promised the delivery of economic incentives to his electoral constituency. At the community level, Lucrecia, a leader from an eastern community and member of the widows' movement CONAVIGUA, bitterly complained, "The mayor of

Chichicastenango says that the government sent fertilizers that were distributed within the *cantones* that voted for the FRG."[44] The delivery of poverty aid projects in exchange for peasants' votes closely mimics the military's paternalistic educational projects provided to supportive communities in the early 1980s.

In 1997, Defensoría Maya, a nationwide human rights group promoting the rights of Indigenous peoples, denounced rightwing political parties for only reaching out to villages every four years when corralling votes. Parties showed no interest in communities' processes of authority selection nor whether these processes had been selected or imposed. Decrying the complicit collaboration of the Chichicastenango Auxiliatura Indígena with political parties corralling votes, Defensoría Maya observed, "Every four years, political parties come with promises, but they fail to facilitate the participation of communities to select their genuine, legitimate and representative authorities."[45]

In July 2000, during a trip when I accompanied an S-5 officer to plant trees (Chapter Three), Roberto, a representative of the National Forestry Institute (INAB), explained the importance of literacy programs in empowering peasants, and urged them to vote for the FRG: "The army, along with other institutions, support[ed] the literacy of people, both morally and intellectually, so they [peasants] can read and write, so they can be a little bit more understanding."[46] Yet, by supporting the military, loyalist amigos continued to perceive the patrol-like structure as a way out of the day-to-day uncertainty of poverty and a way to gain security for their families and communities. As a result, through a system that rewarded collaboration, one more element in shaping the aftermath of violence was maintained: a military mindset that had been coercively shaped and adopted by the poorest communities. The army's local power base was cemented, instead of disarticulated.

A Prevailing Militarized Mindset: Talks and Gratitude

Genocide ideologies prevail and provide further justification for human rights crimes in post-conflict settings and how the oppressed participate in their reproduction. In Africa, René Lemarchand and Maurice Niwese have suggested that efforts for rebuilding war-torn communities must consider how "belief systems are in part shaped by history, and history in turn is inextricably bounded with claims of memory."[47] As Fanon claims about the colonized becoming "a complete replica of the white man," loyalist ex-patrols and ex-military commissioners and their families mimicked their oppressors.[48] Peasants carried with them the army's racist discourse, telling them to be respectful of the law. Ex-patrols' minds were imbued with a one-sided, militaristic worldview that enabled them to impose a regime of death threats. This militarism of the mind, defined by values and ideas about the aggressiveness of human nature and so-cial relationships, was driven by "the disposition to use organized violence."[49]

Aiding in the fueling of this particular mindset was the army's public recog-nition of patrols' duties. For example, on 8 December 1996, at the moment of the official disarmament, some 839 patrollers were decorated for services ren-dered during the war, ranging from dying in combat to "acts above and beyond the call of duty."[50] In turn, demobilized patrols also thanked the army. "For having protected our lives, our families, our material possessions, our traditions and customs," said a leader from Todos Santos Cuchumatan, Huehuetenango on the army's national day. He ended by sending a message of strength and unity to the "big family made up of civil patrols."[51] In this context, the mythical view of the army as "provider and custodian" was perpetuated, as ex-patrollers could now share in the pride of being on the side of the war's winners.

In the unsettled years immediately after the Peace Accords, an authoritar-ian mindset prevailed among groups of ex-militiamen.[52] As the Truth Com-mission unequivocally concluded, "Authoritarianism has taken over the minds and social structures in the city and in the countryside."[53] Explaining this view, Amilcar Méndez Urízar noted, "In the case of Chichicastenango, the army suc-cessfully changed people's mentality," instilling a war mindset and practices that continue to varying degrees, to this day.[54] Other observers noted, "The apparent end of ideological war has not banished many of the structures and the people mobilized to fight this war … cannot be assumed away."[55] In white communities, long years of service in state security forces guarding their fam-ilies against the internal enemy substituted "service to the community" with "service to the army."[56] The latter involves a "military adjustment process" by which the civilian identity "must be inhibited, if not destroyed."[57]

Central to this process of "adjustment" is the depersonalization of ethnic ties through the army's use of "Mayanism" to produce an ethnicity resulting in an alternative identity, imbued with a set of authoritarian beliefs and values. Far from breaking ties, the army's "heroic memories" were concretized into the mindset of ex-patrols and ex-military commissioners who successfully im-posed a top-down vision of internal security and development upon the rest of the community. Contrary to Jennifer Schirmer's claim that the "good Maya" was "deprived of memory" during the genocide,[58] the "good" peasants' collec-tive memory within sectors of Chichicastenango pro-army groups was infused with the army's own heroic memory, displacing the memory of oppression and creating a people bereft "above all of agency in their own affairs."[59]

Orientation Talks by the Army in Communities

Fostering the dramatic revival of militarism were the army's "orientation talks," which preserved the Cold War notion of the internal enemy menacing communities' safety. These talks were a central piece in the military's patriarchal indoctrination of military values: loyalty, uncritical obedience, and camaraderie. As in the past, visits were aimed at surveillance of communities' level of subordination. Although Pablo acknowledged that soldiers had not recently brought tangible projects to his community, he discussed the narrowness of neighborhood orientation in 2000: "Just the four representatives, and they are the ones in charge of passing the information down to the rest of us."[60]

Fueling a militaristic mindset were civil affairs specialists' visits to communities to set agendas and to make sure information was controlled. The stated aim of these continuous visits was to "get feedback from the community"; the reality was to remind them of who was actually in control of their social organization: local representatives acting at the behest of the army. Pablo also described the process the nearest outpost used to liaise with his community in 2000: "Every fifteen days [the army] come[s] to give talks. Our neighbors say that the army gives orientation regarding people, educating a person not to steal, not to kill, that's all … not to do abusive things, not to transgress the law, but to respect the law."[61]

Loyalist ex-patrols repeatedly expressed gratitude to the army for having instilled them with discipline and respect, showing how the oppressed internalizes the myth that their own psychopathological "deficiencies" can only be corrected by the army's patriarchal role and rigid discipline. Vicente, a former patroller and an S-5 collaborator and a staff of the municipal board, proudly told me, "What [the army] has left me is discipline, basically discipline, because in the military they teach you to respect those who are older than you, younger than you, and women. They teach you to greet everyone as they deserve. I respect everyone … that is what the army has left me."[62] Considering that the state and its security forces, including PACs, committed acts of genocide, the ongoing admiration of Maxeños for the army is both troubling and paradoxical.

In a collective interview of human rights groups mobilized in Chupol and Chuguexa II B in 1999, Jeronimo insisted that ties with the military had remained intact within Western communities: "In the area of Saquillá, ex-military commissioners do not even hide. They work in broad daylight because they have the support of the larger community."[63] A survivor of the genocide explained to Victoria Sanford that in the war's aftermath, "those who were the civil patrol chiefs continued to order us around and are always on the side of the military."[64]

From the military's viewpoint, the community had to be subordinated to ex-militiamen, neighbors now in positions of authority, to preserve the same type of behavior embedded with militarized notions of masculinity. Richard Wilson suggests that the hypermasculinization achieved by military training of young Maya men may be "designed to inculcate the state's regulatory norms and values."[65] Masculinity and discipline in which war patrols were trained reenacted war myths in the war's wake, telling poor peasants that their service was paramount to saving Guatemala from the "evil of communism," as told by the army to mobilize peasants into the patrol system.

These myths continued to be internalized by Vicente: "Personally I will never stop being a military man, I will always have respect and discipline … I will not militarize my children, but they have to learn the good ways of the army, which are many."[66] Vicente's pride for his military service included the sacrifices he felt were not recognized by his community. Even so, he shared his experiences with his children, encouraging them to admire his military training: "Thank God, I am very happy … I tell my children my stories, the adventures we had, having to bear cold weather, feel hunger, sleep under a tree, eat seeds."[67]

Samuel, an authority from the Patzibal community told me "When the army comes "people welcome them with *tamalitos* [typical food], beans, rice, because the military means security for the community. People feel safe."[68] According to Samuel, the army was perceived as a supreme guardian: "I believe people respect the army. The military comes and the meeting begins, all the people are seated quietly."[69] This deference for the offer of alleged security and order in the community illustrates the militarized internal colonial order perpetuated by ex-militiamen and expressed in the discipline of the subjugated allies.

Those who held a militaristic ideology shared a common set of misinformation about the army's role in the bloodshed. In this detailed account, Eusebio, from the community of Pocohil, explained the mentality of a neighbor, a former patrol chief, who according to his own assessment, ended up supporting the military's nationalist politics:

> [This neighbor] only thinks about violence. Yesterday, he told me, "I hope that the FRG will win [the 1999 elections so they can] kill the youth."
>
> "What do you think about killings?" I asked him.
>
> "Ah!" he responded, "Because last time the FRG did a good job, [it] took out all the 'suspected hardened criminals' [*manchados*]. I hope it will win to kill a lot of [delinquent] youth."[70]

This militaristic mindset is most eloquently expressed in the words of Rigoberto, the president of the Friends of the Army's Association: "See in my spirit, I feel I am in uniform, the uniform is not worth [anything] to me, what counts is the spirit because if I have a bad spirit, what good would the uniform be?"[71] At the time of the interview, the association was composed of 250 members who in turn liaised with authorities to inform them of their work and the aid they were receiving from the army.

Admiration for the Army: Identifying with the Oppressors

In *Black Skin, White Masks*, Fanon explains the psychology of colonialism and racism as a paradox entailing the internalization by the oppressed of their oppressor's values: the more the colonized assimilates his oppressor's cultural values, the more he would feel the urge to move away from his own culture.[72] This socialization, which Fanon calls "epidermalization," provokes an inferiority complex among the colonized, leading to the destruction and the death of Indigenous culture.

Similarly, the more former patrols identified with the army's culture of discipline and due obedience, the more they felt compelled and proud to pledge their loyalty. Fanon demonstrates that the colonial situation impacts the production of consciousness, as the colonized and the colonizer influence each other's identities.[73] "How could [they] hate the colonizers and yet admire them so passionately?" Memmi has asked.[74]

Families from the poorest communities were trapped in the web of militarism, with their authorities buying into the continuation of the army's genocidal propaganda machine distorting the true origins of the violence. In the process, the amigos betrayed the mission the community assigned to them: to foster solidarity links, respect for ancestral lands. Vicente, from the municipal board, told me, "Efraín Ríos Montt is a man who has fought for Guatemala. I know he's a real man, he is the image of Guatemala."[75] During one of my visits to the military base, a S-5 collaborator, Salvador, added, "Ríos Montt quieted things down."[76] David Stoll also reports on Ríos Montt followers in the early 1990s, who had told him about Ríos Montt: "He was a Campesino as a child. He knows what it's like to haul wood."[77] A war morality spoken in peasant terms, tainted with the notion of the internal enemy, remained deeply entrenched within communities that glorified the military as the savior of their poverty-stricken families.

Reluctance to Let Go of the "Tools of War": A Recolonized Masculinity

Kimberly Theidon asserts that masculinity is an essential component of militarism, linked to weapons and violence and to feelings of superiority, status, prestige, and the power imparted by actually carrying a rifle.[78] Ex-patrollers' reluctance to let go of weapons demonstrates the power of these feelings. During the Colotenango disarmament in Huehuetenango, ex-patroller Ismael Felix Méndez acknowledged, "We are handing in the rifles that were our best friends and companions."[79] Possessing military-issued weapons continued to give ex-militiamen the impression of safety, for themselves and their families, even though the war was over. In her study of demobilized patrollers in the

Cuchumatán mountains, anthropologist Mitsuho Ikeda reports that patrollers cried when the army called them to give up their weapons:

> Numerous militias and former militias gathered in front of the church to partici-
> pate in the ceremony of the disarmament. The sadness of the veteran militias was
> profound. Even though the town recovered the tranquility after the big white cars
> carrying the United Nations observers were gone, the former militias stayed in the
> streets, in the bars, or in front of the houses of their former commanders. That night
> they did not leave the streets. These were filled with the sobs of drunken men. Some
> drank until they passed out on the sidewalks ... in the cold.[80]

Ex-patrols' tears could have been for losing an important element of military identity, a weapon, but they could also have been weeping because turning in the weapons brought back memories of the conflict and service.

In Chichicastenango, encouraged by the army, some ex-patrols failed to give up their arms. In September 1996, Colonel Otto Noack Sierra, the army's spokesperson, announced that the military was advising the allegedly demo-bilized patrollers that they could legalize their weapons through the army's Department of Arms and Munitions (Dirección General de Control de Armas y Municiones [DIGECAM]). Gerson, a community authority from Saquillá II, proudly announced, "We do [have weapons] ... the community [bought them] from before, when the patrols started."[81]

Military sources themselves have admitted that some 9,000 ex-patrollers from forty-one communities in areas untouched by the war, such as Esquipu-las, Chiquimula, and Sololá, did not return their weapons.[82] In mid-September 1996, in Sololá, during a three-day meeting with demobilized patrollers, Francisco Perez Chu, a former PAC leader, pointed out that he had tried to "convince his former comrades in arms to relinquish their weapons," but they refused to because they were angry that the government had signed the Peace Accords with the rebels—whom the army had told them to kill.[83] Resistance to giving back the "tools of war," as termed by Robert Muggah, was largely en-couraged by the military seeking to convince family and community members and authorities to report to the nearest outpost on any "subversive delinquent" activity in the same manner as it had while the slaughter unfolded throughout El Quiché in the early 1980s.[84]

Colonel Noack Sierra noted that those weapons that did not belong to the army, but had instead been bought by the patrollers themselves, were required to be legally registered by the military. He offered this institutional view of the patrols disarming: "The plan laid out for the patrols is very simple. We are going into the villages and telling them: 'Gentlemen, give us your rifles, please.' We cut off all ties. And that is it."[85]

Noack Sierra's cynical views denote, on the one hand, the army's tight con-trol over the ex-patrols' gun possession and, on the other, how the colonel misleadingly portrayed the presumed easiness with which the army could cut off relations with the reservoir of ex-patrols still obedient to the army's commands. But disarming the patrols from white communities proved to be a difficult task since the ex-patrols' ties with the military were complicated by economic and sociopsychological dynamics encouraging loyalty to the military. In fact, the army itself encouraged and sanctioned the possession of arms.

In 1997, a CERJ leader accused former military commissioner Juan Ixcotoyac and former soldier Julio León, from the community of Parraxut, Sacapulas, of forcing Miguel Lux to sign and seal documents legalizing fifty rifles destined for the reorganization of the patrollers, which shows the provision of arms to ex-patrols with the purpose of rearming the population.[86] As the demobilization process was under way in late 1996, Jeronimo Cutillo Panjoj, a restaurant owner from Chichicastenango, told a reporter, "The majority of the people here say it is good to have patrols to protect their communities ... The robbers are afraid of the patrols."[87]

Local Power Structures: Betterment Committees

Over the years, ex-patrol chiefs and commanders took on positions of village authority and held on to their power base: local structures of governance known variously as betterment, pro-development, or self-improvement committees or those named according to the task at hand, like parents committees and road repair committees, and were biased about what outside institutions could or could not approach them. The failed demilitarization of the army's amigos resulted in a rearranged local power structure, passing on from the war a new cadre of militarized K'iché authorities keeping tight control over community structures.

Militarized committees also provide the organizational structure for the continuous surveillance of their communities, and their authorities became the reincarnation of their oppressors by exhibiting extreme patriotism, a common paradox of the colonized. This reconversion, rather than dismantling Cold War structures, enabled ex-PACs and former military commissioners to reorganize under the façade of civilian associations in many areas controlled by the FRG to escape scrutiny from local and international human rights groups.

When following the Maya tradition, authorities comprised a multilayered system of religious and political responsibilities that include *principales*, auxiliary mayors, and betterment committees, which were communally selected to provide "voluntary service." But selection was dramatically transformed from a community-based consensus into a top-down structure, as the army replaced selection processes with the authority of the war patrols, securing long-term control over local power structures. As observers have noted, "The community mechanisms, the oral transmission of their culture, and the infringement of the Mayan norms of community service were replaced with authoritarianism and the arbitrary use of power."[88]

By 2003, some community-based organizations were subordinated to a newly established, highly hierarchical system of local governance known as local development councils (COCODES), or municipal development councils (COMUDES). "Under the administration of these men," argues González, "civil authority was subordinated to military power," in San Bartolomé Jocotenango, El Quiché.[89] In each community, ex-patrols continued to recolonize local spaces of power. Explaining the perverse role of the rural police in colonies, Memmi suggests that authorities--such as the police –are recruited

> from among the colonized [comprises] a category ... which attempts to escape from its political and social condition. But ... by choosing to place themselves in the colonizer's service to protect his interests exclusively, they end up by adopting his ideology even with regard to their own values and their own lives.[90]

Ex-patrol chiefs and ex-military commissioners continued to reenact their role as co-opted caciques, recalling the conquistadors' co-optation of Indigenous allies (Chapter Two), and to hold on to the power the army provided them in exchange for collaboration as a new layer of settler colonialism settled in.[91] Close contacts between ex-patrollers and military officers reinforced the ambivalent relationship of codependency, bringing much-needed infrastructure to remote villages: education, housing, access to goods, and markets. These highly unequal relations continued to bring social and political status to the army's collaborators, leading to the repression of those organizations seeking to empower survivors' groups because they were seen as a menace to their "privileges."

The military convinced community members that their traditional, informal social networks were suspect and inadequate and that the only legitimate social structures were those like the war's PACs. As General Héctor Gramajo told Schirmer, the army had "brought government to the village,"[92] echoing the practices of settler colonialism, which Jürgen Zimmerer analyzed in his study of the Third Reich's policy.[93] Militarism blocked the possibility of anyone falling outside the military power structure to be selected. Jacinto, a leader from Pajuliboy, a hinterland community from the east, revealed, "There are people who are in permanent contact with the army. They are organized into Emergency Committees. The community does not select them. They are a group of about 30 people. They are ex-patrol leaders."[94]

I asked Emilio, an auxiliary mayor, whether members were paid for their services. He replied, "It's voluntary because we are looking out for our families' needs. So we are watching out for our families, nobody is forcing us."[95] Emilio also commented on the ongoing liaison between El Quiché Army Base No. 20

and former patrollers from Saquillá II: "They have kept their contacts. Perhaps they have their meetings with military commanders, I do not know, maybe with the lieutenant. They know each other, they talk with each other."[96] These emboldened postwar authorities made decisions about which institutions and individuals would be allowed to speak to community members about health or economic projects, creating the space for widespread corruption.

Failed Demilitarization: The Mactzul Area

As the postwar neoliberal economy plunged war-torn communities deeper into unemployment and underemployment,[97] the disbanding of the patrol system failed in areas where the military directly encouraged neighbors to retain their patrol structures. As early as September 1997, a year after the official demobilization of patrols, ex-PACs in the village of Paxot were threatening those who attempted to organize into human rights groups with violent deaths.[98]

The CEH found instances of patrol chiefs resisting the demilitarization of their communities, calling upon high-ranking army personnel to support their efforts.[99] Also in Sololá, some communities opposed the disarmament of the patrol system.[100] In Mactzul II, patrols refused to demobilize despite earlier announcements claiming voluntary disarmament. On 13 January 1995, the day of formal disbanding, patrol commanders from forty-six communities gathered together before government authorities and journalists and refused to deactivate. Along with Defensoría Maya, led at the time by Maya-K'iché Juan León, MINUGUA and army representatives were convened to witness the official disarming of some 140 patrols, according to Rosario Pu, a Peasant Unity Committee (CUC) leader.[101]

Siglo Veintiuno reported that "attempts fail in dissolving patrollers in Mactzul II in a tense context."[102] "Leaders from indigenous organizations announced in the capital that the patrols from Mactzul [II] would not only give up their arms, but that they would also burn them because they did not wish to belong to this type of organization," the newspaper stated. However, despite initial claims of voluntarily destroying their arms, patrollers later announced they would disarm only in the military's presence, demonstrating the subordination of patrols to the army in the Mactzules area.

In 2000, Vicente, with the municipal board, proudly recalled the failed demilitarization of the Mactzules' patrols: "Our people are very humble, they are very cooperative, but if you try to harm them or you have other intentions, they will defend themselves. Our community defends what they have."[103] Vicente merged his class and ethnic identity with a militaristic and paternalistic mentality to construct a salable justification for the failed demobilization in Mactzul II, calling patrols "an example for Chichicastenango" and standing in support of the military.[104] This heroic narrative helped cover up the involvement of the army in, for example, the Mactzul massacre of 10 August 1982, when patrollers, reserves, and state soldiers killed at least a dozen peasants, including young children (Chapter Six).

To varying degrees, the failed demilitarization of Mactzul II is illustrative of the larger condition of military control in western communities. In August 1996, representatives from fifty-five communities met with local authorities to protest their imminent disarmament. "The goal of the protest is not to oppose the peace process," they reportedly claimed. Organized patrollers from El Quiché demanded that the URNG rebels give up their weapons first. Replicating the minister of defense Julio Balconi's claims of rebel attacks targeting local military posts in the township of Joyabaj, Raúl Senté Ventura, a former patrol commander, leading the protest, justified the need to protect themselves and their families because of the "increasing attacks made by ex-rebels."[105]

Denoting the ambivalent relations with the military, refusal to give up arms was contested by the defense minister, General Julio Balconi Turcios, who remarked that he was not disconcerted by such apparent signs of rebellion: "They will turn over the weapons when the day comes for them to do so." And he further added, "We will use no method other than persuasion."[106] In 2000, the military litany of an easy and smooth disarmament was echoed by Doroteo, from the community of Pocohil, who claimed, "When [the patrollers] realized the Peace Agreement had been signed, arms were returned and the disarmament was over."[107]

The URNG provided numbers and names of 3,570 personnel to be demobilized on D-15, 16 February 1997.[108] Showing the tense negotiations between the military and ex-militia men, Senté Ventura defiantly reminded the military that patrols had played a prominent role in defeating the insurgency. Disappointed, he told the press that, unlike former rebels, patrols were not compensated with DDR provisions, land grants, vocational training, or health projects.[109] Senté Ventura's complaint resonated with Colonel Samayoa when I interviewed him in his office in 2000.[110] On this occasion, Samayoa wore the infamous Kaibil parachute symbol and offered similar, bitter comments: "The demobilized URNG rebels have been given provisions to disarm; it seems to be a good thing to be a rebel and to be against the government, it brings rewards."[111]

But empirical evidence shows otherwise. Only a year after the 1996 Peace Accords, ex-patrollers made political demands of the FRG regarding disarmament. They claimed that their communities had been abandoned by the central government and requested that the then municipal mayor, Walter Eulogio Alvarado López, provide security for their families. Ex-patrollers threatened to rearm with machetes and clubs and to use violence if their conditions were not met. In their eyes, giving up their weapons had left their remote communities vulnerable to ordinary crime and delinquency, despite the fact that, by

2000, El Quiché showed fewer homicides than other postwar regions but more lynchings (Chapter Nine). Instead of discouraging ex-patrols from rearming and offering locals other means of social support, Mayor Alvarado López pressured former patrollers to regroup for the security of their communities and to make their voices heard. In fact, "the mayor expressed that he did not have the resources to provide for security and therefore it was best that ex-patrols continue to organize themselves as they had done so far."[112] The view that postwar patrolling was a central part of providing security and order in the countryside was also expressed by ex-patrols in Ikeda's study. She recounts:

> Some months after [the Peace Accords], the people expressed their discontent: it seems that the town council did not control the violent events and disputes between drunken neighbors in communities. Even though no open opinions were given that called for the resurgence of the patrol system, some kept a positive image of the system, fondly remembering better times when the patrols kept order in their communities.[113]

In fact, "keeping order" in their communities was used as justification by ex-patrollers. Expressing pride in saving Guatemala from communism, "We have beaten the guerrillas in the war," remarked ex-patrol chief Víctor García from Playa Grande, Ixcán, El Quiché.[114] Yet, while admitting that ex-patrollers still policed their communities after the war, García hoped they would not have to fight anymore. Nevertheless, setting up checkpoints along highways in Huehuetenango, Chimaltenango, and El Quiché in January 1997 in an attempt to combat the rising level of "common delinquency" was not the only sign of enduring militarization in the wake of the war.[115] The far-reaching legacies of militarization and militarism had further concrete and symbolic repercussions, which I discuss in the following chapter.

Notes

1. Feierstein, "Leaving the Parental Home," 262.
2. Maier, *Unmasterable Past.*
3. Biess, *Homecomings,* 46.
4. See, for example, Thacker, *End of the Third Reich.*
5. For the long process of attempts to remove and dismantle the cultural symbols of the Nazi regime, judicial prosecution, and war propaganda, see Maier, *Unmasterable Past;* Frei, *Adenauer's Germany;* and Thacker, *End of the Third Reich.*
6. Biess, *Homecomings,* 1.
7. Hilberg, *Perpetrators, Victims, Bystanders,* 28, 65–74, particularly.
8. Peacock and Beltran, "Hidden Powers," 28. See also MINUGUA, "Status of the Commitments."
9. Taylor and Hall, "Chilean Accused of Murder."

10. Biess, *Homecomings*, 43.
11. According to MINUGUA, "Contacts have continued between former CVDC [as patrollers were renamed] members and both active-service and retired military officers" ("Status of the Commitments," 9).
12. The *palo volador* is a dance linked to pre-Hispanic origins, organized by the *cofradía.* Rojas Lima, "La Cofradía Indígena," 268.
13. MINUGUA, "Thirteenth Report."
14. DDR programs aim to recover military-style weapons, offer initial economic assistance to ex-combatants, and facilitate their reentry as productive citizens into their communities. Gomes Porto, Alden, and Parsons, *From Soldiers to Citizens;* the demobilization, sponsored by USAID among others, cost U.S.$85,272,000. Hauge and Thoresen, *El Destino de los Ex-Combatientes.*
15. For a critical appraisal, see Muggah, "No Magic Bullet."
16. CIRMA, Infostelle, Signatura 84, CDHG, "Demobilization of PACs"; see also, Popkin, *Civil Patrols and Their Legacy,* v.
17. Stedman, "Spoiler Problems in Peace Processes," 7.
18. Figueroa Ibarra, "Militarización, Crimen y Poder."
19. HNG, *Prensa Libre,* "Portillo: Ex-PAC Son Unos Héroes," 5.
20. CIEN, "Informe sobre el Aportes," 9.
21. CIRMA, Infostelle, Signatura 83, CERIGUA, "Despite Demobilization."
22. Peacock and Beltran, "Hidden Powers in Post-Conflict Guatemala," 45.
23. See reports by MINUGUA; Amnesty International, "Civil Defense Patrols Re-Emerge."
24. HNG, *Siglo Veintiuno,* Jimenez, "Un Muerto en Desalojo," 2.
25. CIRMA, Infostelle, Signatura 83, CERJ, "Los Ex-Patrulleros Están Abandonados."
26. "Historical Exchange Rates," OANDA.com. Initially, organized ex-patrols had asked for a total of U.S.$2,531, but under Portillo's years, a final payment of some U.S.$600 was eventually promised to the ex-patrols (after ex-patrols refused to accept an initial Q12 per month) and dispensed by various administrations. Decree 28-04 legalized the "aporte pecuniario" to ex-PACs.
27. See the episode of Pedro Xochimilco and Miguel Damian asking for justice after helping in the conquest in Chuchiak, "Forgotten Allies," 175.
28. World Bank, *Poverty in Guatemala,* 3; SEGEPLAN, "Caracterización del Municipio."
29. PNUD, "Diversidad Etnico-Cultural."
30. Author interview, Father Andrés.
31. Author interview, Pablo.
32. SEGEPLAN, "Caracterización del Municipio."
33. CIRMA, CGD, McAllister, "Chupol," 9.
34. Author interview, Salvador.
35. Author interview, Pablo.
36. REHMI, I.118.
37. Author interview, Rigoberto.
38. Ibid.
39. *El Periódico,* "Ejército a Reforzar Seguridad Interna," 2.
40. "Del Reino de las Armas," Semana.com.
41. Thee, "Militarism and Militarization," 18.
42. Rodas Núñez, "La Nación, la Fabricación."
43. Sáenz de Tejeda, *Victimas o Vencedores?* 17.
44. Author interview, Lucrecia.
45. Defensoría Maya, "Los Verdaderos Enemigos de la Vida y la Paz en Guatemala."
46. Author interview, Roberto.

47. Lemarchand and Niwese, "Mass Murder," 165.
48. Fanon, *Black Skin, White Masks,* 19.
49. Ross, "Dimensions of Militarization," 564; Wendt and Barnett, "Dependent State Formation," 324.
50. CIRMA, Infostelle, Signatura 83, CERIGUA, "PACs Refuse to Disarm."
51. CIRMA, Infostelle, Signatura 84, CDHG, "Discurso Leído por Modesto."
52. Peace and conflict studies focusing particularly on Africa that examine the demilitarization of militiamen have noted the failure to break the strong bonds forged between the army and their collaborators during the war. See, for example, Berdal and Ucko, *Reintegrating Armed Conflict.*
53. CEH, IV.86.
54. Author interview, Méndez.
55. Keen, "Demobilising Guatemala," 2.
56. Macleod and Xiloj Tol, "Justicia, Dignidad y Derechos Colectivos."
57. Hollingshead, "Human Behavior in Military Society," 442.
58. Schirmer, *Guatemalan Military Project,* 103, 113–17.
59. Maybury-Lewis, *Politics of Ethnicity,* xvi.
60. Author interview, Pablo.
61. Author interview, Pablo.
62. Author interview, Vicente.
63. Collective interview, The Mutual Support Group, GAM.
64. Sanford, Buried Secrets, 119; As a woman peasant from San Bartolomé Jocotenango told anthropologist Matilde González, "These groups were the same thing, the same *babosada* under a different name." González, "Ejercicio y Formas de Representación" 17.
65. Wilson, *Maya Resurgence,* 253.
66. Author interview, Vicente.
67. Ibid.
68. Collective interview, Patzibal Betterment Committee.
69. Samuel, Patzibal Authority.
70. Collective interview, Eusebio.
71. Author interview, Rigoberto.
72. Fanon, *Black Skin, White Masks.*
73. On Huehuetenango, see Kobrak, *Huehuetenango;* on the Ixil Area, see Stoll, *Between Two Armies;* and on San Bartolomé Jocotenango in El Quiché, see González, "Man Who Brought the Danger."
74. Memmi, *Colonizer and the Colonized,* x.
75. Author interview, Vicente.
76. Author interview, Salvador.
77. Stoll, *Between Two Armies,* 219.
78. Theidon, "Reconstructing Masculinities."
79. CIRMA, Infostelle, Signatura 84, CERIGUA, "PACs Disarm, with No Remorse."
80. Ikeda, "Reflexiones sobre la Violencia," 193.
81. Author interview, Gerson.
82. CIRMA, Infostelle, Signatura 83, "Violaciones al Derecho."
83. CIRMA, Infostelle, Signatura 83, "Rural Communities Fear Peace."
84. Muggah, "Emerging from the Shadow"; it is worth noting that in thirty Ixcan communities in El Quiché, *campesinos* symbolically gave back their arms to MINUGUA and not to the army since they felt that the army should not be responsible for disarming them. CIRMA, Infostelle, Signatura 83, "PAC en 30 Comunidades."

85. CIRMA, Infostelle, Signatura 83, "Marching toward Peace."
86. CIRMA, Infostelle, Signatura 83, CDHG, "CERJ Pide a MINUGUA."
87. CIRMA, Infostelle, Signatura 83, "Marching toward Peace."
88. Associaió d'Amistat, *Guatemala: A Grandes Trazos*, 7.
89. González, "Ejercicio Y Formas De Representación Del Poder " 16-19, particularly.
90. Memmi, *Colonizer and the Colonized*, 16.
91. Patrick Wolfe has asserted, "Settler colonialism destroys to replace" ("Settler Colonialism," 388).
92. Schirmer, *Guatemalan Military Project*, 63.
93. That contributed to the "complete reorganization of the economy, politics and demography of those territories" occupied in the east. Zimmerer, "Birth of Ostland," 101.
94. APA interview, Jacinto.
95. Author interview, Emilio.
96. Author interview, Emilio.
97. Kurtenbach, "Guatemala's Post-War Development."
98. Amnesty International, "Civil Defense Patrols Re-Emerge," 9.
99. CEH, VII.196.
100. HNG, *Prensa Libre*, "Aldea de Sololá es Inexpugnable."
101. CIRMA, Infostelle, Signatura 84, CDHG, "Frustrada Entrega de Armas."
102. HNG, *Siglo Veintiuno*, "Fracasa Intento"; CIRMA, Infostelle, Signatura 84, PBI, "PAC."; See also, CIRMA, Infostelle, Signatura 84, CERIGUA, "Army Presence." According to CERIGUA, MINUGUA staff, together with the Consultoría Maya, PAC chiefs, and military personnel from Military Zone No. 20 were all convened to witness the official disbanding of the group. Upon their arrival, however, PAC commanders and representatives from forty-six communities refused to be dismantled. Mactzul villagers told a newspaper in 1995, "The only violence was the mysterious deaths of thirteen people and another ten in adjacent communities and death threats against those who refuse to patrol [during the war]." See also CDHG, "Otras Informaciones."
103. Author interview, Vicente.
104. Ibid.
105. HNG, *Prensa Libre*, De Avalos, "Patrulleros de Chichicastenango." In 2000, I was told that Senté Ventura was the former patrol commander for the Mactzul area.
106. CIRMA, Infostelle, Signatura 83, CERIGUA, "PACs Out of Control."
107. Author interview, Doroteo.
108. MINUGUA, "Report of the Secretary-General."
109. Solomon, *Institutional Violence*.
110. I met Senté Ventura once during a collective interview with the Xepocol, Patzibal, and Saquillá II communities. On that occasion, he seemed nervous and dominated the discussion.
111. Author interview, Colonel Samayoa, Asuntos Civiles.
112. CIRMA, Infostelle, Signatura 83; "Patrulleros se Oponen."
113. Ikeda, "Reflexiones sobre la Violencia," 193.
114. HNG, *Prensa Libre*, Hernández, "Le Ganamos."
115. CONADEGUA, "Security Forces?"

8

A "Silence That Hurts"
Garrison Communities

Former PACs not living in organized communities are the first to respond when the military calls up and when the politicians in elections require them.
—Semana.com, "Del Reino de las Armas al Reino del Miedo"

Systems of coercion and exploitation leave a lasting imprint upon vulnerable populations. Economist Melissa Dell has successfully demonstrated the long-term impact of over 200 years (1573–1812) of the *mita* system, an extensive forced mining labor system set up in Peru and Bolivia.[1] Following this approach, in this chapter I focus on the complex, manifold, and long-lasting repercussions of prolonged militarization and militarism.

In reckoning with the question over when processes of genocide end, criminologist Nicole Rafter has noted, "In genocide, one can expect, at best, ragged endings, ragged conclusions."[2] Similarly, I ask, when are the legacies of military control at the grassroots level over? When do militaristic remnants wither away after genocides and wars have ended? How are these socially reproduced by the oppressed? Martin Shaw asserts, "Militarization in its broadest sense is a societal process, affecting civil society as well as the state."[3] The crucial question is how does the supremacy of military culture—loyalty and group cohesion—take over civilian social relations? While scholars and commissions of inquiry have concluded that among the long-standing effects of the genocide was the destruction of communities' cohesiveness, I suggest the opposite: that postwar militarization increased militaristic cohesiveness within what I term "garrison communities." In these local spaces, which have been symbolically built by deep militarization and militarism, military power remained deeply cloistered in the early wake of the genocide and war. The formation of garrison communities refers to Benedict Anderson's "imagined political community," understood as a cultural artifact "both inherently limited and sovereign."[4] Postwar garrison communities differ from, and should not be confused with, the strategic hamlets, or development poles, the army physically built to resettle internally displaced survivors in the Ixil area of El Quiché at the peak of the slaughter (1981–1983).[5] As opposed to this type of war resettlement,[6] postwar garrison communities were symbolically controlled by the army's power, incarnated in ex-militiamen and former military commissioners themselves. This reproduction of lingering legacies took place in the context of ongoing poverty-stricken Maya peasants "who form[ed] the base of [Ríos Montt's] support" due to his promises of security and development.[7]

These types of communities are defined by at least three interrelated sociological traits: first, loyalist ex-militiamen had most deeply internalized the oppressor mentality. Second, within these communities, militarization acted as a motor for social cohesion that is a central feature of the military doctrine, since the shared experience of war (and genocide) forges enduring primary bonds. Third, the leadership of these communities enforced obedience to the army's authority and values.[8] By inscribing military values within the everyday life of communities, the patrol system successfully normalized state violence, restructuring community sociopolitical organizations long after the war was over. I explore four interrelated and long-term repercussions affecting communities: (1) the absence of popular organizations, (2) the halting of sustainable development for small-scale production, (3) the absence of exhumations and, (4) the reproduction of social silence over massacres against the army's loyalist allies.

Garrison Communities' Traits Compared to Nonmilitarized Communities

Although traits of garrison communities existed in eastern Chichicastenango, as in the hinterland community of Chunimá, most of the villages that can best be characterized as garrison communities were located on the northwestern side, the area of the Mactzules, Paxot, and Saquillá. In these communities, collective fear of reprisals from former militiamen continued to shape families' capacity to engage in grassroots action. Among the main symbolic and concrete traits of communities suffering extreme forms of militarization and militarism are (1) the existence of local committees controlled by former patrol chiefs or military commissioners, (2) the lack of social organization and lack of participation in human rights or popular groups, (3) low economic development, (4) militaristic dominating values (blind obedience, loyalty, respect for patriotic symbols and self-sacrifice), and (5) the existence of the law of silence (threats, complicity, secrecy, cohesion, loyalty, and obedience to the army). In contrast, in less militarized communities (such as in the Chupol area), communities are characterized by (1) the existence of local committees being more likely held by communally selected authorities, (2) higher levels of social organization and participation in human rights or popular groups, (3) higher levels of economic development and self-initiatives, (4) resistance against participating in military-oriented groups, and (5) efforts to preserve the memory of the past and to denounce human rights crimes.

Repression and Absence of Human Rights Organizations

Postwar militarism curtailed garrison communities' ability to advocate change and crippled solidarity ties within Maya communities. Local pro-army authorities replicated the war climate of group unity and antagonism against anything that could be related to ex-guerrillas, namely human rights groups with previous ties to rebels. Notions of the threat of the internal enemy continued to exacerbate people's fear of participating in grassroots organizations—a fact that hindered peasants' capacity to become political subjects and, instead, depoliticized communities.

A pivotal trait of garrison communities was the absence of popular and human rights organizations. As I discuss in the previous chapter, in the early postwar years, the "internal enemy" myth remained deeply embedded in the social fabric and mindset, shaping structures and Maya peasant-military relations in rural areas. As a result, the postwar military continued to recast human rights groups as being against the security and development of the country, defining them as less than human and making them vulnerable to deadly reprisals. For example, in Chunimá I, assaults against the few mobilized human rights activists resulted in murderous acts perpetrated by ex-patrollers, a case filed before the Interamerican Human Rights Court in Costa Rica.[9]

Authoritarian practices, such as intimidation and reprisals—like cutting off families' water supplies when refusing former patrol's rules—coexisted within a militaristic culture that promoted a "perverse mutuality" between the oppressors and oppressed.[10] The end result was an intransigent form of military control over local improvement committees, which effectively prevented any manifestation of political dissent. When human rights groups attempted to mobilize within garrison villages, few families participated. Raul, a betterment committee authority from Saquillá I, revealed his dislike for human rights groups: "They are the ones that do not want to cooperate … with the community."[11] A fundamental principle of Maya-K'iché life is to be considered worthy of serving one's community.

In 2000, Francisco García Morales, from the Human Rights Ombudsman Office (PDH), indicated that former patrollers who had become representatives of betterment committees "often threatened their fellow neighbors by shooting in the air," causing panic in an already war-traumatized population.[12] Human rights activists, denouncing corruption and calling for the complete dismantling of the ex-patrols, were targeted for assassinations by loyalist ex-patrols, as during the war. The callous 27 September 2003 killing of Eusebio

Macario Chicoj, who had been a community organizer since 1988 with the Runujel Junam Council of Ethnic Communities "We Are All Equal" (CERJ; see Chapter Five), from Chulumal IV, was just such a case. Macario's death left twelve children as orphans.

The killing of human rights defenders—farmers, trade unionists, students, religious leaders, groups seeking justice—was recast as an ordinary crime rather than as an extension of the war's persecution of grassroots groups and their leaders. In fact, nationwide since 1997, MINUGUA denounced ex-patrol chiefs' attacks on activists from the National Coordination of Widows of Guatemala (CONAVIGUA), Mutual Support Group (GAM), CERJ, and the League of Organizations of the Maya People of Guatemala (COPMAGUA). When activists attempted to mobilize within garrison communities, however, few families joined, suggesting continuity between the absence of critical class and ethnic consciousness before, during, and after the genocide.

By 2000, militarized authorities incarnated the army's staunch opposition to human rights groups, illustrated in their restriction of the right to freely mobilize and organize in the Mactzules, Saquillá, and Paxot areas, since human rights activists were still perceived as the façade of former URNG rebels. That demonstrated the continuity of the national security mindset and the war's mythology.[13] The admiration expressed for the military was a poignant reminder that war myth of the "internal enemy" remained strong. This militaristic mindset precluded the absence of progressive networks, further blocking the participation of victims and survivors in truth-telling processes.[14]

The few peasants in the community of Chunimá who were participating in human rights groups attested to this ongoing perception of a new "internal enemy." Families opposing the military were accused of "failing to cooperate" with the community and, as a result, had their water cut off by the communal authority.[15] This arbitrary punishment resonated with the 1982 counterinsurgency campaigns demonizing organized peasant groups. Rigoberto, a former military commissioner, noted, "Why do we not like organizations? Because [they] only ask for their rights but do not serve their community."[16] This criminalizing view of human rights organizations resonated with Colonel Samayoa, who told me in 2000 that such groups "are on the side of the ex-rebels from the URNG."[17]

At the community level, this criminalization trickled down from Maya authorities identified with the "new Maya," adhering to military values in accordance with the counterinsurgency doctrine.[18] This particular type of postwar Maya maintained a false sense of peace, order, and, ultimately, of normalcy, which the army exploited to deter the mobilization of human rights groups as well as self-generating community development initiatives. Luz, a leader from La Coordinadora de Organizaciones de Desarrollo Integral (CASODI), remarked on the efforts to organize in western communities and the influence of former patrols in shaping local politics:

We have tried to reach the Western area (Mactzules) and we bounced, any institution is rejected. There is army control, manipulation, and divisions. For instance ... regarding the popular consultation [1999 National Referendum], we wanted the ex-PACs to take part. But they protested against the reforms because for them, the army is important.[19]

The notion that institutions "bounced" when seeking to carry out projects corroborates the view of garrison communities as closed. Former patrols' militaristic authority nurtured fear that war could return, shaping the lack of participation in political and development projects. The failed attempts by institutions to take root in these communities also spoke to the way authorities and families viewed political initiatives that promoted autonomous community empowerment—independent from the army.

Furthering this social fear, Salvador, a schoolteacher and army collaborator proud of receiving some military training in Texas, expressed his disdain for COPMAGUA, an umbrella organization concerned with the implementation of the Indigenous Rights Accords. He stated, "In Guatemala, COPMAGUA ... claims to represent the Indigenous population, but that is not true. They are illegal groups ... They are making decisions in the name of the Indigenous people. All these groups belong to the ex-URNG."[20] While Salvador emphasized that he "knows nothing about politics," he nevertheless recast human rights groups to be fronts for the ex-URNG, which revealed the army's effectiveness in molding his perception of them.

In Raul's eyes, community members who opposed the military received funds from groups promoting economic, social, and cultural rights,

Many groups are against the army ... GAM is one example. I believe that [these human rights groups] think the military killed honest, innocent people who were not guerrillas. [But] I already realized that the army doesn't do any harm ... Maybe it's because the other group [the URNG] gives [human rights groups] money. The army instead only gives advice. But [again] I think that human rights groups give them food and that's what makes people confident.[21]

Raul's remarks echoed war propaganda criminalizing groups like GAM and other human rights groups that emerged in the mid-1980s. The argument that, unlike GAM, the army "only gives advice" is challenged by the decrees institutionalizing payments for demobilized patrols and by the unbroken civilian-Maya relations. Pablo concluded that only "bad people" feared the army: "There is a saying that those who fear the military, it is because they have done something wrong. Whoever has nothing to hide is in favor of the military."[22]

Vicente, holding an FRG municipal position, also exemplified the internalized militaristic postwar ideology that called for order and discipline and shaped the symbolic restrictions that discouraged political participation. Vicente denied the ongoing militarization of the town while he praised military values in 2000: "We are not militarizing the municipality or the village, but in each of us there are ethics, responsibility, and discipline. The army had a very important role within Chichicastenango."[23]

For Vicente, the army brought internal security to their communities by arming civil patrols starting in the 1980s. But this neutral stance of "not militarizing communities" was a deception, as authorities largely indicated that they welcomed the army's politics. They adamantly did not allow organized dissent or a strong associational life that may have acted as a counterbalancing force to military control and helped dismantle the war's "internal enemy" myth. Former civilian patrols' continuous authority, flowing from their highly ambiguous, "cozy friendship" with the military, was acting as a symbolic roadblock for those who wanted to participate in developing a sustainable economy that could empower themselves and their communities.

Blocking Constitutional Reforms

The prevailing impunity for the crimes of ex-militiamen enabled the continuation of further violence.[24] Still active, loyalist ex-militiamen continued to harass and intimidate families against joining groups opposed to the army, which frustrated the emergence of shared war, class, and ethnic grievances. This militaristic attitude displayed by authorities may also help explain why amendments to the constitution to include the Peace Accords provisions failed in parts of El Quiché. In May 1999, reforms to the 1985 constitution were included in a national referendum at the ballot box. If passed, they would have secured the legal framework to facilitate implementing the Peace Accords and thus benefit the Indigenous majority, the Maya peasantry. Moreover the referendum rejected "congressional authority to determine when the military would take charge of internal security matters and a civilian defence minister."[25] But instead, the few voters (less than 20 percent of the registered population) rejected the reforms and El Quiché residents overwhelmingly opposed them.[26] One observer noted:

> For the referendum, we brought people who explained to them what the referendum was about; the group must think about it; if they had already registered, they voted; however, most of them were not [registered]; it was then that we realized that they had not been registered. Who is registered? Only two people raised their hands.[27]

To better explain this paradox of peasants rejecting reforms that would have benefitted their families and communities, most scholars argued that fear of retaliation from the army led many to vote against the reforms. While lingering fear was no doubt a factor, too much focus on the role of fear leaves little room to explore how the S-5 specialists delivery of alleged progress and development projects, ended up encouraging the continuity of an ongoing postcolonial relationship with the poorest communities in the countryside (See Chapter Seven). Against this context, I want to suggest that failure to pass the reforms was also shaped by the army's "humanitarian" aid-driven campaigns to corral votes by co-opting Maya authorities to vote against them.

Halting the Development of Their Communities

Scholars have characterized Chichicastenango as, in the words of Anne M. Larson, having "relatively stronger civil society organizations that have constructed participatory structures over a period of several years."[28] Indeed, postwar studies praise the highly organized nature of Chichicastenango's civil society without accounting for those communities where militarization and militarism prevent them from organizing.[29] For example, sociologist Claudia Barrientos de Arriaga, in her study of citizen participation in the township (2002–2006), argues that there were approximately 600 organizations with an average of 7 by community, but she ignores those communities without organizations, except those sanctioned by the army.[30] Few scholars working in the areas of human rights and internationally based health and development NGOs promoting grassroots development in Chichicastenango, however, have noticed how western corner communities refuse to organize, which hinders their participation in development programs. This participation is understood as guaranteeing access to affordable staples as required by international and local humanitarian institutions. While the link between militarism and development has been at the center of much scholarly discussion, some arguing that war brings economic development, few studies have explored how grassroots militarization and militarism adversely affect the local economy of the internally colonized.[31]

Peace economist Jan Drèze has suggested that militarization contributes to halting economic development in addition to chilling grassroots organizing by crushing self-generating collective action.[32] "Wars or rather militarism," asserts Drèze, "is the major obstacle to development in the contemporary world."[33] Militarism shapes the capacity of communities to collectively organize to meet outside institutions' requirements when applying for microcredits: neighbors coming together to carry out self-empowerment projects. This is crucial to acknowledge, since studies have shown that organized peasants benefitting from larger production are more capable of bringing revenues to build infrastructure, raising the possibility of receiving higher revenues.[34] As studies focusing on Andean smallholder farmers suggest, to "strengthen farmers' ability to take advantage of markets ... [any development initiative] needs to address the question of farmers' empowerment." This can be achieved by allowing farmers to choose what "options best suit their needs."[35]

Credycom, an Example of Self-Sabotaging

The experience of NGOs such as Credycom demonstrates the impact of Indigenous peasants' refusal to participate in organized economic activities that could improve their precarious existence. This Italy-based organization sought to encourage peasant participation in projects sponsored by the European Community to bring palliative economic aid. Credycom lent production and commercialization microcredits to small-scale entrepreneurs, financing cold storage units for refrigerating fruits and vegetables. Experts provided advice to peasants interested in exporting to supermarket chains, instructing them on the ins and outs of the export businesses.

While Credycom was not yet present in Chichi during the time of my fieldwork (1997–2000), its most recent initiative can help illustrate the ways in which the lack of communal organization has continued to prevent families from applying for microlending projects to this day. By 2009, Credycom had established microcredit relations with families, largely in the eastern region, to facilitate the cultivation of new crops. In communities such as Agua Escondida (located alongside the Interamerican Highway between kilometers 101 and 105), Credycom helped set up a farm in Pajuliboy and Semejá III[36] and facilitated micro-irrigation (*mini riegos*) projects for diversifying crops.[37]

But the legacy of militarization and militarism sadly restricted peasant families from garrison communities from organizing and taking advantage of potential markets that could bring long-lasting community development. In a comparative study between the township of Cotzal (in the Ixil Triangle) and Chichi, Larson examines Indigenous municipality elders' rejection or acceptance of a new forest policy brought by the National Institute of Forests (INAB).[38] Larson concludes that while the Auxiliatura Indígena met regularly with community representatives, the principals under the Auxiliatura's supervision rejected the central government's forestry policy and kept their informal policy of charging a permit cost for extracting firewood. While Larson recognizes that participatory processes were "met with some opposition from some associations [that] preferred to work individually and former leaders of the [PACs]" she nonetheless leaves unrecognized the long-term implications of militaristic legacies upon these processes.[39]

In contrast to Larson's study, I maintain that peasants' refusal to come together collectively was among the pivotal factors that precluded families from complying with the requirements needed to obtain financial support from Credycom. First, peasants participating had to be literate in Spanish, an obstacle that could be overcome if families were given the opportunity to receive education. Second, to commercialize fruits and vegetables, it was necessary to build a qualified local infrastructure, including a warehouse, temporary collection centers, cold storage rooms, latrines, and a deposit area for chemical waste.[40] Third, and most importantly, Credycom partnered with groups of producers, not individuals, since this had a multiplying effect beneficial to the larger community of 100 to 200 families.[41] That is, being organized into groups of families was required to pull together the initial economic resources needed to apply for larger funds.[42]

While the geography itself limits production of cornfields, the mountainous climate facilitates the planting of new seeds, since shortened fallow times have resulted in soil depletion.[43] Peasants' ability to participate in Credycom's program to obtain credit and technical support was hindered not just by the high lending rates that prevented them from accessing capital to finance a larger enterprise[44] but also by their fear that the army could accuse them of organizing their communities and retaliate to deter their self-initiatives. In 2000, I asked Alberto about the volume of apple production that might provide some income for his community. He replied, "No, I do not think so, we are normal, some have apples, but we do not have a big commercialization."[45] Manuel Sut Lucas, the FRG-aligned mayor of Chichicastenango (2000–2004), commented on some western communities' lack of economic development and contrasted them with communities with access to markets, such as Chupol. "In this area [Chupol], they have greatly improved, [as in] the case of Chicuá, Semejá, where they already have communal telephones, they have secondary high schools, they have professional careers."[46] An example of how better organized communities located off the Interamerican Highway benefitted collectively was given by the Asociación Agua Escondida (ASIADES), which was involved in the cultivation and export of crops to Europe and the United States, including snow peas, sweet peas, and mini-vegetables. For the internal market, they grew maize and beans.[47]

As a result of their organized efforts, some sixty associations were formed, comprising 2,887 people (1,450 women). Revenues were very limited, yet still quite crucial for impoverished families. It is worth noting that by 2002, some 70 percent of Indigenous children under five years old suffered some form of malnutrition and 30 percent from "global malnutrition."[48] By then, 83 percent of the population lived in poverty and 30 percent in extreme poverty.[49]

Sut Lucas further remarked that western communities were in the most need of assistance, "Over there [in the west] what is needed are educational buildings, and economic resources because the people are very poor." The mayor attributed the eastern region's level of development, particularly Chupol's, to external stimulus: "People need stimulus so they can organize in search of aid ... We do not have to wait for people to bring us development. No, on the contrary, we ourselves have to look for it, and if there are institutions willing to help us, we welcome them."[50] This notion of peasants in need of "external stimulus" to start economic development echoes ideas propagated by the 1980s psychological operations (PSYOPs), whereby peasants needed to be encouraged to join the patrols in order to protect their families and their few possessions.

Miguel, a schoolteacher, also compared the ability of families to engage in large-scale entrepreneurial businesses to that of Chupol families: "The Chupol area is more open because they have relations with other groups around here and around the country. People are well informed; they know about a lot of things. [They are] capable of doing big business, not only small businesses but also big ones."[51] Garrison communities, on the other hand were closed to outside organizations, as militarized authorities blocked access to families, echoing Jim Handy's notion that the conquest has laid the basis of a society composed of "guarded individuals, seemingly docile, humble and outwardly obedient to authority—yet harboring bitterness and distrust."[52] To draw membership to their programs, outside organizations were compelled to devise strategies like "recruiting projects" (*projectos de enganche*). These projects consisted of minimal assistance with subsistence production, usually land maintenance for corn production. Emilio, a European Union representative actively seeking communities' support to participate in available development programs, suggested that "recruiting projects" were the initial encouraging steps to "get peasants and their families to work with us."[53] When asked why these particular communities did not join development projects the EU promoted, staff members frequently told me that communities did not want to organize to receive food or health projects.

Corps of Engineering: A Postcolonial Road-Building Mission

Militarism entrenched itself and strangled every effort at building a sustainable economy. For remote communities, the lack of asphalt roads was and continues to be a major obstacle preventing access to export markets, and yet the army continued to take credit for road improvement. Indeed, as the genocide escalated in the early 1980s, the military prioritized the expansion and improvement of roads in the highlands and hinterlands under the guise of fostering economic development for Maya families, with the real intention of defending the territory.[54] Despite the army's spurious claims of caring for communities, whatever road improvements were actually made were intended to guarantee military access to communities to take control and exploit natural resources.

These so-called improvements largely resembled the recolonizing practices of infrastructure development that can be traced to the arrival of the United Fruit Company and its railway construction in the early nineteenth century, when the execution of road repair and vaccination campaigns largely served to legitimize military dominance in rural areas.

Pedro, an army loyalist from Semejá II, further admitted, "Not only was this project [road improvement]," necessary, but "we [also] need another school, we have few classrooms, we need to increase access to drinking water." During our interview, he soon reverted to praising military authority's primary goal: "to fix the main road."[55] On bringing roads to western communities, Pedro put the army's help into an immediate context: "When the Interamerican Highway needs repairs, all the cars and buses are detoured to the Western side ... because the highway is the main way to Chichi." The rerouted traffic and community members "could then take that [alternate] way, so we are concerned with giving that road maintenance [paving it with asphalt]."[56] Pedro's perception of the military as providing infrastructure, however, is fundamentally challenged by the real number of access roads to their communities.

As shown in Table 8.1, for a town of 400 square kilometers, having only two of nine paved roads (except for those communities located along the Interamerican Highway) is a monumental obstacle that hindered efforts for the large-scale commercialization of apples and plums. Nationwide, according to the World Bank, "Thirteen percent of households lack any form of adequate motorable road access,"[57] an isolation that is even worse within Maya communities. This 2010 table shows that the number of dirt roads in the municipality did not improve much, despite the army's systematic claims of bringing "progress" to communities through road construction.

Table 8.1. Poor Rural Infrastructure: Road Access Conditions

No.	Name	Road Access Conditions
1.	Chulumal I	Transitable (asphalt)
2.	Chuguexa II B	Transitable (asphalt, Interamerican Highway)
3.	Chicuá Primero	Transitable (asphalt)
4.	Chupol	Transitable (asphalt, Interamerican Highway)
5.	Mactzul I	Dirt road; 75% of work in order to leave it in good shape
6.	Panquiac	Dirt road
7.	Saquillá I	Dirt road
8.	Xeabaj I	Dirt road
9.	Xecoja	Dirt road

Source: Author's compilation based on DGC, "Listado de Centros Electorales Municipales."

Only two fully asphalted roads go to eastern communities, Chupol and Chicuá I. This vividly illustrates how the army's rhetoric of progress disguised the security goals of military projects conducted by the army's engineer corps, which was created in 1962.[58] In fact, according to a different 2000 World Bank report, given the relatively small 14,000 kilometer road network, less than 4,000 kilometers are mostly paved, proving that Guatemala's roads, compared to those of Costa Rica, are particularly "inadequate."[59] All this means, for example, according to the report, that "the absence of a dependable road network also implies that people have to travel almost an hour to reach a medical center and more than an hour (one-way) to procure wood."[60]

The building of roads, whether or not considered essential by community members, suited military prerogatives and failed to profoundly address the fostering of sustainable economic development. This was already acknowledged in the mid-1950s when members of the Committee for Roads contested the notion of roads being built for the progress of communities with the newly asphalted Interamerican Highway in Chupol: "We welcome this progress ... but want to express that being the region that has some 21 percent of the country's population on an area that comprises 25 percent of the national territory ... yet we only have five percent asphalted." This is a modest figure compared to "the Department of Escuintla, which has 48 percent; Izabal, 53 percent; and our neighbor, Sololá, 31 percent of paved roads."[61] Peasants' complaints unmasked the army's false claims of caring for communities' progress by paving roads.

In the war's wake, the military continued to entice the local population to donate their labor to these projects. Salvador, whom I met during one of my visits to the Quiché Army Zone, connected the history of free Indigenous labor to the army's road construction projects under General Jorge Ubico (1931–1944): "Back then, the Ixcán, during his administration, the Indigenous population was forced to work for free for months; the road from here to Nebaj, and up to Cobán, was opened against the clock."[62]

Halting Exhumations

Massacre victims have frequently been left without proper burials, as survivors fled into hiding. Victoria Sanford argues that survivors have expressed their desire for exhumations, proper burials for their loved ones, justice, and "sometimes revenge."[63] It often takes years of complex legal processes to initiate exhumations. Exhumations play both a legal and a healing role: evidence of military crimes could be recovered and bring closure to families and communities who experienced the mass violence.[64] For some survivors, however, exhumations could instead introduce ambivalence, prompting memories of the bloody past they had experienced and compromising whatever stability they may have achieved since living through the violence. Furthermore, exhumations were a collective process with special meanings for the Maya.[65] According to Sanford, as exhumations unfolded, the sites of mass killings where remains were often found "bec[a]me a community space" for the rebuilding of "larger social relations ... as well as the excavation of individual and collective memory."[66]

Continuous militarism foreclosed these spaces of remembrance, blocking the process of collective grief, closure, and healing and thereby adding yet another layer of silence and fear to the lives of families and communities. Using their militarized authority over communities, former patrols placed restrictions on the exhumation process of victims of the genocide. This was particularly true within garrison communities. According to a report by K'amalb'e Rech Tinamit Ixim Ulew, a human rights organization from Lacamá in the east, there were families that had been "slower in breaking up their silence, fighting against their fear, and seeking exhumations in Saquillá II, Mactzul IV, Paxot II, Mucubaltzip, Mactzul III, and Patulub, ... these [were] the most strict and poor communities."[67] In early 2000, communities from the Ixil area involved in the genocide case against General Ríos Montt were threatened by the ex-patrollers: "Forget the bones, if you want to complain about what happened here in the village, you're going to go through same thing again."[68]

Alejandro, a young forensic anthropologist I interviewed in August 2010, recounted his nightmarish experience in Chichicastenango when accusations of being a *guerrillero* harkened back to wartime attacks on peasant Maya activists. In 2009, as a member of the Guatemalan Forensic Anthropology Foundation (Fundación de Antropología Forense de Guatemala [FAFG]), he participated in exhumations in the western community of Pocohil I, two kilometers from the town's center. This community "had a prior history with restrictions to carry out exhumations ... I believe it was in 1994 or in 1995. It seemed that people believed that an exhumation meant prison for some people."[69] As soon as the forensic team arrived in Pocohil I, a woman whose husband was a COCODES (Consejos Comunitarios de Desarrollo) authority, an Evangelical pastor, and a former patrol accused them of being *guerrilleros* and alerted the rest of the community by chiming a bell to assemble neighbors.

People quickly gathered around, shouting in K'iché. Not understanding what was being said, Alejandro asked those demanding the exhumations to translate. He was told that those blocking the exhumations were the families of war patrols, who did not want the forensic team there. Armed with stones, approximately 200 angry neighbors surrounded Alejandro and his FAFG colleagues, an intimidating tactic also used during lynching (Chapter Nine). Led by the village authority, an ex-military commissioner and auxiliary mayor, neighbors closed in on the forensic team.

The FAFG team had possibly been on the verge of being lynched. Members of the community were not spared from persecution for supporting the exhumation of their relatives. In fact, they suffered severe corporal punishment at the hands of their neighbors: "One of the families is in [the] witness protection [program] because they were not allowed to get in; they got there, and they punished them, they whipped them, they did a lot of things to them, and they had to get out of there and come to the capital."[70] Families were also symbolically punished. For example, as Alejandro recounted, ex-patrollers "cut off water and electricity" to family members mobilized to exhume mass graves in the community. The ringleaders of their attack, he declared, were members of COCODES. He also remarked that during the failed exhumation, ex-militiamen "had total control over the community and over the communities in the area."[71] Within rural communities, traditional village authorities often gathered families to provide them with information about communal projects. This practice was usurped by the military during the war, which then would use the alarm system to convene the patrols and the rest of the community to receive military orders.

Defeaning Silence on the Massacre of Saquillá II

Eviatar Zerubavel suggests that social silence is "more than simply absence of sound."[72] Rather, constructed silence implies a consensual denial and deliberate avoidance concerning the participation in or witnessing of mass atrocities. As cultural theorist Nelly Richard suggests, "Silence does not mean that [there is] nothing to say ... rather, it means that its sounds are regularly silenced by the control exercised by official discourses."[73] But what are the collective silences of the internally colonized, a population terribly humiliated by dehumanizing colonial and neocolonial violence designed to subdue peoples' will?

Pivotal in this phenomenon of constructed social silence is the role of the army's pervasive, ironclad rule over communities, reinforcing the culture of silence covering up past atrocities. In postwar garrison communities, atrocities allegedly committed by the army were hidden from being publicly remembered. This deafening silence concealed, for example, the massacre of the Saquillá II community, showing how rural communities themselves silenced the role of the army, as shared silence is an act that unfolds over time. Unreported to the Truth Commission, this particular case of collective silence was rectified by Chichi's municipal firefighters, who courageously responded to clean up after the massacres and kept an administrative log. Miguel, who had been with the fire department since 1977, tells of the humanitarian duties of "transporting the sick, wounded, traffic accidents, or any dire needs people had" as the violence escalated.[74]

On 18 May 1982, in one pickup truck and one ambulance, Miguel, Juan, and a few others registered forty-two bodies from Saquillá II. Though material perpetrators are not identified, the vicious violence is chillingly illustrated in the log entries.[75] Miguel, one of the founders of the municipal firefighters, recalled, "That was in May 1982. Forty-two corpses, mostly women and children; there were only three or four men. And they all had Galil gunshot wounds." I asked him how he knew the weapon used was a Galil. He reminisced, "Because the Galil has a special way—the body's reaction to Galil bullets is very peculiar, and also, because of the cartridge rounds that had been left behind."[76] Because the firefighters lacked additional vehicles, the corpses were brought to the morgue in piles, one on top of another. "Blood was spilling all over," Miguel remembered sadly when I interviewed him again in 2010.[77] Bodies were distributed into three ambulances, one for men, one for women, and a third for the children.

Pascual, a health promoter from Saquillá II, told me about the massacre, "When the army grabbed the people, with sticks, kicks, and guns, and kidnapped the women ... the army told the community of Saquillá II ... they had betrayed the nation, they had betrayed peace."[78] When asked about the identities of the victims, Miguel replied, "We have no record of the names of the people in that massacre, because nobody knew."[79] Soon after the massacre, survivors fled to other villages or to the capital. "There were only two or three people [left], but they did not want to talk."[80] Similarly, in Santa Maria Tzejá, Manz recounts that the day after the 16 February 1982 massacre, there was "no noise of children playing, no yelling across a field, no chopping word, no morning laugher, no grinding of corn, no smoke, no cooking."[81]

Who was responsible for the Saquillá II Massacre? According to Miguel, "At that time, survivors blamed the army, that is to say, that was something that everyone knew, but nobody dared to say openly, but, rather, it was rumored that the army was to blame." Miguel continued, eventually, "an eyewitness told us that neighbors had seen a small truck, a minivan, had come in from that side leaving after what had happened ... it was painted green-and-white. They later saw that vehicle in the military zone or at the Chupol outpost."[82] Neighbors' refusal to testify to the commission was more telling when considering there appears to have been a prior massacre in the same Saquillá II community, as reported by Amnesty International:

On 8 May 1982 ... Under Ríos Montt the army laid siege to the village of Saquillá II ... Though few men remained in the village, the army killed whomever they could. On 8 May, twenty-three children, fifteen women and six men died in an army raid. Ten days later, the army's elite Kaibiles returned to Saquillá II, conducting a house-to-house search and killing twenty-five more children, fifteen women (three of them pregnant) and three men.[83]

Significantly, the absence of testimonies from this area to the Truth Commission or to REHMI went beyond survivors' silence over this particular atrocity. Of the few cases that were reported is the killing of three young people on 23 June 1993 when patrols from Saquillá II accused Tomás and Santos Pantzay Calel and their cousin Fausto Pantzay Calel, all from the neighboring Xalbaquiej, of being guerrillas and murdered them. Tomás had received death threats for refusing to patrol in his community. They had come to Saquillá II to visit one of the cousins' girlfriend.[84] Before killing them, some twenty patrols from Saquillá II went to the Chichicastenango military outpost to receive orders. The perpetrators used plastic nylon bags to suffocate them, killing them with their bare hands. In 1997, as the work of the commission was under way, efforts to exhume the bodies were obstructed when the remains were removed before a forensic team could unearth them.

The absence of human rights cases reported from western communities should be seen as an indication of the complicit silence over human rights crimes as well as of the covering of the ties binding ex-patrols to the army. In garrison communities, the army replaced Indigenous peoples' shared memory with its own institutional memory, composed of the step-by-step ideological process involved in the militarization of sectors of Indigenous people. By not breaking the silence about the role of the army in their communities, ex-patrols allowed the "culturally genocidal ... dimensions of settler colonialism ... leading to cultural destruction" to continue, as Damien Short discusses in Australia. As a result, any effort to unveil the truth about the past military violence in their communities was obstructed by the subjugated allies.[85]

Notes

1. For this chapter's title, I borrow from geographer George W. Lovell's book, *A Beauty That Hurts*. Dell concludes that the *mita* effect, among others, "lower[ed] household consumption by around 25 percent [and] increase[d] the prevalence of stunted growth," of children living in affected districts today ("Persistent Effects," 1863–1865).
2. Rafter, *Crime of all Crimes*, 181.
3. Shaw, *Post-Military Society*, 71.
4. Anderson, *Imagined Communities*, 6.
5. Unlike in the Ixil Triangle, Chichicastenango families were internally displaced in neighboring communities but not forced into development poles. For the areas where development poles were implemented, see CEH, III.231; REHMI, II.145.
6. This type of colony remained "under the direct supervision of several dozen to one hundred soldiers, and village life [was] permeated by army presence." Americas Watch, *Civil Patrols in Guatemala*, 17.
7. Little and Smith, *Mayas in Postwar Guatemala*, 155.
8. This term refers to political scientist Harold D. Lasswell's "garrison state," foreseeing the supremacy of the men in uniform for whom "the duty to obey, to serve the state ... are cardinal virtues." Lasswell, "Garrison State," 460.

9. The case was brought for the murder of Sebastián Velásquez Mejía, a member of GAM and CERJ who was bludgeoned to death in 1990 by Manuel Perebal Ajtzalam III, patrol chief of Chunimá. Case 10.674 of the Interamerican Commission of Human Rights. See, for example, the OAS, *Interamerican Yearbook on Human Rights.* Carlota McAllister also reports that in hinterland communities, such as Chunimá, authorities continued to have ties with the army. CIRMA, CGD, McAllister, "Chupol," 9.

10. Gandhi, *Postcolonial Theory,* 11.

11. Collective interview, Betterment Committee Saquillá I and Xepocol.

12. HNG, *Prensa Libre,* Elder Interiano, "CONIC Alerta por Marcha," 8.

13. Schirmer, *Guatemalan Military Project,* 178.

14. Foweraker, *Theorizing Social Movements.*

15. As recorded by human rights groups and the Interamerican Court. See, Interamerican Institute of Human Rights, "Revista IIDH." As late as 2010, the Chunimá ex-militiamen continued to harass their neighbors. "Demandan al Estado," Siglo21.com.gt.

16. Author interview, Rigoberto.

17. Author interview, Colonel Samayoa.

18. Keen, "Demobilising Guatemala."

19. Author interview, Luz.

20. Author interview, Salvador.

21. Author interview, Raul.

22. Ibid.

23. Author interview, Vicente.

24. A human rights worker in Ixcan, El Quiché, commented, "When groups who hijack buses are arrested, often ex-PACS, they say 'So what? We have friends in the military.' That's an attitude we encounter." Keen, "Demobilising Guatemala," 15.

25. "Guatemala Squeezed," 8.

26. According to Susanne Jonas, "The voter turnout was only 18.5 percent, blocking the reforms by a margin of 55/45. Those highland departments affected by the war voted yes (not all) and had higher participation than the national average." Besides the FRG, opposing the reforms were those organizations "presenting themselves as the guardians of the Constitution," such as the rightwing Liga Pro-Patria and Evangelical Alliance, which Jonas terms the "Dinosaurs" (*Of Centaurs and Doves,* 10, 195, 203–4).

27. Author interview, Miguel.

28. Larson, "Indigenous Peoples," 43.

29. Barrientos de Arriaga does not problematize the fact that of thirty-six participants, only eight claimed to belong to a political party. She rightly suggests that due to participants' extreme poverty and difficult road access, they would not take time off to participate in her study but leaves unexplored authorities' refusal to participate in projects that could benefit their families and communities (Barrientos de Arriaga, "Participación Ciudadana," 12–13).

30. Barrientos de Arriaga, "Participación Ciudadana," 62.

31. At the macrolevel, development and security has been examined by scholars of Latin American military. See, for example, Pion-Berlin, *Civil Military Relations.*

32. Drèze and Sen, *Hunger and Public Action;* Drèze, "Militarism, Development and Democracy."

33. Drèze, "Militarism, Development and Democracy," 1171.

34. Wollni and Zeller, "Do Farmers Benefit?" This does not mean, however, that agriculture will serve as a major vehicle for drastic poverty reduction. According to the World

Bank, "While the poor are highly dependent on agriculture … [which] is not likely to be a dynamic source of new employment opportunities … Poor farming households are primarily involved in the production of subsistence crops." World Bank, *Poverty in Guatemala*, 6.

35. Hellin and Higman, "Crop Diversity and Livelihood Security," 172.
36. Located along the 130-kilometer marker and the 138-kilometer marker, respectively.
37. This could vary from 15 to 30 percent of the total investment. Included within this percentage is the beneficiaries' labor. Credycom provides microcredit to organize groups to finance the storage of thousands of cases of fruit. Credycom.org.
38. She notes that the program Strengthening of Forestry Incentive Program for Small Forest Owners is directed at the municipalities most affected by poverty and hunger. "It prioritizes groups of producers, men and women, whose lands together add up to 15 hectares but that individually hold very small plots, usually less than 2 hectares." Larson, "Indigenous Peoples," 16.
39. Larson, "Indigenous Peoples," 41.
40. Fruits like apples, peaches, and plums and vegetable like peas, potatoes, broccoli, cabbages, carrots, and beans. Credycom notes an example of small-scale agricultural investment represented by a group of women, the Cooperativa Ut'z K'aslemal (the Health and Wellness Cooperative).
41. "In order to more effectively reach the target population, the Project has particularly focused on helping groups of producers/production companies, their businesses, either formally or informally founded, producers' cooperatives, etc., but without excluding the individual producers." A Credycom study shows how the program had a favorable impact on Maya women, who were 50 percent of the beneficiaries, but it largely ignores the difficulties in mobilizing communities, or at least did not openly acknowledge it.
42. It also required meeting international norms and undergoing a verification process by certified institutions. Granado, Mérida, and Scappini, "Proceso de Producción."
43. Ibid., 85.
44. Interests rates were 20 or 30 percent annually, which, individually, prevented poverty-stricken families from applying.
45. Author interview, Alberto.
46. Author interview, Sut Lucas.
47. They also manufactured and sold textiles and commercialized farm animals, such as pigs and hens. ASIADES had a storage center and furnished offices to serve their membership. Families were able to subsist by relying on basic crops and commercialization within twenty-eight hectares, or sixty-nine acres of land; farmers grew on farms with an average of 0.55 hectares, or one acre. Asdiaes.com.
48. PNUD, "Diversidad Etnico-Cultural."
49. Gobierno de Guatemala, "Mapas de Pobreza," 41; according to Barrientos de Arriaga, neighbors possessed fincas of two *manzanas*. Some 92 percent of the population own their own plot of land; 5 percent rent land, while 1 percent is communal land (*Participación Ciudadana*, 50).
50. Author interview, Sut Lucas.
51. Author interview, Miguel.
52. Handy, *Gift of the Devil*, 15, 34.
53. Of the four Chichicastenango participating communities, only one western community, Patzibal, reportedly received aid to improve the production and commercialization of apples. Mactzul, Mactzul IV, and Paxot II were the others.

54. "The goal is to improve the terrain for the organization of the defense," 47. Ejército de Guatemala, "Plan de Campaña Victoria 82."
55. Author interview, Pedro.
56. Author interview, Pedro.
57. World Bank, *Poverty in Guatemala,* 4.
58. HNG, *Revista Militar,* "Sobre Actividades del Ejército," 29.
59. Puri, "Transport and Poverty in Guatemala," 3–4.
60. Ibid., 4.
61. CIRMA, *El Imparcial,* "Galera, Ramón Blanco." He reportedly concluded, "Therefore, Quiché occupies the twentieth position among the 22 departments of the nation, regarding kilometers of roads per kilometers of territory."
62. Author interview, Salvador.
63. Sanford, "Grey Zone," 401.
64. Author interview, Ricardo.
65. For some families, "this means having the certainty of death and a place of reference for their rites." REHMI, I.31.
66. Sanford, "Buried Secrets," 17.
67. Kamalb'e registered the following exhumations initiated by their members: Lacamá II, Lacamá I, Tzanimacabaj Chuchipacá II, Xabillaguach, and Xecoja. Asociación K'amalb'e, Eco-Spirituality.org.
68. Amnesty International, "Civil Defense Patrols Re-Emerge," 18–19.
69. Author interview, Alejandro.
70. Ibid.
71. Ibid.
72. Zerubavel, "Social Sound of Silence," 32.
73. Richard, "El Tumulto de las Fronteras."
74. Author interview, Miguel.
75. See Esparza, "Santo Tomás Chichicastenango's Municipal Firefighters," 57–78.
76. Author interview, Miguel. *Prensa Libre* also reported that forty-three, not forty-two, cadavers were the victims of the massacre and said, "Unknown men who pretended to be soldiers arrived in the village, in the morning, still asleep when the neighbors were surprised. A survivor said that the strangers asked the patrol to be formed because they would leave to hunt guerrillas. When they did, they were held at gunpoint and then systematically mass murdered." HNG, *Prensa Libre,* Echeverría, "Otras 43 Personas," 8.
77. Author interview, Miguel.
78. Author interview, Pascual.
79. Author interview, Miguel.
80. Ibid. *Prensa Libre* reported on the massacre: "Chichicastenango municipal firefighters came to the village with its rescue units working under a constant rain managed to transport the bodies of the 43 victims to the Santa Elena hospital. Neighbors made a plea to state institutions to help buy the coffins." HNG, *Prensa Libre,* Echeverría, "Otras 43 Personas."
81. Manz, *Paradise in Ashes,* 124.
82. Author interview, Miguel.
83. Quoted in Ball, Kobrak, and Spirer, *State Violence in Guatemala,* 81.
84. CEH, VII.193–98.
85. Short, "Australia: A Continuing Genocide?" 46, 51.

9

Militaristic Legacies
Lynching and La Cadena

Even if perpetrators are highly constrained in some circumstances,
they remain active subjects who construct meaning and assert
their self-identities through their violent practices.
—Alexander Laban Hinton, *Genocide: An Anthropological Reader*

Damien Short has pointed out that "genocide is a continuing process in an Australia that has failed to decolonize and continues to assimilate."[1] Similarly, Raphael Lemkin, as Short asserts, was more concerned with the loss of culture than the loss of life, and he "came to view cultural and physical destruction as interrelated, interdependent elements of a singular genocidal process."[2] Following this perspective, in this chapter I argue that the practice of lynching enabled the genocide to continue by desecrating Maya reciprocity values such as service to the community, dishonoring ethnic and class loyalties, disrupting social ties, pitting Indigenous peasants against each other, reactivating collective fear, and perpetuating the Cold War "internal enemy" mythology in remote areas.

As sociologist Angelina Godoy concurs, state terrorism ruptured and replaced preexisting civil society spaces with authoritarian ones.[3] The violence that arose in the wake of the war—assassinations, lynchings, kidnappings, and drug trafficking, among other acts of violence—made 2002 one of the most violent years of the country's postwar period. In just the month of December that year, 426 deaths—thirteen per day—were recorded.[4]

Lynching is a complex crime encompassing torture, homicide, and the destruction of property[5] and a phenomenon not unique to postwar Central America; the term was coined in the United States, in the Jim Crow South.[6] Martha K. Huggins defines lynchings as popular tribunals in which victims are sentenced to torture and death without due process of law.[7] By definition, vigilantism involves actions carried out beyond the established legal framework, a "communal desire and willingness to enforce existing law or to precipitate a new necessary and proper order by popular rule in order to meet social exigencies."[8] Scholars argue that lynchings are of short duration, lack an ideological underpinning, and are usually led by community elites.[9] Although it is tempting to identify lynching with criminal actions carried out by vigilante groups, the manipulation of fear aimed at the repression of social and criminal justice demands derived from the war and genocide legacies should be seen as the key element distinguishing vigilante actions and state-sponsored terror encouraging the practice of lynchings.

In Todos Santos Cuchumatán, Huehuetenango, during a market day on 29 April 2000, the lynchings of a Japanese tourist accused of baby stealing, Saison Tetsuo Yamahiro, and Edgar Castellano, a Guatemalan bus driver, sent waves of chilling terror beyond the nation's borders.[10] Two prior incidents of lynching are reported: one referring to the 1984 attempted lynching in Tierra Nueva, Chinautla—a region known for its militaristic stance—when "a group of men armed with knives, sticks and machetes, tr[ied] to lynch the deputy mayors of Tierra Nueva, Chinautla,"[11] while another refers to the lynching of three neighbors on 7 January 1996 in Patzún Chimaltenango as the first case of lynching.[12]

Through the lens of the Xalbaquiej lynching, perpetrated by a network of ex-patrol groups known as La Cadena, "the Chain," I argue that, while on the surface lynchings present vigilante characteristics, ex-patrols also used them to settle war accounts with human rights groups seeking to exhume bodies and to request justice for crimes committed in the past by the state.[13] That is, rather than spontaneous eruptions of mob violence, some instances of lynchings and attempted lynchings could also be considered political crimes, organized and premeditated events, which is also suggested by the United Nations Observer Mission to Guatemala (MINUGUA).

I tease out the reenactment of the genocide's public spectacle of cold-blooded executions to show the "still present counterinsurgency structures,"[14] broadening the analytical scope beyond a "vigilante culture" approach to include those planned lynchings motivated by political reasons. Relying on militaristic cohesion rooted in primary bonding facilitating the reproduction of the myth of the "savage primitive Indian," the practice of lynching enabled the further reproduction of cultures of "terror and fear," "violence," and "silence," which was fabricated by the oppressor for the internally colonized.[15] "Latin America still lives with the legacy of the 1970s," suggested Dirk Kruijt in the early 2000s.[16]

An early analysis of lynching exposing the army's derisive views of Indigenous peasants blamed Maya "customary law," a term that refers to unwritten traditional legal norms, which need to be distinguished from the positive law.[17] However, Maya customary legal practices are, far from being punitive, guided by the principles of reconciliation, as scholars have pointed out. This means that the focus is on the victim and not on the victimizer—a view that markedly departs from the Western criminal justice perspective. Like Godoy, I trace "the lynchings' roots in state terror"[18] in the context of a vengeful aftermath and growing economic inequality, as described by anthropologist Jennifer Burrell.[19] People's perceptions of public insecurity and corruption and mistrust of the criminal justice system are also factors that partially account for lynching.[20] According to a survey by Vox Latina published in *El Periódico*, 42 percent of those interviewed thought that the reasons behind the lynching were distrust of the criminal justice system, followed by 10 percent indicating that it was lack of authority.[21]

Lynching: A General Statistical Profile

In 1999, MINUGUA reported that lynchings took place in areas with low rates of homicides and where high rates of extreme poverty and social exclusion were most deeply felt.[22] By 2003, the number of lynching victims "dropped sharply," but the practice continues to this day.[23] All of this must be considered in the context of a postwar period in which "average peacetime violence [was] worse than wartime violence."[24] This includes Black Tuesday, 24 July 2003, about a month after the Supreme Electoral Tribunal ruled that former General Jose Efrain Rios Montt's aspirations for presidency was "inadmissible." As a result, "thousands of peasants were bused from rural areas to protest the Tribunal's decision, leaving at least two reporters dead."[25] By 2000, Guatemala's homicide rate was twice that of Latin America as a whole.[26] Overall, more men than women became victims of lynching and most victims of lynching were reportedly Indigenous.[27]

Between 1996 and 2000, MINUGUA stated that 176 lynchings took place, resulting in 185 deaths and 448 injuries. In 1999 alone, 236 victims were registered.[28] Between 2004 and 2011, reports show the prevailing levels of lynching. Eerily similar, the types of wounds resulting from assaults with bare fists and the burning of victims alive resemble some of the causes of death shown in the Chichicastenango Fire Department municipal log registered by its crew during the war. Geographically, those highlands' departments most affected by the war were El Quiché, with a total of sixty-four incidents leaving 123 people dead or injured, followed by Alta Verapaz, with a total of fifty-four incidents leaving a total of 113 people dead or wounded. These departments were particularly hard hit by state violence in the early 80s.[29]

In contrast, lynchings were almost absent in non-Indigenous departments, such as Jutiapa and Santa Ana.[30] In El Quiché, in 2003, the rates for lynching were higher, but it had lower homicide rates (12) due to firearms than did the non-Maya regions, such as Izabal (226 deaths).[31]

Widespread Circulation of Weapons: Gun Culture

The use of small weapons was embedded in the practice of lynching. According to the Asociación para el Estudio y Promoción de la Seguridad en Democracia (SEDEM), there has not been an arms collection (*despolitización*) since the signing of the Peace Accords in 1996.[32] Against this context, from "1997 to the end of 2005, a total of 33,814 people were murdered."[33] Disguised under the veneer of "disarmament" was the widespread circulation of small weapons. In 2002, there were over 180,000 registered weapons in the country, and MINUGUA estimated there were an additional 1.8 million illegal firearms circulating in the country.[34]

The availability of small weapons shows the failure to disarm militarized structures in rural areas. In the community of Las Trampas, Sololá, neighboring southern El Quiché (see Map 2), two brothers in their twenties accused of stealing a tape recorder and some textiles were lynched in 1997. One fusil Galil AK-47 and two charges were found in their backpacks. *Prensa Libre* reported the incident by highlighting the "low instincts" of the criminals and the role of the army keeping close to protect public authorities such as the Public Ministry and the Presidential Human Rights Office (COPREDEH).[35] In 1997, in Joyabaj, El Quiché, where the patrol system was known for its belligerence, an AK-47 rifle was also found involved in the lynching of an alleged robber by angry neighbors, along with a toy gun.[36]

In addition to allegations of stealing babies, the lynched were accused of committing various forms of crime, from misdemeanors to serious offenses: stealing livestock, stealing petty sums of quetzals from local groceries, robbing passengers in rural buses, stealing light refreshments from distribution trucks, and being involved in family disputes. Political conflicts in remote areas were also resolved by the lynching of authorities accused of corruption.[37] Accusations of kidnappings for ransom also justified the lynching in San Juan Sacatepéquez in 1998.[38] In general, lynching victims were most often poor men, both urban and rural, but are known to occasionally include pregnant women and the elderly. For example, in Santa Lucia Utatlán, Sololá, together with two other victims, a seven-month-pregnant woman was lynched.[39]

During the War: La Cadena, Army Sweeps

Originating with the formation of the patrol system, La Cadena, or the Chain, was a network composed of patrollers from various communities across Chichi from the east and the west. "Chained" to one another through strong militaristic cohesion and activated to attack those who challenged the army, at the time of this study, this network was one of the many "clandestine structures dedicated to organized crime."[40]

This cohesion was achieved by the army's reliance on forced recruitment, trained obedience, strict control over groups, and complicity in past atrocities. As a result, patrols were given an ideological justification, which "fostered a sense of group unity and morale, and a preconditioned hostility toward anything that could be related to the guerrillas."[41] This criminal network was rooted in military sweeps for "subversives" in dispersed settlements throughout mountains in targeted areas during the height of the genocide (1981–1983) that brought together militiamen from distant communities to defeat the "internal enemy," the poorly armed rebels and their sympathizers from Chichicastenango.[42] In Huehuetenango, according to the Truth Commission, patrols would also go "in a big line of approximately 400–500 people. Soldiers would go in the middle of patrols, then a soldier, and then again another two patrols."[43]

During military operations, patrols "went on army-accompanied sweeps that lasted up to several weeks" to hunt *guerrilleros*.[44] Also, Americas Watch reported that during the war, "in northern Quiché, men were called out for *rastreos* [sweeps] on the town loudspeaker or with a firecracker, and patrols [we]re not allowed to go home to say goodbye to their wives and children."[45] Although the exact location and year of this photograph (Fig. 9.1) is unknown, it depicts elements of patrols jointly hunting for alleged guerrillas with Indigenous soldiers dressed in camouflage ordering them to carry out their internal security duties.

Figure 9.1. Anonymous Soldiers and members of PACs. © CIRMA, Fototeca Guatemala. Archivo fotográfico Comité Holandés de Solidaridad con el pueblo de Guatemala.

Also in the municipality of Zacualpa, in 1994, 500 patrols from assorted communities demanded the release of a patrol accused of human rights violations. Americas Watch also reported during the war:

> One February incident in which civil patrols from different villages around Nebaj were called up by army commanders. Some fifty soldiers and two hundred patrollers walked to a small village, which had been established recently without army permission near Sumal Grande. The patrollers were ordered to burn buildings and crops, and to march the inhabitants to the town of Nebaj, where they were interned in government camps, along with the others flushed out of the mountains, to await resettlement in army-approved "model villages."[46]

Victoria Sanford also reports that "while the army carried out ground and aerial attack against the unarmed civilians, in the valleys below the civil patrollers searched out and destroyed nearby planted crops, stole whatever livestock they found, and burned any stored food they unearthed from buzones."[47] The participation of patrols in the *rastreos* resulted in the incursion of neighboring patrols into adjacent communities. The army relied on the patrols' intimate knowledge of the wooded, rural footpaths that connected remote communities.

Gerson, a betterment committee authority from Saquillá, remarked on the mobilization of patrols from other communities into their villages to kidnap neighbors presumed to be involved with guerrillas:

> A group of people from [the Eastern communities] of Xabiyaguach and Chipacá came. From the community of Xabiyaguach, José Riquiac was the chief of the military commissioners. He not only visited the communities, but also kidnapped those who were involved with the guerrilla in Pajuliboy. Ten people were beaten with sticks and tied to trees.[48]

Vicente, a Municipal board staff, spoke of the kind of informal solidarities that acted to protect people's complicity with criminal activities: "I believe that the Chain is still working. If the chief is accused, he would go to prison, and the rest of the people, like a Chain, would follow him. That's why they [former patrols] have to protect each other."[49]

Protecting each other from criminal accountability, this cohesion echoes the non-Maya army's shared pacts of silence that it enforces with its subjugated allies to protect the institution—and allegedly the country—from judicial proceedings related to war crimes. In short, ex-militiamen were bound together by years of association, connected by shared feelings of pride. All of these factors converged in a lethal early legacy of war that endures to this day, twenty years after the Peace Agreements were signed.

Postwar Revival

Angelina Godoy argues that in Latin America, "citizens also clamor for state enforcement in the form of zero tolerance," giving legitimacy to unlawful acts.[50] What Godoy fails to note is the underlying militarism that fosters vigilantism and calls for a *mano dura*, a "strong hand," in the first place.[51] Rather than a weak state, as posited by scholars such as Godoy, the renewed mobilization of La Cadena shows that an authoritarian state enabled the practice of lynching in the postwar years.[52]

The Chain, according to Godoy, was a "formed during the war and served as a way for civil patrol commanders to coordinate their actions between communities and the army."[53] The Chain was a clandestine military force characterized by its militaristic cohesion, as illustrated in the many coordinated acts of support shown by patrollers when demanding that other patrollers accused of human rights crimes be released from jail.[54] Cohesion, military sociologist Morris Janowitz has pointed out, relates to "the feeling of groups' solidarity and the capacity for collective action—[it] is an essential aspect of the military profession's internal organization that conditions its political behavior ... [it] rests on primary groups' solidarity and on personal loyalties that men develop toward each other."[55] The Chain illustrates the long-term cohesion forged within former militiamen that integrated the east and the west regions into a "brotherhood of violence," to paraphrase Fanon, even in the war's early wake.

The Reproduction of Fear and Violence

The renewal of La Cadena relied on primary group bonding leading to the group's internal cohesion. By 2000, this coordinated military structure was not yet disentangled, bringing a horrifying unity to Chichicastenango. Domingo, an ex-military commissioner from an eastern community observed, "The military mentality tells us we go together and united."[56] Neighbors feared being executed or punished if they refused to participate with La Cadena, coercing them into becoming accomplices of human rights abuses.

Former patrols continued to unite under the army's orders. Father Andrés, from the El Quiché Archdiocese, summarized how postwar militarization brought neighbors together in violent action: "There are moments that all of them rally together without any division." He further emphasized people's capacity for "standing up at any moment ... doing anything and acting in a bloc."[57]

To verify the existence of the Chain, human rights representatives provided me with *actas,* also known as "memorials," or written petitions to the state, containing the thumbprints and signatures of S-5 military officers liaising with communities. These *actas,* filed at the Public Ministry, were evidence of the rational and planned coordination of a lynching leadership, compelling neighbors to bear witness to the abuse against those not complying with officers' laws. For example, on 28 November 2000, in the hamlet of Las Conchas in the Department of Las Verapaces, a crowd of 500 people lynched five men accused of stealing the equivalent of U.S.$50. A notebook with the signatures and fingerprints of 100 people supporting the execution was turned over to the police by community authorities.[58]

Fast Communication and Unity

In Pocohil I, Catholic followers told me that at least twenty-three hamlets were part of the Chain while other informants pointed to an estimated forty communities, out of the seventy-six communities at the time of this study in 2000. The authorities were former PACs chiefs. Alfonso, a former patrol leader who participated in the Chain, noted that "there were four general chiefs for each hamlet selected [by] the army. These men are now in the community."[59] "When one is involved [in La Cadena], one does not think anything good," Tomás from Chicuá asserted.[60] La Cadena facilitated a rapid intracommunity communication, unifying the population. Gerson, from Saquillá, stated:

> When the subversion came, all those communities got together to work with the army: Saquillá I, II, all the six Mactzules, the three Paxot, Xalbaquiej, Xepocol, and Patzibal. Some communities were united, like Chucojom, Pocohil, and Xeabaj. There were like twenty-seven cantons that went together to the Army [Base No. 20] to receive orientation.[61]

"For any unexpected event, yes, we have unity."[62] This remark, by Vicente, from the municipal board, reveals the militaristic cohesion embedded in the Chain, compelling neighbors to participate in sweeps. "The key word in Chichicastenango is internal security, and if that is what we want, we have to be coordinated," Vicente asserted.[63] Tomás described how consistently community members support his network in the western area: "Around Saquillá, Patulup, Paxot, all that area and until today." He pointed out that "if you look at the behavior of ex-civil patrols chiefs, there isn't a big change from past years. In Chicuá, there is a 40 percent change."[64]

Vicente also explained how the Chain used means of communication that were deeply rooted in Maya rural community traditions, especially those in remote and widely dispersed mountain areas:

> I do not remember the type of messages that other cultures used in other times, such as the Peruvians, but they did pass the message one to another, running. They would leave it in the [next] person's hand and he would run and take it to the next point … Well that's how we communicate. Remember we are a Mayan culture,

purely Mayan, and we have our own different ways of communicating in the mountains. We communicate with screams—we can identify when it is a scream of help, happiness or sadness.[65]

To explain the system of communication, he recounted how the Chain was used to inform other communities:

On that side of the town, we do not bother. Suppose that right now a UFO landed in the middle of Saquillá I; in less than twenty or twenty-five minutes it would be known in Pachot, it would be known in the Mactzules, and it would be known in *el pueblo*.[66]

Referring to communities in the east, also tied to this militarized structure, Vicente told me, "We would inform Quiejel [in the event that something happened] and in the lapse of two to three hours, the seventy-six communities would be chained."[67]

Showing how the practice of lynching endured beyond the years directly following the Peace Accords, in 2010, I interviewed Alejandro, a member of the Fundacion de Antropología Forense de Guatemala or the Guatemalan Forensic Anthropology Foundation (FAFG) and a survivor of the Pocohil I near lynching on 29 May 2009. In this community, a few families organized in CONCODIG (Asociación de las Comunidades para el Desarrollo Integral de Guatemala) claimed to have identified the site of a clandestine grave containing the remains of at least seven of their relatives killed during the war.[68] According to REHMI, many war remains are buried in the backyards of their own or former patrols chiefs or ex-military commissioners' ranches or in the yards of their villages' elementary schools.[69]

When the FAFG exhumation team and CONCODIG human rights activists arrived at the site and realized that the grave had been removed, they decided to call Diego Martín Salvador, former patrol chief, ex-auxiliary mayor at the time of the massacre, and by then an Evangelical leader. After being told that Diego Martín was not home, the team was leaving when they heard neighbors shouting, "Guerrillas entered the house of Diego Martín, bring gasoline." What unraveled from that point on was a terrifying reenactment of the genocidal violence and the lynching of the early aftermath. Alejandro recounts the story:

Neighbors started to accuse us of wanting to kidnap the ex-military commissioner that we wanted to put him in jail. We told them that it was not so, that we were not police officers or anything of that sort. By that time, there were already, I do not know how many, eight or ten people; they already had machetes and all that.[70]

Those against the exhumation process demanded that the FAFG cease their work. Statements made to the Unidad de Protección a Defensoras y Defen-sores Derechos Humanos (UDEFEGUA) show that Diego Martín's relatives asked, "Why do you want to help the 'bad people'?" The absence of the National Police authority that ended up encouraging the abuse of family members requesting the exhumation was highlighted in Alejandro's account:

> People asked us what we were doing there. I explained everything to them all over again, saying that the District Attorney's Office had authorized us to be there ... They told us that the Office did not consider, that we were supposed to have asked permission to enter from the community. We told them that we had permission. But [the community authorities] were there, and they began to beat up this [young person] ... for having organized the exhumations.[71]

Relatives requesting the exhumation were kept during this time by their neighbors, tortured, and made to pay Q500 for the problems they had brought to the community.[72] During our interview, Alejandro praised his forensic team members for having quieted down neighbors, who were ready to set them on fire: "This fellow—who was an archaeologist—managed to shut them all up. He explained to them what we were going to do and he apologized to them on our behalf." At the end, however, they had to tell the authorities, "You were right; we apologize for not abiding by your [community] laws"[73] of requesting permission from authorities.

But the gathered neighbors did not believe what the anthropologists were saying. CONCODIG members eventually managed to escape to safety to share the frightening experience that had transpired in Pocohil I. Among them was Angelica Macario, whose father, a Rujunel Junam Council of Ethnic Communities "We Are All Equal" (CERJ) leader in his Chulumal IV community, had been killed in front of his house (Chapter Eight). By reinforcing an ideological justification, pro-army community authorities replicated the war's sense of group loyalty and morale toward anything that could be related to the ex-rebels, namely human rights groups.[74] As one Guatemalan human rights lawyer from the Instituto de Ciencias Comparados (ICCPG), remarked, "Lynchings are created to give a feeling of insecurity and strengthen authoritarian structures, especially the presence of the army in the streets."[75]

The Chain: Keeping Militarization and Militarism Alive

By stressing a vengeful aftermath, rather than reconciliation, I emphasize the ongoing reproduction of a culture of violence, defined by Brandon Hamber as a society that endorses the use of violence as a legitimate means to resolve social conflict.[76] The Chain reactivated at least two layers of fear in people: of being labeled "bad people" by army loyalists and of the return of the violence that could plunge them and their families into further poverty and social despair.

The first fear reduced villagers' choices to playing the role of either victim or victimizer, which pressured them to join the patrols. The peasants' second fear was of the return of deadly violence, by which they could be manipulated.

The use of small arms in lynching highlights the army's role in licensing and failing to restrict the use of weapons. According to SEDEM, "In 2004, of all illegal activities reported by the National Police, 80.8 percent of homicides were perpetrated with weapons; out of the wounded, 65.8 percent corresponded to the use of weapons."[77] One trade unionist commented: "With so many private police, you don't need an army, and the private police have got better arms … There are 50,000 private security police, many of them illegal. They are directly organized by the military and ex-military. The prerequisite for involvement in private security is that you are an ex-soldier."[78]

The Xalbaquiej Lynching: The Reactivation of the Chain

Interviews with survivors of the Xalbaquiej lynching show that persistent militarization, through the socialization of military values and the reproduction of militaristic cohesion,[79] directly connects with Chichicastenango's historical east/west division. That is, paradoxically, through lynching, militarization closed the gap between the geographically and politically divided areas, as former militias widened the sense of community through intercommunity criminal complicity. This is illustrated by the lynching that took place in the western community of Xalbaquiej on 8 July 2000. Eight peasants from the same Panzay family were publicly whipped and burned before a cheering crowd of some 200 villagers.[80] About this harrowing spectacle of violence, I interviewed two K'iché survivors in Santa Cruz, thanks to the help of the local Catholic priest, Ramon Peréz, who called the lynching a "postwar massacre."[81] As mentioned in Chapter One, the names used in interviews with survivors of the lynching are identified in secondary sources by their real names and therefore are not pseudonyms.

The peasants recounted how a crowd of residents with plastic containers of gasoline were waiting for them at a roadblock and dragged from their minivans when the ringleaders asked the crowd whether the terrified victims should be doused. In its aftermath, the local El Quiché TV station repeatedly showed the charred corpses, and the newspaper, *Prensa Libre,* reported how the victims became human torches, reminding peasants of the horrors of the genocide (1981–1983).[82]

The gathering of hundreds of peasants was not spontaneous, given the scattered geographical locations of communities. Rather, it shows that the Xalbaquiej lynching was linked to a newly created "Security Committee," which facilitated the reactivation of La Cadena.[83] It showed forms of cruelty informed by dehumanizing practices learned earlier in a context of counterinsurgency violence that engulfed communities. Rather than a senseless postwar "ethnic conflict" executed in "pervasively persistent" multiethnic settings, the practice of lynching should be seen as a deliberate militaristic mechanism that perpetuated terror and fear within highland communities.

Former patrols from fourteen to thirty hamlets (the number varies depending on the source) were once again "chained" to one another from distinct communities.[84] To get neighbors to gather, ringleaders used *gorgoritos*, quickly gathering the whole community: men and women, including the elderly, and children. Neighbors' knowledge of footpaths connecting hamlets facilitated this collective gathering, as people crossed innumerable paths at the Xalbaquiej bridge, previously established by perpetrators as a "security checkpoint." A few days later, one of the two survivors, Juan Panzay, shared with me details of the nightmare that had engulfed them.

Repeatedly, the victims were accused by ringleaders of not serving the community: "'You do not work for the community, you don't cooperate, and you don't serve the community.' 'That's not true,' I told him. 'I recently brought some development projects to the community.'"[85] These accusations of not serving the community eerily evoked the accusations made during the war, justifying the killings of popular organizations' leaders and nonpatrollers who refused to obey the army's orders. Juan reported on the military mentality in the community of Xalbaquiej:

> They went into a community to loot everything, with a military mentality. In the year 1982, they took the community of Xalbaquiej. Three thousand patrols murdered around 150 people: men, women and children with this well-organized group that was called the patrols' Chain. They had received orders from the captain.[86]

The second survivor, Diego Panzay, who was left lying on the ground, severely beaten, remembered that one of the leaders of the mob shouted:

> "What should we do, guys? Should we throw the gasoline?" "Yes!" [was the answer]. Everyone lifted their hands! I saw how they doused the [victims] with gasoline, on their faces and on their bodies. Then I heard a noise like a truck. Soon after, I realize[d] that the noise was from the burning bodies.[87]

Diego Panzay recalled his dialogue between himself and one the attackers:

> "So, what do you think? Are you going to go and denounce us to human rights?"
>
> "No," I replied.
>
> "OK, you will not go to denounce us to human rights, because if you do, we are going to kill you like we did with these seven people. There is no more gasoline for you. You are lucky you are alive."

And the rest of the people said, "No!! Let's kill them right now. Let's kill them with kicks and fists."

And the man from Xalbaquiej said again, "I know you will go to report the incident to human rights organizations."[88]

This gruesome reference to the lack of gasoline is disturbingly also found in other cases of lynching.[89] The victims' ages in this brutal attack ranged from sixteen to sixty years old, all Maxeño males, all relatives, grandchildren, and nephews of a family that had testified to the Truth Commission.[90] Showing the legacies of the unresolved crimes of the past, the Xalbaquiej lynching claimed the lives of five family members from Saquillá II who had denounced the patrols system in early 1990.[91] For the Panzay family, this was the third state-sanctioned massacre by former patrols they had experienced. On 23 June 1993, patrols from a bordering western community killed three young family members.[92] Relatives had challenged the participation of civilian patrollers before human rights groups. As a result, in September 1997, along with members from MINUGUA, a forensic team carried out an exhumation in their Saquillá II community. After digging, however, they found only one piece of evidence since the victims' remains had been removed days before.[93]

When I asked what he thought about justice, Juan Panzay convincingly replied, "I want to request from the authority, from the Public Ministry to bring to justice those responsible for the death of my family. But I believe there is no justice. But still I want them to pay for the lives they took."[94] Justifying the lynchings as a form of vigilantism, "taking justice into their own hands," served to support the military's claims of bringing "security" and peace to otherwise uncivilized rural Maya communities.

Juan sadly expressed concerns about his daughter, now a widow with two children. "Who will take care of them?" he asked. "Now, who will answer for the orphans?" As an old man, he acknowledged he could no longer work. He reflected on the perpetrators: "Do those responsible for the lynching believe that only they have the right to life? What were the terrible crimes committed by my grandchildren, my sons, that they were killed in such a horrible way? They were human beings, but were treated as things or animals."[95]

Juan continued remarking on justice:

> If my family committed a crime, why didn't they bring them to justice? Do they have evidence? Now I am tired with the law. Instead of justice, the authority benefits from crimes. If one denounces these crimes to the criminal justice system, the offenders go to jail a couple of days, months, but then they are set free again. I say there is no justice.[96]

Juan also described "the arrival of a white truck with a green cabin transporting the same villagers who killed my son in 1983 and then my other two sons in 1993."[97] This witness also reported that early in the morning of 8 July, men were seen buying gasoline in the town center, which clearly shows premeditation and planning. There is clear evidence that suggests the planned nature of the lynching by the La Cadena leaders, as also asserted by Godoy.

Relatives of those lynched could not afford the coffins for proper burial, *Prensa Libre* reported,[98] as their extreme poverty became even more accentuated by the deaths of the families' males. A few days later, in a defiant public appearance, around 7,000 men, women, and even young children from twenty-nine Chichicastenango communities justified the lynching.[99] Traditional authorities signed with thumbprints a written statement (known as *actas*) stating villagers' frustration with the lack of justice in their communities. Justice, they argued in this statement, could only be achieved if they took matters into their own hands:

> Being 10:30 am on Friday 21 July, 2000. Meeting in the Xalbaquiej Bridge. Present communities were: Paxot I, Paxot II, Paxot III, Xeabaj I, Xeabaj II, Mactzul I, Mactzul VI, Xalbaquiej, Pocohil I, and Patzibal. All together related the lynching that took place on July 8, 2000, we state being tired of suffering at the hands of thieves, the many armed robberies and rapes of women, leaving people disabled. We acknowledge that MINUGUA, the Office of the Ombudsman and other officials, except for the Mayor of Chichicastenango, had failed to visit our communities to investigate. We hope that these authorities would not then blame the poor peasants who only know how to work and wanted to defend their rights.[100]

Invoking the "good Maya," who "only works" and therefore should not be blamed, community authorities justified the lynching, as an eerie climate of silence prevailed in the aftermath of the incident. For several days, local El Quiché television broadcast video images of the charred corpses in the morgue. Only a few days after the lynching, I went with the European Community Development Program on a visit to a community near Xalbaquiej. On our way, we passed by the narrow crossroad where the grisly lynching took place. I still could see several piles of ashes from victims' remains.

Lack of Accountability: Impunity for the Past and Present

In marked contrast to the aftermath of the lynchings of Saison Tetsuo Yamahiro and Edgar Castellano—analyzed in depth by Burrell—in the days following the Xalbaquiej lynching, local authorities requested the presence of President Alfonso Portillo.[101] A few days later, in an unprecedented trip to a postlynching site, Portillo visited Chichicastenango. Leaders claiming to represent thirty of the seventy-six communities gathered in a crossroad in the western area and sent a message to the president saying that "he had no moral authority to prosecute them for the lynching."[102] After all, he himself had been accused of killing two Mexican citizens in 1982.

Moreover, villagers defiantly warned the president that if a single arrest against those participating in the lynching was made, "there would be consequences."[103] The neighbors' silence in the aftermath of the lynching was highlighted in newspapers.[104] As one informant once told me, "If one is caught and accused, the rest of the ex-patrollers will go, too." The mayor of Chichicastenango, Manuel Sut Lucas, blamed the lynching on the existence of the Mara 18, Mara 13, and Mara Salvatrucha but said he hoped that with the Security Board (Juntas de Seguridad), local lynchings would be prevented.[105]

In March 2001, a judge issued forty-one arrest warrants for the alleged ringleaders of the Xalbaquiej lynching. By year's end, however, the police had not arrested a single suspect. As with other lynching cases, in the case of Xalbaquiej, impunity protected every Indigenous villager implicated in La Cadena. The lynching echoed the genocidal violence, when army soldiers would burn alive those deemed "subversives," thus dealing another psychosocial blow to communities already traumatized. In 2010 and in 2012, during my short visits to the country, I was told by acquaintances that the Chain continued to operate semiunderground (*bajo agua*). The adoption of the militaristic, authoritarian iron fist attitude manifested itself in the belief that lethal violence continued to be seen as a legitimate method of conflict resolution and crime prevention.

Notes

1. Short, "Australia: A Continuing Genocide?" 46.
2. Ibid., 49.
3. Godoy, "Lynching," 641.
4. "Guatemala Civil War," GlobalSecurity.org.
5. I am not defining lynching in the sense of hanging a person from a tree as conventionally defined in North America. In the Guatemalan penal code it is defined as *muchedumbre,* a collective crime committed by people gathered for the act of killing. OAS, "Codigo Penal."
6. Zinecker, "Violence in Peace."
7. Huggins, *Vigilantism and the State.*
8. Culberson, *Vigilantism: Political History,* 13–19.
9. Ibid.; Rosenbaum and Sederberg, *Vigilante Politics.*
10. For a discussion of this particular lynching and about baby stealing in Central America, see Godoy, *Popular Injustice,* 3.
11. HNG, *Prensa Libre,* 19 March 1984. "Attempted Lynching."
12. HNG, *Prensa Libre,* Flores, "Presunto Asaltante Fue Linchado," 8.
13. Carey and Torres, "Precursors to Femicide."
14. Keen, "Demobilising Guatemala," 2.
15. For the reproduction of a culture of fear, see Figueroa Ibarra, "Militarización, Crimen y Poder."
16. Kruijt, "Low Intensity Democracies," 409.

17. See Sieder, "Derecho Consetudinario"; sociologist Carlos Mendoza argues for a "spatial diffusion of lynching," the density of Indigenous population concentration ("Structural Causes and Diffusion").

18. Godoy, *Popular Injustice.*

19. See Burrell, "After Lynching."

20. Zinecker, "Violence in Peace," 12–13; Burgerman, "Making Peace Perform," 245.

21. HMP, *El Periódico,* "Falta de Justicia," 3.

22. MINUGUA, "Ninth Report," 22.

23. Zinecker, "Violence in Peace," 12–13.

24. Ibid., 3.

25. Little and Smith, *Mayas in Postwar Guatemala,* 154, 155.

26. Richani, "State Capacity."

27. MINUGUA, "Tenth Report."

28. MINUGUA, "Informe de Verificación."

29. Ibid.

30. Godnick, Muggah, and Waszink, "Stray Bullets," 19.

31. Homicides by Department in 2003. PDH. "Informe Anual Circunstanciado," 132, 280.

32. SEDEM, "Mapa Centroamericano," 23, fn41.

33. Zinecker, "Violence in Peace," 4. The definition of small arms and light weapons encompasses both military-style weapons and commercial firearms (handguns and long guns), such as revolvers and self-loading pistols, rifles, and carbines (Faltas et al., "Removing Small Arms from Society"). To compare, during his first trip to Cambodia in 1992, Hinton asserts that the country was also "awash with munitions, ranging from handguns and AK-47s to unexploded ordinance … in villages and rice paddies" (*Why Did They Kill?* 6).

34. MINUGUA, "Caught in the Crossfire," 68.

35. HNG, *Prensa Libre,* Saenz Archila, "Dos Hermanos," 39.

36. HNG, *Prensa Libre,* Ramírez Espada, "Turba Lincha." The execution took place in San Juan Los Llanos, Joyabaj.

37. HNG, *Prensa Libre,* Samayoa and Mario Garcia, "Ejército y Policia," 3.

38. HNG, *Prensa Libre,* "Linchado era Secuestrador." In San Juan Sacatepéquez, the victim confessed that he had carried out the "assignment" to kidnap Rosalio Canel Pirir, son of a contracting carrier, for which he had been paid Q400 in cash.

39. HNG, *Prensa Libre,* Chapas Pérez and Saenz Archila, "Embarazada entre Linchados."

40. MINUGUA, "General Assembly Agenda Item 9."

41. REHMI 1998, I.36; REHMI 1999, 129.

42. Americas Watch, *Civil Patrols in Guatemala,* 56; CEH, II.213.

43. CEH, II.214.

44. Allison and Goldman, "Civil Patrols," 81.

45. Americas Watch, *Civil Patrols in Guatemala,* 57.

46. Ibid., 6.

47. Sanford, *Buried Secrets,* 100.

48. APA interview, Gerson.

49. Author interview, Vicente.

50. Godoy, *Popular Injustice,* 39.

51. For literature on vigilante groups, see Huggins, *Vigilantism and the State.*

52. About the absence or "the limited presence of government institutions," see also Godnik et al., "Stray Bullets," 19.

53. Godoy, *Popular Injustice,* 86.

54. For example, observers have noted, "On April 30, 1999 some one thousand villagers

traveled to Huehuetenango to free their condemned patrollers." Kobrak, "Long War in Colotenango," 233–34; see also, Solomon, *Institutional Violence,* 26.

55. Janowitz, *Military in the Political Development,* 67–70.
56. Author interview, Domingo.
57. Author interview, Father Andrés.
58. *Newsday,* 18 March 2001.
59. Author interview, Alfonso.
60. APA interview, Tomás.
61. APA interview, Gerson.
62. APA interview, Tomás.
63. Author interview, Vicente.
64. APA interview, Tomás.
65. Author interview, Vicente.
66. Ibid.
67. Ibid.
68. Some of the victims were Sebastián Martin Guarcas, Manuel Jorge Ordonez, Miguel Macario Xaper, Sebastiana Maria Morales González, Diego Martin Salvador, Sebastián Martin Chitic, Sebastián Tevelan Panjoj.
69. REHMI, 1998, I.23.
70. Author interview, Alejandro.
71. Ibid.
72. HMP, UFEDEGUA Archive.
73. Author interview, Alejandro.
74. The REHMI noted that involvement in violent act fostered "genuine blood pacts," 1999, 130.
75. Author interview, Edgardo.
76. Hamber, "Have No Doubt."
77. SEDEM, "Mapa Centroamericano," 22.
78. Keen, "Demobilising Guatemala," 11.
79. Siebold, "Essence of Military Group Cohesion."
80. HMP, *Prensa Libre,* Campos and Matias, "Silencio tras Masacre," 3.
81. See also Godoy, *Popular Injustice,* 39.
82. For a discussion of México, see Vilas, "(In)Justicia por Mano Propia."
83. HMP, *El Periódico,* Llorca, "El Reestreno de las PAC," 3.
84. With a population of 422 residents in the mid-1990s.
85. Author interview, Panzay, Juan.
86. Ibid.
87. Author interview, Panzay, Diego.
88. Ibid.
89. "A crowd attacked teenagers Cristobal Néstor Xum, and Diego Gómez Colom for having robbed Q600 from a store owner in front of the Municipality. The assailants did not have more gasoline sparing them with the awful death." HNG, *Prensa Libre,* "Linchan a Dos Presuntos," 75.
90. See MINUGUA, "Eighth Report," 10.
91. The fatal victims were identified as Juan Panzay Ajpop (60), Manuel Panzay Calel (23), Diego Panzay Calel (16), Cirilo Panzay Calel (16), Sebastián Suy Saquic (22), Anibal Panzay Choma (17), Diego Sucuque Aj (25), and another unidentified victim whose body was burnt beyond recognition. HMP, *Prensa Libre,* Campos, "Moviles sin Ser Aclarados," 8.

92. Some twenty patrols took them to the school and decided to request advice from the military zone. After ninety minutes they came back to murder Tomás, Santos, and Fausto, suffocating them with nylon plastic bags. CEH, VII.193–98.

93. CEH, IV.277.

94. Author interview, Panzay, Juan.

95. Ibid.

96. Ibid.

97. Ibid.

98. Lack of money also prevented families from Saquillá II from burying their victims.

99. HMP, *Prensa Libre*, "Buscan Justificar Muertes"; Godoy, *Popular Injustice,* 92.

100. HMP, Xalbaquiej.

101. Burrell, "After Lynching," 2013.

102. HMP, *Prensa Libre*, Ramírez Espada, "Lanzan Desafio," 3.

103. Godoy, *Popular Injustice,* 92.

104. HMP, *Prensa Libre*, Campos and Matias, "Silencio tras Masacre," 3.

105. Born in the aftermath of El Salvador's twelve-year war, the *maras* comprised marginalized groups engaged in illegal activities. See, for example, Hume, "Armed Violence and Poverty."

10

A Forseen Aftermath
Decree 3-2014

> *Once the crime has been committed, we can only console the victims, not undo the crime. But we can have an effect on the criminals, on those who committed crimes in the past, so that they don't repeat their crimes, and on future criminals.*
> —Tzvetan Todorov, *Memory as a Remedy for Evil*

> *How can we forget both military commissioners, members of the G2, S5, S2, private guards, soldiers, generals, colonels, Kaibiles, spies, who lived and became enriched killing and massacring people who dreamed and thought different. How to forget the moments spent in a military police station in Civil Self-Defense Patrols' checkpoints, at Military Reserve units, military zones and military detachments where the planning of the disappearance of men and women, dreamers and rebels took place.*
> —Centro de Medios Independientes, "Oda a Ti"

Two decades after the Peace Accords were signed, postcolonial contradictions remain as alive as they were in the early aftermath of the war and genocide. As Omer Bartov has concluded, "A historical event can only be understood within its context, just as its significance can be grasped only at some historical distance."[1] The time that elapsed since I interviewed survivors of the 1980s genocide in the late 1990s, and soon after pro-army authorities, was crucial in countless ways to gain the needed sociological and interdisciplinary perspective. Over the years, to complete the book, I went back to the interviews and field research notes to "refresh the manuscript." Every time I asserted my findings, I grew even more convinced of the poisonous legacies of militarism and militarization and of the need to encourage future analysis of the corrosive postcolonial relationships the army promotes in the countryside.

In this book, I have sought to address what is, essentially, a sociological phenomenon: the reproduction of militarization and militarism and its long-term repercussions affecting rural Maya communities. Rather than being withered away, militarism has been hardened by the failure to dismantle the Cold War machinery, particularly its bellicose mythology, which is little analyzed in the global literature of genocide and military sociology. Framing the ongoing militarism and militarization in intersecting ways helps highlight the commonalities of oppression and resonates loudly with the extreme marginalization impacting rural Indigenous communities elsewhere in the Americas.

When the commission called for all witnesses to provide their testimonies, it was presumed that this record would contribute to challenging widespread impunity and the state's denial of human rights crimes as well as to achieving justice for victims. Among the undeniable merits of the CEH was its painstaking documentation of the more than 200,000 people who had been tortured, killed, or forcibly disappeared and its conclusion that the non-Indigenous state had committed genocide against four Maya groups (1981–1983). As Matilde González has asserted, however, the commission's report does not "enable us to understand how the people of the various ethnic groups and places that were affected lived and understood the conflict."[2]

Retrospectively, the commission's large-scale investigation took place in the context of a United Nations peace process negotiated with an army that had little remorse for its past crimes against humanity perpetrated on disarmed rural communities. From a postcolonial standpoint, the signing of the 1996 Peace Accords was a typical neocolonial smokescreen disguising the army's hypocrisy, as demonstrated by its lack of political will to overhaul its militaristic doctrine. Few scholars have considered that the negotiated transition masked the sad truth that, by virtue of militarily defeating the URNG, the army was emboldened to keep encouraging support from disempowered sectors of the Maya population, in the context of conditions of internal colonialism.

In fact, the poorest have continued to be saddled with exploitative wages, to be denied access to cultivable land, to suffer staggering unemployment rates and deficient road conditions, and to lack health and educational infrastructure. Perhaps the most telling evidence of the continuities, rather than rupture, of military control at the state and local level is the official return—through the ballot box—of the army to state power through elections, as I discuss below.

This negotiated ending to the prolonged war silenced local peasant-army relations, while the army continues to manipulate international public opinion, in part through its participation in the UN peacekeeping operations in Haiti and the Democratic Republic of Congo, which are little problematized by transitional justice practitioners and scholars. Though accused of human rights violations by the UN, the "new" postwar army has clad itself in the political rhetoric of a professional military and has successfully integrated its Kaibil special forces units, bringing with them their deep-seated racist doctrine as they deliver "security and development" in post-conflict societies in Africa.

This alleged transformation was an attempt not only to erase from national consciousness the army's callous crimes but also to render hidden from public scrutiny the highly unequal relationship the army had continued to encourage with illiterate peasants in the countryside. As Tzvetan Todorov asserts, evil seems to "have survived intact from all the efforts to fight them with memory."[3] Between "irruptions of memory," as Steve J. Stern points out in his study of Chile's collective memory, and enduring silence over the past, there are important lessons to draw from the silences found in Guatemala in the early aftermath of the war.

First, it shows how the genocide reinforced the Ladino racial supremacy and the army's triumphant memory. Second, a discussion of the politics of remembrance and silence in Guatemala shows how the ongoing alleged threats to national security have overshadowed a national reckoning of the painful issues of national responsibility and collaboration. Third, in this context, not only does the role played by the patrols, as a militaristic structure made up of the internally colonized, deserve attention, but so do the underlying historical conditions shaping Indigenous peoples' genocide roles. Both could easily be obliterated from the collective memory of the war and genocide if the footprints of militarization and militarism are left unaddressed.

Last, and perhaps the most telling lesson to draw when understanding entrenched militarization, is that the oppressed, organized in courageous human rights groups, have resisted the state's efforts to obliterate the past. Organizations such as CERJ, GAM, CONAVIGUA, FAMDEGUA, CALDH, Asociación de Justicia y Reconciliation (Association for Justice and Reconciliation [AJR]), and many others have denounced, exposed, and sought justice for war atrocities. An example of collective efforts is the project of ongoing exhumations at the Peace Operations Training Institute (Comando Regional de Entrenamiento de Operaciones de Mantenimiento de Paz [CREOMPAZ]).

Previously the Military Zone No. 21 of Cobán, Alta Verapaz, CREOMPAZ now functions as a training site for UN-sponsored peacekeeping troops.[4] Most recently, some 500 war remains were found there. Further efforts to preserve the memory of the past are also under way, as seen in commemorations of the Massacre of the Cumbre de Alaska, Totonicapán on 4 October 2012, when peasants blocked highways to protest against "excessive electricity rates, changes to the professional teacher training requirements, and proposed constitutional rceforms."[5] At least six were killed by militarized police forces.

An Unrelenting Past

Between 2000 and 2004, popular support for the army continued unabated. Postwar legacies of militarization and militarism have persisted beyond the postwar years of Alfonso Portillo's pro-military, rightwing FRG political party explored in this study. At the local level, by 2011, the FRG had lost direct control of its supporters in Chichicastenango, but loyalist ex-militiamen and their families continued to be corralled during election times. Ex-patrollers contin-ued to pressure different administrations, including the Otto Pérez Molina ad-ministration, for their last payment for war services in the midst of allegations of being used by political parties who distributed food bags in exchange for votes.[6] The subsequent governments have given continuity, to varying degrees, to the military's prerogatives. These government included Óscar Berger (2004–2008), Álvaro Colom (2008–2012), former general Pérez Molina (2012–2016), and, more recently, Jimmy Morales. Inaugurated in 2016, Morales is a known comic performer representing the National Convergence Front [FCN], which is led by retired military officers implicated in the genocide and by AVEMIL-GUA [Asociación de Militares Veteranos de Guatemala].

Óscar Berger (2004–2008)

The persistence of the past is illustrated by the ongoing activities of the former patrols and ex-military commissioners pressuring for complete payment of their war compensation in exchange for their participation in reforestation programs in their communities. In October 2006, according to Claudia Sa-mayoa, leader of UFEDEGUA (Unidad de Protección a Defensoras y Defen-sores de Derechos Humanos de Guatemala), of one million people who had comprised the PACs in 1983, "still, to date, about 25,000 are under military control ... activated as *sicarios*," or hitmen.[7]

Some of the progress under the Berger administration includes the recov-ery of *El Diario Militar* and the *Archivos de la Policia Nacional* in 2005, the latter containing 70 to 80 million documents of the disbanded National Police, including files on victims murdered and disappeared during the war.[8] This was a landmark step toward recovering the historical memory. Material found in these archives has been used as evidence in the recent local trials.

Álvaro Colom (2008–2012)

Under the Álvaro Colom (2008–2012) administration, representing the more progressive National Unity for Hope (Unidad Nacional de la Esperanza [UNE]) party, the Military Archive Declassification Commission was created and as-signed sorting and declassifying military documents from 1954 to 1996. In 2009, Colom ordered the army to submit four counterinsurgency plans: Plan Sofía, Operación Ixil, Plan Victoria 82, and Firmeza 83. At the same time, a limited policy of reparation was instituted that left out ex-patrollers and their families, who did not qualify as victims.[9] Notably, on 1 August 2007 the con-gress ratified plans to establish the United Nation's International Commis-sion Against Impunity in Guatemala (CICIG), which, with varying degrees of success, still exists to the moment of this writing. Also in 2007, General José Efraín Ríos Montt became a member of congress, which gave him immunity from legal actions over war crimes. In early January 2012, he stepped down from congress, losing his congressional immunity.

The Return and Demise of the Kaibiles (2012–2016)

In 2011, I returned to southern El Quiché as an electoral observer for the Organization of American States (OAS). In one of the meetings convened by OAS with the army to discuss authorities' security plans in areas of El Quiché considered "potentially problematic" during election times, I took the occasion to chitchat with Colonel Carlos Juventino Saavedra Carrascosa, director of the Institute Adolfo Hall, and Sargent Ulises, general secretary of army reserves for El Quiché, who explained to me the system of military reserves prevalent in the country as the country elected a retired general as its new president. Later on that day, Sunday, 6 November, I had dinner at El Chalet, the same restaurant in Santa Cruz where peers and I from the commission had often dined back in the late 1990s.

From here, I watched on TV as General Otto Pérez Molina won the election. While my OAS colleagues were stunned, for me, Pérez Molina did not mean the "remilitarization" of the countryside because a real and substantial demilitarization of structures and ideologies had never taken place at all. As president he called for "national unity," telling Guatemalans to forget the past during his presidential swearing in ceremony on 14 January 2012.

Soon after, his government undertook the audacious move to approve Decree 3-2014, which calls for "the executive office to carry out public measures to promote reconciliation" and for the judicial system to "administer justice in a way that is unbiased and does not affect particular influences recently made public." The decree was approved on 12 May 2014.[10] This effort to silence the genocide was added to the postwar scholarship of denial and revisionism—illustrated particularly by the scholarship of David Stoll, which sadly undermines the courageous efforts undertaken by communities to keep the memory of the past alive and active.[11]

Under the government of Pérez Molina, the military has continued to recast itself as the "army of peace," but recent events show otherwise. In connivance with transnational corporations, the oligarchy, and multinational financial institutions such as the World Bank, the army has sustained criminalization of peasants to push them off their territories and exploit natural resources. At the same time, the postwar state has continued to militarize its responses to organized resistance to the construction of hydroelectric dams "denoting the cannibalistic nature of capitalism."[12] In fact, ex-Kaibil Pérez Molina's tenure was eerily reminiscent of the first decade of the militaristic trend that has been taking place since the war's end. On 30 June 2013, at celebrations for Army Day at Base Militar Mariscal Zavala in Guatemala City, a new national defense policy was announced that involved the participation of advisors and experts from other countries. At the event, the chief of the Southern Command of the U.S. forces, John F. Kelly, shared the balcony with the president and the vice-president, Roxana Baldetti.

This shows that the U.S. interventionist approach in internal affairs has been encouraged through Plan Colombia, the Andean Regional Initiative, the Mérida Initiative, and the Initiative for Regional Security of Central America, among others. These security pacts include training programs and capacity-building lessons, in addition to the sale of arms and equipment and the involvement of U.S. security agencies, such as the DEA (Drug Enforcement Administration) and the FBI, and private corporations in providing the resources for militaries and police forces of Latin American countries.[13] Currently, the U.S. armed forces are present in more than seventy military bases in the region.

To keep its mass-based support, in October 2011, Pérez Molina offered to increase the Ministry of Agriculture's budget to provide fertilizer and technical support and to bring water projects to patrol bastions Paquix and Capellanía, Chiantla, Huehuetenango.[14] Not coincidentally, it was in Capellanía in 2009, under Colom's regime, when ex-patrols took hostages, demanding payment for reforesting their communities, a strategy that was used to quiet down criticisms from internal and national human rights groups.[15]

Unsurprisingly, Pérez Molina closed his presidential campaign in Chichicastenango on 5 November 2011, an occasion he used to encourage ex-patrollers' loyalty. As in 1999, when the FRG corralled votes, Pérez Molina was elected on similar promises to pay war compensation to former patrollers. By relying on its old and renewed, entrenched ideology, the military continued to folklorize Chichicastenango's cultural traditions and its co-opted authorities. Showing their support for the general, the *principales* from the Auxiliatura Indígena offered him the ancestral dance the Caballito of Tzijolaj.[16] By celebrating the general with the Tzijolaj, the township's highest Maya authorities continued to legitimize the Kaibil president implicated in the carnage of the early 1980s.

Twenty years after the signing of the Peace Agreements, the army has continued to skillfully adapt its rhetoric to "times of peace," persuading its supporters internationally of its Hambre Cero (Zero Hunger) policy, which was hailed by the Bill Clinton Foundation. Contradicting the International Index against Hunger, Guatemala's Hambre Cero claims to "shepherd" the fight against this scourge. The 2013 *Report on Indigenous Peoples*, however, notes that the introduction of programs such as the Zero Hunger Pact "do not seem to be contributing to poverty reduction or reduced malnutrition."[17]

Trials: Memory Crisis and Revisionism

Thanks to the international pressure and support to local organizations–such as the Center for Human Rights Legal Action (CALDH)—taking judicial processes upon themselves by working with survivors associated with human rights groups, the perpetrators of crimes against humanity have been brought to national courts.[18] In the most telling Guatemalan politics of resistance—showing once again fiery resistance against forgetting the past by organized sectors of survivors—José Efraín Ríos Montt and José Mauricio Rodriguez Sánchez were brought to trial in 2013, accused of the killing and torture of 1,771 Ixil people and the forced displacement of tens of thousands when he was president and commander in chief. The original sentence was handed down on 10 May, but only ten days later the constitutional court overturned the sentence and declared that a partial retrial was necessary because of presumed due process violations.

Though the trial was hailed as unprecedented by observers, its annulment made a mockery of the feeble democratic fabric of the country, despite the courageous efforts of conscientious local and international lawyers. In 2015, Ríos Montt again appeared in a local court of law; this time he was wheeled in on a hospital gurney and the trial was suspended due to "legal anomalies," as alleged by the accused's legal defense team. Observers have noted that the elite, including then-president Pérez Molina and powerful Guatemalan companies implicated in the genocide, have "voiced their concern over any genocide ruling" in which they could be implicated for abetting or facilitating the genocide.[19]

Roddy Brett, in a recent *Journal of Genocide Research* volume dedicated to the Ríos Montt trial, argues that it "is more than a legal process in that it represents a thermometer for Guatemala's peace process and, ultimately, for testing the nature and stability of the post-genocide/post-conflict conjuncture." Brett concludes that a "partial rights culture," has been achieved, one that has been challenged by the overturning of its verdict.[20] More cautious of transitional justice, Jo-Marie Burt, in the same volume, situates the genocide trial within the "broader transitional justice process in Guatemala [where] the current setbacks should be viewed as a backlash to initial transitional justice success that is neither unexpected nor fatal to the accountability process."[21]

From a postcolonial point of view, however, even these laudable transitional justice efforts need to be more carefully scrutinized. This is especially true when considering postcolonial subjects, since Western-style trials might end up inscribing Indigenous peoples merely as "victims" and not as resistant to conditions of oppression.[22] Second, rather than seeing the success of transitional justice, I would argue there is a failed transition—if there ever was a meaningful transition at all.

Since aftermaths have to do with political agendas of national interroga-tion, that is, reckoning with historical responsibility and national conscious-ness, have recent criminal trials elucidated the war's unpalatable truths? How have local trials unveiled the pacts of silence forged between military commis-sioners and patrols? The trial against Felipe Cusanero Coj, a former military commissioner accused of abducting and disappearing six victims between September and October 1982, in Choatalúm, Chimaltenango, illustrates the pacts of silence forged with the army: he only spoke once during the more than twelve days of trial, as he claimed to be innocent of the criminal charges. He was, nevertheless, found guilty and sentenced to years in prison. His lawyer, Humberto Smith, provided by AVEMILGUA and commissioned by the army, refuted the conviction, and the judge acknowledged that, due to his extreme poverty, Cusanero Coj could not pay bail.[23]

Failed demilitarization and widespread corruption in the armed forces, im-punity, and ongoing violence are intimately related. In fact, one of the most spectacular challenges to military power took place when Pérez Molina was arrested on charges of corruption in September 2015 (before that, Roxana Bal-detti, his vice-president, had been arrested on similar charges). As the *New York Times* reported, all in one day, "such a scene would have been unimagi-nable: a president forced to resign, then sit in open court to hear charges lev-eled against him and ultimately spend the night in a prison he once might have overseen as a top general." [24]

The arrest was the result of the CICIG efforts supported by thousands of demonstrators gathering at the Plaza Central in Guatemala City to end Pérez Molina's multimillion dollar fraud scheme, known as "La Linea," involving customs bribes. The irony is that Pérez Molina has been charged merely for corruption and not the callous crimes against humanity in the Ixil area during the genocide in which he has been implicated. That means that, to this day, not one head of state has been imprisoned for the genocide.

Future Research

In this section, I highlight the various venues for future research linking post-colonial studies and military sociology interrogating Indigenous-military relations. First, the subfield of military sociology could benefit from an ex-amination of the underlying ideological mechanisms and dominant memories holding armies together, which can contribute to the current understanding of conclusions queried by past research, all this from a postcolonial perspec-tive. All too often, postcolonialism is invoked to explain current conditions of exploitation; few scholars have examined precisely what, if any, were the long-term socioeconomic, cultural, and political consequences of militariza-tion and militarism for rural communities.

Indeed, the formation and reproduction of pacts of silence between the military rank and file and the officer corps in post-Cold War Latin America, hiding the ugly truths of the past from the public, has received little attention. While studies that have contributed to remembering Indigenous peoples as rebellious contribute to the deconstruction of racialized stereotypes—such as the myths created by the oppressor about the oppressed being lazy and bloodthirsty—few studies have documented how armies reproduce their institutional memory. My current project comparatively analyzing military museums in the post-Franco era and in Latin America attempts to do just that.

To be sure, however, armies' memories are not homogenous and have competing interpretations of the past. In Chile, I have examined these memories between the minority memory of the military members who refused to support the coup d'état that brought General Augusto Pinochet and his junta to power and the triumphalist memory of the military's high command. Moreover, the memories of both conscripts and reservists accuse the army of exploiting them through forced conscriptions while nevertheless keeping their militaristic identity.[25] Through archival research examining newspapers and military journals, as well as critical ethnographic research revealing the ongoing use of the military in internal and civilian affairs in the post-Cold War years, we could challenge problematic assertions that Latin America's armed forces have dismantled their Cold War internal enemy doctrine.

A military annotated bibliography currently in progress reveals that, since 2000, there has been a gaping hole in studies examining the collective and institutional memory of armies promoting the notion of shared glory and sacrifices, notions that shape current civilian-military relations in the region, long after state violence has ended.[26] What narratives about the role of the military in their communities have been forced upon peasants' memories by counterinsurgency campaigns? This type of question can help reveal how social silence camouflages institutional loyalty and the complicity of the oppressed, the rippling—and long-term—social effects of militarization and militarism.

Second, the war mythology embodied by notions of the "internal enemy" has prevailed because there is an ideological registry that was imprinted through fear but also through a reward system (namely, but not exclusively, through civic action programs). Further studies should consider examining how genocidal ideologies are not easily dissolved in the postwar years and how historically vulnerable Indigenous populations are rendered part of the same murderous designs put forward by transnational capitalism and financial institutions.

In Guatemala, systems of oppression, shared silence, and historical memory are all crucial and interconnected themes necessary to understanding the lingering effects of militarization and militarism. The ongoing, deadly aftermath in Guatemala shows that nearly twenty years after I relocated to New

York City, the end of the Cold War did not quite translate into vanquishing neocolonial ties the army actively fostered, and fosters, with its loyalist subjugated allies.

Third, while genocide studies have long noted the close relationship between genocide and settler colonialism, few, if any, have ethnographically explored the intimate relations between long-term legacies of grassroots militarization and militarism to conditions of internal colonialism and the deafening silence kept by the oppressed.[27] This line of study can uncover a state's political will (or lack thereof) to rebuild war-torn communities, except in those areas where families and communities have come together undertaking efforts to demand truth, memory, and justice. In addition, it can elucidate how in those areas where the former patrols and military commissioners kept their ties with the army, a shared silence was built that contributed to further institutional cohesion, closing any space for the recognition of the immense human and material damage it has done to rural communities, damage that goes beyond the Cold War years.

Limitations

There are at least two important methodological considerations when planning for the replication of this study in Guatemala or elsewhere. First, its replication in Chichicastenango will depend on levels of military control in the township, particularly since entry into militarized communities depended on access to the nearby military zone. Second, as long as research does not endanger the researcher and all those involved in the study, both further critical ethnography and archival research are required to learn about localities' political allegiances during and after prolonged periods of state violence, genocide, and war. Hopefully, future studies will be able to solve some of the methodological limitations that this work presents regarding access to historical events prior to state violence in communities under military control to learn about local systems of authority affected by violence.

Given more time in the field, researchers are encouraged to undertake censuses of communities that can reveal, with some precision, their socioeconomic profiles (especially in places where national censuses fail to report community-based statistics, if they are taken at all).

As I complete this manuscript in mid-2017, the multiple footprints of militarism and militarization still defy sociological and historical understanding. Thinking about the problems of today's militarization and militarism, and their relationship to the early aftermath of the war, is crucial to tackling the devastation currently affecting communities: disregard for human life, widespread corruption, mistrust for state institutions, and clientelism have similarly continued to beset Latin American countries.

The Guatemalan army has grown from 14,193 troops in 2008 to 22,326 in 2014, and increase of 57 percent.[28] Against this ongoing militarization, as long as the extreme disparities persist, the most oppressed are poised to act out their roles during genocidal violence, deepening the internal colonialism that ties them to the very military and Ladino oligarchy that germinated the internal colonial situation exploited for the recruitment of Indigenous peoples. Today, thirty-five years after the height of the bloodbath, under the façade of neoliberal democracy, messy postcolonial and postwar relations and endemic military control over communities have endured. This façade is sustained in coalition with the oligarchy and multinational corporations, perpetuating the scourge of internal colonialism against a globalized context and extractive capitalism rooted in disturbing colonial legacies, uprooting and militarizing entire generations.

Notes

1. Bartov, *Mirrors of Destruction*, 6.
2. González, "Man Who Brought the Danger," 318.
3. Todorov, *Memory as a Remedy*, 7.
4. "ONU encomia a Guatemala."
5. Guatemala Human Rights Commission, "GHRC Condemns Massacre."
6. "Ex-PAC Rechazan Compromisos."
7. Restrepo Echeverri, "Los Ex-PAC Agentes de Tension."
8. See an insightful account by Kirsten Weld, *Paper Cadavers*.
9. COHA, "Combating Impunity," 71; Secretaría de la Paz, "Informe 2009."
10. "Congreso Niega Genocidio." Siglo21.com.gt.
11. Stoll, "Guatemala—Was It Genocide?"
12. Césaire, *Discourse on Colonialism*, 28.
13. Romano, "Natural Presence."
14. "Otto Pérez Viaja Huehuetenango," *Prensa Libre*. Reportedly, Pérez Molina had already visited Chiantla on 14 May of that year, promising the ex-patrols the final payment.
15. "Fijan Ultimatum," *Prensa Libre*.
16. "Partido Patriota Realiza Cierre," *Noticias de Quiché*.
17. "International Index against Hunger." *The Indigenous World*, 80. According to HANCI, by 2013, Guatemala had the most widespread hunger for two years running ("Key Findings").
18. One of the very active human rights groups has been the Families of the Detained and Disappeared of Guatemala (FAMDEGUA).
19. Gligorevic, "Ríos Montt Genocide Trial Delayed."
20. Brett, "Peace without Social Reconciliation?" 285.
21. Burt, "From Heaven to Hell," 143.
22. For an insightful discussion, see Dill, "International Human Rights."
23. "Condena Contra Ex Militar," Noticias.com.gt.
24. Ahmed and Malkin, "President Otto Pérez Molina."
25. Esparza et al., "Antagonistic Memories."
26. Esparza and Woodill, "A Latin American Military Sociology Bibliography."
27. Kuper, *Pity of It All*; Moses and Stone, *Colonialism and Genocide*.
28. Fox News, "Growth of Central American Armies."

Appendix

Table 11.1. Before the Genocide: Sociodemographic Profile for Red and White Communities

Community	Population			Census (Percentages) 1973 Population by Age						Literacy	Economically Active	Indigenous Population
	Total	Men	Women	Under 7	7 to 9	10 to 12	13 to 17	18 & Over				
White												
Mactzul	2,389	49.9	50.1	23.8	9.3	8.5	10.4	48.0	12.6	65.7	99.9
Paxot	1,132	49.9	50.1	25.4	7.7	6.6	10.4	49.8	7.5	64.0	99.7
Saquillá	34	58.8	41.2	35.3	0.0	2.9	11.8	50.0	8.8	58.8	100.0
Red												
Agua Escondida	1,039	51.1	48.9	23.9	9.2	7.6	11.5	47.7	16.8	66.9	99.3
Chugüexa I	159	49.7	50.3	22.0	8.8	8.8	17.6	42.8	11.3	86.8	99.4
Chupol	1,308	49.5	50.5	27.8	8.6	7.4	10.2	45.9	6.9	71.5	99.3

Source: Centro De Información y Documentación Técnica I.N.E. (Census 1973).

Notes: The percentage economically active was calculated by dividing the total headcount of persons economically active for each community by the working age population, ages 18 and over. Author's elaboration with the collaboration of Kristy Sanandres.

Table 11.2. Postwar Socioeconomic Profile: White Communities

Community	White Communities—Census (Percentages) 2002												
	Population			Distribution of Population by Age				Literacy	Economically Active	Education Level			Comments
	Total	Men	Women	0 to 6	7 to 14	15 to 64	65 & Over			No Schooling	Pre-primary	Primary	
Mactzul I	820	46.8	53.2	24.4	22.8	50.0	2.8	41.8	46.0	33.2	0.9	41.0	
Mactzul II	1,507	47.0	53.0	25.2	21.9	49.6	3.3	45.3	74.9	29.3	0.1	44.8	
Mactzul III	488	44.3	55.7	25.2	21.7	48.4	4.7	31.1	49.0	43.6	—	30.9	On census name appears as "Mactzuloxib III"
Mactzul IV	1,271	46.8	53.2	26.8	21.5	48.5	3.2	35.7	76.3	37.3	0.5	35.1	On census name appears as "Mactzulcajib IV"
Mactzul V	851	48.5	51.5	26.0	23.5	47.6	2.9	40.7	65.1	31.3	2.1	39.5	On census name appears as "Mactuloob V"
Paxot I	852	47.2	52.8	24.2	25.9	47.2	2.7	35.2	49.4	38.3	2.3	33.2	
Paxot II	884	48.5	51.5	19.3	24.8	50.9	5.0	48.4	48.2	32.2	0.3	47.6	
Paxot III	882	48.0	52.0	22.6	22.6	51.5	3.4	40.0	28.9	37.4	0.1	38.0	
Saquillá	1,084	46.7	53.3	25.0	20.7	51.8	2.6	43.1	46.5	31.3	0.7	41.0	On census name appears as "Saquiya"

Source: XI Censo de Población, VI de Habitación 2002.

Notes: The percentage economically active was calculated by dividing the total headcount of persons economically active for each community by the working age population, ages 15 and over. Author's elaboration with the collaboration of Kristy Sanandres.

Bibliography

Key Sources

CEH. Commission for Historical Clarification [*Comisión para el Esclarecimiento Histórico*]. *Guatemala: Memory of Silence*, 1999. 12 Vols.

REHMI. *Guatemala: Nunca Más*. Oficina de Derechos Humanos del Arzobispado de Guatemala, Informe Proyecto Interdiocesano de Recuperación de la Memoria Histórica. 4 Vols. Guatemala City: ODAGH, 1998.

REHMI. *Guatemala: Nunca Más*. Recovery of Historical Memory Project, The Official Report of the Human Rights Office. New York: Maryknoll, 1999.

Archives

AHG (Academia de Historía y Geografía). Ciudad de Guatemala, Guatemala.

    Leticia González, Magda. "Revueltas Indígenas." In *Siglo XVIII hasta la Independencia*. Vol. ed. Ernesto Chinchilla Aguilar. *Historia General de Guatemala*. Gen. ed. Jorge Luján Muñoz. 6 Vols. Guatemala City: Asociación de Amigos del País para la Cultura y el Desarrollo, Vol. III, 1995, 1, 712–1, 820.

CIRMA (Centro de Investigaciones Regionales de Mesoamérica) Archivo Histórico. La Antigua, Guatemala.

———. Archivo de Inforpress Centroamericana. No. 561.

———. Archivo de Inforpress Centroamericana, No. 1903.

———. CGD (Colección General de Documentos).

    Colección 57, Personal Collection, Marcie Mersky.

    McAllister, Carlota. "Chupol. Informe." 2000. 73 folios, No. 4258.

———. Colección de Documentos y Publicaciones del Ejército. Document #65. "Objectives of the Guatemalan Civic Action Program."

———. Colección de Revistas Departamentales. "El Héroe Indiano." Fiestas Elenas, August 1938, 49.

———. Colección Familia Figueroa Ibarra. Guatemala, Memoria de Labores del Gobierno Militar, No.2. 1964–1965. Guatemala (Col. Figueroa Ibarra, No. 66) 27, 43.

———. CONAVIGUA. Archivo del Comité Holandés de Solidaridad con Guatemala. Folder No. 58. "Resolver la Problematica de las PAC es Indispensable para que en Guatemala se Termine la Impunidad, se Cumpla la Ley se Respeten los Derechos Humanos." 10 November 1993.

———. CONAVIGUA. Archivo del Comité Holandés de Solidaridad con Guatemala. Folder No. 60.

    Guatemala, Introducción, August 1993.

"Qué es CONAVIGUA." Undated.
Prensa Libre. 7 June 1989.
"Viudas o Guerrilleras. Directivas de CONAVIGUA Insisten en Afirmar que la Organización es un Derecho que les Corresponde." 2 July 1989.
"Fui Combatiente no Genocida." Nacionales. 21 July 1991.
Julio Domingo Mendez Testimony, Guatemala. 15 May 1995.
————. Fondo Infostelle. Archivo de la Coordinadora Alemana de Solidaridad con Guatemala. 07.03.01. Signatura 84.
CDHG.
"Frustrada Entrega de Armas de 140 Patrulleros que Decidieron Dejar las PAC." 11 January 1995.
"320 Campesinos Renuncian a las PAC." 1 March 1995.
"Demobilization of PACs." *Central America Update.* 15–30 June 1996.
"Discurso Leído por Modesto Mendoza." *Informe Diario.* 30 June 1996.
"Gobierno Fija Fecha para Desarme de PAC." 13 August 1996.
"Violaciones al Derecho Internacional Humanitario." Seguiremos Armados: Patrulleros Civiles. 6 September 1996.
CERIGUA.
"Date Set for PAC Disarming." Number 30. *Cerigua Weekly Briefs.* 1 August 1996.
"PACs Disarm, with No Remorse for Role as Big Brother." *Cerigua Weekly Briefs.* Number 32. 15 August 1996.
Informe Diario. "PAC de Colotenango Entrega sus Armas al Ejército." 11 August 1996.
"Disolución de Grupos Paramilitares Debe Ser Total: Agrupación Maya."
CERJ. "Presentación Primer Informe sobre la Situación de Derechos Humanos." Report 31 July–31 October 1988.
"Army Presence Stops Planned PAC Disbandment."
Interpress Service. Zubieta, Celina. "Guatemala, Dudas ante Desmovilización de Patrullas de Autodefensa." 15 August 1996.
————. Fondo Infostelle. Archivo de la Coordinadora Alemana de Solidaridad con Guatemala. 07.02.02 al 07.03.01. Signatura 83.
CDHG. "CERJ Pide a MINUGUA Verificar Surgimiento de PAC en Quiché." 20 January 1997.
CERIGUA.
"Despite Demobilization, PACs and Military Still Feared." *Cerigua Weekly Briefs.* Number 34. 29 August 1996.
"PACs Out of Control." *Cerigua Weekly Briefs.* Number 35. 5 September 1996.
"PACs Glorified, Ombudsman Charges." *Cerigua Weekly Briefs.* Number 41. 17 October 1996.
"Civil Patrols Pass into History." *Cerigua Weekly Briefs.* Number 47. 5 December 1996.
"PACs Refuse to Disarm." *Cerigua Weekly Briefs.* Number 48. 12 December 1996, Informe Diario.
"Patrulleros se Oponen a Entregar Armas antes de Firma de la Paz." *Informe Diario.* 18 August 1996.
"Se Desmovilizan PAC de San Marcos y Alta Verapaz." *Informe Diario.* 13 October 1996.
"PAC en 30 Comunidades de Ixcan Quedarán Desmanteladas Mañana." *Informe Diario.* 12 November 1996.
CERJ. "Los Ex-Patrulleros Están Abandonados." *Informe Diario.* 12 May 1997.
"Marching toward Peace; Weapons Turn-in Gives Hope to Terrorist-Torn Guatemalan Villages." *The Houston Chronicle.* 13 October 1996.

"Rural Communities Fear Peace in Guatemala Could Bring More Violence." *Agence France Press*. Santa Catárina, Ixtahuacán. 9 September 1996.

———. Fondo Infostelle. Archivo de la Coordinadora Alemana de Solidaridad con Guatemala.

07.02.02 al 07.03.01. Signatura 82.

"Noticias de Guatemala: Entrevista a Campesino Forzado en Patrullas Civiles."

———. Fototeca, Guatemala

Araminta Gálvez García. Archivo of the United Nations' Observer Mission in Guatemala (MINUGUA). Solemn disbanding ceremonies, during which patrols gave back their arms, took place on 9 August 1996 in Colotenango, Huehuetenango.

Araminta Gálvez García. Archivo of the United Nations' Observer Mission in Guatemala (MINUGUA). One of the first official army ceremonies that, with the participation of representatives from local government, the United Nations, and the Catholic Church disbanded the patrols.

Archivo Fotográfico del Comité Holandés de Solidaridad con el Pueblo de Guatemala. Anonymous soldiers and members of PACs.

Archivo Fotográfico del Comité Holandés de Solidaridad con el Pueblo de Guatemala. Unknown location. Soldiers giving talks to civil self-defense patrols (PACs), 1984–1990.

Juan Rolando González Díaz. Members of the civil patrols, armed with rifles, adorning the Queen of Beauty of the PACs in Huehuetenango during a demonstration in support of the government and protesting the war in 1993.

———. *El Gráfico*, "17 Facciosos Mueren en Enfrentamiento," 17 December 1981, 5.

———. Publicación *Diario El Imparcial*. Serie La Morgue (Recortes de Periódico). Tema: Militares y Judiciales.

"Acción Cívica del Ejército de Guatemala Observada por Peruano, a Recomendación de Fort Georgia." 22 November 1961.

"85 Centros de Alfabetización para Adultos y 4 174; 7 Centros para la Cultura Básica." 25 August 1962.

"Ministro de la Defensa lo Inaugura en Zacapa." 23 April 1963.

"Acción Cívica del Ejército a Quezaltenango con Equipo AID." 6 June 1963.

"Carretera: Encuentros Chichicastenango." 17 August 1968.

"Galera, Ramón Blanco." 19 August 1968.

"Acción Cívica Militar en Actividades. En Beneficio de la Región Occidental." 12 April 1969.

Cortez Ruiz, Hermana. "Chichicastenango y sus Tradición Indígena." 20 December 1971.

"El Ejército es un Agente de Cambios Sociales." 25 June 1975.

"Vinculación de la Seguridad Militar con el Desarrollo." 26 April 1980.

"Ofensiva Anti-Guerrillera se Inicia en Chimaltenango Hoy." 20 November 1981.

"Ejército en Reparto de Navidades, con Cantidades de Juguetes." 31 December 1981.

———. Publicaciones.

Revista Gumarcaah. 1969.

Ejército, "*Lo que Puede el Espíritu de Solidaridad*," May 1965, Vol. 3, No. 33, 7.

HMP (Historical Memory Project). CUNY John Jay College of Criminal Justice. New York.

CEH Internal Memorandum.

CERJ Archive.

"Historia Chichicastenango." 26 February 1997.

"Historia Chichicastenango." 1999.

Collection: Chichicastenango. Chutzorop Archive.

Collection: Chichicastenango. Historical Battalion.

Collection: Ejército de Guatemala.

"Manual de Guerra Contrasubversiva." 1980.

"Plan de Campaña Victory 82." 1982.

"Plan de Campaña Firmeza 83." 1983.

"Plan de Campaña Firmeza 83–1." 1983.

———. *El Periódico.*

Llorca, Juan Carlos. "El Reestreno de las PAC en Quiché." 3 October 2000.

"Falta de Justicia." 11 November 2000.

"Ejército a Reforzar Seguridad Interna." 1 July 2000.

———. *Prensa Libre.*

"Buscan Justificar Muertes." 22 July 2000.

Campos, Erick. "Moviles sin Ser Aclarados." 11 July 2000.

Campos, Erick and Raul Matias. "Silencio tras Masacre." 10 July 2000.

Ramírez Espada, Alberto. "Lanzan Desafío." 29 July 2000.

———. UFEDEGUA Archive.

HNG (Hemeroteca Nacional de Guatemala), National Clemente Marroquín Rojas, Ciudad de Guatemala, Guatemala.

———. *Memorial de la Escuela Militar.* 31 January, 1891.

———. *Prensa Libre.*

"Municipalidad de Chichicastenango Quemada." 20 July 1981, 6.

"Acciónes Terroristas Dejaron 2 Millones de Pérdida." 21 July 1981, 4.

"Paro Turistico Afecta a 30,000 Personas." 22 July 1981, 4.

"Benedicto Lucas García Critíca Sugerencia de Armar Civiles." 3 November 1981, 4.

"El Ejército Dará Armas a Campesinos Para Su Defensa." 19 November 1981, 2.

"Campesinos Quieren Armas, Baja Verapaz." 5 December 1981.

"800 Peteneros Se Unen al Ejército." 23 March 1982.

"Más de 40 Muertos en Acciones Antisubversivas." 3 April 1982.

Echeverría, Claudia. "Otras 43 Personas Masacradas en Chichicastenango." 19 May 1982.

"Chichicastenango: Iniciada Construccion de Casetas Sanitarias con el Financiamiento del BID," 19 December 1982.

"Integrantes de Patrullas Civiles Recibirán Víveres del Ejército." 5 January 1983.

"Juramentan a Más Patrulleros." 18 April 1983.

"Denuncian Abusos de Patrulla Civil." 22 June 1983.

"Attempted Lynching." 19 March 1984.

"Aldea de Sololá es Inexpugnable por Oposición de Autodefensa Civil." 13 September 1996.

De Avalos, Elizabeth. "Patrulleros de Chichicastenango se Oponen a Entregar sus Armas antes de Firma de la Paz." 28 August 1996.

Hernández, Ramon S. "Le Ganamos la Guerra a la Guerrilla, Dicen Patrulleros antes de Entregar sus Armas." 20 November 1996.

Sáenz Archila, Edgar René. "Dos Hermanos Fueron Linchados Ayer por Turba en Sololá." 2 January 1997.

Flores, Samuel. "Presunto Asaltante Fue Linchado en San Cristobal." 4 January 1997.

"Linchan a Dos Presuntos Asaltantes en Sololá." 10 January 1997.

Chapas Pérez, Arnulfo and Edgar René Saenz Archila. "Embarazada entre Linchados." 6 March 1997.

Samayoa, Sergio and Jorge Mario Garcia. "Ejército y Policia Rescatan al Alcalde de Huehuetenango." 2 December 1997.

Ramírez Espada, Alberto. "Turba Lincha a Presunto Asaltante." 7 February 1998.
"Linchado era Secuestrador." 30 May 1998.
16 May 2000.
Elder Interiano. "CONIC Alerta por Marcha de Ex-PAC." 4 October 2000.
"Portillo: Ex-PAC Son unos Héroes." 28 September 2003.
Seijo, Lorena. "Víctimas a Resarcir Superarán 250 mil." 22 December 2004.
———. *Revista Militar.* Ciudad de Guatemala.
"Guatemala Renace a la Vida Activa y de Progreso." XII, Nos. 1–3 (January–March 1935).
"Expedición Administrativa del Presidente de la Republica por la Zonas del Occidente y Sur." Vol. XIV, 5ta época Nos. 1–3 (January–March 1937).
"La Función del Ejército: El Problema de la Educación, La Acción Civilizadora del Ejército." Nos. 7–8 (July–August 1940).
"Reservas Militares, Graphic Section," April–June Issue. 1960.
Navarino, Mela. "Que Es y Como Nació Acción Cívica Militar." No. 24 (October–December 1961).
"Acción Cívica un Arma Muy Efectiva." Vol. 65 (July–September 1970).
García C., Infantry Lieutenant Mario Roberto. "Una Experiencia Involvidable." Vol. 65 (July–September 1970).
"Sobre Actividades del Ejército se Informó en Conferencias de Prensa." Vol. 65 (July–September 1970).
"Contribución del Ejército al Progreso de Caminos Vecinales." Vol. 66 (October–December 1970).
"Acción Cívica, El Desarrollo de los Ciudadanos" (October–December 1971).
———. *Siglo Veintiuno.*
Jimenéz, Jorge. "Un Muerto en Desalojo." 3 October 2002.
"Fracasa Intento para Disolver PAC en un Cantón del Quiche." *Siglo Veintiuno,* 14 January 1995.

Interviews

Author Interviews

Alberto. Health promoter.
Alejandro. FAFG. Guatemala City, August 2010.
Alfonso. Chain participant and former patroller. Chicuá, July 1999.
Andrea. Catholic health promoter and midwife. Chichicastenango, July 1999.
Andrés, Father. Chichicastenango, March 1998.
———. Santa Cruz, El Quiché, March, 1998.
Asuntos Civiles. Military Zone No. 20. El Quiché, 5 July 2000.
Candelario. Chuchipacá, June 1999.
Domingo. Former military commissioner. Chicuá II, June 2000.
Doroteo. Pocohil Directivos de Accion Católica. June 1999.
Duarte. Lieutenant. Military Base No. 20. Chichicastenango, July 2000.
Edgardo. Human rights lawyer. Instituto de Estudios Comparados (ICCPG). Guatemala City, 2000.
Emilio. Auxiliary mayor. Saquillá II, July 2000.
Esteban. Marista Brotherhood. Chichicastenango, 1999.
Fernando. Ex-Peasant League leader and ex-military commissioner. Chupol, July 2000.

García, José. Lieutenant. Civil affairs officer. Tzocoma Stadium, Chichicastenango, 2000.
Gerson. Betterment Committee. Chichicastenango, 1999.
Human Rights organizer (Anonymous). Lacamá II, December 1997.
Ignacio. CERJ, regional coordinator. Guatemala City, February 1997.
Jesús. Former URNG. Chichicastenango, 1998.
Julio. Ex-Peasant League member. Chichicastenango, June 1999.
Lucrecia. CONAVIGUA leader. Chontolá, Chichicastenango, 2000.
Luis. A. Health Post director, 1999.
Luz. CASODI. Chichicastenango, June 1999.
Manuel. Former patrol chief and reservist from Saquillá I, June 1999.
Méndez. Amilcar. CERJ founder. Santa Cruz El Quiché. 1998.
Miguel. Schoolteacher and municipal firefighter. Chichicastenango, March 1998.
———. Chichicastenango, 2000.
———. Chichicastenango, August 2010.
MINUGUA Staffer. 8 July 2000.
Morales, Sebastián. CUC founder. Chuguexa I, Chichicastenango, July 1999.
Pablo. Human rights lawyer, Instituto de Ciencias Penales. Guatemala City, 1999.
Pantzay, Diego. Survivor of the Xalbaquiej Massacre. El Quiché, July 2000.
Pantzay, Juan. Survivor of the Xalbaquiej Massacre. El Quiché, July 2000.
Pascual. Health promoter, SIAS (Sistema Integral de Atención en Salud). Saquillá II, July 2000.
Pedro. Former URNG. Chichicastenango,1998.
Pedro. Military expert. Guatemala City, August 2010.
Pinzón, Government Office for Human Rights (COPREDEH). Guatemala City. 2000.
Pixcar, Candelaria. CONAVIGUA. Chontolá, December 2012.
Polanco. Mario. GAM cofounder. Guatemala City, 1994.
Raúl. Betterment Committee. Saquillá I, 13 July 2000.
Reginaldo. Betterment Committee, Chupol, August 2000.
Ricardo. Guatemalan Forensic Anthropology Foundation (FAFG).
Rigoberto. President, Friends of the Army Association. Ex-PAC, ex-military commissioner, Patzibal II. Santa Cruz, Military Zone No. 20's Civil Affairs Office, 14 July 2000.
Roberto. INAB. Chichicastenango, July 2000.
Salvador. Teacher. Intelligence. Military Zone No. 20. El Quiché, July 2000.
Samayoa. Colonel. Asuntos Civiles. Military Zone No. 20. El Quiché, 5 July 2000.
Samuel. Authority Patzibal. Chichicastenango, July 2000.
Staff, Justice Program, USAID, June 2000.
Sut Lucas, Manuel. Mayor of Chichicastenango, July 2000.
Tomás. Peasant leader. Chicuá, Chichicastenango, 1999.
Vicente. Municipal board secretary, former patrol chief, key army informant. Chichicastenango, July 2000.
———. Chichicastenango, August 2000.

Collective Interviews

Betterment Committee. Saquillá I and Xepocol, Chichicastenango, 13 July 2000.
CONAVIGUA. Chuguexa, 1999.
CONAVIGUA. Margarita. Chupol, 1999.
CONAVIGUA. Yolanda, Chupol, 1999.
Doroteo. Directivos de Acción Católica. Pocohil I, June 2000.

Emanuel. Survivor, Directivos de Acción Católica. Pocohil I, June 2000.
Eusebio. Pocohil. Directivos de Acción Católica, June 1999.
Evaristo. Directivos de Acción Católica. Pocohil I, June 2000.
Fernando. Ex-Peasant League, Ex-Military Commissioner, Ex-Patrol Chief, CERJ, Chupol, July 2000.
GAM. Chichicastenango, June 1999.
GAM. Chupol, 1 June 2000.
Nicolás. GAM. Chupol, 1 June 1999.
Patzibal Betterment Committee. Chichicastenango, 2000.
Pixcar, Candelaria and Maria Tum. CONAVIGUA. Chontolá, 1999.
Raúl. Chichicastenango, June, 2000.

APA Interviews (Conducted by Juan, APA Member)

Gerson. Saquillá, July 1999.
Jacinto. Auxiliary mayor and principal. 8 July 1999.
Tomás. Ex-peasant leader. Chicuá, July 1999.

Sources

Acan-efe. "Exhumarán restos paramilitares ajusticiados en Guerra." Radio La Primerisima, Nicaragua, 15 March 2010. Retrieved 20 February 2017 from http://www.radiolaprim erisima.com/noticias/72610/exhumaran-restos-paramilitares-ajusticiados-en-guerra.
Achugar, Mariana. "Between Remembering and Forgetting: Uruguayan Military Discourse about Human Rights (1976–2004)." *Discourse Society* 18, no. 5 (September 2007): 521–47.
Adams, Richard N. *Integración Social en Guatemala.* Guatemala City: Seminario de Integración Social Guatemalteca, 1956.
———. *The Development of the Guatemalan Military.* No. 90 Offprint Series. Institute of Latin American Studies. Austin: University of Texas Press, 1969.
———. *Crucifixion by Power: Essays on Guatemalan National Social Structure, 1944–1966.* Austin: University of Texas Press, 1970. Kindle edition.
———. "Conclusions: What Can We Know about the Harvest of Violence?" In *Harvest of Violence: The Maya Indians and the Guatemalan Crisis,* edited by Robert M. Carmack, 274-291. Norman: University of Oklahoma Press, 1988.
———. "Ethnic Images and Strategies in 1944." Paper No. 88-06. Pre-publication working papers of the Institute of Latin American Studies. Austin: University of Texas, 1988.
Agüero, Felipe. *Soldiers, Civilians and Democracy: Post-Franco Spain in Comparative Perspective.* Baltimore: Johns Hopkins University Press, 1995.
Aguilera Peralta, Gabriel. "La Guerra Interna." In *Epoca Contemporánea: De 1945 a la Actualidad. Historia General de Guatemala,* Vol. VI, 135–50. Guatemala: Asociación de Amigos del Pais, Fundación para la Cultura y el Desarrollo, 1997.
Ahuja, Ravi. "The Bridge-Builders: Some Notes on Railways, Pilgrimage and the British 'Civilizing Mission' in Colonial India." In *Colonialism as Civilizing Mission: Cultural Ideology in British India,* edited by Harald Fischer-Tiné and Michael Mann, 95–116. London: Anthem South Asian Studies, 2004.
Akçam, Taner. *A Shameful Act: The Armenian Genocide and the Question of Turkish Responsibility.* Translated by Paul Bessemer. New York: Metropolitan Books, 2006.

Alden, Chris, Monika Thakur, and Matthew Arnold. *Militias and the Challenges of Post-Conflict Peace: Silencing the Guns*. London: Zen Books, 2011.

Allison, Ewen, and Robert K. Goldman. "Civil Patrols." In *Crimes of War: What the Public Should Know*, edited by Roy Gutman and David Rieff, 81. New York: W.W. Norton, 1999.

Alvarez, Alex. *Genocidal Crimes: Key Ideas in Criminology*. London: Routledge, 2010.

Americas Watch. *Civil Patrols in Guatemala*. New York: Fund for Free Expression, 1986.

Americas Watch Committee. *Guatemala: The Group of Mutual Support, 1984–1985*. Americas Watch Report, New York, 1985.

Amnesty International. "Further Information on UA 128/00 (AMR 34/15/00, 22 May 2000) Fear for Safety: Ana María Pichol, et al." AI Index: AMR 34/49/00. 8 December 2000. Retrieved 8 July 2012 from http://www.amnesty.org/fr/library/asset/AMR34/049/2000/fr/6528923e-9bd2-4d67-95da-1e13d5dd328d/amr340492000en.pdf.

———. "Guatemala: The Civil Defense Patrols Re-Emerge." AI Index: AMR 34/053/2002. 4 September 2002. Retrieved 6 June 2017 from https://www.amnesty.org/en/documents/amr34/053/2002/en/

———. "Fear for Safety/Possible Extrajudicial Execution: Amílcar Méndez, et al." AI Index: AMR 34/060/2003. 2 October 2003. Retrieved 22 April 2015 from http://www.amnesty.org/ptbr/library/asset/AMR34/060/2003/fr/ec1ed67e-fac8-11dd-b6c4-73b1aa157d32/amr340602003en.pdf.

Anders, Gary. "Internal Colonization of Cherokee Native Americans." *Development and Change* 10, no. 1 (January 1979): 41–55.

Anderson, Benedict. *Imagined Communities: Reflections on the Origin and Spread of Nationalism*. New York: Verso, 1991.

Anderson, Thomas P. *Politics in Central America: Guatemala, El Salvador, Honduras, and Nicaragua*. Santa Barbara: Greenwood Publishing Group, 1988.

Archer, Christon I. "Bourbon Finances and Military Policy in New Spain, 1759–1812." *The Americas* 37, no. 3 (January 1981): 315–50.

Arendt, Hannah. *Eichmann in Jerusalem: A Report on the Banality of Evil*. New York: Penguin Classics, 2006.

Arens, Richard, ed. *Genocide in Paraguay*. Philadelphia: Temple University Press, 1976.

Arevalo de León, Bernardo. "Civil-Military Relations in Post-Conflict Guatemala." *Revista Fuerzas Armadas y Sociedad* 20, no. 1 (2006): 63–103.

Arias, Arturo. "El Movimiento Indígena en Guatemala, 1970–1983." In *Movimientos Populares, Centroamerica*, edited by Daniel Camacho and Rafael Menjivar, 62–119. San José: EDUCA, 1985.

Arrabure, Manuel, Marcelo Vieto, and Daniel Schugurensky. "The New Cooperativism in Latin America: Worker Recuperated Enterprises and Socialist Production Units." *Studies in the Education of Adults* 43, no. 2 (Autumn 2011): 181–96.

Asdiaes.com. Retrieved 21 January 2013 from http://asdiaes.com/quienes.html. [Obsolete link.]

Asociación Kamalbe Rech Tinamit Ixim Ulew. Eco-Spirituality.org. 2008. Retrieved 6 May 2015 from http://www.eco-spirituality.org/es-qch-ass.htm.

Asselberg, Florine G.L. "The Conquest in Images." In *Stories of Tlaxcalteca and Quauhquecholteca Conquistadors*, edited by Laura E. Matthew and Michel R. Oudijk, 65–101. Norman: University of Oklahoma Press, 2007.

Associaió d'Amistat amb el Poble de Guatemala. *Guatemala: A Grandes Trazos*. Guatemala: Associaió d'Amistat amb el Poble de Guatemala, 2005. Retrieved 5 June 2017 from http://www.aapguatemala.org

Asturias Montenegro, Gonzalo, and R. Gatica Trejo. *Terremoto 76: S.O.S. Guatemala.* Guatemala: Editorial Girblán, 1976.

Ball, Patrick, Paul Kobrak, and Herbert F. Spirer. *State Violence in Guatemala, 1960–1996: A Quantitative Reflection.* Washington, D.C.: American Association for the Advancement of Science, 1999.

Barber, Willard F., and C. Neale Ronning. *Internal Security and Military Power: Counterinsurgency and Civic Action in Latin America.* Dayton: Ohio State University Press, 1966.

Barrientos de Arriaga, Inés Claudia. *Participación Ciudadana y Construccion de Ciudadanía desde los Consejos de Desarrollo: El Caso de Chichicastenango.* Licenciada en Sociología. Guatemala: Universidad de San Carlos de Guatemala, Escuela de Ciencias Politicas, 2007.

Bartov, Omer. *Mirrors of Destruction: War, Genocide, and Modern Identity.* New York: Oxford University Press, 2000.

Bastos, Santiago, and Manuela Camus. *Quebrando el Silencio: Organizaciones del Pueblo Maya y sus Demandas (1986–1992),* 3rd ed. Guatemala: Flacso, 1996.

Bauman, Zygmunt. *Modernity and the Holocaust.* Ithaca, NY: Cornell University Press, 1991.

Behar, Ruth. *The Vulnerable Observer: Anthropology that Breaks Your Heart.* Boston: Beacon Press, 1997.

Behrens, Susan Fitzpatrick. "Confronting Colonialism." Working Paper #338. Kellogg, May 2007. Retrieved 5 June 2017 from https://kellogg.nd.edu/publications/workingpapers/WPS/338.pdf.

Berdal, Mats, and David H. Ucko, eds. *Reintegrating Armed Conflict: Politics, Violence and Transition.* Routledge Studies in Intervention and State Building. Abingdon: Routledge, 2009.

Bethell, Leslie, ed. *Latin America: Politics and Society since 1930.* New York: Cambridge University Press, 1998.

Bhabha, Homi K. "Forward." In *Black Skin, White Masks,* by Frantz Fanon. Translated by Charles Lam Markmann. London: Pluto Press, 2008.

Biess, Frank. *Homecomings: Returning POWs and the Legacies of Defeat in Postwar Germany.* New Jersey: Princeton University Press, 2006.

Black, George, Milton Jamail, and Norma Stoltz Chinchilla. *Garrison Guatemala.* London: Zed Books, 1984.

Blauner, Robert. "Internal Colonialism and Ghetto Revolt." *Social Problems* 16, no. 4 (spring 1969): 393–408.

Boff, Leonardo, and Clodovis Boff. *Introducing Liberation Theology.* New York: Orbis Books, 1998.

Bram, Joseph. *An Analysis of Inca Militarism: Monographs of the American Ethnological Society.* Seattle: University of Washington Press, 1966.

Brett, Rachel, and Irma Specht. *Young Soldiers: Why They Choose to Fight.* Boulder, CO: Lynne Rienner, 2004.

Brett, Roddy. "Peace without Social Reconciliation? Understanding the Trial of Generals Ríos Montt and Rodriguez Sánchez in the Wake of Guatemala's Genocide." *Journal of Genocide Research* 18, nos. 2–3 (2016): 285–303. DOI: 10.1080/14623528.2016.118 6955.

———. Social Movements, Indigenous Politics, and Democratisation in Guatemala (1985-1990). Leiden, the Netherlands: Koninklijke, Brill, 2008.

Brill, William Handford. "Military Civic Action in Bolivia." Unpublished Ph.D. dissertation. Philadelphia: University of Pennsylvania, Political Science, 1965. ProQuest Dissertations and Theses.

Brook, Timothy. *Collaboration: Japanese Agents and Local Elites in Wartime China*. Cambridge, MA: Harvard University Press, 2005.

Brotherton, C. David. *Youth Street Gangs: A Critical Appraisal. New Directions in Critical Criminology*. London: Routledge, 2015.

Browning, Christopher. *Ordinary Men: Reserve Battalion 101 and the Final Solution in Poland*. New York: Harper Collins, 1998.

Bunzel, Ruth. *Chichicastenango*. Guatemala: Editorial Jose Pineda Ibarra, 1981.

Burgerman, Susan. "Making Peace Perform in War-Transition Countries: El Salvador, Guatemala and Nicaragua." In *Short of the Goal: U.S. Policy and Poorly Performing States*, edited by Nancy Birdsall, Milan Vaishnav, and Robert L. Ayres, 245–84. Washington, D.C.: Center for Global Development, 2006. Retrieved 4 May 2015 from http://www.cgdev.org/doc/shortofthegoal/chap8.pdf.

Burrell, Jennifer. "After Lynching." In *War by Other Means. Aftermath in Post-Genocide Guatemala*, edited by Carlota McAllister and Diane M. Nelson, 241–60. Durham: Duke University Press, 2013.

Burt, Jo-Marie. "From Heaven to Hell in Ten Days: The Genocide Trial in Guatemala." *Journal of Genocide Research* 18, nos. 2–3 (2016): 143–69. DOI: 10.1080/14623528.2016.1186437.

Cahill, David. "Genocide form Below: The Great Rebellion of 1780–82 in the Southern Andes." In *Empire, Colony, Genocide: Conquest, Occupation, and Subaltern Resistance in World History*, edited by A. Dirk Moses. New York: Berghahn Books, 2009. Kindle edition.

Calero, Luis F. *Chiefdoms under Siege: Spain's Rule and Native Adaptation in the Southern Colombian Andes, 1535–1700*. Albuquerque: University of New Mexico Press, 1997.

Carey, David Jr. *Our Elders Teach Us: Maya-Kaqchikel Historical Perspectives. Xkib'ij Kan Qate' Qatata'*. Tuscaloosa: University of Alabama Press, 2001.

———. "Who's Using Whom? A Comparison of Military Conscription in Guatemala and Senegal in the First Half of the 20th Century." *The Comparative Study of Conscription in the Armed Forces* 20 (2002): 171–99.

———. *I Ask for Justice: Maya Women, Dictators, and Crime in Guatemala, 1889–1944*. Austin: University of Texas Press, 2013.

Carey, David Jr., and M. Gabriela Torres. "Precursors to Femicide: Guatemalan Women in a Vortex of Violence." *Latin American Research Review* 45, no. 3 (2010): 142–64.

Carmack, Robert M. "The Story of Santa Cruz Quiché." In *Harvest of Violence: The Maya Indians and the Guatemalan Crisis*, edited by Robert Carmack. Norman: University of Oklahoma Press, 1988.

———. *Rebels of Highland Guatemala: The Quiché-Mayas of Momostenango*. Norman and London: University of Oklahoma Press, 1995.

Carruthers, Susan L. *Winning Hearts and Minds: British Governments, the Media and Colonial Counter-insurgency 1944–1960*. Leicester: Leicester University Press, 1998.

Catholic Church. "Y Dieron la Vida por El Quiché." *Colección Testigos Fieles No. 1*. Guatemala: Diocésis del Quiché, 2000.

Catholic Church, Diocese of Santa Cruz del Quiché. *El Quiché, el Pueblo y su Iglesia*. Santa Cruz del Quiché, Guatemala: La Diócesis, 1994.

CEDFOG (Centro de Estudios y Documentación de la Frontera Occidental de Guatemala). *Primera Jornada de Estudios y Experiencias sobre Territorio, Poder y Politica*. Huehuetenango: CEDFOG, 12–13 October 2006.

Centro de Medios Independientes. "Oda a Ti." 6 January 2016. Retrieved 30 July 2016 from https://cmiguate.org/oda-a-ti/.

Césaire, Aimé. *Discourse on Colonialism.* Translated by Joan Pinkham. New York: Monthly Review Press, 2000.

Chatterjee, Partha. "The Nation and Its Peasants." In *Mapping Subaltern Studies and the Postcolonial,* edited by Vinayak Chaturvedi, 8–23. New York: Verso, 2000.

Chavez, Lydia. "Guatemala Mobilizes over 700,000 Civilians in Local Patrols." *New York Times (1923–Current File),* 18 November 1983.

Christiansen, Betty Barton. *The United States Air Force in Southeast Asia.* Washington, D.C.: Air Force History and Museums Program, 1998.

Chuchiak, John F., IV. "Forgotten Allies: The Origins and Roles of Native Mesoamerican Auxiliaries and Indios Conquistadores in the Conquest of the Yucatan, 1526–1550." In *Indian Conquistadores: Indigenous Allies in the Conquest of Mesoamerica,* edited by Laura E. Matthew and Michel R. Oudijk, 175–226. Oklahoma City: University of Oklahoma Press, 2012.

CIEN. "Informe Sobre el Aporte de Capital a Ex-PAC." Guatemala, 16 July 2003. Retrieved 16 July 2016 from http://old.congreso.gob.gt/plumainvitada/11.pdf.

"Cinco Grupos Clandestinos Dominan Crimen Organizado en Guatemala." *Noti Mundo,* 8 March 2007. Retrieved 20 January 2012 from http://midar.wordpress.com/2007/03/08/cinco-grupos-clandestinos-dominan-crimen-organizado-en-guatemala/.

Civico, Aldo. "Portrait of a Paramilitary: Putting a Human Face on the Colombian Conflict." In *Engaged Observer: Anthropology, Advocacy and Activism,* edited by Asale Angel-Ajani and Victoria Sanford. New Brunswick, NJ: Rutgers University Press, 2007, 131–148.

Clark, Robert A. "Aggressiveness and Military Training." *The American Journal of Sociology* 51 no. 5 (March 1946): 423–32.

COHA. "Combating Impunity, Violence, and Crime in President Colom's Guatemala." 17 March 2009. Retrieved 12 December 2011 from http://www.coha.org/combating-impunity-violence-and-crime-in-president-colom's-guatemala/.

Cojtí Cuxil, Demetrio. *Configuración del Pensamiento Politico del Pueblo Maya.* Vol. 2. Guatemala: Seminario Permanente de Estudios Mayas, 1995.

———. "The Politics of Maya Revindication." In *Mayan Cultural Activism in Guatemala,* edited by Edward Fischer and R. McKenna Brown. Austin: University of Texas Press, 1996, 19-50.

CONADEGUA. "Security Forces Involved in Illegal Activities." *Cerigua Weekly Briefs* 7–13, May 1990. Retrieved 4 May 2015 from http://www.tulane.edu/~libweb/RESTRICTED/CERIGUA/1990_0507.txt.

———. "Violencia y Represión en Guatemala." *Cerigua Weekly Briefs* 4–10. June 1990. Retrieved 19 April 2015 from http://www.tulane.edu/~libweb/RESTRICTED/CERIGUA/1990_0604.txt.

———. "Security Forces, or Source of Insecurity?" *Cerigua Weekly Briefs,* No 5. 30 January 1997. Retrieved 10 October 2011 from http://www.tulane.edu/~libweb/RESTRICTED/CERIGUA/1997_0130.txt.

CONAVIGUA. "El Reclutamiento Militar Forzoso en Guatemala." 26 February 1999. Retrieved 3 June 2011 from http://conavigua.tripod.com/reclutamiento.html.

"Condena Contra Ex Militar, Felipe Cusanero, abre Esperanzas de Justicia por Crímenes de Guerra." Noticias.com.gt, 31 August 2009. Retrieved 10 May 2015 from http://noticias.com.gt/nacionales/20090831-condena-contra-ex-militar-felipe-cusanero-abre-esperanzas-de-justicia-crimenes-de-guerra.html.

"Congreso Niega Genocidio en Guatemala." Siglo21.com.gt, 13 May 2014. Retrieved 8 May 2015 from http://www.s21.com.gt/nacionales/2014/05/13/congreso-aprueba-punto-resolutivo-que-niega-existencia-genocidio.

Corradi, Juan, Patricia Weiss Fagen, and Manuel Antonio Garretón, eds. *Fear at the Edge: State Terror and Resistance in Latin America.* Berkeley: University of California Press, 1992.

Crahan, Margaret E., ed. *Human Rights and Basic Needs in the Americas.* Washington, D.C.: Woodstock Theological Center, George Washington University Press, 1982.

Credycom.org. Retrieved 12 January 2012 from http://www.credycom.org/ES/attivita.php?id=3. [Obsolete link.]

CUC. "Lucha, Resistencia e Historia." Guatemala: Editorial Rukemik Na'ojil, 2007. Retrieved 28 April 2015 from http://www.cuc.org.gt/materiales/historiadelcuc.pdf.

Culberson, C. William. *Vigilantism: Political History of Private Power in America.* New York: Greenwood Press, 1990.

Defensoría Maya, "Los Verdaderos Enemigos de la Vida y la Paz en Guatemala." Chuj Walijo'q Informacion Mensual De La Defensoría Maya No. 3 GUATEMALA, Abril de 1997 Retrieved June 18, 2017 from http://www.puebloindio.org/Defensoria_Maya/Maya_boletin3.htm.

Degregori, Ivan, Jose Coronel, Ponciano del Pino, and Orin Starn. *Las Rondas Campesinas. La Derrota de Sendero Luminoso.* Estudios de la Sociedad No. 15, Lima: IEP Ediciones, 1996.

Del Carmen Velazquez, María. "Los Indios Flecheros." *Historia Mexicana* 13, no. 2 (October–December 1963): 235–43.

"Del Reino de las Armas al Reino del Miedo." Semana.com. Agencia de Prensa IPC, 10 October 2006. Retrieved 12 April 2015 from http://www.semana.com/imprimir/81382.

Dell, Melissa. "The Persistent Effects of Peru's Mining Mita." *Econometrica* 78, no. 6 (Nov 2010): 1863–903. Retrieved June 18, 2017 from http://ez.lib.jjay.cuny.edu/login?url=http://search.proquest.com/docview/821289954?accountid=11724

DeLugan, Robin Maria. *Reimagining National Belonging: Post-Civil War El Salvador in a Global Context.* Tucson: University of Arizona Press, 2012.

"Demandan al Estado Tomar Control de Chunima." Siglo21.com.gt. Retrieved April 2015 from http://m.s21.com.gt/nacionales/2010/08/30/demandan-estado-tomar-control-chunima.

DGC (Dirección General de Caminos). "Listado de Centros Electorales Municipales (CEMS) y Condiciones de Acceso," n.d.

Dill, Kathleen. "International Human Rights and Local Justice in Guatemala: The Rio Negro (Pak'oxom) and Agua Fria Trials." *Cultural Dynamics* 17, no. 3 (2005): 323–50. DOI:10.1177/0921374005061993.

Divinzenso, Maria Alicia, "La transformación de las relaciones cívico-militares: la "Accion Cívica" del Ejército (1960–1983)," 69–98. In Águila, Gabriela; Garaño, Santiago; Scatizza, Pablo (Eds.) (2016). Represión estatal y violencia paraestatal en la historia reciente argentina : Nuevos abordajes a 40 años del golpe de Estado. La Plata: Universidad Nacional de La Plata. Facultad de Humanidades y Ciencias de la Educación. (Estudios/ Investigaciones; 57) Retrieved June 9 2017 from http://www.libros.fahce.unlp.edu.ar/index.php/libros/catalog/book/63

Drèze, Jan. "Militarism, Development and Democracy." *Economic and Political Weekly* 35, no. 14 (April 1–7, 2000): 1171–83.

Drèze, Jan, and Amartya Sen. *Hunger and Public Action.* New York: Oxford University Press, 1989.

Drouin, Marc. "To the Last Seed: Atrocity Crimes and the Genocidal Continuum in Guatemala. 1978-1984." M.A. Thesis. Montreal, Canada: Concordia University, Department of History, August 2006.

———. "The 1982 Guatemalan Genocide." In *State Violence and Genocide in Latin America*, edited by Marcia Esparza, Henry R. Huttenbach, and Daniel Feierstein, 81103. London: Routledge, 2011.

Du Bois, W.E.B. *The Souls of Black Folk*. New York: Dover Publications, 1994.

Ejército de Guatemala "Ley Constitutivo del Ejército de Guatemala." 7th ed. Guatemala, 1997. Retrieved 17 April 2015 from http://www.mindef.mil.gt/leyes_reglamentos/leyes_y_reglamentos/ley_constitutiva_ejercito.pdf.

———. "Army General Order on Assimilated Officers No. 12–92." Department of National Defense, National Palace. Articles 7–8. Retrieved 21 August 2013 from http://www.mindef.mil.gt/ftierra/emdn/sage/directivas/directivas/leyes_reglamentos/Leyes_Reg_PDF/A.G._No._1047-92_Reg._Of._As._30DIC1992.pdf. [Obsolete link.]

———. "Seguridad." Retrieved 4 January 2014 from http://www.mindef.mil.gt/organizacion/fuerzas%20tierra/comandos/creompaz/historia.html. [Obsolete link.]

———. "Mariscal Gregorio Solares." Retrieved 26 April 2016 from http://mindef.mil.gt/brigadas/5brigada/historia.html.

Ekern, Stener. "The Modernizing Bias of Human Rights: Stories of Mass Killings and Genocide in Central America." *Journal of Genocide Research* 12, nos. 3–4 (December 2010): 219–41.

Engel Masoliver, Carlos. *Historia de las Divisiones del Ejército Nacional 1936–1939*. Madrid: Alemana Ediciones, 2000.

Engelking, Barbara. "Murdering and Denouncing Jews in the Polish Countryside, 1942–1945." *East European Politics and Societies* 25, no. 3 (2011): 433–56. DOI: 10.1177/0888325411398912.

Enloe H., Cynthia. *Maneuvers: The International Politics of Militarizing Women's Lives*. Berkeley: University of California Press, 2003.

———. *Ethnic Soldiers: State Security in Divided Societies*. New York: Penguin Books, 1980.

Escobar, Jenny. "Memoria Viva: State Violence and the Movement for Memory in Colombia." Ph.D. dissertation. Santa Cruz, CA: University of California, Psychology, December 2013.

Maria Jose Espana. Ex-PAC Rechazan Compromisos con Otto Pérez Molina Retrieved 16 June 2017 from http://lahora.gt/hemeroteca-lh/ex-pac-rechazan-compromisos-con-otto-perez-molina/

Esparza, Marcia. "Post-War Guatemala: Long-Term Effects of Psychological and Ideological Militarization of the K'iché Mayans." *Journal of Genocide Research* 7, no. 3 (2005): 377–91.

———. "Courageous Soldiers (Valientes Soldados). Politics of Concealment in the Aftermath of State Violence in Chile." In *State Violence and Genocide in Latin America*, edited by Marcia Esparza, Henry R. Huttenbach, and Daniel Feierstein, 196–208. New York: Routledge, 2011.

———. "Globalizing Latin American Studies of State Violence and Genocide." In *State Violence and Genocide in Latin America*, edited by Marcia Esparza, Henry R. Huttenbach, and Daniel Feierstein, 1–20. New York: Routledge, 2011.

———. "Impossible Memory and Post-Colonial Silences: A Critical View of the Historical Clarification Commission (CEH in Spanish) in Guatemala." In *Indigenous Peoples' Access to Justice, Including Truth and Reconciliation Processes*, edited by Chief Wilton Littlechild and Elsa Stamatopoulou, 170–80. Institute for the Study of Human Rights. New York City: Columbia University Press, 2014.

———. "The Santo Tomás Chichicastenango's Municipal Firefighters: Green Pines Covering the Dead Bodies." In *Remembering the Rescuers of Victims of Human Rights Crimes in*

Latin America, edited by Marcia Esparza and Carla de Ycaza, 57–78. Maryland: Lexington Books, 2016.

Esparza, Marcia, and Carla DeYcaza, eds. *Remembering the Rescuers of Victims of Human Rights Crimes in Latin America.* Maryland: Lexington Books, 2016.

Esparza, Marcia, Henry R. Huttenbach, and Daniel Feierstein, eds. *State Violence and Genocide in Latin America: The Cold War Years.* London: Routledge, 2010.

Esparza, Marcia and Woodill. Post-Cold War Annotated Bibliography of Military Sociology in Latin America. Unpublished.

Esparza, Marcia, Nathaniel Woodill, and Zacharias McKiernan. Antagonistic Memories. Unpublished.

Ewen, Allison, and Robert K. Goldman. "Civil Patrols." In *Crimes of War: What the Public Should Know,* edited by Roy Gutman and David Rieff. New York: W.W. Norton, 1999. Retrieved 16 July 2016 from http://www.crimesofwar.org/a-z-guide/civil-patrol/.

"Exhumarán los Restos de unos Paramilitares Asesinados por la Guerrilla Guatemalteca." *Qué!* 15 March 2010. Retrieved 2 February 2017 from http://www.que.es/ultimas-no ticias/espana/201003152014-exhumaran-restos-unos-paramilitares-asesinados.html.

Falla, Ricardo. "We Charge Genocide." In *Guatemala: Tyranny on Trial. Testimony of the Permanent People's Tribunal.* Translated by Susanne Jonas, Ed McCaughan, and Elizabeth Sutherland Martinez. San Francisco: Synthesis Publications, 1984.

———. *Massacres in the Jungle: Ixcan, Guatemala (1975–1982).* Translated by Julia Howlan. Boulder: Westview Press, 1993.

———. *Quiché Rebelde: Religious Conversion, Politics and Ethnic Identity in Guatemala.* Translated by Phillip Berryman. Austin: University of Texas Press, 2001.

Faltas, Sami, Glenn McDonald, and Camilla Waszink. "Removing Small Arms from Society: A Review of Weapons Collection and Destruction Programmes." Small Arms Survey, July 2001. Retrieved 21 April 2015 from http://www.smallarmssurvey.org/file admin/docs/B-Occasional-papers/SAS-OP02-Weapons-Collection.pdf.

Fanon, Frantz. *The Wretched of the Earth.* Translated by Richard Philcox. New York: Grove Press, 2004.

———. *Black Skin, White Masks.* Translated by Richard Philcox. New York: Grove Press, 2008. Kindle edition.

FAO.org. "Guatemala: Agricultural Census." 2003. Retrieved 4 May 2015 from http://www .fao.org/fileadmin/templates/ess/documents/world_census_of_agriculture/countries _for_website/GUATEMALA_2003.pdf.

Feierstein, Daniel. "Leaving the Parental Home: An Overview of the Current State of Genocide Studies." *Genocide Studies and Prevention: An International Journal* 6, no. 3 (2011): 256–69.

———. "National Security Doctrine in Latin America: The Genocide Question." In *The Oxford Handbook of Genocide Studies,* edited by Donald Bloxham and A. Dirk Moses, 489–509. New York: Oxford University Press, 2013.

———. *Genocide as Social Practice: Reorganizing Society under the Nazis and Argentina's Military Juntas. Genocide, Political Violence, Human Rights.* Translated by Douglas Andrew Town. New Brunswick: Rutgers University Press, 2014.

Fein, Helen. *Accounting for Genocide: Victims and Survivors of the Holocaust: National Responses and Jewish Victimization in the Holocaust.* New York: The Free Press, 1979.

———, ed. *Genocide Watch.* New Haven, Yale University Press, 1992.

———. *Genocide: A Sociological Perspective.* Thousand Oaks, CA: Sage Publications, 1993.

Ferrell, Jeff. "Criminological Verstehen: Inside the Immediacy of Crime." In *Ethnography at the Edge: Crime, Deviance, and Field Research,* edited by Jeff Ferrell and Mark S. Hamm, 20–42. Boston: Northeastern University Press, 1998.

Figueroa Ibarra, Carlos. "Militarización, Crimen y Poder Invisible en Guatemala: el Retorno del Centauro." In *Movimientos Sociales y Conflictos en América Latina,* edited by José Seoane, 86–93. Buenos Aires: CLACSO (Consejo Latinoamericano de Ciencias Sociales), 2003. Retrieved 19 June 2017 from http://bibliotecavirtual.clacso.org.ar/ar/libros/osal/seoane/figueroa.rtf

———. "The Culture of Terror and Cold War in Guatemala." *Journal of Genocide Research* 8, no. 2 (June 2006): 191–208.

"Fijan Ultimatum: Patrulleros Liberar Retenidos." *Prensa Libre.* Retrieved 23 February 2015 from http://www.prensalibre.com/noticias/Fijan-ultimatum-patrulleros-liberar-retenidos_0_151187012.html.

Foreign Broadcast Information Service. "Military Zone No. 3 Inaugurated with Headquarters in Chimaltenango." *Latin America Report 2690,* 13 June 1983.

Foster, Don, Paul Haupt, and Maresa de Beer. *The Theater of Violence: Narratives of Protagonists in the South African Conflict.* Oxford: James Currey, 2005.

Foweraker, Joe. *Theorizing Social Movements.* Colorado: Pluto Press, 1995.

Fox News. "Growth of Central American Armies Poses Threat to Democracy." Retrieved 17 February 2017 from http://latino.foxnews.com/latino/politics/2016/08/24/growth-central-american-armies-poses-threat-to-democracy/print.

Franco, Jean. *Cruel Modernity.* Durham: Duke University Press, 2013.

Frei, Norbert. *Adenauer's Germany and the Nazi Past: The Politics of Amnesty and Integration.* New York: Columbia University Press, 2002.

Freire, Paulo. *Education for Critical Consciousness.* New York: Continuum, 1986.

———. *Learning to Question: A Pedagogy of Liberation.* Translated by Tony Coates. New York: Continuum, 1989.

Fromm, Erich, and Michael Maccoby. *Social Character in a Mexican Village: A Socio-psycho Analytical Study.* New Jersey: Prentice Hall, 1970.

Gaillard, Regina. *Civic Action Versus Counterinsurgency and Low Intensity Conflict in Latin America: The Case for Delinkage.* Carlisle Barracks, PA: Strategic Studies Institute: Army War College, 1990. Retrieved June 5 2017 from http://www.dtic.mil/dtic/tr/fulltext/u2/a222180.pdf.

Gandhi, Leela. *Postcolonial Theory: A Critical Introduction.* New York: Columbia University Press, 1998.

García, Glenda Mabelyn. "Herederos de la Guerra: Ex Paramilitares y Víctimas de la Contrainsurgencia en Guatemala." In *Informe Final del Concurso: Movimientos Sociales y Nuevos Conflictos en América Latina y el Caribe.* Programa Regional de Becas: CLACSO, 2002. Retrieved June 5 2017 from http://bibliotecavirtual.clacso.org.ar/ar/libros/becas/2002/mov/garcia.pdf.

Garrard-Burnett, Virginia. *Protestantism in Guatemala: Living in the New Jerusalem.* Austin: University of Texas Press, 1998.

———. *Terror in the Land of the Holy Spirit: Guatemala under General Efraín Ríos Montt (1982–1983).* New York: Oxford University Press, 2010.

Garretón, Manuel Antonio. "Fear in Military Regimes: An Overview." In *Fear at the Edge: State Terror and Resistance in Latin America,* edited by Juan Corradi, Patricia Weiss Fagen, and Manuel Antonio Garretón, 13–25. Berkeley: University of California Press, 1992.

Genocide Studies and Prevention: An International Journal. (GSP) Special Volume Genocide Studies: Debates from the Latin American Margin 8, no. 1 (2013).

Gill, Leslie. *The School of the Americas: Military Training and Political Violence in the Americas.* Durham: Duke University Press, 2004.

Gligorevic, Tihomir. "Ríos Montt Genocide Trial Delayed." Jul 24, 2015. INSERBIA Retrieved June 15 2017 from https://inserbia.info/today/2015/07/rios-montt-genocide-trial-delayed-again-for-medical-observation/

Ginio, Ruth. "African Silences: Negotiating the Story of France's Colonial Soldiers, 1914–2009." In *Shadows of War: A Social History of Silence in the Twentieth Century,* edited by Efrat Ben-Ze'ev, Ruth Ginio, and Jay Winter, 138–52. Cambridge, UK: Cambridge University Press, 2010.

Gobierno de Guatemala, Secretaria de Planificación y Programación del la Presidencia. "Mapas de Pobreza en Guatemala al 2002." Retrieved 18 July 2016 from https://www.ine.gob.gt/sistema/uploads/2014/01/14/Vv8VNwvdE1SnO5ebSClI8coZGPcEq9OJ.pdf.

Godnik, William, Robert Muggah, and Camilla Waszink. "Stray Bullets: The Impact of Small Arms Misuse in Central America." Small Arms Survey Occasional Paper 5. Geneva: Graduate Institute of International Studies, October 2002.

Godoy, Angelina Snodgrass. "Lynchings and the Democratization of Terror in Postwar Guatemala: Implications for Human Rights." *Human Rights Quarterly* 24, no. 3 (August 2002): 640–61.

———. *Popular Injustice: Violence, Community, and Law in Latin America.* Stanford: Stanford University Press, 2006.

Gomes Porto, João, Chris Alden, and Imogen Parsons. *From Soldiers to Citizens: Demilitarization of Conflict and Society.* Burlington, VT: Ashgate, 2007.

Gómez-Barris, Macarena. *Where Memory Dwells: Culture and State Violence in Chile.* Berkeley: University of California Press, 2009.

González Casanova, Pablo. "Colonialismo Interno: Una Redefinición." 2006. Buenos Aires: CLACSO. Retrieved 17 May 2015 from http://biblioteca.clacso.edu.ar/ar/libros/campus/marxis/P4C2Casanova.pdf.

———. El colonialismo interno. En publicación: Sociología de la explotación." 2006. Buenos Aires: CLACSO. Retrieved June 18, 20117 from http://bibliotecavirtual.clacso.org.ar/ar/libros/secret/gonzalez/colonia.pdf

González, Matilde. "The Man Who Brought the Danger to the Village Representations of the Armed Conflict in Guatemala from a Local Perspective." *Journal of South African Studies* 26, no. 2 (June 2000): 317–35.

———. "Ejercicio y Formas de Representación Local Ligada a las Fuerzas Armadas 1980–1996." Presented at LASA 2001 XXIII International Congress. Washington, D.C.: Avancso, 2001.

González, Sarah. "Guatemalans Refuse to Serve in Civil Patrols 1988–1993." Global Nonviolent Action Database, 9 April 2013. Retrieved April 22, 2015 from http://nvdatabase.swarthmore.edu/content/guatemalans-refuse-serve-civil-patrols-1988-1993.

Gottesman, Eva. *Cambodia: After the Khmer Rouge. Inside the Politics of Nation Building.* New Haven: Yale University Press, 2003.

Gramajo Morales, Héctor Alejandro. "Political Transition in Guatemala, 1980–1990: A Perspective from Inside Guatemala's Army." In *Democratic Transitions in Central America,* edited by Jorge I. Dominguez and Marc Lindenberg, 111–38. Gainesville: University of Florida Press, 1997.

Gramsci, Antonio. *Selections from the Prison Notebooks.* Edited by Quintin Hoare and Goffrey Nowell Smith. New York: International Publishers, 1971.

Granado, Ottoniel, Maucelio Mérida, and Alessandro Scappini. "Proceso de Producción y Certificación de Semilla de Papa (Solanum Tuberosum var. Loman), por el Programa Acceso al Crédito y Apoyo a la Comercialización de la Producción Agrícola en Quiché -CREDyCOM- en el Municipio de Chichicastenango, Guatemala." *Journal of Agriculture and Environment for International Development* 105, no. 2 (2011): 83–102.

Grandin, Greg. *The Last Colonial Massacre: Latin America in the Cold War.* Chicago: University of Chicago Press, 2004. Kindle edition.

———. *Empire's Workshop: Latin America, the United States, and the Rise of the New Imperialism.* New York: Metropolitan Books, 2006.

———. *Who Is Rigoberta Menchu?* New York: Verso Books, 2011.

———. "Five Hundred Years." In *War by Other Means: Aftermath in Post-Genocide Guatemala,* edited by Carlota McAllister and Diane M. Nelson, 49–70. Durham: Duke University Press, 2013.

"Guatemala Civil War." GlobalSecurity.org. 2000–2015. Retrieved 21 April 2015 from http://www.globalsecurity.org/military/world/war/guatemala.htm.

Guatemala Human Rights Commission/USA. "Army Has Disproportionate Budget." *Guatemalan Human Rights Update* 19, no 15. August 1–15, 2007. Retrieved 16 July 2016 from http://www.ghrc-usa.org/wp-content/uploads/2011/12/vol19no15.pdf.

———. "GHRC Condemns Massacre." Retrieved 26 July 2016 from http://www.ghrc-usa .org/resources/press-room/totocomunicado/.

"Guatemala Squeezed between Crime and Impunity." Latin American Crisis Group Report No. 33. 22 June 2010.

Guha, Ranajit. "The Prose of Counterinsurgency." In *Selected Subaltern Studies,* edited by Ranajit Guha and Gayatri Chakravorty Spivak, 45-86. New York: Oxford University Press, 1988.

Guoz, Abner. "Entrevista—Rosalina Tuyuc: 'Debemos Saber Quiénes Fueron los Asesinos y Torturadores.'" Albedrío.org, 22 March 2004. Retrieved 1 April 2015 from http://www .albedrio.org/htm/entrevistas/ep-001.htm.

Gurney, Joan Neff. "Not One of the Guys: The Female Researcher in a Male Dominated Setting." *Qualitative Sociology* 8, no. 1 (spring 1985), 42-62.

Halbwachs, Maurice. *The Social Frameworks of Memory.* Edited and translated by Lewis A. Coser. Chicago: University of Chicago Press, 1992.

Hale, Charles. "Consciousness, Violence, and the Politics of Memory in Guatemala." *Current Anthropology* 38, no. 5 (December 1997), 817-838.

Hamber, Brandon. "Have No Doubt It Is Fear in the Land: An Exploration of the Continuing Cycles of Violence in South Africa." *Zeitschrift für Politische Psychologie* 7, nos. 1–2 (1999): 113–28.

HANCI (Hunger and Nutrition Commitment Index). "Key Findings." HanciIndex.com, 2013. Retrieved 10 May 2015 from http://www.hancindex.org/the-index/research-findings.

Handy, Jim. *Gift of the Devil: A History of Guatemala.* Brooklyn: South End Press, 1984.

———. *Revolution in the Countryside: Rural Conflict and Agrarian Reform in Guatemala, 1944-1954.* Chapel Hill: University of North Carolina Press, 1994.

———. "Democratizing What? Some Reflections on Nation, State, Ethnicity, Modernity, Community and Democracy in Guatemala." *Canadian Journal of Latin American and Caribbean Studies* 27, no. 53 (2002): 35–71.

———. "Rights in Guatemala." 14 July 2008. Retrieved 15 February 2015 from http://www .hria-guatemala.com/es/docs/Impact%20Assessment/Rights_in_Guatemala-Sp_fi nal_10_17_08.pdf.

Hanhimaki, Jussi M., and Odd Arme Westad, eds. *The Cold War: A History in Documents and Eyewitness Accounts.* Oxford: Oxford University Press, 2004.

Hansen, Arlen J. *Gentlemen Volunteers: The Story of the American Ambulance Drivers in the Great War, August 1914–September 1918.* New York: Arcade Publishing, 1996.

Hauge, Wenche, and Beate Thoresen. *El Destino de los Ex-Combatientes en Guatemala: Obstaculizadores o Agentes de Cambio?* Guatemala: Magna Terra Editores, 2007.

Hayner, Priscilla B. *Unspeakable Truths: Transitional Justice and the Challenge of Truth Commissions.* New York: Routledge, 2011.

Heller, Henry. *The Cold War and the New Imperialism, a Global History, 1945–2005.* New York: Monthly Review Press, 2006.

Hellin, Jon, and Sophie Higman. "Crop Diversity and Livelihood Security in the Andes." *Development in Practice* 15, no. 2 (2005): 165–74.

Hess, Gary R. *Vietnam: Explaining America's Lost War.* Hoboken: Blackwell Publishing, 2009.

Higonnet, Etelle, ed. *Quiet Genocide: Guatemala 1981–1983.* New Brunswick: Transaction Publishers, 2009.

Hilberg, Raul. *Perpetrators, Victims, Bystanders: The Jewish Catastrophe 1933–1945.* New York: Harper Collins, 1993.

Hinton, Alexander Laban, ed. *Genocide: An Anthropological Reader.* Malden: Blackwell Publishers, 2002.

———. *Why Did They Kill? Cambodia in the Shadow of Genocide.* Berkeley: University of California Press, 2005.

———. "Critical Genocide Studies." *Genocide Studies and Prevention* 7, no. 1 (April 2012): 4–15.

"Historia." Feria Departmental de Quiché: Fiestas Elenas, 2008–2014. Retrieved 28 December 2012 from http://www.fiestaselenas.com/historia.php.

"Historical Exchange Rates." OANDA.com, 2015. Retrieved 30 April 2015 from http://www.oanda.com/currency/historical-rates/.

HMP (Historical Memory Project). CUNY John Jay College of Criminal Justice. New York. Collection: Flyer Ejército de Guatemala.

Hokowhitu, Brendan. "Producing Elite Indigenous Masculinities." *Settler Colonial Studies* 2, no. 2 (2012): 23–48. DOI: 10.1080/2201473X.2012.10648840.

Hollingshead, August B. "Human Behavior in Military Society." *The American Journal of Sociology* 51, no. 5 (March 1946): 439–47.

Holm, Tom. "Militarization of Native America: Historical Process and Cultural Perception." *The Social Science Journal* 34, no. 4 (1997): 461–74.

Hough, Richard, John Kelley, Steve Miller, Russell DeRossier, Fred L. Mann, and Michael Seligson. "Land and Labor in Guatemala: An Assessment." Washington, D.C.: USAID, 1982. Retrieved 22 September 2014 from https://my.vanderbilt.edu/seligson/files/2013/12/Land-and-Labor-in-Guatemala-An-Assessment.pdf.

Hristov, Jasmin. *Paramilitarism and Neoliberalism: Violent Systems of Capital Accumulation in Colombia and Beyond.* London: Pluto Press, 2014. ProQuest ebrary. Retrieved 27 June 2016 from https://ebookcentral.proquest.com/lib/johnjay-ebooks/reader.action?docID=3386782

Huggins, Martha K., ed. *Vigilantism and the State in Modern Latin America: Essays of Extralegal Violence.* New York: Praeger, 1991.

Huggins, Martha K., and Marie-Louise Glebbeek. "Women Studying Violent Male Institutions: Cross-Gendered Dynamics in Police Research on Secrecy and Danger." *Theoretical Criminology* 7, no. 3 (2003): 363–87.

———. "Studying Violent Male Institutions: Cross-Gender Dynamics in Police Research—Secrecy and Danger in Brazil and Guatemala." In *Women Fielding Danger: Negotiating Ethnographic Identities in Field Research,* edited by Martha K. Huggins and Marie-Louise Glebbeek, 353–78. New York: Roman Littlefield, 2009.

———, eds. *Women Fielding Danger: Negotiating Ethnographic Identities in Field Research.* New York: Roman Littlefield, 2009.

Huggins, Martha K., Mika Haritos-Fatouros, and Philip G. Zimbardo. *Violence Workers: Police Torturers and Murderers Reconstruct Brazilian Atrocities.* Berkeley: University of California Press, 2002.

Hume, Mo. "Armed Violence and Poverty in El Salvador: A Mini Case Study for the Armed Violence and Poverty Initiative." Bradford: CICS Centre for International Cooperation and Security, 2004.

Huntington, Samuel P. *The Soldier and the State: The Theory and Politics of Civil-Military Relations*. Cambridge: Belknap/Harvard University Press, 1957.

Huyse, Luc. "Introduction: Tradition-Based Approaches in Peacemaking, Transitional Justice and Reconciliation Policies." In *Traditional Justice and Reconciliation after Violent Conflict: Learning from African Experiences*. Stockholm: International Institute for Democracy and Electoral Assistance, 2008. Retrieved 22 April 2015 from http://www.idea.int/publications/traditional_justice/upload/Chapter_1_Introduction_traditionb ased_approaches_in_peacemaking_transitional_justice_and_reconciliation_policies.pdf.

Hydle, Ida. "An Anthropological Contribution to Peace and Conflict Resolution Studies." *Contemporary Justice Review* 9, no. 3 (September 2006): 257–67.

Ikeda, Mitsuho. "Reflexiones sobre la Violencia Política y la Antropología: La Actualidad Guatemalteca." In *El Mundo Maya: Miradas Japonesas*, 179–209. Mérida: Universidad Nacional Autónoma de México, 2006.

INE (Centro de Información y Documentación Técnica). *Census 1973*. Guatemala City, Guatemala: Gobierno de Guatemala, 1973.

Interamerican Institute of Human Rights. "Revista IIDH." Order of the Interamerican Court of Human Rights, 15 July 1995.

International Work Group for Indigenous Affairs. *The Indigenous World*. IWGIA: Copenhagen, 2013.

Janowitz, Morris. *The Professional Soldier: A Social and Political Portrait*. Glencoe, IL: Free Press, 1960.

———. *The Military in the Political Development of New Nations: An Essay in Comparative Analysis*. Toronto: University of Toronto Press, 1964.

Jay, Alice. *Persecution by Proxy: The Civil Patrols in Guatemala*, edited by Kerry Kennedy Cuomo, Helet Merkling, and Nan Richardson. Boston: The Robert F. Kennedy Human Rights Center, 1993.

Jeffrey, Paul. "Restorative Justice Worldwide." *New World Outlook: The Mission Magazine of the United Methodist Church*, July/August 1999. Retrieved June 5 2017 from archives.gcah.org/xmlui/bitstream/.../1999-07-08-July-Aug-NWO.pdf?

Jelin, Elizabeth. *State Repression and the Labor of State Memory*. Translated by Judy Rein and Marcial Godoy-Anativia. Contradictions, Volume 18. Minneapolis: University of Minnesota Press, 2003.

Jilani, Hina. "Report by the Special Representative of the Secretary-General on the Situation of Human Rights Defenders in Guatemala." United Nations. 6 December 2002. E/CN.4/2003/104/Add.2.

Jonas, Susanne. *The Battle for Guatemala: Rebels, Death Squads, and U.S. Power*. Latin American Perspective Series, No. 5. Boulder: Westview Press, 1991.

———. *Of Centaurs and Doves: Guatemala's Peace Process*. Boulder: Westview Press, 2000.

———. "Guatemala: Acts of Genocide and Scorched-Earth Counterinsurgency War." In *Century of Genocide: Critical Essays and Eyewitness Accounts*, edited by Samuel Totten and William Parsons, 376–411. New York and London: Routledge, 2009.

Jonas, Susanne, and Nestor Rodriguez. *Guatemala-U.S. Migration: Transforming Regions*. Austin: University of Texas Press, 2015.

Jones, Seth G. "The Strategic Logic of Militia." Working Paper. Rand National Defense Research Institute, January 2012. Retrieved 9 January 2014 from http://www.rand.org/content/dam/rand/pubs/working_papers/2012/RAND_WR913.pdf.

Keberlein Gutiérrez, Douglas R. "The Guatemalan Liberal Revolution of 1871 and the

Founding of the Escuela Politécnica." *International Journal of the Humanities* 3, no. 7 (2005/2006): 145–54.

Keen, David. "Demobilising Guatemala." Working Paper no. 37. Crisis States Programme. London: Development Research Centre (LSE), November 2003.

Kirkpatrick, Michael D. "Optics and the Culture of Modernity in Guatemala City since the Liberal Reform." Ph.D. dissertation. Saskatoon: University of Saskatchewan, Department of History, 2013.

Klein, Kerwin Lee. "On the Emergence of Memory in Historical Discourse." *Representations* no. 69, Special Issue: Grounds for Remembering (winter 2000): 127–50.

Klepak, Hal, Francisco Rojas Aravena, and David Mares. "Relaciones Hemisféricas." In *Atlas Comparativo de la Defensa an América Latina y Caribe.* Buenos Aires: Resdal, 2012. Retrieved 16 July 2016 from http://www.resdal.org/atlas/atlas12-05-relaciones-hemis fericas.pdf.

Kobrak, Paul. *Huehuetenango: Historia de una Guerra.* Huehuetenango: CEFDOG, 2003.

———. "The Long War in Colotenango: Guerrillas, Army and the Civil Patrols." In *War by Other Means: Aftermath in Post-Genocide Guatemala,* edited by Carlota McAllister and Diane M. Nelson, 218–40. Durham: Duke University, 2013.

Konefal, Betsy Ogburn. "May All Rise Up: Highland Mobilization in Post–1954 Guatemala." Ph.D. dissertation. Pittsburgh: University of Pittsburgh, 2005.

———. *For Every Indio Who Falls: A History of Maya Activism in Guatemala, 1960–1990.* Albuquerque: University of New Mexico Press, 2010.

Kovats-Bernat, J. Christopher. "Negotiating Dangerous Fields: Pragmatic Strategies for Fieldwork amid Violence and Terror." *American Anthropologist* 104, no. 1 (March 2002): 208–222.

Kruijt, Dirk. Low Intensity Democracies: Latin America in the Post-Dictatorial Era. *Bulletin of Latin American Research, 20, no.* 4 (2001) 409-430. Retrieved June 19 2017 from http://www.jstor.org.ez.lib.jjay.cuny.edu/stable/3339022

Kuper, Leo. *The Pity of It All: Polarization of Racial and Ethnic Relations.* Minneapolis: University of Minnesota Press, 1977.

———. *Genocide: Its Political Use in the Twentieth Century.* New Haven: Yale University Press, 1982.

Kurtenbach. "Guatemala's Post-War Development: The Structural Failure of Low Intensity Peace." Project Working Paper No. 3. Social and Political Fractures DSF, German Foundation for Peace Research, 2008. Retrieved 2 May 2015 from https://inef.unidue .de/cms/files/wp3_guatemala_low_intensity_peace_druckversion.pdf.

LaDuke, Winona, and Sean Aaron Cruz. *The Militarization of Indian Country.* Minneapolis: Honor Earth Publication, 2011.

Laguerre, Michel S. *The Military and Society in Haiti.* Knoxville: University of Tennessee Press, 1993.

Lang, Kurt. *Military Institutions and the Sociology of War: A Review of the Literature with Annotated Bibliography.* London: Sage Publications, 1972.

Larson, Anne M. "Indigenous Peoples, Representation and Citizenship in Guatemalan Forestry." *Conservation and Society* 6, no. 1 (2008): 35–48.

———. Guatemala Country Case Study, January 2008. Rights and Resources, Retrieved June 12 2017 from http://rightsandresources.org/en/publication/llsl-country-case-study-guatemala/#sthash.laCk5qZN.dpbs

Lasswell, Harold D. "The Garrison State." *American Journal of Sociology* 46, no. 4 (January 1941): 455–68.

Lazzara, Michael. *Chile in Transition: The Poetics and Politics of Memory.* Gainesville: University Press of Florida, 2006.

Le Bot, Yvon. *La Guerra en Tierras Mayas: Comunidad, Violencia y Modernidad en Guatemala (1970–1992).* Translated by Maria Antonia Neira Bigorra. Mexico City: Fondo de Cultura Economica, 1997.

Legree, Peter J., Paul A. Gade, Daniel E. Martin, M.A. Fischl, Michael J. Wilson, Veronica F. Nieva, Rod McCloy, and Janice Laurence. "Military Enlistment and Family Dynamics: Youth and Parental Perspectives." *Military Psychology* 12, no. 1 (2000): 31–49.

Lemarchand, René. *Burundi: Ethnocide as Discourse and Practice.* Cambridge, UK: Cambridge University Press, 1995.

———. *Forgotten Genocides: Oblivion, Denial, and Memory.* Philadelphia: University of Pennsylvania Press, 2011.

Lemarchand, René, and Maurice Niwese. "Mass Murder, the Politics of Memory and Post-Genocide Reconstruction: The Cases of Rwanda and Burundi." In *After Mass Crime: Rebuilding States and Communities,* edited by Beatrice Pouligny, Simon Chesterman, and Albrecht Schnabel, 165–89. New York: United Nations University Press, 2007.

Levenson-Estrada, Deborah. *Trade Unionists against Terror: Guatemala City, 1954–1985.* Chapel Hill: University of North Carolina Press, 1994.

Levi, Primo. "Primo Levi's Heartbreaking, Heroic Answers to the Most Common Questions He Was Asked about 'Survival in Auschwitz.'" Interview. *The New Republic.* Translated by Ruth Feldman. 17 February 1986. Retrieved 2 January 2017 from https://newrepub lic.com/article/119959/interview-primo-levi-survival-auschwitz.

———. *The Drowned and the Saved.* New York: Vintage International, 1989.

Lifton, Robert Jay. *Home from the War: Vietnam Veterans: Neither Victims nor Executioners.* New York: Simon and Schuster, 1973.

Little, Walter E., and Timothy J. Smith. *Mayas in Postwar Guatemala: The Harvest of Violence Revisited.* Tuscaloosa: University of Alabama Press, 2009.

Löfving, Staffan. "Silence and the Politics of Representing Rebellion: On the Emergence of the Neutral Maya in Guatemala." In *No Peace No War: An Anthropology of Contemporary Armed Conflicts,* edited by Paul Richards, 77–97. Dayton: Ohio University Press, 2005.

Lovell, George. *A Beauty That Hurts: Life and Death in Guatemala.* Austin: University of Texas Press, 2000.

Loveman, Brian. *For La Patria: Politics and the Armed Forces in Latin America.* Wilmington: A Scholarly Resource, 1999.

———. "Historical Foundations of Civil-Military Relations in Spanish America." In *Civil Military Relations in Latin America: New Analytical Perspectives,* edited by David Pion-Berlin, 246–74. Chapel Hill: University of North Carolina Press, 2001.

Loveman, Brian, and Thomas M. Davies, Jr., eds. *The Politics of Antipolitics: The Military in Latin America.* New York: Rowman and Littlefield, Revised Edition, 1997.

Lozowick, Yaacov, and Rollbahn Mord. "The Early Activities of Einsatzgruppe C." *Holocaust and Genocide Studies* 2, no. 2 (1987): 221–41.

Luckert, Steven, and Susan Bachrach. *State of Deception. The Power of Nazi Propaganda.* Washington, D.C.: United States Holocaust Memorial Museum and New York: W.W. Norton, 2009.

Lykes, M. Brinton. "Children in the Storm, Psychosocial Trauma in Latin America." In *Surviving beyond Fear, Women, Children and Human Rights in Latin America,* Marjorie Agosin (Ed) 152–61. Fredonia, NY: White Pine Press, 1993.

Machel, Graca. *The Impact of War on Children.* London: C. Hurst & Co., 2001.

Macleod, Norma, and Josefa Xiloj Tol. "Justicia, Dignidad y Derechos Colectivos: Acompañando a las Comunidades y a la Alcaldia Indígena de Chichicastenango." In *Justicia y Diversidad en América Latina. Pueblos Indígenas ante la Globalización,* Edited by

Victoria Chenaut, Magdalena Gómez, Héctor Ortiz y María Teresa Sierra. México: Centro de Investigaciones y Estudios Superiores en Antropología Social (CIESAS).

Mader, Heather. "Dracula, the Turks, and the Rhetoric of Impaling in Fifteenth-and Sixteenth-Century Germany." In *Death, Torture and the Broken Body in European Art (1300–1650)*, edited by John R. Decker and Mitzi Kirkland Ives, 164–90. Burlington: Ashgate, 2015.

Madlingozi, Tshepo. "On Transitional Justice Entrepreneurs and the Production of Victims." *Journal of Human Rights Practice* 2, no. 2 (2014): 208–28.

Maier, Charles S. *The Unmasterable Past: History, Holocaust, and German National Identity.* Cambridge, MA: Harvard University Press, 1998.

Malešević, Siniša. *Sociology of War and Violence.* Cambridge, UK: Cambridge University Press, 2010.

Ahmed, Azam, and Malkin, Elisabeth. "Otto Pérez Molina Of Guatemala is Jailed Hours After Resigning Presidency." *New York Times*, 3 September 2015. Retrieved 16 June 2017 from https://www.nytimes.com/2015/09/04/world/americas/otto-perez-molina-guatemalan-president-resigns-amid-scandal.html

Mamdani, Mahmood. *When Victims Become Killers: Colonialism, Nativism, and the Genocide in Rwanda.* Princeton: Princeton University Press, 2001.

Manz, Beatriz. *Paradise in Ashes: A Guatemalan Journey of Courage, Terror and Hope.* Berkeley: University of California Press, 2005.

———. "Continuum of Violence in Post-war Guatemala." In *An Anthropology of War,* edited by Alisse Waterston, 151–64. New York: Berghahn Books, 2009.

Margalit, Avishai. *The Ethics of Memory.* Cambridge, MA: Harvard University Press, 2002.

Martín-Baró, Ignacio. *Writings for a Liberation Psychology.* Edited by Adrianne Aron and Shawn Corne. London: Harvard University Press, 1994.

Martínez Pelaez, Severo. *Motines de Indios.* Guatemala: Ediciones en Marcha, 1991.

Matthew, Laura E., and Michael R. Oudijk, eds. *Indian Conquistadors: Indigenous Allies in the Conquest of Mesoamerica.* Oklahoma City: University of Oklahoma Press, 2012.

Maybury-Lewis, David, ed. "Editor's Introduction." In *The Politics of Ethnicity: Indigenous Peoples in Latin American States.* Cambridge, MA: Harvard University Press, 2002.

———. "From Elimination to an Uncertain Future: Changing Policies toward Indigenous Peoples." In *At the Risk of Being Heard: Identity, Indigenous Rights, and Postcolonial Studies,* edited by Bartholomew Dean and Jerome M. Levi, 324–34. Ann Arbor: University of Michigan, 2003.

McAllister, Carlota. "Rural Markets, Revolutionary Souls, and Rebellious Women in Cold War Guatemala." CERLAC Working Paper Series, May 2005.

McAllister, Carlotta, and Diane M. Nelson, eds. *War by Other Means: Aftermath in Post-Genocide in Guatemala.* Durham: Duke University Press, 2013.

McClintock, Michael. *The American Connection: State Terror and Popular Resistance in Guatemala.* London: Zed Books, 1985.

McCoy, Katherine E. "Trained to Torture: A Statistical Analysis of Human Rights Violations Committed by Graduates of the U.S. Army School of the Americas, 1960–2000." M.A. Thesis. Madison: University of Wisconsin, July 2003. Retrieved June 5 2017 from http://www.soaw.org/docs/KateMcCoy.pdf.

McCreery, David. "State Power, Indigenous Communities, and Land in Nineteenth Century Guatemala." In *Guatemalan Indian and the State: 1540–1988,* edited by Carol Smith. Austin: University of Texas Press, 1990.

McDoom, Omar. "Rwanda's Ordinary Killers: Interpreting Popular Participation in the Rwandan Genocide." Crisis State Research, Working Paper No. 77. Development Studies Institute (LSE), December 2005.

McGregor, Katharine E. *History in Uniform: Military Ideology and the Construction of Indonesia's Past.* Singapore: National University of Singapore Press, 2007.

McSherry, J. Patrice. *Incomplete Transition: Military Power and Democracy in Argentina.* New York: St. Martin Press, 1997.

———. "The Evolution of the National Security State: the Case of Guatemala." Socialism and Democracy Vol. 6, Iss. 1, 1992.

Mechbal, Adnan. "Los Moros de la Guerra Civil Española: Entre Memoria e Historia." *Amnis* 2 (2011). Retrieved 14 February 2017 from http://amnis.revues.org/1487.

Melville, Thomas R. *Through a Glass Darkly: The U.S. Holocaust in Central America.* Bloomington, IN: Xlibris Corporation, 2005.

Memmi, Albert. *The Dominated Man: Notes toward a Portrait.* Boston: Beacon Press, 1968.

———. *The Colonizer and the Colonized.* Boston: Beacon Press, 1991.

———. *Decolonization and the Decolonized.* Translated by Robert Bononno. Minneapolis: University of Minnesota Press, 2006.

Menchú, Rigoberta. "Rigoberta Menchú." 30 November 2010. Retrieved 5April 2015 from http://rigobertamenchu123.blogspot.com/2010/11/rigoberta-menchu_30.html.

Mendoza, Carlos A. "Structural Causes and Diffusion Processes of Collective Violence: Understanding Lynch Mobs in Post-Conflict Guatemala." Graduate Student Department of Political Science University of Notre Dame. Presented at the 2006 Meeting of the Latin American Studies Association San Juan, Puerto Rico, 15–18 March 2006. Retrieved June 5 2017 from https://www.researchgate.net/publication/237235035_Structural_Causes_and_Diffusion_Processes_of_Collective_Violence_Understanding_Lynch_Mobs_in_Post-Conflict_Guatemala

Merry, S.E. *Human Rights and Gender Violence: Translating International Law into Local Justice.* Chicago: University of Chicago Press, 2006.

Mignolo, Walter. "Coloniality of Power and Subalternity." In the *Latin American Subaltern Studies Reader,* 424-444edited by Ileana Rodriguez. Durham: Duke University Press, 2001. Kindle edition.

Mills, C. Wright. *The Power Elite.* London: Oxford University Press, 1958.

———. *The Sociological Imagination.* New York: Oxford University Press, 1959.

MINUGUA (United Nations Verification Mission in Guatemala). "Report of the Secretary-General on the Group of Military Observers Attached to MINUGUA Distr. GENERAL." S/1997/432. 4 June 1997.

———. "Eighth Report." June 1998.

———. "Ninth Report, Verification of Compliance." New York: United Nations, March 1999.

———. "Tenth Report, Verification of Compliance." New York: United Nations, January 2000.

———. "Informe de Verificación: Los Linchamientos: Un Flagelo Contra la Dignidad Humana." Guatemala City: United Nations, December 2000.

———. "Status of the Commitments of the Peace Agreements Relating to the Armed Forces." Guatemala City, May 2002.

———. "Thirteenth Report: Covering 1 July 2001 to 30 June 2002." Reported to the General Assembly 10 July 2002.

———. "General Assembly Agenda Item 9 Fifty-seventh Session, Item 38 of the Provisional Agenda." United Nations Distr. General. A/57/336. 22 August 2002.

———. "Caught in the Crossfire: Crime and Development in Central America." United Nations Office on Drugs and Crime. May 2007.

———. "Promise and Reality: Implementation of the Peace Accords." Retrieved 27 September 2011 from http://lanic.utexas.edu/project/hemisphereinitiatives/promise.htm#armed.

Mjoset, Lars, and Stephen Van Holde, eds. *The Comparative Study of Conscription in the Armed Forces.* Comparative Social Research, Volume 20. New York: Elsevier Science, 2002.

Moore, Barrington Jr. *Social Origins of Dictatorship and Democracy: Lord and Peasant in the Making of the Modern World.* Boston: Beacon Press, 1966.

Moses, A. Dirk, ed. *Empire, Colony, Genocide: Conquest, Occupation, and Subaltern Resistance in World History.* New York: Berghahn Books, 2008. Kindle Edition.

Moses, A. Dirk, and Dan Stone, eds. *Colonialism and Genocide.* Abingdon: Routledge, 2007.

Muggah, Robert. "No Magic Bullet: A Critical Perspective on Disarmament, Demobilization and Reintegration (DDR) and Weapons Reduction in Post-Conflict Contexts." *The Round Table* 94, no. 379 (April 2005): 239–52.

———. "Emerging from the Shadow of War: A Critical Perspective on DDR and Weapons Reduction in the Post-Conflict Period." *Contemporary Security Policy,* 27, no. 1 (April 2006): 190–205.

Nagar, Richa, and Susan Geiger. "Reflexivity and Positionality in Feminist Fieldwork Revisited." In *Politics and Practice in Economic Geography,* edited by Adam Tickell, Eric Sheppard, Jamie Peck, and Trevor Barnes, 267–278. London: Sage, 2007.

Nelson, Diane M. *A Finger in the Wound: Body Politics in Quincentennial Guatemala.* Berkeley: University of California Press, 1999. Kindle edition.

———. "Means and End/s of Clandestine Life." Hemispheric Institute. Retrieved 7 August 2013 from http://hemisphericinstitute.org/hemi/en/e-misferica-72/nelson.

Newton, Esther. "My Best Informant's Dress: The Erotic Equation in Fieldwork." *Cultural Anthropology* 8, no. 1 (February 1993): 3–23.

Nisbett, Richard E., and Timothy Decamp Wilson. "The Halo Effect: Evidence for Unconscious Alteration of Judgment." *Journal of Personality and Social Psychology* 35, no. 4 (1977): 250–56.

Nora, Pierre. "Between Memory and History: Les Lieux de Mémoire." *Representations,* no. 26, Special Issue: Memory and Counter Memory (Spring 1989): 7–24.

Nordstrom, Carolyn. *A Different Kind of War Story.* Philadelphia: University of Pennsylvania Press, 1997.

Oakley, Ann. "Interviewing Women: A Contradiction in Terms?" In *Doing Feminist Research,* edited by Helen Roberts, 30–61. New York: Routledge, 1981.

OAS (Organization of American States). *Interamerican Yearbook on Human Rights.* Netherlands: Martinus Nijhoff Publishers, 1998.

———. "Los Comités Voluntarios de Autodefensa Civil." *Comisión Interamericana de Derechos Humanos.* Retrieved 18 June 2012 from http://www.cidh.org/countryrep/Guatemala93sp/cap.6.htm.

———. "Codigo Penal de Guatemala Decreto No. 17–73." Retrieved 12 June 2016 from http://www.oas.org/dil/esp/Codigo_Penal_Guatemala.pdf.

OAS (Organization of American States). "Inter-American Commission on Human Rights. Report No. 21/98 Case 11.435, José Sucunú Panjoj," 2 March 1998. Retrieved 28 April 2015 from http://www.cidh.oas.org/annualrep/97eng/Guatemala11435.htm.

———. "Report No. 19/00 Case 11.435, José Sucunú Panjoj," 24 February 2000. Retrieved 19 April 2015 from http://www.cidh.org/annualrep/99eng/Friendly/Guatemala11.435.htm.

Oglesby, Elizabeth. "Historical Memory and the Limits of Peace Education: Examining Guatemala's 'Memory of Silence' and the Politics of Curriculum Design." New York: Carnegie Council on Ethics and International Affairs Fellows Program, History and the Politics of Reconciliation, June 2004.

Organización de las Naciones Unidas. "ONU encomia a Guatemala por juicio a ex militares responsables de atrocidades." Retrieved June 15 2017 from http://www.un.org/span ish/News/story.asp?NewsID=34252#.WUPuVbGZOHo

Organizaciones de la Sociedad Civil. "Hacía El Siglo XXI. Unidos Construyendo el Desarrollo de Chichicastenango." Una Propuesta de Desarrollo Municipal desde Las Organizaciones de la Sociedad Civil. Chichicastenango, 10 October 1999.

Orraca Corona, Marcela. "Ejército, Subjetividades y Memoria Colectiva en Ayutla de los Libres, Guerrero." *Tramas* 38 (2012): 105–22.

"Otto Pérez Viaja Huehuetenango." *Prensa Libre.* Retrieved 23 February 2015 from http://www.prensalibre.com/decision_libre_-_actualidad/Otto-Perez-viaja-Huehuetenan go_0_578342319.html.

Paige, Jeffrey. *Coffee and Power: Revolution and the Rise of Democracy in Central America.* Cambridge, MA: Harvard University Press, 1997.

"Partido Patriota Realiza Cierre de Campaña de Quiche." *Noticias de Quiche,* 5 November 2011. Retrieved 10 May 2015 from http://noticiasquiche.blogspot.com/2011/11/part ido-patriota-realiza-cierre-de.html.

Pasqualucci, Jo M. "Medidas Provisionales en la Corte Interamericano de Derechos Humanos." Organization of American States (OAS). Retrieved 4 May 2015 from http://www.juridicas.unam.mx/publica/librev/rev/iidh/cont/19/dtr/dtr2.pdf.

Patch, Robert W. *Maya Revolt and Revolution in the Eighteenth Century (Latin American Realities).* New York: Routledge, 2002.

Payne, Leigh A. *Unsettling Accounts: Neither Truth nor Reconciliation in Confessions of State Violence.* Durham: Duke University Press, 2008.

Peacock, Susan C., and Adriana Beltran. "Hidden Powers in Post-Conflict Guatemala: Illegal Armed Groups and the Forces Behind Them." Washington, D.C.: Washington Office on Latin America (WOLA), 2003.

Pebley, Anne R., and Noreen Goldman. "Social Inequality and Children's Growth in Guatemala." *Health Transition Review* 5 (1995): 1–20.

Perera, Victor. *Unfinished Conquest: The Guatemalan Tragedy.* With Photographs by Daniel Chauche. Oakland, CA: University of California Press, 1995.

PHD (Procuradoria de Derechos Humanos [Human Rights Ombudsman Office]). "Actuación de los Patrulleros en Situación de Emergencia, Nunca o Casi Nunca." 1994.

———. "Informe Anual Circunstanciado 2003." Guatemala, January 2004. Retrieved 19 July 2016 from http://www.pdh.org.gt/archivos/descargas/Biblioteca/Informes%20 Anuales/informe2003.pdf.

Pinto Soria, J.C. *Nación, Caudillismo y Conflicto Étnico en Guatemala (1821–1854).* Guatemala: Universidad de San Carlos de Guatemala, 1996.

Pion-Berlin, David, ed. *Civil Military Relations in Latin America: New Analytical Perspectives.* Chapel Hill: University of North Carolina Press, 2001.

Plant, Roger. *Guatemala: Unnatural Disaster.* London: Latin American Bureau, 1978.

PNUD (Naciones Unidas, Programa de Desarrollo). "Diversidad Etnico-Cultural: La Ciudadania en un Estado Plural." *Informe Nacional de Desarrollo,* 2005. Retrieved 24 July 2016 from http://desarrollohumano.org.gt/wp-content/uploads/2016/04/INDH_2005_1.pdf.

Pollack, Aaron. *Levantamiento K'iche' en Totonicapan, 1820: Los Lugares de las Politicas Subalternas.* Guatemala: Avancso, 2008.

Popkin, Margaret. *Civil Patrols and Their Legacy: Overcoming Militarization and Polarization in the Guatemalan Countryside.* Washington, D.C.: RFK Human Rights Center, 1996.

"Populist President Takes Over in Guatemala." *BBC News,* 14 January 2000. Retrieved 16 July 2016 from http://news.bbc.co.uk/2/hi/americas/604184.stm.

Pouligny, Béatrice, Simon Chesterman, and Albrecht Schnabel, eds. *After Mass Crime: Rebuilding States and Communities*. Tokyo: United Nations University Press, 2007.

Powell, Philip Wayne. *Soldiers, Indians, and Silver: North America's First Frontier War*. Tempe: Arizona State Press, Center for Latin American Studies, 1975.

Purcell, Fernando. "Connecting Realities: Peace Corps Volunteers in South America and the Global War on Poverty during the 1960s." *Revista Historica Crítica* 53 (May–August 2014): 129–54.

Puri, Jyotsna. "Transport and Poverty in Guatemala: A Profile using Data from the Encovi 2000, Technical Paper No. 8." Retrieved 23 July 2016 from http://www.wds.world bank.org/external/default/WDSContentServer/WDSP/IB/2006/05/30/000090341_2 0060530090326/Rendered/PDF/362080GU0GUAPA0Transport1Paper801PUBLIC1 .pdf.

Puwar, Nirmal. "Sensing a Post-Colonial Bourdieu: An Introduction." *The Sociological Review* 57, no. 3 (2009): 371–84.

Quijano, Anibal, and Michael Ennis. "The Coloniality of Power, Eurocentrism and Latin America." *Nepantla: Views from South* 1, no. 3 (2000): 533–80.

Rafter, Nicole. *The Crime of All Crimes: Towards a Criminology of Genocide*. New York: New York University Press, 2016.

Redress Trust. "Child Soldiers before the International Criminal Court: Victims, Perpetrators or Heroes?" September 2006. Retrieved June 5 2017 from http://www.redress.org/downloads/publications/childsoldiers.pdf.

Reichardt, Sven. "Fascist Movements." In *The Wiley-Blackwell Encyclopedia of Social and Political Movements*, 453–59. New York: Blackwell, 2013.

Reisz, Matthew. "High and Popular Culture to Meet in New Postcolonial Studies Centre." *Times Higher Education,* 20 November 2014. Retrieved 26 July 2016 from https://www .timeshighereducation.com/news/high-and-popular-culture-to-meet-in-new-postco lonial-studies-centre/2017016.article.

Remijnse, Simone. *Memories of Violence: Civil Patrols and the Legacy of Conflict in Joyabaj, Guatemala*. Amsterdam: Rozenberg Publishers, 2002.

RESDAL (Red de Seguridad y Defensa de América Latina). *Libro de la Defensa Nacional de la República de Guatemala (Libro Blanco)*. Buenos Aires: RESDAL, 2003. Retrieved 15 April 2015 from http://www.resdal.org/Archivo/guate-libdef03-parte4.html.

Restrepo Echeverri, Juan Diego. "Guatemala: Los Ex-PAC Agentes de Tension." Semana .com, 10 October 2006. Retrieved 7 March 2015 from http://www.semana.com/on-line/articulo/del-reino-armas-reino-del-miedo/81382-3.

Reynolds, Louisa. "¿Por qué Votaron por Pérez Molina las Zonas Asoladas por la Guerra?" Retrieved 2 May 2015 from http://www.adital.com.br/site/noticia_imp.asp? lang=ES&img=S&cod=63139.

Richani, Nazih. "State Capacity in Post Conflict Settings: Explaining Criminal Violence in El Salvador and Guatemala." *Civil Wars* 12, no. 4 (2010): 431–55.

Richard, Nelly. "El Tumulto de las Fronteras." Hemispheric Institute E-Misférica, 2009–2013. Retrieved 29 July 2013 from http://hemisphericinstitute.org/hemi/en/e-misferica-72/richard.

Rigby, Andrew. *Justice and Reconciliation: After the Violence*. Boulder: Lynne Rienner Publishers, 2001.

Rivas Vasconcelos, Maribel. "La Guerra Fría y su Doctrina Contrainsurgente, una Visión Caleidoscópica de la Represión en América Latina a Través de las Patrullas de Autodefensa Civil: Guatemala 1981–1983." M.A.Thesis. Mexico, D.F.: Instituto de Investigaciones, October 2012.

Rivera Cusicanqui, Sylvia. *Oppressed but Not Defeated: Peasant Struggles among the Aymara and Qhechwa in Bolivia, 1900–1980.* Geneva: United Nations Research Institute for Social Development, 1987.

———. "Aymara Past, Aymara Future: The Horizons of Internal Colonialism." *NACLA* 25 no. 3 (December 1991).

———. Rivera Cusicanqui, Sylvia. *Oprimidos pero no Vencidos: Luchas del Campesinado Aymara y Qhechwa. 1900–1980.* La Paz: La Miranda Salvaje, 2010. Retrieved June 5 2017 from http://www.ceapedi.com.ar/imagenes/biblioteca/libros/294.pdf.

Robben, Antonius C.G.M. "The Politics of Truth and Emotion." In *Fieldwork under Fire: Contemporary Studies of Violence and Survival,* edited by Carolyn Nordstrom and Antonius C.G.M. Robben, 81–104. Berkeley: University of California Press, 1995.

Rodas Núñez, Isabel. "La Nación, la Fabricación del Voto y los Patrulleros de Autodefensa Civil." 2009. Retrieved 1 May 2015 from https://www.academia.edu/5672965/2009_La_nación_la_fabricación_del_voto_y_los_patrulleros_de_autodefensa_civil.

Rojas Lima, Flavio. "La Cofradia Indígena Reducto Cultural de los Mayas." *Los Mayas de los Tiempos Tardios,* edited by Miguel Rivera, Andres Ciudad Ruiz, 253–82. Toledo: Sociedad Española de Estudios Mayas, 1986.

Romano, Silvina. "The Natural Presence of US Armed Forces in Latin America." Monday 18 January 2016. Retrieved 13 July 2016 from http://upsidedownworld.org/main/international-archives-60/5557-the-qnatural-presence-of-us-armed-forces-in-latin-america.

Rosenbaum, John H., and Peter C. Sederberg, eds. *Vigilante Politics.* Philadelphia: University of Pennsylvania Press, 1976.

Ross, Andrew. "Dimensions of Militarization in the Third World." *Armed Forces and Society* 13, no. 4 (1987): 561–78. DOI: 10.1177/0095327X8701300405.

Ruhl, J. Mark. "The Guatemalan Military since the Peace Accords: The Fate of Reform under Arzú and Portillo." *Latin American Politics and Society* 46, no. 4 (spring 2005): 55–85.

Sáenz de Tejeda, Ricardo. *Víctimas o Vencedores? Una Aproximación al Movimiento de los Ex PAC.* Guatemala: Flacso, 2004.

Salvi, Valentina. "Entre Héroes y Torturadores: Subjetividad y Memorias de Oficiales Retirados del Ejército Argentino sobre la Represión." *Tramas* 38 (2012): 15–39.

Sanford, Victoria. *Buried Secrets: Truth and Human Rights in Guatemala.* New York: Palgrave McMillan, 2003.

———. "The 'Grey Zone' of Justice: NGOs and the Rule of Law in Postwar Guatemala." *Journal of Human Rights* 2, no. 3 (September 2003): 393–405.

———. "From Genocide to Feminicide: Impunity and Human Rights in Twenty First Century." *Journal of Human Rights* 7, no. 2 (2008): 104–22.

———. "Gendered Observations: Activism, Advocacy, and the Academy." In *Women Fielding Danger: Negotiating Ethnographic Identities in Field Research,* edited by Martha K. Huggins and Marie-Louise Glebbeek, 123–46. New York: Roman Littlefield, 2009.

Scheper-Hughes, Nancy, and Philippe I. Bourgois. *Violence in War and Peace: An Anthology.* Malden: Blackwell, 2004.

Schirmer, Jennifer. "Seeking of Truth and the Gendering of Consciousness: The CoMadres of El Salvador and the CONAVIGUA Widows of Guatemala." In *Viva: Women and Popular Poorest in Latin America,* edited by Sarah A. Radeliffe and Sallie Westwood, 30–64. London and New York: Routledge, 1993.

———. "'Those Who Die for Life Cannot Be Called Dead': Women and Human Rights Protest in Latin America." In *Surviving Beyond Fear: Women, Children and Human Rights in Latin America,* edited by Marjorie Agosín, 31–57. Fredonia, NY: White Pine Press, 1993.

———. *The Guatemalan Military Project: A Violence Called Democracy.* Philadelphia: University of Pennsylvania Press, 1998.

———. "Prospects for Compliance: The Guatemalan Military and the Peace Accords." In *Guatemala after the Peace Accords,* edited by Rachel Sieder, 21–32. London: University of London, Institute of Latin American Studies, 1998.

———. "From the Horse's Mouth: Research on Perpetrators in Guatemala." *State Crime Journal* 1, no. 1 (spring 2012): 27–44.

Schlesinger, Stephen, and Stephen Kinser. *Bitter Fruit: The Untold Story of the American Coup in Guatemala.* New York: Anchor Books, 1982.

Schneider, Nina. *Brazilian Propaganda: Legitimizing an Authoritarian Regime.* Gainesville: University Press of Florida, 2014.

Schneider, Nina, and Marcia Esparza. "Whose Transition? Whose Voices: Latin American Responses to Transitional Justice." In *Legacies of State Violence and Transitional Justice in Latin America: A Janus-Faced Paradigm?,* edited by Nina Schneider and Marcia Esparza, xi–xxviii. New York: Lexington Books, 2015.

Seckinger, Ron. "The Central American Militaries: A Survey of the Literature." *Latin American Research Review* 16, no. 2 (1981): 246–58.

Secretaría de la Paz. "Informe 2009 sobre el Cumplimiento de los Acuerdos de Paz." Guatemala: Secretaría de la Paz de la Presidencia de la República de Guatemala, 2009. Retrieved 24 October 2014 from http://www.guatemalaun.org/bin/documents/info rme-2009-secretaria-de-la-paz.pdf.

SEDEM (Asociación para el Estudio y Promoción de la Seguridad en Democracia). *Mapa Centroamericano de Instituciones de Seguridad.* 3rd ed. Guatemala: SEDEM, 2006. Retrieved 19 July 2016 from http://www.sedem.org.gt/sedem/sites/default/files/archivos/ Mapa%20centroamericano.pdf.

SEGEPLAN (Secretaria Planificación y Programación). "Caracterización del Municipio de Chichicastenango." *El Quiché,* December 2001.

Semelin, Jacques. "Towards a Vocabulary of Massacres." *Journal of Genocide Research* 5, no. 2 (2003): 193–210.

———. *Purify and Destroy: The Political Uses of Massacre and Genocide.* Translated by Cynthia Schoch. New York: Columbia University Press, 2007.

Shaw, Martin. *Post-Military Society: Militarism, Demilitarization and War at the End of the Twentieth Century.* Philadelphia: Temple University Press, 1991.

———. *What Is Genocide?* Malden: Polity Press, 2007.

Short, Damien. "Australia: A Continuing Genocide?" *Journal of Genocide Research* 12, nos. 1–2 (2010): 45–68. DOI: 10.1080/14623528.2010.508647.

Siebold, Guy L. "The Essence of Military Group Cohesion." *Armed Forces & Society* 33, no. 2 (January 2007): 286–95.

Sieder, Rachel. *Derecho Consuetudinario y Transicion Democrática en Guatemala.* Guatemala City, Guatemala: FLASCO, 1996. Retrieved June 5 2017 from http://racheluk .domain.com/wp-content/uploads/2012/08/Sieder-derecho-consuetudinario1.pdf.

Silva, Patricio, ed. *The Soldier and the State in South America. Essays in Civil-Military Relations.* New York: Palgrave, 2001.

Simon, Jean Marie. *Guatemala: Eterna Primavera, Eterna Tiranía.* Retrieved 19 April 2105 from http://www.primavera-tirania.com/museovirtual.php.

Sluka, Jeffrey A. "Reflections on Managing Danger in Fieldwork: Dangerous Anthropology in Belfast." In *Fieldwork under Fire: Contemporary Studies of Violence and Survival,* edited by Carolyn Nordstrom and Antonius C.G.M. Robben, 276–94. Berkeley: University of California Press, 1995.

———, ed. *Death Squad: The Anthropology of State Terror.* Philadelphia: Penn University Press, 2001.

Smith, Carol A. "The Militarization of Civil Society in Guatemala: Economic Reorganization as a Continuation of War." *Latin American Perspectives* 17, no. 4 (autumn 1990): 8–41.

———, ed. *Guatemalan Indians and the State: 1540 to 1988.* LLILAS Symposia on Latin America Series. Austin: University of Texas Press, 1994. Kindle edition.

Smith, Gary H. *Forty Years in the Altiplano: A Cross-Cutting Evaluation of Aid-Financed Assistance in Guatemala's Altiplano (from the 1940s to the Present).* Vol. 1. Guatemala City: USAID, 1989.

Smyth, Frank. *Painting the Maya Red: Military Doctrine and Speech in Guatemala's Genocidal Acts.* Washington, D.C.: U.S. Holocaust Memorial Museum, 2010.

Solomon, Joel A. "Institutional Violence: Civil Patrols in Guatemala, 1993–1994." Edited by James J. Silk. Washington, D.C.: Robert F. Kennedy Memorial Center for Human Rights, 1994.

Solomon, Joel A., and James Silk. *Violencia Institucional: Las Patrullas de Autodefensa Civil en Guatemala 1993–1994.* Washington, D.C.: The Robert F. Kennedy Center, 1994.

Sosa Velásquez, Mario Enrique. *Rupturas y Construcción de Poder en Santiago Atitlan.* Guatemala: SERJUS, 1998.

Stavenhagen, Rodolfo. "Class, Colonialism, and Acculturation." In *Masses in Latin America,* edited by Irving L. Horowitz, 235–88. New York: Oxford University Press, 1970.

Stedman, Stephen John. "Spoiler Problems in Peace Processes." *International Security* 22, no. 2 (fall 1997): 5–53.

Stern, Steve. *The Memory Box of Pinochet's Chile.* Vols. 1–3. Durham: Duke University Press, 2006.

Stoll, David. *Is Latin America Turning Protestant? The Politics of Evangelical Growth.* Los Angeles: University of California Press, 1990.

———. *Between Two Armies in the Ixil Towns of Guatemala.* New York: Columbia University Press, 1993.

———. "The Obligatory Indian." *Dialect Anthropology* 35, no. 2 (2011): 135–46. DOI 10.1007/s10624-011-9226-x.

———. "Guatemala—Was It Genocide?" 2013. Retrieved 3 March 2015 from http://sites .middlebury.edu/dstoll/files/2013/10/Guatemala-Was-It-Genocide.pdf.

Taylor, Marisa, and Kevin G. Hall. "Chilean Accused of Murder, Torture Taught 13 Years for Pentagon." *Miami Herald,* 12 March 2015. Retrieved 16 June 2016 from http://www .miamiherald.com/news/nation-world/world/americas/article13814051.html.

Tedlock, Dennis, trans. *Popol Vuh: The Definitive Edition of the Mayan Book of the Dawn of Life and the Glories of Gods and Kings.* New York: Simon and Schuster, 1996.

Thacker, Toby. *The End of the Third Reich: Defeat, Denazification & Nuremberg, January 1944–November 1946.* Mount Pleasant, SC: The History Press, 2008.

Thee, Marek. "Militarism and Militarization in Contemporary International Relations." In *Problems of Contemporary Militarism,* edited by Asbjorn Eide and Marek Thee, 15–35. New York: St. Martin's Press, 1980.

Theidon, Kimberly. "Intimate Enemies: Reconciling the Present in Post-war Communities in Ayacucho, Peru." In *After Mass Crime: Rebuilding States and Communities,* edited by Béatrice Pouligny, Simon Chesterman, and Albrecht Schnabel, 97–121. New York: United Nations University Press, 2007.

———. "Reconstructing Masculinities: The Disarmament, Demobilization, and Reintegration of Former Combatants in Colombia." *Human Rights Quarterly* 31, no. 1 (February 2009): 1–34.

Thomas, Jim. *Doing Critical Ethnography*. Newbury Park, CA: Sage Publications, 1993.

Todorov, Tzvetan. *Facing the Extreme: Moral life in the Concentration Camps*. Translated by Abigail Pollak and Arthur Denner. New York: Henry Holt & Co, 1996.

———. *The Conquest of America: The Question of the Other*. Translated by Richard Howard. Oklahoma City: University of Oklahoma Press, 1999.

———. *Memory as a Remedy for Evil*. Translated by Gila Walker. London: Seagull Books, 2010.

Todorov, Tzvetan, and David Bellos. *Hope and Memory: Lessons from the Twentieth Century*. Princeton: Princeton University Press, 2003.

Tuhiwai Smith, Linda. *Decolonizing Methodologies: Research and Indigenous Peoples*. New York: Zed Books, 1999.

Tunnell, Kenneth D. "Honesty, Secrecy and Deception in the Sociology of Crime: Confessions and Reflections from the Backstage." In *Ethnography at the Edge: Crime, Deviance and Field Research,* edited by Jeff Ferrell and Mark S. Hamm, 206–20. Boston: Northeastern University Press, 1998.

UNICEF. "Chronic Malnutrition: Stunting." Retrieved 28 March 2012 from http://www.unicef.org/nutrition/training/2.3/20.html.

Vagts, Alfred. *A History of Militarism: Civilian and Military*. Revised ed. London: The Macmillan Company, 1959.

Van de Sandt, Joris. "Mining Conflicts and Indigenous Peoples in Guatemala." The Hague: CORDAID, 2009.

Vela Castañeda, Manolo. *Masas, Armas y Elites: Guatemala, 1820–1982*. Colección de Ciencias Sociales, vol. III. Guatemala: Flacso, 2008.

———. "Los Pelotones de la Muerte: La Construcción de los Perpetradores del Genocidio Guatemalteco." Ph.D. thesis. Mexico City: El Colegio de México, 2010.

Viaene, Lieselotte. "Dealing with the Legacy of Gross Human Rights Violations in Guatemala: Grasping the Mismatch between Macro Level Policies and Micro Level Processes." *The International Journal of Human Rights* 15, no. 7 (October 2011): 1160–81.

———. "Voices from the Shadows: The Role of Cultural Contexts in Transitional Justice Processes: Maya Q'eqchi' Perspectives from Post–Conflict Guatemala." Ph.D. dissertation. Ghent, Belgium: Ghent University, Department of Public Law, 2011.

Vilas, Carlos M. "(In)Justicia por Mano Propia: Linchamientos en el México Contemporáneo." *Revista Mexicana de Sociología* 63, no. 1 (January–March 2001): 131–60.

Vinson, Ben. "Race and Badge: Free-Colored Soldiers in the Colonial Mexican Militias." *The Americas* 56, no. 4 (2000): 471–96.

Vizenor, Gerald, ed. *Survivance: Narratives of Native Presence*. Lincoln: University of Nebraska, 2008.

War Resisters' International (WRI). "Country Report and Updates: Guatemala." 30 April 1998. Retrieved 16 July 2016 from http://www.wri-irg.org/programmes/world_survey/country_report/en/Guatemala.

Weld, Kirsten. *Paper Cadavers: The Archives of Dictatorship in Guatemala*. Durham: Duke University Press, 2014.

Wendt, Alexander, and Michael Barnett. "Dependent State Formation and Third World Militarization." *Review of International Studies* 19, no. 4 (1993): 321–47.

Wilson, Richard. *Maya Resurgence in Guatemala: Q'eqchi' Experiences*. Norman: Oklahoma University Press, 1995.

Winter, Jay. "Thinking about Silence." In *Shadows of War: A Social History of Silence in the Twentieth Century,* edited by Efrat Ben-Ze'ev, Ruth Ginio, and Jay Winter, 3–31. Cambridge, UK: Cambridge University Press, 2010.

Wolf, Eric R. *Peasant Wars of the Twentieth Century.* New York: Harper and Row, 1969.

Wolfe, Patrick. "Settler Colonialism and the Elimination of the Native." *Journal of Genocide Research* 8, no. 4 (2006): 387–409.

Wollni, Meike, and Manfred Zeller. "Do Farmers Benefit from Participating in Specialty Markets and Cooperatives? The Case of Coffee Marketing in Costa Rica." Contributed paper prepared for presentation at the International Association of Agricultural Economists Conference, Gold Coast, Australia, 12–18 August 2006. Retrieved 14 November 2012 from http://ageconsearch.umn.edu/bitstream/25670/1/cp061062.pdf.

Wood, Charles H., and Marianne Schmink. "The Military and the Environment in the Brazilian Amazon." *Journal of Political and Military Sociology* 21, no. 1 (summer 1993): 81–105.

World Bank. *Poverty in Guatemala: A World Bank Country Report.* Washington, D.C.: World Bank, 2004.

Wright, Barbara. "Guatemala's Civilian Patrols Help Quash Leftist Rebels in North." *Christian Science Monitor,* 13 December 1983. Retrieved 30 March 2015 from http://www.csmonitor.com/1983/1213/121324.html.

Zbikowski, Andrzei. "Night Guard: Holocaust Mechanisms in the Polish Rural Areas, 1943–1945: Preliminary Introduction into Research." *East European Politics & Societies* 25, no. 3 (August 2011): 512–29.

Zerubavel, Eviatar. "Social Memories: Steps to a Sociology of the Past." *Qualitative Sociology* 19, no. 3 (1996): 283–99.

———. "The Social Sound of Silence: Toward a Sociology of Denial." In *Shadows of War: A Social History of Silence in the Twentieth Century,* edited by Efrat Ben-Ze'ev, Ruth Ginio, and Jay Winter, 32–46. Cambridge, UK: Cambridge University Press, 2010.

Zimmerer, Jürgen. "The Birth of Ostland out of the Spirit of Colonialism: A Postcolonial Perspective on the Nazi Policy of Conquest and Extermination." In *Colonialism and Genocide,* edited by A. Dirk Moses and Dan Stone, 101–23. Abingdon: Routledge, 2007.

Zinecker, Heidrun. "Violence in Peace: Forms and Causes of Postwar Violence in Guatemala." PRIF Reports No. 76. Translated by Gerard Holden. Frankfurt: Peace Research Institute (PRIF), 2006. Retrieved 20 April 2015 from http://www.fes-seguridadregional.org/images/stories/docs/4736-001_g.pdf.

Index